MURDERERS' ROW

MURDERERS' ROW

G. H. FLEMING

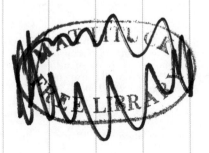

WILLIAM MORROW AND COMPANY, INC.
New York

All entries in this book come from newspapers of 1927. In no instance did I change the wording of a passage, but sometimes for the sake of readability, I deleted words, phrases, and sentences that I regarded as irrelevant, nonessential, or repetitious. G.H.F.

Library of Congress Cataloging in Publication Data

Fleming, Gordon H., 1920–
Murderers' row.

Includes index.
1. New York Yankees (Baseball team)—History.
I. Title.
GV875.N4F56   1985   796.357'64'097471   84-25385
ISBN 0-688-04804-8

Printed in the United States of America

First Edition

1 2 3 4 5 6 7 8 9 10

TO
the Memory of Waite Hoyt,
1899–1984

Foreword

[*On April 17, 1984, four months before his death, Waite Hoyt completed this foreword. It came to the author with a covering letter that said, in part, "Since I have no facilities for research, I have written mostly from memory. I feel I have gone as far as I can under the circumstances. . . . I worked many hours trying to assemble my facts and thoughts. I ran, I believe, far beyond a normal foreword. . . . I trust everything has turned out as you hoped for, and that I have helped somewhat in the quality of the tome. Good luck."*]

The week of July 21, 1969, remains vividly in my memory. Neil Armstrong took his giant step for mankind, and, more personally, along with Stanley Coveleski, Roy Campanella, and Stanley Musial, I was inducted into baseball's Hall of Fame.

The year 1969 was professional baseball's centennial year, and the executives of the national pastime celebrated with a lavish banquet at the Shoreham Hotel in Washington, D.C., on July 21. (The Hall of Fame induction ceremonies occurred one week later.) After a keynote address by Commissioner Bowie Kuhn and appropriate speeches by other notables came the highlight of the evening. The Baseball Writers Association of America announced the results of its poll to select the best players at each position and the greatest team in baseball's first hundred years.

As an invited guest, I sat on the edge of my chair listening with rapt attention. It is difficult to describe my emotions when the master of ceremonies clarioned, "The greatest team ever was . . . the New York Yankees of 1927!" It was one of the most exciting moments in my more than sixty years' association with baseball. I was in a state of sheer exuberance.

I was indeed fortunate to have pitched on that team, my seventh season with the Yankees. I hope I am not being immodest in saying that I led the American League that year. [*Waite Hoyt had the highest winning percentage, .759, and the lowest earned run average, 2.63. Had the Cy Young Award then been in existence, Hoyt would surely have been the winner.*] Actually, the first four pitchers in winning percentage were Yankees—Waite Hoyt, Urban Shocker, Wilcy Moore, and Herb Pennock.

I have no desire to go further with facts and figures. They are covered by G. H. Fleming in this book and should without doubt substantiate the vote of the Baseball Writers Association of America in 1969.

As I write, I look at an enlarged group picture on my wall captioned *The Greatest Team of All Time,* three rows of the '27 Yankees. I look first to the rear where, standing side by side, are Lou Gehrig, Bob Meusel, and Babe Ruth. I stare at the gang with much misgiving. A slight tremor runs through me as I sadly realize that only four members of that wonderful club are still alive: George Pipgras, pitcher; Mark Koenig, shortstop; Ray Morehart, utility infielder; and I.

That awesome club wasn't created overnight. The roots went back as far as 1921, 1922, and 1923. Ruth, Meusel, Bob Shawkey, manager Miller Huggins, and I had been members of the 1921 club, the first Yankee team to win a league championship. Joe Dugan, our third baseman, came from our supply house, the Red Sox, in 1922, and Herb Pennock followed in 1923. [*The Red Sox were called the Yankees' supply house because eight of the Yankees' star players in the twenties had been traded from Boston. On the 1927 team there were Ruth, Hoyt, Pennock, and Dugan. Additionally, these Red Sox alumni had played on earlier championship Yankee clubs: Everett Scott (1922, 1923), Wally Schang (1921, 1922, 1923), Carl Mays (1921, 1922), Sam Jones (1922, 1923, 1926). And in 1930 Red Ruffing would join the parade.*] Gehrig arrived in 1923 but was farmed out until 1925, when, on June 1, he began his famed consecutive-game string of 2,130 games. Also arriving in 1925 was our center fielder, Earle Combs, purchased from Louisville in the American Association. In the winter of 1925, we got our second-base combination: Tony Lazzeri was bought from Salt Lake City, in the Pacific Coast League, and his fellow San Franciscan Mark Koenig came from St. Paul, in the American Association. This baseball team was thus skillfully assembled by Miller Huggins and general manager Ed Barrow.

We won the pennant in 1926, but the World Series ended dismally. Needing but one victory in the last two games against the St. Cardinals, to be played on our own home field, we blew it. The Cards, with Grover Cleveland Alexander on the mound, won, 10–2, on Saturday. In Sunday's finale, I pitched for the New Yorkers. Leading 1–0, we fell apart in the fourth inning, as our defense permitted three runs to score on three errors. In the seventh came that memorable moment when "Old Pete" Alexander, coming back without a day of rest, struck out Lazzeri with the bases loaded. And that was that.

If I may be permitted to digress for a moment, I should like to note that earlier in 1926 I had had another unfortunate experience, when for the one and only time in my twenty-two years of pitching professional baseball I acquired a sore arm. The injury had come about rather colorfully.

One day after a game in Philadelphia, Babe Ruth, Joe Dugan, and I accepted an invitation from Herb Pennock, our star left-handed pitcher, to accompany him to his hometown of Kennett Square, about twenty-five miles away, where the townspeople were putting on a big celebration for their local hero. We took part in a parade in Herb's honor, ate a big dinner, and then visited a street fair.

There were many colorfully decorated booths where various types of merchandise were sold. (Babe Ruth, recognizing that worthy charities were the beneficiaries, spent a bundle of cash in these booths.) One booth especially attracted our attention; it was one in which you threw baseballs at pyramids of papier-mâché bottles. If you could knock the entire pyramid off the bench in three throws, you would win a baby doll, a box of candy, a pennant, or some such prize. It was rather easy. As we were surrounded by a semicircle of people who were curious to see professional ballplayers throwing at these small targets, each of us knocked off those pyramids with a couple of tosses, and Esther Pennock, Herb's wife, soon had her arms loaded with our winnings.

Then a representative of the proprietor came out.

"Take it easy, guys. Will ya?'" he said. "You'll have us broke. We ain't makin' a nickel."

Babe, Dugan, Pennock, and I then moved back some ten feet. Not content with merely throwing the ball, we began curving it. Or trying to. The balls were small, light in weight, like ten-cent balls, stuffed with kapok with oilcloth covers. Eventually, we tired of this and moved on, but not before we had returned to the majordomo of the booth most of the prizes we had won.

The next morning, on awakening, I had a queer feeling in my pitching arm. I looked at it. The elbow was swollen to three times its normal size. I showed it to my roommate, Joe Dugan, and he said, "The curves did it—and the lightweight balls."

I had to tell manager Huggins that I had injured my arm, but I told him that I must have hurt it on the field. We went from Philadelphia to Washington, where I was sent to a specialist who said that I wouldn't pitch again for the rest of the season. That opinion didn't satisfy Huggins, who sent me to Doc Knight, a bonesetter in Rochester, New York. He had me soak my arm every day in a tank of near-scalding water, and he massaged it, rotated it, and covered it with the hottest salve I have ever felt. It even caught fire at night. After three weeks of this treatment, he gave my elbow an upward flip while rotating the arm. Something clicked audibly. The injury was corrected, but the arm was very weak. Knight arranged for me to take light workouts with the Rochester club of the International League. After a week of this, I returned to the Yanks, and ten days later, I was our starting pitcher.

I can truthfully claim that I never hurt my arm in a professional baseball game. But street fairs? That's another story.

Now for 1927. There have been challenges to the title The Greatest Team by fans, media, and players, but I will be so bold as to defend the Yankees' designation on the basis of my experience as an active major league player for twenty years [*1919–38*] and, further, as the radio play-by-play broadcaster for the Cincinnati Reds for another twenty-five years [*1942–65, 1972*]. Although there have been many outstanding teams, especially with old-line organizations such as the Dodgers, Giants, Cubs, Athletics, Red Sox, Indians, Pirates, and Reds, I must say that I have never, never seen a team that I thought could beat the '27 bunch.

Instead of delving into facts and figures, I should like to deal with the even more important collective state of mind of our team. Huggins termed it well. He preached "attitude." Sometimes he used a similar word, *disposition,* "the natural tendency to an action or state of mind," as Webster's dictionary defines it. There could not have been a group with a better attitude and disposition than that ball club. There was no flamboyant display, no back slapping, no cheering, for this was before the days when professional athletes reacted to teammates' accomplishments with congratulatory enthusiasm. Our only concession to high-spirited behavior occurred after a victory in Yankee Stadium. On the way from the players' bench to the clubhouse we chanted, "Roll Out the Barrel," which became our theme song. [*The song in question is "The Beer Barrel Polka."*]

In 1927, the Yanks took first place on the second day of the season and held it for the rest of the way. There was no mystic force working; it was simply a nearly perfect, dynamic machine. We were not perfect. We did lose forty-four games, often beating ourselves. But, then, no athletic team I know of has been perfect—nor, for that matter, has any individual or group or company. We supplied that which had to be supplied, and in abundance when it was needed.

We were a contingent of twenty-five divergent personalities, yet each of us was totally dedicated to a peak effort and result. In effect, we had the same dedication to purpose for which Pete Rose is so properly famed today, and in our performance each of us maintained a sophisticated dignity. We were never rough or rowdy, just purposeful. [*The team never engaged in a fight on the field, and only once during the season was a Yankee, Joe Dugan, ejected from a game by an umpire.*]

Huggins instituted a rigid program of behavior for those men who were not in the starting lineup. If you were an extra for the day, you were expected to pay attention to the game. There was to be no talk about anything but baseball, no sitting slouched with feet up and chin resting on cupped hands. We sat like third-grade kids in front of a hard-shelled teacher. I recall one incident vividly. Our bull pen was out in left field, atop a slightly graded embankment in the open space between the main grandstand and the bleachers, and it was provided with a wooden bench. A telephone was installed so that Huggins could phone down to "get so and so ready." There was also a connecting telephone in the mezzanine box of Ed Barrow, who, from that vantage point, could oversee the whole stadium. One day, Barrow cast a critical eye toward the bull pen. It was a hot day, and one player was stretched out on the bench, apparently taking a snooze. The bull-pen phone rang. Barrow snorted, "Tell that lazy (bleep) to sit up straight. Get his feet on the ground. What the hell does he think we're paying him for?"

Miller Huggins could be firm, but he could also be gentle. I recall an incident in Philadelphia in 1927. After a great start, when he led the league in batting for a while, Mark Koenig suddenly went into a slump. After he had a disastrous day at the plate in a game at Shibe Park, Mark, who was an emotional person, sat slumped in the clubhouse, his head in his hands, a picture of dejection. Huggins walked over to the downcast Koenig. "It's all right, Mark," he said. "Don't worry. Remember, we're not paying you to hit four hundred. We're paying you to play shortstop. If you hit two seventy-five, that's all we expect." Hug said the right word at the right time, and Mark came out of his slump. (He batted .281 that year, and then, in 1928, he hit .319.)

Huggins tolerated some levity when the Yanks were well ahead. It was the custom of the regulars, after two were out in their turns at bat, to scale to the second step of the dugout, ready to charge out to their positions when the third out had been made. In 1927, the Yankee bench was on the third-base side of the field, not on the first-base side, as in more recent years. Ruth usually carried a large bandana handkerchief in a rear uniform pocket, and one day the rag was hanging over the rim. Tony Lazzeri, who enjoyed needling the Babe, borrowed a match from a spectator in an adjacent box seat and set fire to the rag. After the third out had been made, Ruth trotted to right field with actual smoke issuing from his rear. It took the big guy several moments to discover the joke, and the "bench" was hysterical.

As the season progressed, a gimmick came into being that proved rather prophetic and, I might add, destructive to opponents. It was given a name, five o'clock lightning. The games at that time began at 3:30 P.M. The Yankees did not always jump in front. Frequently, we had to come from behind. A sportswriter pointed out that we scored many of our runs and started many of our winning rallies in the eighth inning, which usually came up around 5:00. Earle Combs latched on to this ominous threat to the opposition. Almost every day, whether we were behind or in front, before our time at bat in the eighth, Earle came trotting in from center field yelling, "C'mon gang. Five o'clock lightning, five o'clock lightning." The superstition spread, and it frequently rang true. More than once I heard an opponent say that he feared the five o'clock Yankee onslaught.

Along these lines, I was often told, "You're a lucky guy to be pitching for that club. They score a lot of runs for you." Admittedly, I was lucky, but I must qualify this statement. As I have just said, the Yankees did not always score in the early innings, and so if you were not giving a good performance in the pitcher's box, you wouldn't be around for five o'clock lightning.

Indeed, you had to keep performing well to maintain your place in the pitching rotation. The club played at a high standard, and you were expected to measure up to that standard.

The Mite Manager [*Huggins was five feet four inches in height*] insisted on only a few rules, but he enforced them with rigidity. Hug was broad-minded about curfew on the road. Most clubs stipulated midnight as the time to be in your hotel room. Hug stated that that did not allow enough time to return from a show or some other form of entertainment. He set 1:00 A.M. as the deadline, and he held to it. Once, while we were in Philadelphia, I was invited to a birthday party in the suburb of Cynwyd. This was before the days of superhighways, and so it was a good forty minutes from our hotel. At 12:15, I asked for transportation back to the hotel. None was to be had, so I called for a cab. I walked through the lobby at 1:10. (I glanced at the clock above the main desk.) The next morning, I was invited to Huggins's room. Said he tersely, "Would you be willing to lose a thousand dollars if I can prove that you weren't in this hotel by one A.M.?" I said, "Sir, I got in at one-ten." Then I explained my dilemma. He replied, "Okay. I just wanted to know if you would tell the truth." [*How did Huggins know when Hoyt had arrived? It was a common practice for managers to bribe bellmen and room clerks to be alert to late arrivals.*]

At home we had to report to Yankee Stadium at 10:00 A.M., not to practice, just to sign in. This was a device, we supposed, to cut down on late hours the night before.

We were allowed no food in the clubhouse between games of doubleheaders, not even ice-cream sandwiches. And, of course, there was no beer [*even though the club owner, Jacob Ruppert, had become a millionaire through the manufacture and sale of beer.*]

As a club we generated a supreme confidence in our own amazing way. As a group of individuals we were a free-wheeling bunch. With only a few exceptions, centering around Lou Gehrig, we were night owls. But we were not nightclub addicts. [*Most of the nocturnal fun making occurred in the homes of people who enjoyed entertaining the Yankees.*] Not even Babe Ruth. Babe reigned like the king that he was—the King of Swat. He held night court in his suite in the hotels on the road, attired in a flowing red robe, red Moroccan slippers, with a hale and hearty laugh for all visitors. Like most Yankees of all eras, we enjoyed our fun. The penchant for entertainment was an escape from the intensity with which we had played in the afternoon. But it must be quickly established that neither Ruth nor any of the rest of us ever gave a poor performance because of anything that had happened the night before. We had, fortunately, a certain dignity that was reflected in our on-field performance.

[*In a letter to the author shortly before his death, Waite Hoyt enlarged upon the preceding paragraph: "There were three social segments on the club. There were those whom we can label the movie-going set, and there were those who were inclined toward house parties and social gatherings, and then there was Babe Ruth, who stood alone. The movie-going set was comprised of Gehrig, Combs, Paschal, Durst, Moore, and, usually, Koenig. The rest of the gang had substantial numbers of friends in each city on the road, and in New York, and we enjoyed sophisticated enter-tainment, lively though harmless. As for Ruth, he was a loner."*]

The New York Yankees of 1927 won the world chamionship from the Pittsburgh Pirates in four straight games. Then, in 1928, we again won the pennant and the World Series, from the St. Louis Cardinals, in four straight games. We were simply con-firming the vote of the Baseball Writers of America that awarded us the proud title of The Greatest Team of All Time.

For the World Series supplement to the October 9, 1982, issue of the *TV Guide* I wrote, "Occasionally in all branches of athletics, one team becomes a sort of freak outfit, or one individual comes along and is able to perform beyond all conception of normal thinking. The '27 Yankees were like that." But not only did we have great players. We were guided by the man I consider to be one of the best—if not *the* best—managers of all time, a man who in twelve years with the club won six pennants and three world championships and only once finished lower than third place. Because he was so self-effacing, unheralded, underrated, unacclaimed, unpublicized, I should like to end my contribution to this book with an extended tribute to and appreciation of Mil-ler Huggins.

The diminutive little guy came to New York in 1918. The Yanks finished third that year, and they were second in 1919 and again in 1920. The club was then owned by two colonels, the portly, affable T. L. Huston and the serious, precise German brewer Jacob Ruppert. Huston did not think much of Huggins, but Ruppert liked the little fellow. Huston wanted to get rid of the manager, and Ruppert fought for his retention. With the two colonels fighting, Hug's position in command was shaky indeed. In 1921 [*Waite Hoyt's first year with the club*], the Yankees won their first pennant, and the excitement spread a blanket of peace and contentment over the scene. [*In the World Series Hoyt won two games and lost the seventh and deciding contest, 1–0, because of an unearned run. His earned run average for the three games was 0.00, a record he shares with Christy Mathewson.*] Then, in 1922, everything went haywire. Ruth was tough to handle. He and teammates Bob Meusel and Fred Hofmann were suspended by Commissioner Kenesaw M. Landis for the first month of the season for disobeying an order by Landis. There were three or four fistfights on the bench. Players took their pleasures where they found them. Hug's influence was at its lowest ebb. He was held in slight esteem by his men, especially Ruth. The Babe was no bargain then—he was not liked by his peers or his manager.

In 1923, Huston sold his half interest in the club to Ruppert, and an abrupt change took place. Ruppert declared that Huggins was his manager and had full power to legislate, maintain discipline, and impose fines. The Mite Manager became the Mighty Manager despite his 5 feet 4 inches and 138 pounds. In a clubhouse meeting he asserted himself, and from then on the Yanks took on polish and dignity.

Huggins became our father confessor, our financial adviser, and our confidant, but never to excess, nor when he felt the occasion was not advantageous.

Pitching under Huggins was in many ways a learning experience. My first lesson came early in the 1922 season. I was laboring in a fifteen-inning game against the Boston Red Sox. In the first of the fifteenth the Sox had a man on second with two out and a left-handed batter at the plate. Even though he batted left-handed, he was a man against whom I had had excellent success. [*Left-handed batters are considered to have an advantage against right-handed pitchers, and vice versa.*] As I stood on the pitching rubber, I heard frantic yells from our bench. Huggins and his coaches were waving wildly toward first base, meaning "put him on." I was to give the batter an intentional walk, a piece of strategy I did not want to follow. I walked to the foul line and in a brash way yelled, "If you want to talk to me, come out here." A coach charged out with the message, and I walked the man at the plate. Joe Dugan, the next batter, doubled, and I lost a fifteen-inning game.

When I arrived at our bench, I had worked up a hot anger. Huggins poured fuel on it by saying, "You acted out there as if you didn't want to pitch."

I replied, "If I didn't want to pitch, I wouldn't have worked for fifteen innings."

The argument grew more bitter, and I raised my arm as if I was about to belt Huggins. At this time the press box at the Polo Grounds was on the field level. [*The Yankees played their home games at the Polo Grounds until 1923, when Yankee Stadium was opened.*] It was possible for the writers to look into the players' benches. The next day, Fred Lieb, writing for a New York paper, claimed that Huggins had suspended me for two weeks. This statement Huggins denied by saying, "I merely had a meeting with Hoyt. I told him he was neither fined nor suspended. He's just a kid, and I feel he's learned his lesson."

On another occasion, in Washington, I came out through the runway with our center fielder, Earle Combs. I told Earle, "When Sam Rice and Joe Judge come to bat, play them in left center field." They were both left-handed batters. [*And thus the center fielder would normally be expected to play toward right center field.*] Earle forgot what I had said, and then in the fourth inning both Judge and Rice tripled into left center field on balls that should have been outs. I was lifted. When I reached the bench, I shouted, "Why the hell don't you take the outfielders out once in a while. They shouldn't have had a run." Another argument with my manager took place, whereupon Huggins snorted, "You're fined a hundred dollars."

Wise guy me, I sarcastically cracked, "Only a hundred! How cheap. The grand, lofty Yankees!"

Huggins then obliged by saying, "All right, it's two hundred."

In Huggins's Yankee Stadium office there was a desk, a desk chair, and a leather-covered couch. It was sort of a psychiatrist's setup. I once said that I spent more time in that office than on the field. I heard many lectures in there, many admonitions, all of which were logical if sometimes unheeded.

On one occasion, he told me, "You know, Waite, a ballplayer should look around him. Try to discover some worthwhile occupation. Perhaps serve the public in some way, or humanity. You can become a man of substance if you apply yourself." [*Interestingly, Waite Hoyt became one of the very first ballplayers to take up radio announcing as a profession. For twenty-five years, he was the*

extremely successful play-by-play announcer for the Cincinnati Reds,
whose fans always welcomed rain delays so that they could hear his spon-
taneous reminiscences.]

Then I recall the time in Chicago in August 1929. Huggins,
Herb Pennock, a couple of other fellows, and I were in a taxicab
riding from the railroad station to our hotel, and the subject of
the stock market arose. Miller, in his quiet but affirmative way,
said, "Ya know, fellows, how many of you have money in the
market?" Without waiting for an answer, he went on, "I have
sold all my Florida holdings [*he had extensive properties around St.*
Petersburg]. This thing can't last. There's got to be an explosion
in the market. If I were you guys and I owned any stock, I'd get
rid of it. It's just going to boil over."

This was exactly two months before the stock market crash.

And then I recall an earlier occasion, in 1925, when Huggins
felt that I needed a few words of caution. He called me into his
stadium office and gave me a lecture on behavior patterns. He
said, "You're too friendly with people. You have your head in
the stands looking for friends. Cut that out. Concentrate. This is
your business, not a walk in the park. Also, learn to control your
emotions—and your habits." This last reference seemed to carry
a word of caution.

I answered, "Why are you saying all this to me. At that outing
at the inn there were other players besides me. Did you lecture
them?" [*The "inn" was a favorite Yankee hangout, a suburban*
"roadhouse" on the Boston Park Road called the Blossom Heath Inn.
Big bands often played there, and sometimes two or three musical Yan-
kees, like Benny Bengough, a catcher who played the saxophone, sat in
with the musicians. The occasion referred to here was one in which the
players celebrated a little more than usual, and reports of the incident
reached owner Jacob Ruppert, who spoke of it to Huggins, who in turn
mentioned it to Hoyt.]

He said, "Look, I'm counting on some ten or twelve players as
the core of next year's club, and in the future. I want men I can
depend on. The guys you referred to will not be with us next
year."

This was a reassuring lecture.

The scene that still most vividly colors my memories occurred
about September 15, 1929. I had pitched that day, but not for
long, having been knocked out by Cleveland in the middle of the
game. Huggins wasn't on the bench that day because he had

been suffering from what was thought to be a painful carbuncle on one cheek.

As I entered the clubhouse following my exit from the game, I saw him sitting next to the training table with a heat lamp penetrating the infected area. He looked very weak, downcast.

"What happened to you?" he asked in a hoarse whisper. [*Unlike some other clubs, the Yankees did not yet permit radio broadcasts of their games.*]

"Oh, Joe Hauser hit one in the seats with a couple on," I said. "So here I am."

He hesitated, applied a small towel to his cheek, and then asked, "How old are you?"

"I was thirty a week ago."

"There is something you should think about," he said. "You can never do after thirty what you could do so easily before thirty. You just don't come back that quickly. Not from physical strain, mental stress, or what have you. I told Colonel Ruppert last spring that you'd have an off year. [*In 1929, Hoyt won ten games and lost nine.*] You just weren't in shape. I told Pennock [*who had a sore arm*] and I'm telling you. Tomorrow go down and get your paycheck. You're through for the season. Get in good shape this winter. Come down next spring and have the year I know you can have."

That was the last time I saw Miller Huggins. His affliction was erysipelas, a fatal, torturous disease. The Mite Manager was taken to the hospital the next day, and he died on September 25, 1929. Part of me went with him. I had come to look upon him as my baseball father. Had he lived, I'm sure I would have remained to end my career with the Yankees. [*On May 30, 1930, Hoyt, along with Mark Koenig, was traded to Detroit.*] And had Hug inherited Joe McCarthy's players from the minor leagues [*in the middle and late thirties*], I'm certain he would have established a secure position as one of the finest managers ever to direct a major league baseball team.

WAITE C. HOYT

Cincinnati, Ohio
April 17, 1984

Preface

As Waite Hoyt recalled, in the centennial year of 1969 America's baseball writers chose the New York Yankees of 1927 as the greatest of all teams. I doubt that anything has happened since 1969 to call for a new election. The 1927 Yankees are still the greatest. This book tells the story of that team.

The Yankees of 1927 have hardly been ignored by other writers, but I think that there is room for another volume with a different format. Several years ago, I put together a book, *The Unforgettable Season*, that deals with the pennant race of 1908—the year of the so-called Merkle Blunder—from the viewpoint of the New York Giants, and my only source materials were contemporary news reports. More recently, I used the same approach with the 1934 St. Louis Cardinals in *The Dizziest Season*. There seems to be enough juice left in this method for one final fling, and where better to turn than to The Greatest Team ever?

Again, the real authors of a book whose title page bears my name are the men (and, occasionally, women) who were there on the spot to tell of what they had seen and heard and thought. They include, most prominently, the New York regulars on the Yankee beat, writers like James R. Harrison and John Drebinger of *The Times*; Frank Graham of the *Sun*; Fred Lieb of the *Post*; Ford C. Frick of the *Evening Journal*; Charles Segar of the *Daily Mirror*; Dan Daniel of the *Telegram*; "Monitor" (George E. Daley) of the *World*; Rud Rennie of the *Herald-Tribune*; Bill Slocum of the *American*; and Marshall Hunt of the *Daily News*. Joining them from time to time are such non-regulars as Grantland Rice, Damon Runyon, Paul Gallico, Dan Parker, John Kieran, Ed Sullivan, W. O. McGeehan, Bozeman Bulger, and even Ring Lardner. And there are visiting firemen from each of the Yankees' seven road cities, such as Austen Lake of the Boston *Evening Transcript*; Edward Burns of the Chicago *Tribune*; Stuart Bell of the Cleveland *Press*; H. G. Salsinger of the Detroit *News*; Bill Brandt of the Philadelphia *Public Ledger*; Martin J. Haley of the St. Louis *Globe-Democrat*; and John B. Keller of the Washington *Evening Star*.

The star of the book, naturally, is George Herman "Babe" Ruth, who is viewed from every conceivable position, on and off the field, beginning with his making of a motion picture in Hollywood in February and ending with his hitting of a home run in the final game of the World Series at Yankee Stadium in October. (Each of his record-breaking sixty home runs will be described by an eye witness.) The Babe is here in all his glory, but he isn't alone. It may be true that the 1927 Yankees without Ruth would be like *Hamlet* without Hamlet, but just as the Prince of Denmark had his indispensable supporting cast—Claudius, Gertrude, Polonius, Ophelia, Laertes, Horatio, Rosencrantz, Guildenstern—so too was the Sultan of Swat backed up by exceedingly able colleagues: Lou Gehrig, Bob Meusel, Tony Lazzeri, Earle Combs, Mark Koenig, Joe Dugan, Waite Hoyt, Herb Pennock, George Pipgras, Wilcy Moore, and, of course, manager Miller Huggins. They are all here, just as they were when each was part of the "greatest."

Because the action is mainly in New York in 1927, the heart of the Roaring Twenties, there are inevitable cameo appearances by personalities who were very much part of the mise-en-scène: Charles Lindbergh, Mayor Jimmy Walker, Jack Dempsey and Gene Tunney, Texas Guinan, Paul Whiteman, Bill Tilden, Tammany Young, Wayne B. Wheeler of the Anti-Saloon League, and a fifteen-year-old evangelist named Uldine Utley.

Again like *Hamlet*, everyone knows how this story turns out, but this should not spoil the pleasure of readers who would enjoy having the opportunity to turn back the clock and to live and work and play and travel, day by day, with those men who gained sports immortality on The Greatest Team ever.

Acknowledgments

My biggest debt of gratitude is to the American League's leading pitcher of 1927, a member of Baseball's Hall of Fame, Waite Hoyt. Not only did Waite Hoyt generously accept my invitation to write the Foreword and then produce far more than I might reasonably have expected, but, additionally, he was most gracious in dipping into his unusually vivid store of recollections in order to answer many questions of mine during several telephone conversations. Then, to top it off, he read the entire book while it was still a manuscript and offered numerous valuable suggestions. If this book has any merits, they derive in part from the efforts of Waite Hoyt. The finished product, however, is mine, and I must accept full responsibility for its organization and for the opinions that are expressed.

Several other people also assisted me. George Pipgras, who is the sole surviving '27 Yankee pitcher, responded promptly and fully to a letter of inquiry. Hall of Fame broadcaster Red Barber also answered a query immediately and in detail. Charles Segar, a principal contributor to this volume, was another who replied to my questions, and he provided me with one piece of information that I would not have obtained elsewhere. And Robert E. Skinner was most helpful on a medical matter.

Once more, everybody was accommodating at the newspaper division of the New York Public Library. This has been the main research library for my last three books, and I have yet to experience any unpleasantness within its borders—a rather good record of performance for any library. Another library in which I was treated with great hospitality is that of the National Baseball Hall of Fame in Cooperstown, New York. I am indebted to all of its staff members, most particularly Thomas Heitz and Donna Cornell. At the public libraries in Boston and Chicago, local history specialists quickly and accurately replied to my requests for information. And at my home base of operations, in New Orleans, three individuals continued, as in days gone by, to be as reliable as Yellowstone's Old Faithful: Evelyn Chandler and Gregory Spano, interlibrary loan librarian and microfilm librarian at the University of New Orleans, and the crème de la crème of research assistants, Paula Caruso Bryars.

On the other side of the coin, the most seemingly probable source of help, the New York Yankees' public relations office, was unresponsive to my telephone calls and ignored my letters. Sorry, but I must tell it "like it is."

THE NEW YORK YANKEES OF 1927

CATCHERS

	Birth Date	B	T	G	AB	R	H	HR	RBI	BA
Bengough (Benny)	7-27-98	R	R	31	85	6	21	0	10	.247
Collins (Pat)	9-13-96	R	R	92	251	38	69	7	36	.275
Grabowski (Johnny)	1-7-00	R	R	70	195	29	54	0	25	.277

INFIELDERS

	Birth Date	B	T	G	AB	R	H	HR	RBI	BA
Dugan (Joe)	5-12-97	R	R	112	387	44	104	2	48	.269
Gazella (Mike)	10-13-96	R	R	54	115	17	32	0	9	.278
Gehrig (Lou)	6-19-03	L	L	155	584	149	218	47	175	.373
Koenig (Mark)	7-19-02	B	R	123	526	99	150	3	62	.285
Lazzeri (Tony)	12-6-03	R	R	153	570	92	176	18	102	.309
Morehart (Ray)	12-2-99	L	R	73	195	10	20	1	20	.256
Wera (Julie)	2-9-02	R	R	38	42	7	10	1	8	.238

OUTFIELDERS

	Birth Date	B	T	G	AB	R	H	HR	RBI	BA
Combs (Earle)	5-14-99	L	R	152	648	137	231	6	64	.356
Durst (Cedric)	8-23-96	L	L	65	129	18	32	0	25	.248
Meusel (Bob)	7-18-96	R	R	135	516	75	174	8	103	.337
Paschal (Ben)	10-13-95	R	R	50	82	16	26	2	16	.317
Ruth (Babe)	2-6-95	L	L	151	540	158	192	60	164	.356

PITCHERS

	Birth Date	T	G	IP	SO	BB	W	L	ERA
Giard (Joe)	10-7-98	L	16	27	10	19	0	0	8.00
Hoyt (Waite)	9-9-99	R	36	256	86	54	22	7	2.63
Moore (Wilcy)	5-20-97	R	50	213	75	59	19	7	2.28
Pennock (Herb)	2-10-94	L	34	210	51	48	19	8	3.00
Pipgras (George)	10-20-99	R	29	166	81	77	10	3	4.11
Ruether (Dutch)	9-13-93	L	27	184	45	52	13	6	3.38
Shawkey (Bob)	12-4-90	R	19	44	23	16	2	3	2.89
Shocker (Urban)	8-22-90	R	31	200	35	41	18	6	2.84
Thomas (Myles)	10-22-97	R	21	89	25	43	7	4	4.87

1927

Monday, January 3

Babe Ruth's salary, like Babe Ruth's appetite, has long been a matter of public interest, and the boys are discussing it plenty this winter. Some of the lads think that the Babe will demand and should get $150,000 for a season's work. Others argue that $75,000 is a goodly sum and should be sufficient.

This writer is inclined to agree with the latter group. While Mr. Ruth may draw a half million dollars at the gate, the fact remains that most ball clubs cannot afford to pay the sum mentioned—and, frankly, this writer isn't yet convinced that any player is worth it.

[In 1921, when Babe Ruth set major league records with 59 home runs and 171 runs batted in, he was paid $30,000. Before the start of the 1922 season, Ruth signed a three-year contract calling for $52,000 a year, with an option for two additional years. The club exercised its option, and thus the contract ended with the 1926 season, with Ruth's home run and RBI records still standing.

In 1927, Ford C. Frick was a thirty-two-year-old baseball writer. In the summer of 1934, he would leave sportswriting to become the National League's publicity director, and in November of the same year, he succeeded John Heydler as league president. Early in 1951, after the resignation of Albert "Happy" Chandler, Frick became baseball's third commissioner. This piece might provide a clue as to why Frick was chosen by club owners to fill two of the highest positions in their establishment.]

Ford C. Frick, New York Evening Journal

Wednesday, January 12

Col. Jacob M. Ruppert
Yankee Stadium
New York City, N.Y.

Dear Col. Ruppert:

Looka, Col., if Babe Ruth wants $75,000 a year, maybe you had better give it to him. I'll explain. Or rather, supposing that I ask you a question instead: Why not give it to him? He's worth it, isn't he? You've got it, haven't you? Well, then—Everything is settled splendidly, eh? This column believes in paying a man what he is worth, especially if the money comes from somebody else's pocket. Practically, Ruth is worth almost anything he asks for. The profit on him at $52,000 a year must be simply enormous and at $75,000 will not be very much less. What do you say we give it to him, huh?

I don't want to hurt the feelings of anyone on your team, Col., but the Babe is just about the whole show. I don't know what your yearly profits are on baseball, but I do know that if you have no Ruth on your team they will be just about 95 per cent less than they have been. Why shouldn't the Babe share in the financial success of your team since he is directly responsible for it?

Dawgonnim, he's the greatest press agent any athletic team ever had. Everything he does is a story. When he strikes out, it is as big a story as when he hits one. He can hit more home runs than anyone else and he can pick more crucial spots to strike out than anyone. He is ready copy day and night. You will never have enough money to buy the annual space that Babe Ruth gets for nothing in the press throughout the country. Does he get the dough?

Well, Col., if this will help decide you to give Babe the extra smackers, it won't have been in vain. The fellers don't want to see a row between you and Ruth over dough and they don't want to see anything happen that might cause him to leave the Yanks.

I suppose I'm butting in and it's none of my business, Col., but I just wish you'd come right out in the open and tell the newspaper boys that you are going to give Ruth $75,000 and then we'll all rest easily.

[*Although Babe Ruth, in fact, had a financial adviser, Christy Walsh, all of baseball's salary negotiations at this time were carried out by the parties directly involved, players and club owners, without the intervention of agents, attorneys, and accountants. The club owners, moreover, actually paid the salaries with their own money instead of taking advantage of tax loopholes to pass on the expense to their fellow citizens.*

The fifty-nine-year-old Jacob Ruppert owned the brewery bearing his name, which he had inherited from his father, and he had served four terms (1901–08) as a Democratic congressman. In 1915, he and an *associate, T. L. Huston, purchased the Yankees for $450,000, and in 1922, Ruppert bought Huston's interest for $1.2 million to become the club's sole owner. Yankee Stadium opened the following year. A lifelong bachelor, Ruppert lived in a twelve-room apartment at 1120 Fifth Avenue, where his staff of servants included a butler, maid, valet, cook, and laundress. In 1889, at the age of twenty-two, he was appointed a colonel on the staff of New York Governor David B. Hill, and thereafter he was always known as Colonel Ruppert.]*

Paul Gallico, New York *Daily News*

Wednesday, January 19

There is a fault in the armor of the greatest slugger of them all, the man who has inspired more fear in the breasts of more pitchers than any other hitter, present day or past. For several years up to this last, when Tony Lazzeri snatched the doubtful honor from him, Babe Ruth led the American League and usually all baseball in the number of strikeouts.

Miller Huggins, manager of the Yankees, declares that the Babe's "whiffings" are due to two causes—mental strain and the desire to make good because he feels the responsibility on his shoulders, and the fact that he nearly always disdains "safety first," or the producing of a mere single, and takes his full, long swing for a home run. Huggins asserts that if Ruth shortened his swing and tapped or "placed" the ball he would make more hits, have a bigger batting average, and cut his strikeouts practically to nothing. But then the Babe wouldn't be the gate attraction he is for the Yankees. The fans want that old over-the-fence sock.

[*Actually, Babe Ruth did not strike out as often as is popularly believed. Only three times prior to 1927, and only five times during his entire career, did he lead the American League in strikeouts, whereas Jimmy Foxx led in this category seven times. Ruth's top mark was reached in 1923, when he whiffed ninety-three times. Contrast this with more recent performances. Including even the strike-shortened year of 1981, the American League's strikeout leader for every year since 1957 and the National League's leader for every year since 1958 has fanned more than a hundred times. In 1969, and again in 1970, Bobby Bonds of the*

*San Francisco Giants had more than twice the number of strikeouts that
Ruth had in 1923.*]

Monitor [*pen name of George Daley*], New York *World*

Sunday, January 23

Hollywood—Babe Ruth has decided to enter the motion picture
field. It was announced here today that Ruth had signed a contract with the First National Corporation and would be starred in
a picture to be called *Babe Comes Home*. It was stated that he
would start working within a few days.

Ruth has been on the vaudeville circuit during the winter season and has been appearing in Southern California for the past
month.

[*Several stories have been told of how George Herman Ruth acquired
his nickname. According to one, Jack Dunn, who signed him to his first
professional contract, with the Baltimore club in the International
League, gave him the name because he looked so young. A more likely
explanation is that he gained his sobriquet when he was a small boy
living in a charity school in Baltimore. According to this version, he
could not hold back his tears when he was picked on by older boys, who
thereupon called him Babe.*]

The New York Times

Thursday, February 3

Members of the Prudential Insurance Company Athletic Association, an organization of 6,000 members, are renewing their
appeal for the modification of the rule governing the intentional
walk. Commissioner Kenesaw M. Landis and the various presidents have been petitioned to consider the matter at the next
meeting of the playing rules committee.

"We feel," says George Rostock, president of the association,
"that a great deal of the romance of baseball is lost when pitchers
deliberately pass the heavy hitters.

"Men and women travel from the suburbs to the ball parks

and put up with great inconvenience of travel. It doesn't appeal to their sense of sportsmanship to see a heavy hitter deliberately walked three of the four times he goes to the plate."

The revision suggested is that when a batter is deliberately walked, he may decline to take first base and stay at bat. Then if three additional balls are thrown, the batter would be permitted to take third base, all runners on the bases automatically scoring.

Babe Ruth would whoop with joy if such a rule were ever adopted. He's the boy who is handed most of the free tickets to first base. [*Babe Ruth was not only the most frequent recipient of the intentional walk; he was responsible for its becoming a recurrent feature of the game. In pre-Ruthian days, pitchers rarely issued intentional walks.*]

Will Wedge, New York Sun

Monday, February 7

Babe Ruth has the most-talked-of waistline in the world. Not since Big Bill Taft [*who weighed about three hundred pounds*] adorned the presidential suite in the White House [*from 1909 until 1913*] has belt-line corpulence received such play in the newspapers, and it is a question whether Big Bill's weight would have been the more talked about had the Babe been "bustin' 'em" in Big Bill's political era. The public interest in the case of Taft was different from Ruth's. Taft provided merriment and good humor with his rolling avoirdupois. But every extra pound on the Bambino causes fidgets and alarm to the Babe's public. Fandom, at this season of the year, lies awake at night wondering if Babe's career will die of fatty degeneration of the batting average.

The fear is not without foundation. Ruth wasn't in shape for the 1925 season, with the result that he was a complete flivver as a home run artist—or any other kind, for that matter. [*"Flivver" came into the language about ten years earlier as a slang term for a Ford car. Soon it was used to refer to all dilapidated automobiles. In 1925, Ruth was not in shape to play baseball, and he had his worst season, with a batting average of .290 and only 25 home runs and 66 runs batted in.*] His adoring public naturally has been sceptical of the big fellow's willingness to "do the right thing" in the off season.

Last season Ruth was great and all because he attended to his knitting with plenty of gym work and careful attention to his diet. [*In 1926, which, as noted earlier, was the last year of his five-year contract, Ruth batted .372, with 47 home runs and 145 RBIs.*] Ruth's program this year is not so encouraging. He is fooling around in Hollywood, expending his energies in picture making. Babe maintains he will be right for the coming season. So, too, do Artie McGovern, his trainer, and Christy Walsh, his manager. Both are smart fellows who also have a financial interest in the girth of Ruth's waistline.

Ed Hughes, New York *Telegram*

Wednesday, February 9

Babe Ruth celebrated his thirty-third birthday yesterday in Los Angeles by establishing a trust fund of $33,000 for himself in the Bank of Manhattan Company, New York.

This is part of the money he has saved from vaudeville and picture making this winter. In a telegram to the bank, George Herman said that he is planning a $100,000 trust fund but is holding off until he has signed a Yankee contract.

If all goes well, Babe said, he will increase the fund to $50,000 by June 1 and make it an even $100,000 by the end of the year.

New York *Evening Journal*

Thursday, February 10

Babe Ruth, now in Hollywood, has returned his contract for this season and threatened to quit baseball because it called for the same salary he received for the past five years—$52,000.

"I think the New York club used exceedingly poor judgment," Ruth said, "and I have no intention of signing.

"I don't care to mention how much I expect to get, but if the Yankee management refuses to meet my terms I may get out of baseball altogether.

"I don't know what I will do if I quit baseball, but I'm not going to worry about that until I see whether the Yankees will meet my terms."

[*The Yankee management had indeed sent Ruth a contract for $52,000 a year, but this was a mere formality. Baseball rules stipulated that if a contract was not mailed to a player on or before February 15 he would become a free agent. Since the Yankee management could not confer with Ruth until March, he was sent a duplicate of his 1926 contract.*

As for what Ruth would do if he left baseball, an Associated Press story published in various newspapers on February 11 stated that he was thinking of "opening a string of gymnasiums and starting a correspondence course on how to keep fit physically and how to play baseball."]

New York *Evening World*

Saturday, February 12

We have an interesting letter from Arthur A. McGovern, the physical engineer who went to Hollywood to take charge of the Babe Ruth belt line. [*McGovern was the proprietor of a gymnasium at 41 East Forty-second Street.*] He says:

"When I came out here to take the Babe in hand, I thought the publicity concerning Ruth's being in good physical condition, due to golf, tennis, and other sports, was the bunk. But when I caught up with the big fellow I received a very pleasant surprise. He really is in good physical condition. I figured that a fourteen-week vaudeville tour was likely to put the rollers under anybody. The truth is that most of Ruth's tour was in this part of the country, and he has taken every opportunity to get out on a golf course, not for the exercise, but because he loves the game.

"The Babe is ten pounds lighter than he was a year ago. He is down to 231 pounds and his best weight is around 220 or 222, so there is not a great deal of work for me to do beyond a general systematic toning up and a concentration on the abdominal muscles. This will be easy in conjunction with the vast amount of exercise he is getting in the picture. The studio has constructed for Ruth a handball court and exercise room, supplying all that is necessary for us to work with. My job will be not so much to put the Babe in shape as to prevent him from becoming stale or overtrained.

"Ruth books out of here on February 25, directly for the training camp, and if he goes right through the season he will have had two years of solid work without a letup. In spite of this vigorous regime, I am glad to report that he is in splendid condition."

So that is that. The Babe apparently intends to go right to the training camp, and you will notice that nothing is intimated about his being a holdout. At any rate, nobody is better qualified to speak of Ruth's condition than Arthur McGovern, who knows the Babe inside out. If McGovern says he is fit and ready, the Sultan of Swat should have a big year.

[*The most popular of the various nicknames given to Babe Ruth was Sultan of Swat, the creation of Grantland Rice.*]

Walter Trumbull, New York *Evening Post*

Sunday, February 13

Los Angeles—Filmdom's latest sensation, Babe Ruth, has stood the test of popularity in the Far West.

Friday night Ruth was introduced at the Hollywood Stadium, that select show place of boxing. The fans, accustomed to celebrities and inclined to politely snub most of them, gave Ruth an ovation that threatened to ruin the roof. For a full five minutes the big boy stood in the middle of the ring, bowing and smiling nervously, while his friends of Hollywood thundered their greeting.

It was a wonderful tribute, and it caught Ruth right in the throat. He choked up, blushed, and mumbled a brief, husky thanks to his "fellow motion picture workers."

Martin Burke, New York *American*

"Not a chance," said Ed Barrow when informed of a report from the Coast that Ruth had been assured that he would get a two-year contract.

"No more contracts for more than a year," Barrow went on. "We have discovered that men who tie themselves up for long terms immediately relax and take it easy. They only hustle in the last year of the term when they are fighting for a renewal. I could name ten players who cajoled their clubs into long contracts and at once fell off in their work. And so Ruth's contract will be for one year."

[*The sixty-year-old Barrow was the Yankees' general manager and, more than any other single person, was responsible for the club's success. Never a professional player, he served in almost every other capacity in baseball. In 1896, as manager of the Paterson, New Jersey, team in the newly formed Atlantic League, he signed to his first contract Honus Wagner, who would become the greatest infielder of all time. He piloted various other teams until, in 1918, he became manager of the Boston Red Sox, one of whose pitchers was George Herman "Babe" Ruth. Until 1918, Ruth had never appeared in a professional game except as a pitcher (or a pinch hitter), but Barrow at once began to convert him into an outfielder. After the 1919 season, Ruth was sold to the Yankees, and a year later, he was joined by Barrow, who began to create a dynasty. Before his arrival, the Yankees had never won a pennant and had seldom finished in the first division; during his twenty-six years with the club, it won fourteen pennants and only once finished out of the first division. He encouraged Jacob Ruppert to build Yankee Stadium; he laid the groundwork for the club's vast farm system; and he established the authority of the field manager, even prohibiting Ruppert from entering the clubhouse. Indeed, because of Barrow's abhorrence of night baseball, light towers were not seen in Yankee Stadium until 1947, the year after his retirement.*

Barrow, incidentally, moved Ruth from the mound to the outfield, despite the fact that the Babe was a superb pitcher who had had twenty-three victories in 1916 and twenty-four in 1917, who had had a league-leading ERA of 1.75 in 1916, and who had set a World Series record for consecutive scoreless innings that remained unbroken for more than forty years. If the designated hitter rule had been in effect then, Ruth would never have come to bat and he would have ended his career without hitting even one home run. And he was not the only hurler to make the shift. George Sisler, winner of two batting championships with averages over .400; Lefty O'Doul, winner of two batting championships; and Stan Musial, winner of seven batting championships, all began their professional careers as pitchers, and like Ruth they demonstrated their prowess with a bat. One can only speculate as to how many mute, inglorious American League sluggers will forever remain buried because of the designated hitter.]

Monitor, New York *World*

The Yankees are not likely to repeat as pennant winners this year. Their pitching corps is lacking in well-distributed quality as compared to the Philadelphia, Chicago, Cleveland, and Detroit staffs. The Yankees have a fine lot of veterans, but it is uncertain how much more good baseball there is left in them.

The Athletics, Senators, and Tigers threaten to beat them out.

W. B. Hanna, New York *Herald-Tribune*

Wednesday, February 16

Practically the entire Yankee ball club has enlisted in the Holdout Brigade of 1927. This became official when Ed Barrow issued a list of those whose signed contracts had been received. This communiqué showed that 21 players had boarded the bandwagon. A simple process of subtraction developed the fact that 16 were recalcitrant.

The holdouts include three outstanding pitchers, two regular catchers, the infield with the exception of first baseman Lou Gehrig, and the entire outfield. In short, the only regulars of 1926 who have signed are pitcher Waite Hoyt, pitcher Bob Shawkey, and Gehrig.

The Yankee situation is the most aggravated of its kind which yet has affected the club at this stage of the off season. It is a reaction to the surprising success of the club last year. Here are the lads who are having their little wrangle with Ruppert and Barrow and their estimated salaries for 1927:

Pitchers: Herb Pennock, $16,000; Walter Ruether, $11,000; Urban Shocker, $11,000; Walter Beall, $6,000; Henry Johnson, $5,000; Wilcy Moore, $5,000.

Catchers: Benny Bengough, $8,000; Pat Collins, $8,000.

Infielders: Tony Lazzeri, $9,000; Mark Koenig, $9,000; Joe Dugan, $14,000; Spencer Adams, $7,000.

Outfielders: Babe Ruth, $65,000; Bob Meusel, $15,000; Earle Combs, $12,000; Bob Paschal, $8,000.

Dan Daniel, New York *Telegram*

Thursday, February 17

Hollywood—The echoes of some 230 pounds of man mountain, as it bounced up and down on the floor, reverberated through the corridors of the Hollywood Plaza Hotel. Patrons of the hotel were at a loss to determine the reason for such noise and shakes and finally came to the conclusion that another earthquake had hit town.

Earthquakes, especially Hollywood earthquakes, give a shake, or perhaps two, and then cease. But nothing of the sort happened this morning. The rumbling and noise continued for several minutes before an investigation was started.

It was finally found that Babe Ruth, with a few idle moments on his hands before breakfast, was taking some exercise. Because of the rain Ruth found it impossible to do any outdoor work and was strutting his stuff within the four walls of his room. Upon request he finished in the basement.

Martin Burke, New York *American*

Saturday, February 19

What will be the salary demands of major league players when asked to sign new contracts for 1928? Frenzied finance, unless it is checked, is bound to make serious trouble for the magnates.

During the coming season players who draw comparatively low salaries will envy Ruth, Ty Cobb, Tris Speaker, Rogers Hornsby, Eddie Collins, Ed Roush, Grover Cleveland Alexander, Zack Wheat, Frankie Frisch, and others, who will draw from $18,000 all the way up to $75,000.

Inasmuch as magnates have allowed money to dominate baseball, the ordinary players cannot be blamed when they put on the screws with the determination to get larger slices of their employers' wealth. The magnates will open their eyes when it's too late!

Joe Vila, New York *Sun*

Sunday, February 20

Enraged at reports that Manager Miller Huggins is seeking a first baseman who bats right-handed, Henry Louis Gehrig, the Yankee Strong Boy, has decided to go South with the first squad of Yanks this week. Lou declares that he has ordered 77 bats for 1927 and will swing them wickedly as soon as the Yanks get to St. Petersburg [*the Yankees' spring training site since 1925*].

The Yankee rookies will leave on Friday, and ordinarily a "regular," as Gehrig is now classed, wouldn't associate with the rookies. But Lou wants to go. He is chafing, eager, "rarin'."

"I don't know what all this talk of a right-handed hitting first baseman is about. It can't be that anyone who can field any better than I do is needed, and if this mysterious guy is being considered because he may be more effective in hitting left-handed pitching, why that's a laugh. I can hit left-handers as well as right-handers, and just as far."

[*If, indeed, there had been any intention of replacing or complementing Gehrig at first base with a right-handed player, the idea was quickly dropped. A native of upper Manhattan and the son of German immigrants, Gehrig was a football and baseball star at the High School of Commerce, where his biggest moment came in his senior year, in 1921, in a so-called prep school "World Series" game in Chicago. The game was won by Commerce over Chicago's Lane Tech, when in the ninth inning with the bases loaded Gehrig hit a home run. From Commerce High Gehrig enrolled in Columbia College, where he continued to play football and baseball and was sometimes called the "Babe Ruth of Columbia." Baseball proved to be a greater lure than the classroom, and at the end of his sophomore year, in 1923, Gehrig signed a contract with the Yankees. In 1923 and 1924, he played a few games in New York, but he spent most of those seasons learning his trade with the Yankees' farm club at Hartford, in the Eastern League. After batting .369 in 1924, with 37 home runs, Gehrig was called up to the Yankees. He began the 1925 season as understudy to first baseman Wally Pipp. When, on June 2, Pipp had a headache and asked for an aspirin tablet, he was replaced by Gehrig, who in 1927 had not missed a game since that day. In 1925, he batted .295, with 20 home runs and 68 RBIs, and in 1926, he batted .313, with 16 home runs and 107 RBIs. He was as yet no threat to Babe*]

Ruth as a home-run hitter. As for fielding, Gehrig was a good but not great first baseman.]

Monitor, New York World

Monday, February 21

Babe Ruth winds up his picture Friday and takes a train on Saturday for New York to talk matters over with Col. Jake Ruppert. For his seventeen days in front of the camera Ruth is being paid $25,000 with a percentage of gross sales over $400,000.

Mark Kelly, Los Angeles Examiner

When asked to comment on the report that the sixteen who were listed as holdouts last week were still holding out, Ed Barrow said, "There will be no information as to who has and who hasn't signed. No more publicity for the birds who think they can hold up this ball club. We have no holdouts."

Dan Daniel, New York Telegram

Tuesday, February 22

The conviction is inescapable that baseball salaries are running into altogether too much money. Too much money breeds a lot of children who often get out of hand and become unruly.

Dan Daniel, New York Telegram

Friday, February 25

Hollywood—Babe Ruth is working hard until two and three in the morning to complete his picture. Hundreds of extras are being handled in relays. to keep up with America's hero as he hustles through his scenes.

"That picture will have to be completed Saturday because I'm going to New York Saturday evening at six o'clock," was Babe's ultimatum to First National officials.

New York American

Saturday, February 26

San Diego—George Herman "Babe" Ruth was found not guilty in Police Court today on charges of violating the State Child Labor Law, preferred by Stanley Gue, deputy labor commissioner, in connection with Ruth's appearance at a local theater the week of January 10.

Testimony at the trial showed that Ruth used children on the stage during his performance, but that none of them had been paid to appear and that none of them had been asked by him to come upon the stage.

New York American

Sunday, February 27

Los Angeles—The Big Bambino they call him, and that's just what he is. [*Residents of New York's Little Italy were the first to call Ruth* bambino, *the Italian word for "babe."*] A great, big, overgrown kid! Happy-go-lucky, bubbling over with pep, an all-around good fellow and a "bull" artist deluxe. That's how you find him when he's not playing, thinking, or dreaming of baseball.

A few days ago at First National Studios we got the big dope on Mr. Ruth "at ease."

Ruth has his mind made up on what he's going to do when he's through, and he hasn't any objection to letting the world in on it.

"None of that minor league ball for me," Ruth says. "When I feel myself slipping I'm going to get out before they start writing sob stories about how the Bambino is near the end.

"I want my best days remembered by the fans. I don't want to be referred to as a has-been. You can bet the family jewels that there'll be no minors for yours truly." [*It had been customary for*

*major league players to end their careers on one of the dozens of minor
league teams then in existence.*]

About this time a lunch whistle blew, and we beat it off the set
to grab a sandwich. While the rest of us were putting away the
groceries, Ruth and his trainer, Arthur McGovern, did some
road work. No lunch for the Bambino. [*That Ruth could skip a
meal might seem surprising in light of the popular legend concerning his
allegedly voracious appetite. Actually, Ruth was not an avaricious eater,
and certainly there is no truth to the frequently told stories of his devouring as many as a dozen hot dogs at one sitting.*] When we got back on
the set, Ruth loosened up again. When somebody asked him if
he read very much, he replied:

"No, reading, like picture shows, is almost taboo. They're both
hard on the eyes, and I've got to watch the old optics closer than
anything else. [*Another player who protected his eyes by scrupulously
avoiding motion picture theaters was Rogers Hornsby, who had a lifetime
batting average of .358 and is generally regarded as the best right-
handed batter of all time.*] Whose stuff do I like best? That's a
pretty tough question, but altogether I think Charles Van Loan
wrote the best sport stories ever put out. That guy knew baseball
and could write plenty." [*Van Loan, who died of nephritis in 1919 at
the age of forty-two, had been a sportswriter in Los Angeles and New
York and an editor of the* Saturday Evening Post. *He wrote many
sports stories and novels, including* The Big League, The Lucky Seventh, *and* Ten Thousand Dollar Arm.]

Babe had to leave for a few minutes. After a half hour of gam-
bolling before the camera, he returned and wiped the sweat off
his forehead and made us all sleepy with a huge yawn.

"Great life this," he interjected between gapes. "It's awful
tough but darned interesting. If somebody'd make a John Barrymore [*perhaps, at this time, America's finest actor*] out of me, I'd like
this movie game as a steady diet. But we can't all be handsome
and have brains, too. Lucky thing for me I don't need either."

Ruth was interrupted by his director. He was handed a mouth
organ and told to drape himself over a bench and play away
while they shot a closeup. And, much to our surprise, Babe
obliged by getting some honest-to-goodness music out of the ancient instrument.

"My only musical accomplishment," he shouted as we left
the set.

Our last glimpse of the great Babe Ruth showed him seated on the bench, grinning and blowing away on the harmonica as if he was having the time of his life.

Edmund C. Luster, New York American

Babe Ruth is demanding a two-year contract calling for $100,000 a year. After waiting 48 hours to give Col. Jacob Ruppert ample time to think over his request, Ruth made his demands public as he stepped on a New York train last night. He did so by releasing his reply to Ruppert's offer of $52,000 a year.

In his letter, Ruth wrote,

"Colonel Ruppert—Dear Sir: I am prepared to report at St. Petersburg, but only on the basis of $100,000 per year for two years, plus refund of $7,700 held out from my salary in the past. [*The reference is to fines assessed by the club for misbehavior.*] I think you are entitled to know what terms I honestly expect and, therefore, the figure is not padded with intentions of accepting less.

"The New York club has profited from five of my best years. During that period my earning power to the club has greatly increased while my salary has remained unchanged. If 1926 had been a poor playing year my salary for 1927 would now most likely be reduced. If I were in any other business I would probably receive a new contract at higher salary without request. Or rival employers could bid for my services. Baseball law forces me to work for the New York club or remain idle, but it does not prevent a man from being paid for his value." [*Until the successful legal challenge of baseball's reserve clause in 1974, a player was bound to the club by whom he was employed. Literally, when the club made an offer, he had to "take it or leave it."*]

"Taking all things into consideration, I sincerely believe I am entitled to $100,000 per season. I realize your expense and risks and want to be fair and friendly as you have always been to me. I have made no threats to quit baseball. Such threats are not necessary because unless I accept your figure I will be prohibited from playing with another club and barred from baseball, regardless of my desires.

"(Signed) BABE RUTH"

As he boarded the train, Ruth was cheered by a big crowd from his film company—actors, actresses, extras by the hundreds, cameramen, electricians, carpenters, and messenger boys.

It was just a genuine expression of good fellowship from a crowd which has found Ruth to be all a national idol should be. It's worth a fellow's life to utter one word against Babe Ruth on the First National lot.

Ruth declared he was going to sleep all the way to New York. For the past week he has been obliged to work far into the night in order to finish his picture. He closed his make-up kit at 3:30, just two and one-half hours before train time.

Trainer Arthur McGovern broke in to remark that the Babe's sleep would be broken up by some exercises calculated to keep the big fellow in trim. McGovern has been persistent at his job and has seldom let a day slip by without making his charge go through a long group of strenuous setting-up exercises.

Unless his train is delayed, Ruth will be in New York Wednesday to confer with Colonel Ruppert.

Martin Burke, Los Angeles *Examiner*

Spring prices quoted yesterday by New York betting commissioners made the Giants and Athletics favorites to win their respective 1927 pennant races.

The New York Times

Monday, February 28

Baseball is on the threshold of the most interesting salary controversy in its long history. As the outstanding turnstile attraction in the game, a player who has broken and rebroken every attendance record in the league, Mr. Ruth is cheap at $100,000. He has contributed more to the group wealth of American League magnates in the last five years than all the other stars combined.

It is on this point that the Colonel has a justifiable squawk. While Mr. Ruth's artistic gifts enhance the business interests of all the magnates, the Colonel alone pays the freight.

Joe Williams, New York *Telegram*

The transcontinental negotiations between Babe Ruth and Colonel Jacob Ruppert have reached what the diplomats would call an impasse. Recovering slightly from a siege of fever and chills which attacked him as he read that Ruth's ultimatum was a two-year contract calling for $100,000 a year, with the remission of $7,700 which had been deducted from the Babe's salary as a punitive measure, Colonel Ruppert gradually became coherent enough to say, "Unreasonable." Then his vocabulary gave out as he lapsed into hoarse whispers.

The Colonel has not yet begun to deliver his counter-ultimatums, but he intimates that there will be considerable intimating as soon as Ruth arrives. "I will say nothing," declared the Colonel, "until Ruth gets here, then the thing will be thrashed out."

"Do you consider Ruth's terms reasonable or unreasonable?" he was asked.

Colonel Ruppert gasped at the banality of the question, then replied with considerable emphasis, "Unreasonable."

As the ultimatum of Colonel Ruppert seems quite as ultimate as the ultimatum of Babe Ruth, it would seem that Ruth was not to start the season with the Yankees. If the mood which was on Colonel Ruppert yesterday continues it looks as though Ruth would return to Hollywood and continue to hurl left-handed pies in the interests of the silent drama. [*In October, the era of talking pictures would begin with the showing of* The Jazz Singer.] Also it looks as though there would be a great saving in the matter of ticket takers at the Yankee Stadium.

W. O. McGeehan, New York *Herald-Tribune*

The only stunning surprise in G. Herman Ruth's demands on Colonel Jacob Ruppert is the revelation that the Yankee club actually deducted those famous fines from his paychecks. This will leave some of baseball's closest observers gasping with astonishment. [*Usually, fines levied against players remained uncollected.*]

The $5,000 fine imposed on G. H. Ruth when the home-run king jumped the club in 1925 was in real money, as it turns out. [*On August 29, 1925, when the club was in Washington, Yankee manager Miller Huggins suspended Ruth indefinitely and fined him $5,000 for persistently breaking training rules. This was the largest fine ever imposed against any player. Two days later, in New York, Ruth conferred with Ruppert, who totally supported his manager. Ruth then apologized for his conduct; he was reinstated as a player, but the fine was not*] *revoked.*] And there was a fine of something like $2,000 way back in 1922 which the Babe hasn't forgotten. That was the time that many of the Yankee players made a boon companion of an amusing and obliging chap who turned out to be a detective in the employ of the Yankee owners. [*This man pretended to be a base-ball writer for one of New York's fourteen daily newspapers.*]

Nobody can remember offhand where the odd $700 part of the $7,700 demand for restitution was assessed. Perhaps it's com-pound interest at 5 per cent since the original assessment.

The letter mailed by Ruth to Colonel Ruppert is a logical doc-ument, which is proof positive that the Babe didn't write it. Doubtless it contains his real sentiments and a genuine signature, but the fine hand of the publicity agent is apparent all through the composition.

That demand for the return of the $7,700 in fines, however, is something that only a ballplayer would think of inserting. It sprang from the heart. It's the personal touch.

John Kieran, *The New York Times*

Tuesday, March 1

St. Petersburg—The collapse of the Florida boom has developed a silver lining for some of the Yankee party [*those who had already reported for spring training*].

Rents are so cheap that those who brought their wives along have forsaken the official hotel for the quiet of family life in an apartment. Others are finding that this method of living will make it economically possible to send for their honeys. [*For vari-ous reasons, including detected fraud, a number of Florida real-estate companies had gone bankrupt during the winter of 1926–27, causing property values to plunge disastrously.*]

After the first week of hotel life it becomes increasingly easy for the married men to devise ways and means of getting their helpmates down here. For, regardless of the propensity to con-sider all people in public life inclined toward wildness, your base-ball men are family men.

They are compelled to be away from home for 77 days during the regular season, in addition to this 7-week training jaunt, which is almost half the year. People who envy the easy life of the ballplayer might talk this item over at the dinner table tonight.

People talk freely to strangers here. Last year it was a titillating romance of quick and heavy profits; this year it is a dirge of cheap rents and empty apartments.

You can get three rooms and a bath furnished in the heart of town for from $40 to $60 per month. I heard of a 5-room house with $5,000 furnishings renting at $26 a month.

The boys and girls are trying to get in a few golden hours down here to compensate somewhat for those many lonely ones of the campaign.

Frank Wallace, New York *Evening Post*

The boys in the Roaring Forties [*a reference to streets in midtown Manhattan*] will bet you that Babe Ruth doesn't get the hundred thousand. They are willing to lay 2 to 1 the home-run monopolist signs for less than $100,000 despite the fact that he has publicly stated he will quit the game rather than accept a compromise salary.

Ruppert's pride is fully as great as the Babe's. Insiders say he is not unwilling to give the Babe's salary a vigorous boost, but he'll fight to the last money bag to keep him out of the $100,000 class.

New York *Telegram*

As George Herman Ruth draws nearer and nearer his home, his two employers, Col. Jacob Ruppert and Ed Barrow, appear to be close to a panic for fear they will have to pay him what he is worth. If the boys who run the Yankees are anxious to alienate the sympathy of the public, they are doing very nicely. If it is just the well-known thumping of the tomtoms, they are not doing badly either. Ruth and his owners are due for tons of newsprint space in the next few days. The problem of the owners is to emerge from the fray without looking like pikers.

Baseball and the newspapers are curiously related. The sport gets more free space than does any other business in the world. Due to the tremendous national interest in baseball, the newspapers have become the helpless tools of the magnates. They lie to us, give out false information, withhold news, and generally lead us a merry dance because they know that we are forced to print reams of baseball news or take a licking from our competitors.

However, woims have been known to toin. If Ruth is not with the Yankees when the season rolls around, this column will be delighted to inaugurate, foster, and whoop up a campaign to make the season's local opening Stayaway-from-the-Yankee-Stadium day. The rebellion is liable to be popular around the business offices of many of our best publications and if three or four join in there will be hell to pay on the baseball front.

Paul Gallico, New York Daily News

According to reports from the western front, here is what Babe Ruth earned since this time a year ago: Yankee salary, $52,000; World Series and post-season exhibitions, $20,000; vaudeville tour, $65,000; movie contract, $75,000; syndicate stories, $10,000; incidentals, $10,000.

Some of these figures may be open to discussion, but the total of $232,000 can be scaled down considerably and still leave enough to arouse the envy of the ordinary wage slave.

John Kieran, The New York Times

Herb Pennock, conceded to be the best southpaw pitcher in the majors, is staging a "holdout" that is worrying the Yankee owners every bit as much as that of Babe Ruth.

Pennock's weapon is not of such heavy caliber as that of the Babe's, but it is by no means a pop gun. He is asking the largest salary ever paid to a twirler [*that is, a pitcher*].

Walter Johnson is generally regarded as the most costly gunner [*pitcher*] in baseball. It is understood that Walter collects $15,000 a season. [*Often called the best pitcher of all time, Johnson had spent twenty seasons with the Washington Senators, for whom he had won more than four hundred games. Until 1983, Johnson was baseball's all-time leader in strikeouts. In fact, his salary was currently about $25,000.*]

According to those who know, Pennock is demanding $20,000, which would put him in a class with President Nicholas Murray Butler of Columbia University and Mayor Jimmy Walker of New York.

[*Thirty-three-year-old Herb Pennock, who had begun his professional career in 1912 with the Philadelphia Athletics, was now looking forward to his fifth season with the Yankees, for whom, in 1926, he had had twenty-three victories and two World Series wins. He was perhaps baseball's best control pitcher: in 266 innings pitched in 1926 he had issued only 43 bases on balls. He was also, in the words of Arthur Mann, "the most graceful pitcher in the game. His is the poetry of motion, without wasted effort"* (New York *Evening World,* January 6, 1927). *Pennock was almost certainly the best left-handed pitcher in either league.*]

New York *Evening Journal*

Wednesday, March 2

Chicago, March 1—G. Herman Ruth today was putting final touches on his preparations for the epochal huddle to be held in New York tomorrow.

Ruth made a triumphant and ceremonious entrance into Chicago; flashlights boomed in the chilly station, chattering reporters hopped agilely about the immense figure. [*It was not then possible to travel from the West Coast to New York without changing trains, and stations, in Chicago.*]

"Do you really hope to get $200,000 for two years, plus $7,700 back salary?" queried one of the younger Chicago writers.

Mr. Ruth surveyed the youth for a moment, cleared his throat, and answered, "I hope to tell you."

More questions, all of which have been asked Ruth a score of times, and more flashlights.

Edging her way through an admiring throng was a little girl reporter.

"O, Mr. Ruth," she trilled, "I'm so glad to meet you. I have heard a lot about your work in the movies. You're a baseball player, too, aren't you?"

The Bambino grinned and replied, borrowing a Hollywood expression: "Well, I'm at liberty at present."

"Have you any suggestions for reforms in Hollywood?" asked the little girl reporter, as she adjusted note paper on which to scribble Babe's historic reply.

"No," Babe said. "Hollywood was just like a church center."

"Were there many pretty girls in your moving picture cast?"

"Naw," Babe answered, with a tone of disgust, and toothing into his eating tobacco. "Not half enough."

The Babe departed on the Twentieth Century and will arrive in New York at 9:40 o'clock in the morning.

Marshall Hunt, New York *Daily News*

Babe will blow in like a lion today on the Twentieth Century Limited.

But he'll have to go to the Yankees like a lamb. They're not going to move the mountain to Mahomet—even to such a Mahomet as George Herman Ruth, who thinks his services are worth $100,000 a year.

Cousin Egbert Barrow, secretary of the club, flew off all seven of his handles when asked if the club would have an emissary at the train to meet Babe and arrange an interview with him. [*Although Egbert was no part of his name, Barrow's nickname was Cousin Egbert.*]

"Emissary nothing," fumed Ed. "Let him come to us. We're not looking for a raise."

Though the Babe says he will not compromise, the "shrewd dough," as the wise money is sometimes called, is of the opinion that Babe will have to be content with less than $100,000. He may get a $75,000 or $85,000 contract. But whatever his salary will be, the contract will run for only one year. The Yanks found out from past experience that Babe doesn't do his best stuff when protected by a long-term contract. The shadow of the old ax must be constantly over his neck. [*As already noted, Ruth's worst season was that of 1925, which was the first year of a two-year renewal of his earlier contract.*]

Dan Parker, New York *Daily Mirror*

How much is Babe Ruth worth to the New York Yankees, the American League, and organized baseball in general? The Babe, who suddenly has developed into a serious financier, says that he is worth $100,000 a year for two years. Colonel Jacob Ruppert, who never has been accused of being a piker, says that is too much.

In this crisis I find myself moved to stand shoulder to shoulder with oppressed labor, as represented by Mr. Ruth, and in unwilling opposition to oppressive capital, as represented by Colonel Ruppert. If this is Bolshevism, make the most of it.

Of course, baseball is a team game and Babe Ruth by himself cannot play a full nine innings of the national pastime; neither could Caruso have sung all of an opera by himself. But it seems fairly certain that quite as many customers, if not more, have been paying to see Ruth's speciality as have been paying to see baseball games. Baseball is a show business rather than a sport, and the Babe is the big show as far as the Yankees are concerned and, in fact, as far as the game is concerned.

Oh yes, I know that the statesmen and the authors of the game have declaimed and written to the effect that no man is bigger than the national pastime. But the box office says different, and the box office speaks with authority.

[*The argument repeatedly advanced to defend Babe Ruth's salary demands, and revived seven years later with Dizzy Dean, was that the player deserved the money because he single-handedly brought patrons into the various ballparks. Such a contention would hardly be relevant to the astronomical sums being paid today to professional athletes, some of whom, indeed, receive their megabucks for sitting on a bench.*]

W. O. McGeehan, New York *Herald-Tribune*

Thursday, March 3

He came. He saw. He compromised.

And Babe Ruth will get $210,000 for hitting home runs for the New York Yankees for the next three seasons.

After weeks of threatening dire consequences to the Yankees if they didn't give him a two-year contract at $100,000 per, the Babe came to terms with Colonel Jacob Ruppert in less than half an hour. Tomorrow morning he will sign a contract, binding himself to play with the Yankees for three years at a salary of $70,000 per year.

This is the highest salary in baseball. It tops Commissioner Landis's by $5,000; Ty Cobb's by $10,000, and Tris Speaker's by $20,000. [*In December 1926, at baseball's annual winter meeting in Chicago, the club owners awarded Landis a new seven-year contract, with his salary increased from $50,000 to $65,000. After the 1926* *season, the forty-year-old Cobb was released by the Detroit Tigers, for whom he had played for twenty-two seasons, and the thirty-eight-year-old Speaker, a nineteen-year veteran of major league play, resigned as manager of the Cleveland Indians. Cobb then signed a contract with the Philadelphia Athletics, and Speaker agreed to play for the Washington Senators. If one were to select an all-time all-star baseball team, the outfield probably would consist of Ruth, Cobb, and Speaker.]* So, all things considered, George Herman Ruth didn't do so badly by himself.

The history-making conference took place in the office of Colonel Ruppert's brewery [*at the corner of Ninety-Second Street and Third Avenue*].

The three-year feature of the contract is a big victory for Babe. Three years from now, he may be ready for the baseball boneyard. But the Colonel, advised by Ed Barrow, one of baseball's shrewdest judges of players, is willing to take that gamble. Barrow thinks Babe has over three more years of stardom left. [*In fact, Ruth would have six more years of "stardom," and in the Depression years of 1930 and 1931, his salary would reach its apex, $80,000 a year.*]

Babe's capitulation was like a tonic to Colonel Ruppert, who left a sick bed to attend the conference. He braced up after the conference as if he had just received an injection of goat-gland serum. [*A serum recently had been developed from goat testicles, the purpose of which was to enable men to maintain their youthfulness and sexual potency.*] Ed Barrow, who usually wears a serious look, was grinning like a bagful of Cheshire cats when he came out of the council chamber to announce the Babe had come to terms.

Babe was more pleased than either of his masters. He registered delight, approval, peace of mind, and a half dozen other kindred emotions which he learned to interpret during his sojourn in Hollywood.

"Jake did the right thing as I knew he would," said Babe. "Of course I had no intention of quitting baseball. I knew everything would be all right. The Yankees have always treated me right, and I knew they would this time. You can say for me that I'll earn every cent of my salary. There'll be no more monkey business for me [*a reference to his past off-field antics, which often had been a source of annoyance to the club's field manager, general manager, and owner*]. I learned my lesson and I'm going to do the right thing from now on."

While all the felicitations were being bandied about, a young man who remained in the background during the negotiations was having his hour of triumph in private. He is the man behind the Bam, the man who relieves Babe of the burden of thinking— Christy Walsh.

A few years ago, Christy was a struggling youth, the son of poor but honest parents, trying to make his way in the big city. He didn't have enough money at times to take him up to the Yankee Stadium by subway. But he happened into Babe's life, and the partnership has proved most profitable to both.

Until Christy Walsh came along, Babe didn't know how to make use of his by-products. But what Armour did to the pig and the cow, Christy did for the Babe.

[*Born in 1891, Christy Walsh grew up in Los Angeles and graduated from St. Vincent's College in that city. He spent his early years after graduation as a Los Angeles sportswriter, and then, late in 1921, his life changed when he teamed up with Babe Ruth after he and Ruth conferred briefly together in Grand Central Station. Walsh would also manage the financial affairs of other sports celebrities, including Lou Gehrig and Knute Rockne.*]

He showed him how to be an author. He taught him the profitable science of endorsing underwear [*at least twenty years before the birth of Jim Palmer*], showed him the road to wealth by having candy named after him, touring the provinces during the off-season with an all-star team, and, finally, turning movie star.

When Babe got the holdout bug, Christy was behind the scenes telling him what to say to his public. He built up the best ballyhoo a ballplayer has ever had to pave the way for a salary increase.

Christy has grown rich himself showing Babe how to get rich. It is the most equitable partnership ever established in athletics. Christy fathers Babe. He steers him away from the phoney investments that formerly lured Babe and his lucre. He has taught him that there is a rainy day ahead and that it behooves even a demigod to lay aside an odd penny for that evil day. Babe has a trust fund in the making, thanks to Christy's efforts, that will make him independent when his baseball career is over. [*The major league pension scheme did not come into being until 1947, and it did not cover players whose careers ended before that year.*] They will not have to hold benefit games for the Babe, though he has been the most profligate athlete since John L. Sullivan [*the first universally*

*recognized heavyweight champion of the world, who held the title from
1882 until he was defeated by James J. Corbett in 1897].*

Babe stole an hour away from business to make a visit to his
wife [*his first wife, Helen, whom he had married on October 17, 1914,
when he was nineteen and she was seventeen*], who is recovering from
a serious operation in St. Vincent's Hospital [*on West Twelfth
Street in New York City*]. There was enacted one of those scenes
for which the Babe and his wife are famous.

Helen's pale, thin arms were uplifted from her sick bed to en-
gulf the man mountain who rushed to meet them. The big
movie star and home-run man dropped a few honest tears on his
wife's face, and if there was a movie camera on hand it would
have recorded one of the most unaffected love scenes on record.

Babe scowled, on leaving the hospital, when some tactless reporter asked him if he and his wife were to be divorced.

"That old story is still going the rounds," snapped Babe.
"There's nothing to it. But I wish the scandal mongers would let
a man enjoy a little privacy in his family affairs." [*In fact, for more
than a year, Ruth and his wife had been separated, but because he was a
Roman Catholic who had been married in a Roman Catholic church he
would not consider divorce. He had many, many female friends, the favorite of whom was a young widow, Claire Hodgson. In January 1929,
Helen Ruth would die in a fire, and three months later, on the morning
of the baseball season's opening day, in St. Gregory's Roman Catholic
Church, on West Ninetieth Street, Claire Hodgson became the second
(and last) Mrs. George Herman Ruth.*]

Dan Parker, New York *Daily Mirror*

Ruth's entrance into the city yesterday was a welcome home
event. The Babe arrived on the first section of the Twentieth
Century Limited at Grand Central Station at 9:40 A.M. Despite
the efforts of half a dozen gate tenders and a squad of private
police, a hundred or so ardent fans had gained access to the
platform and were the first to gaze upon Ruth as he stepped
from the train, topped off with a brown cap and overcoated in a
tan affair that made him look like a man mountain about to fall
upon the crowd. Outside the entrance 2,000 more spectators
awaited Ruth's appearance, and as he came through the doorway
cheered him loudly.

Babe walked through the crowd, smiling broadly, and hurried

half a block to the building in which [*on the eleventh floor*] his
trainer, Arthur McGovern, has a gymnasium. There Babe held
open house for three-quarters of an hour while his picture in
various poses was snapped by an army of photographers.

Babe's first act was to make a telephone inquiry regarding the
condition of Mrs. Ruth. His next move was to telephone Colonel
Ruppert and arrange for the all-important conference, and his
next move was a flying call to St. Vincent's Hospital and a chat
with Mrs. Ruth.

Promptly at 12:30 Babe appeared at the Ruppert Brewery.
There he again posed for photographers, while Colonel Ruppert
paced nervously up and down his private office.

Ruth never looked more fit at this early stage of the season.
He weighed 221 pounds when he left Los Angeles, but gained
four pounds en route East. His waistline now measures 39
inches, but still can stand to be reduced by at least two inches,
according to McGovern.

The Home Run King's physical fitness surprised Colonel Ruppert and Barrow. Babe himself was surprised that he had had no
great trouble in cutting off eight inches of girth.

"I have worked harder in the past four weeks than I ever did
in my life," declared Babe. "This making a moving picture is no
joke. Maybe you think it's all play, but, take it from me, it is
nothing but twelve to fifteen hours' hard work every day."

The New York Times

Kings, even home-run kings, have their troubles in a suspicious
democracy, Babe Ruth learned yesterday when he telephoned
the Hotel Alamac to engage a room. [*Some visiting baseball teams
used the Hotel Alamac, at West Seventy-first Street and Broadway, as
their New York residence, and it was also a favorite with many local
players when they needed hotel accommodations.*]

"Name please?" the clerk asked.

"Babe Ruth."

A pause.

"Spell it," directed the clerk.

Babe's face was reddening. "B-" he growled, "A-B-E R-U-"

"Aw, quit kidding," the clerk interrupted. "We haven't got any
room."

Ruth found his tongue then and made the clerk understand a thing or two. His Majesty received profuse apologies and a choice room.

New York *World*

St. Petersburg—"If any figure in baseball ever has been worth pay like that it is Babe Ruth," said Miller Huggins, Yankee manager, commenting on Ruth's contract.

"I think the club treated Ruth most liberally," Huggins said, "and such terms are in accord with the liberal manner in which Colonel Ruppert always has run his ball club. Of course, no other player ever could have been worth any such sum, or any sum approaching it. But everyone admits there is only Ruth, and baseball may never see his like again.

"He is the master showman, and the club can afford to pay him a figure because of his tremendous drawing powers. It is nevertheless a tremendous salary, and with our other big salaries gives us a payroll which would daze a club owner."

"Do you think it was wise for the club to tie up so much money in a player of 32 when it is considered that Ruth already has had trouble with his legs the past two seasons?" Huggins was asked.

"I believe Colonel Ruppert took that into consideration. Unquestionably, Ruth showed up in New York in fine shape. He is a much more sensible fellow now than he was when he signed his five year contract in 1922. He now realizes the necessity of keeping in shape.

"We now have him tied up until he is 35 years old. There is no reason why he should not continue a topnotcher during that entire period.

"You know Ruth is as much a hero to this club as he is to the kids of the nation. They know he is the outstanding figure of their profession, and that despite his reputation, drawing power, and big salary, he is just one of the team."

[*Before coming to New York, the forty-seven-year-old Miller Huggins had been a major league second baseman for twelve years, with Cincinnati and the St. Louis Cardinals, and was known as baseball's best lead-off man. He had also managed the Cardinals for five years (1913–17). Although he was the smallest man in the major leagues, and was one of the quietest persons in baseball, there was no question about his being*

*in complete charge of his team, a matter settled beyond any doubt in
1925 when Colonel Ruppert unhesitatingly upheld his fine and suspension of Babe Ruth. (Ruppert's action might be contrasted with that of
a more recent Yankee owner who settled a dispute between a manager
and a couple of extremely well-paid players by sacking the manager.)
Highly intelligent on and off the field, Huggins had graduated from
the University of Cincinnati Law School and was licensed to practice
law in Ohio. Because of shrewd investments, he was a man of considerable wealth. Like Ruppert, Miller Huggins had been a lifelong
bachelor.]*

Fred Lieb, New York *Telegram*

Friday, March 4

On hearing that Mr. George Herman Ruth had signed for an
annual salary of $5,000 less than that of the President of the
United States [*who was then paid $75,000 annually*], a dirty-faced
little boy approached the flopping idol as he left his employer's
brewery. "Say it ain't true, Babe! Oh, say it ain't true!" pleaded
the little lad in a shrill treble of anguish. [*Eight Chicago White Sox
players, including the great "Shoeless Joe" Jackson, were banished from
organized baseball for "throwing" the 1919 World Series to Cincinnati,
and at the time of the players' trial a small boy encountered Jackson
outside the courtroom and cried out, "Say it ain't so, Joe."*]

The great left-hander bowed his head. He could not meet the
accusing gaze of the little lad. His lips trembled as he tried to
frame a reply. Then he dashed the tears from his eyes and hurried away, leaving the little boy slumped across the steps of the
brewery, sobbing as though his childish heart would break. It
must be true! [*The incident described is totally fictitious.*]

The effects of these revelations will become obvious in the
very near future. This is a commercial age, and the youth of the
land will want to become Presidents instead of Babe Ruths. Of
course there will be a few who will retain enough of their boyhood ideas to exclaim, "I would rather be left-handed than President" [*an echo of Henry Clay's assertion after he had lost a presidential
election for the third time, "I would rather be right than President*], but

the majority will look upon the Babe as an idol with plaster of paris feet. The political outlook for the future is ominous.

You can work out your own statistics as to what the Babe's new salary may mean. One statistician figures that the Babe is being paid $4.33 a minute. What of it? As Mr. Tennyson did not put it, "Better fifty years of Babe Ruth than a cycle of the other batters." [*In Alfred Tennyson's "Locksley Hall" (1842), the young jingoistic narrator declares, "Better fifty years of Europe than a cycle of Cathay."*] A lot of young men are swinging bats in the big leagues, about four hundred of them, but there is only one Babe Ruth. The opinion in the ivory market is that Colonel Ruppert got a bargain.

The payment of this salary to the former cigarmaker of Baltimore will cause much deploring and viewing with alarm concerning the distortion of relative values. [*Ruth's vocational training at St. Mary's Industrial School, in Baltimore, included the technique of making cigars.*] It will be pointed out that a good head of the department of psychology in an average university gets only about $5,000. But Ruth is being paid $70,000 a year because he is worth more in the matter of making gate receipts accumulate. It may be true that we are a nation of morons, but we are a nation of well-to-do morons with the cash to pay for our entertainers.

W. O. McGeehan, New York *Herald-Tribune*

A three-year contract was one thing that Babe Ruth did not dare ask for, but I think it was what he wanted more than anything else. Only the other day I wrote that the problem of Barrow and Ruppert was to get out of this thing without looking like pikers. They solved the problem. They gambled with Ruth for a three-year term when he did not have the temerity to ask it himself. It is a marvelous contract for Ruth and a fine one for the Yankee owners. It is the perfect draw. Ruth asked for $207,700 for two years. The Yankees are giving him $210,000, but are getting an extra year's work for it. Ruth gets the protection of a long-term contract.

One hears that the Babe capitulated a little too easily. That is not so. One must know Ruth to appreciate how swiftly and how cleverly he was won over. If Ruppert and Barrow had tried to

sign him for $70,000 for two years they never would have suc-
ceeded. Ruth is stubborn. He would have fought it out if it had
taken all summer, although his boy's soul would have hungered
for baseball dreadfully.

But Babe has something of a one-track mind. The Yankee
owners threw him off the track by offering a three-year contract.
Ruth had no carefully built up defense against that, and his defense crumbled. The thing was splendidly handled by all concerned. The ending was perfect.

Paul Gallico, New York *Daily News*

Saturday, March 5

Babe Ruth yesterday signed a contract binding himself to play
three seasons of baseball for the New York Yankees at $70,000 a
year. [*On Wednesday, the parties had come to an agreement, but the
contract itself was not signed until two days later.*]

It had been heralded that the illustrious Bambino would autograph a contract at 11 o'clock yesterday in Col. Ruppert's
brewery.

Now, one might wonder, just how do magnates and players
get together about signing contracts?

Picture yourself in the marble lobby of a huge building, recently given to the distribution of joyous brew, now catering to
less discriminating palates. [*During the days of Prohibition, the alcoholic content of beer was limited to one-half of one percent.*]

The elevator stops at the sixth floor of the imposing building.
From the elevator there emerges a vast figure in rah! rah! raiment. [*Ruth was wearing a raccoon-skin coat, which in the 1920's was
popular on college campuses.*]

It is G. Herman Ruth, who is ushered into the handsome offices of Col. Ruppert.

Photographers are invited in.

Moving picture men, carrying heavy flat lights which will defy
the sun, are requested into the offices of Col. Ruppert. [*The pictures would be shown in newsreels, which in pre-television days regularly
accompanied feature films in motion picture theaters.*]

There are flashes. The blinding huge lights cast an eerie, peculiar light about the offices.

Mr. Ruth has shed his coon rinds. He takes pen in hand and is about to sign a contract making him the highest priced player in the history of baseball.

Mr. Ruth has been caught by photographers in the act of taking pen in hand. They depart, happy that they registered on film the signing of the epochal "papers."

But there was a catch. Mr. Ruth was only acting. It remained for news reporters to see Mr. Ruth, left-handed at the plate, left-handed in the outfield, to sign his contract with a firm RIGHT hand.

Col. Ruppert piloted his name across the bottom of the contract. Cousin Egbert Barrow inked a witness signature, and there was an audible sigh of relief.

Marshall Hunt, New York *Daily News*

Lord! how weary it maketh me when petty persons compare Babe Ruth's salary to the President's or to their own, saying, "How hard I work, and how little I earn!" But this man chooseth to be a writer or a truckman, and that one a ballplayer, and if he is fortunate enough to have the qualities that a great public will pay to see displayed, who is anybody to complain at that? For all I would have to do, I tell myself, to get a larger salary than Babe Ruth's would be to be a greater ballplayer, and if I am not, I have no right to complain, nor do I, but say "Huzzah for Mr. Ruth!" Now that he hath accepted $70,000 a year that will make persons happy, forasmuch as they will justify their own incompetence by saying he is losing $30,000 a year, which is more than most of us have to lose.

[*A daily feature of the editorial page of the* World *was "The Conning Tower," a column with the byline FPA, the initials of Franklin P. Adams. The column often included a personal diary in the manner and style of the seventeenth-century diarist Samuel Pepys.*]

FPA, "The Conning Tower," New York *World*

St. Petersburg—The hitting of the entire Yankee squad was surprisingly good yesterday, especially Lou Gehrig, who was in there with five solid smashes every time he walked to the plate.

[*On each trip to the plate in batting practice, a player would swing at five pitches.*] If trying will get him anywhere, Lou is bound for that place right now. There isn't a harder working athlete on the squad, while his muscles are hard and firm as steel.

Gehrig looks bigger and better than he did last year. He is down on the roster for 200 pounds, but he probably weighs 210 easily and maybe more. The former Columbia star's shoulders are broader and his legs are heavier muscled and he swings away at a ball with everything he's got. Three of his drives went far down into right field and in the Stadium would have gone into the bleachers.

New York *Morning Telegraph*

Sunday, March 6

Babe Ruth left town last night, and today he is speeding toward St. Petersburg.

"I am glad to get going," said the Babe as he stepped aboard the Seaboard Air Line train at Pennsylvania Station at 7:10. "These last three days have been the busiest I ever remember. However, I feel fine. Everything has turned out great. I will be out hitting 'em on the nose Monday morning."

The Babe's departure caused a furor among the younger population which had gathered at Pennsylvania Station. Some fifty youngsters surrounded him as he marched into the station flanked by a couple of large grips. The Babe was photographed by an army of cameramen who have dogged his trail for several days and then sought relief by dashing to the lower train platform.

There, however, he was the center of another group of youngsters and had to make half a dozen special poses before he could satisfy them, and in addition autographed half a dozen baseballs. The Babe smiled broadly as the kids descended upon him. He refused no request and posed for the last picture beside a messenger boy just as the train began moving out.

The New York Times

Monday, March 7

St. Petersburg—His majesty Babe Ruth, Sultan of Swat, descended in regal fashion from the train this morning.

Twenty-four gaping rookies stood at attention as he sauntered through the lobby of the hotel, and flocks of femininity dogged his footsteps to the very portals of the elevator where a flunkey in uniform barred the way.

It was a great reception, with even the native crackers showing an excitement that was almost enthusiasm. But the Babe bore his laurels gracefully. He smiled and bowed, and smiled again and shouted hoarsely to his teammates as he passed through the lobby. He has a right to smile. Never before has a ballplayer paraded into camp with a contract for $210,000 safe in his hip pocket.

Ford C. Frick, New York *Evening Journal*

St. Petersburg—Babe Ruth played golf on his first morning in camp.

The action apparently violated the training rule which prohibits golf on all days except Sunday, but Miller Huggins said he had given Ruth permission to play. [*Four Yankees were rather good golfers: Benny Bengough, Waite Hoyt, Bob Shawkey, and, the best of the four, Babe Ruth, who played to a three handicap—which means that his scores were usually in the mid-seventies—and could drive the ball farther than many professionals.*]

Frank Wallace, *New York Post*

Speaking of golf and baseball, Mr. Huggins elaborated on previously expressed sentiments.

"It's all right physically," he expounded, "but these fellows have got to think baseball. You and I know that there are not half enough young fellows today who do anything near enough thinking about baseball—not half enough."

[*As Waite Hoyt noted in the Foreword to this book, players who were sitting on the bench during a game were not permitted to converse on any subject but baseball.*]

Roscoe McGowen, New York *Daily News*

Tuesday, March 8

Mr. George Herman Ruth, the well-known tragedian, is not suffering from Klieg eyes.

For the round sum of five dollars your correspondent learned the truth yesterday in 18 holes of golf. Mr. Ruth, ever big hearted and generous, played this writer and Mr. Marshall Hunt, another itinerant scribbler, for $5 each, giving handicaps of 10 strokes on the 18 holes.

At the end of the match George Herman pulled up with a neat 72 for the round, at least 12 drives of more than 300 yards, and $10 in cash.

Mr. Ruth lost no time in starting his exercises. Fifteen minutes after his arrival he was headed for the golf club—without any breakfast, mind you. The shock of seeing the Bambino pass up a meal was almost too much for the sanity of the old-timers. Joe Dugan [*the team's regular third baseman since 1922*], seeing the Bam go past the dining room without so much as a glance, immediately sought out an oculist to have his eyes tested. And Bob Shawkey [*a member of the pitching staff since 1916, who had been uninterruptedly with the Yankees longer than any other player*], informed of the fact, sought out a shady place and called for an ice pack. [*Perhaps Ruth had had breakfast on the train.*]

But it's on the level, and yesterday the Babe passed up lunch as well. The rumor spread around the hotel that it was all a plot of Colonel Ruppert to cut down expenses.

Following his golf, the Babe came back to the hotel, took a brisk rub, and went immediately to the ball park. And what a load of paraphernalia he brought with him. First he donned a rubber corset. Then for ten minutes he lay flat on his back while Doc Woods massaged his anatomy with a trick rolling pin. [*Al "Doc" Woods was now in his twenty-seventh year as a team trainer in organized baseball. From 1901 until 1913, he had served in the American Association, and then in 1914, he began his association with Miller*

Huggins. He was with Huggins in St. Louis until 1918, when they both joined the Yankees.] After that Ruth donned a sweat shirt, two sweaters, and a rubber waistcoat before he strolled forth to engage in the business of fielding bunts.

Ford C. Frick, New York *Evening Journal*

St. Petersburg, March 7—George Herman "Babe" Ruth came out to Crescent Lake Park [*the Yankees' training field*] this afternoon and demonstrated that the Klieg lights in Hollywood had not affected his batting eye by slamming one of Bob Shawkey's fast balls a mile high in the air.

It was a characteristic Ruthian drive which landed on the outskirts of right field. In Yankee Stadium the ball would have landed well up in the right field bleachers, and at the Polo Grounds it would have hit the top of the upper tier.

Apparently Mr. Ruth was well satisfied with the distance that he got, for he came to the bench smiling like a kid and shouting, "Boys, I kissed that one."

He "kissed" two more before he finished his batting, and then to show that he was here for business he marched out to the pitcher's mound and flipped them up to the plate for 15 minutes.

Ruth has a remarkable throwing arm. Although this was his first game in camp, he cut loose on the mound and whizzed the ball with plenty of speed.

"That big fellow has an iron arm as well as an iron bat," remarked "Jumping Joe" Dugan as one of the rookies almost broke his bat trying to hit one of Ruth's fast ones. [*As a major league pitcher, mainly with the Boston Red Sox, Ruth had had 94 victories and 46 losses as well as 3 World Series wins without a setback. His regular season winning percentage of .671 was higher than that of such legendary pitchers as Christy Mathewson (.664), Sandy Koufax (.655), Dizzy Dean (.644), Grover Cleveland Alexander (.643), Three Finger Brown (.636), Carl Hubbell (.622), Cy Young (.617), Walter Johnson (.599), and Warren Spahn (.597). And Ruth's earned run average of 2.28 surpassed that of all of these men but Mathewson (2.13) and Johnson (2.17). If he had never gone from the mound to the outfield, Ruth almost certainly would have been elected to baseball's Hall of Fame as a pitcher. He had last pitched, and won, a game, as a Yankee, in 1921, and twice in the future he would gain pitching victories.*]

"I never felt better in my life," said Ruth on his arrival. "I weigh 223 pounds and will lose only 3 pounds while here."

Asked if he would set a new home run record this year, Ruth replied, "Well, it all depends upon the other fellow. If they pitch to me I'll beat my record and hit over 60 home runs." But the trouble is that they won't pitch to him. And you can't make home runs when you can't hit 'em.

It was at 1:20 P.M. that Ruth officially started work on his new contract.

"The king is here! Long live the king!" shouted the other players. The Babe seemed to enjoy the "kidding."

"Hello, Sheik," said second baseman Tony Lazzeri. "There's still some paint under your eyes." [*In the mid-twenties, a ladies' man or a handsome matinee idol would be called a "sheik," because of Edith Hull's best-selling novel of 1924* The Sheik, *and the exceedingly popular motion picture version of the book, starring Rudolph Valentino.*]

"Well, there was paint in your eyes when you missed that one that Alex threw in the World Series," came back the Bambino. [*This refers to the most famous strikeout in baseball history when Grover Cleveland Alexander fanned Lazzeri with the bases loaded and two outs in the seventh inning of the seventh game of the 1926 World Series, enabling the St. Louis Cardinals to win the Series.*]

Ruth wore a white sweater and a pair of golf pants, golf socks, and a low-cut pair of shoes. After getting into his uniform, Babe walked out on the field, and the greatest player that baseball has ever known was ready to start practice.

William Hennigan, New York World

St. Petersburg—There is nothing "high hat" about Babe Ruth. After the Babe jumped into a uniform yesterday, he called over Benny Bengough, the little catcher and saxophone player. [*Now in his fifth season as a Yankee catcher, Bengough was a good saxophonist.*]

"Round up all the rookies," Ruth said. "I want to meet them."

Benny got the rookies together, and the Babe greeted them with a big handshake and a "Howdy-do, sir."

New York World

St. Petersburg—The king is here, and the populace flocked to the ball park to look at him. Men, women, and children came on foot, in wheel chairs, in motor cars, and on bicycles.

Rud Rennie, New York *Herald-Tribune*

Wednesday, March 9

St. Petersburg—Some of the natives were real concerned when Babe Ruth was wheeled into morning practice in a rolling chair. But it was only another stunt by the busy photographers, who cluster around Ruth like so many bees.

New York *Telegram*

Thursday, March 10

St. Petersburg—Babe Ruth is the wow of the training camp, and he's the same democratic fellow he was when he was getting only $52,000 per.

"Hello, Kid, how are you?" is the way Babe welcomes everybody. Members of the Yanks were greeted in this way, and a man in his late 70's was given the same welcome. [*One reason for calling everyone Kid is that Ruth had a notoriously bad memory for names. When, along with Mark Koenig, Waite Hoyt was traded to Detroit during the 1930 season, Ruth said to his teammate of more than ten seasons, "Good luck with the Tigers, Walter."*]
During practice Babe is a riot. Yesterday he worked on the mound during the batting drill. He got so much fun in fooling the batters that you couldn't remove him from the box without threatening to get a derrick or a cannon.

Charles Segar, New York *Daily Mirror*

St. Petersburg—Babe Ruth is the hardest worker in the outfit and he's setting a pace that is making the others look like wooden Indians. [*In these days of racial insensitivity, one often saw in front of a tobacco store a wooden statue of a native American who seemed*

to have just stepped out of an old western movie.] The big Bam shags
flies to begin the day's work, fields bunts, and then warms up
with a catcher. By this time he is ready to go into the box, and
there he remains, pitching for 25 minutes. His batting practice
consists of about 12 good wallops.

Arthur Mann, New York *Evening World*

In the last two years one of the defensive defects on the Yanks
was the confusion around first base. A ball would be hit to
Gehrig, and neither Lou nor the pitcher could decide who
should cover. So frequently the base was left vacated, and when
someone finally decided to cover, invariably it was too late.

The first routine of morning practice is to station Gehrig at
first base and one of the young pitchers in the box. Charley
O'Leary [*a one-time Detroit Tiger shortstop, who was now one of the
Yankees' three coaches*] or someone else hits those short choppers
between Gehrig and the box. Lou usually fields them, and the
pitcher covers. Perhaps they will know the lesson by the time the
regular season rolls around.

Fred Lieb, New York *Telegram*

Friday, March 11

Orlando, March 10—When Mr. McGovern, the well-known
trainer, was ministering to the physical needs of Babe Ruth recently he should have devoted slightly more time to Mr. Ruth's
underpinning. Although the famous movie actor is sound of
wind and stalwart from the waistline up, he is not so good from
the knees down.

In the first exhibition played by the Yanks—as a matter of
fact, in almost the first bit of serious sprinting that Mr. Ruth has
had to do this spring—he pulled the same old "charley horse"
that afflicted him in the left leg last season.

Attempting to go into high from a standing start, G. Herman
hurt himself so painfully that he was compelled to leave the
game in the fourth inning, much to the annoyance of a record
crowd of 4,000 who gathered to watch the Yanks flail the Cincinnati Reds, 8 to 5. [*A base runner on second base, Ruth ran full speed*

in an attempt to score on a single and pulled up lame while rounding third base.]

It is a trivial injury as injuries go, but it only goes to prove that the home-run king is still brittle below the kneecaps and will probably have his customary run of leg injuries. [*Ruth's legs had been, and would continue to be, a frequent source of irritation to him and provide one reason for the fact that in 15 seasons as a full-time outfielder, only 6 times would he appear in more than 145 games.*]

Although Trainer Doc Woods has massaged the injured member vigorously, Ruth's leg was still paining him tonight. The muscles have knotted into a large lump which sticks out like an ostrich egg.

James R. Harrison, *The New York Times*

Orlando—"I wanted to continue in the game for the sake of those kids who came out to see me," said the Babe tonight. "That's the reason I started out for center field in the last half of the fourth inning, but the pain was too great and I was forced to quit. [*During the regular season, Ruth always played left or right field, but in exhibition games he was sometimes in center field.*] When I saw all those kids in the park I knew that they wanted me to treat them to a home run. I'm sorry I had to disappoint them." [*There was nothing spurious or affected about Ruth's fondness for children, toward whom he always felt a genuine affection.*]

William Hennigan, New York *World*

Saturday, March 12

[*The following is taken from an interview of Babe Ruth.*] Q. Do you expect to break your home run record of 59 made in 1921?

A. That's a gamble. It depends on how much the pitchers pitch to me. I'm hopeful, but I'm not making predictions.

Q. How many do you expect to hit this season?

A. Can't answer. Perhaps 50.

Q. How many more years do you expect to play baseball?

A. Expect to be good for five more years at least.

[*In fact, Ruth would play regularly for another eight seasons. When he hit fifty-nine home runs in 1921, the record he broke was fifty-four,*]

*set in 1920 by himself, which in turn broke the record of twenty-nine, set
in 1919 by himself.*]

New York *Evening Journal*

St. Petersburg—The ranks of the holdouts were reduced by one
as Earle Combs, the Kentucky Colonel, telegraphed that his contract was on its way and that he would be here in two or three
days. Whether Combs was a winner in the battle with the club,
whether he compromised or surrendered, was not announced.

With Combs in line, only Bob Meusel, Herb Pennock, and Urban Shocker are outside the fold. [*Combs, who had lived all of his
life in Kentucky and had graduated from Eastern Kentucky State Teachers College, was starting his third season as the Yankees' center fielder.*]

Bill Slocum, New York *American*

Sunday, March 13

St. Petersburg—Another break in the ranks of the Yankee holdouts was announced after a conference between Miller Huggins
and Urban Shocker. Both came out smiling, and Huggins gave
out the word that Shocker had signed.

No announcement was made by Huggins as to whether the
club had met Shocker's demands or whether the pitcher had
come down in his request.

[*Urban Shocker had pitched for eleven years in the American League.
He began with the Yankees in 1916, and two years later, he was traded
to the St. Louis Browns, where he remained for seven years, returning to
New York in 1925. With the Browns, where he was noted for beating the
Yankees, Shocker had four consecutive seasons of winning twenty games
or more, including a league-leading twenty-seven in 1921. In 1922, he
led American League pitchers in strikeouts with 149, and now, in 1927,
he had the best winning percentage of all pitchers who had been in the
major leagues for at least five years.*

*When the spitball pitch was outlawed in 1920, seventeen men were
permitted to continue using the pitch, and seven were still in the major
leagues, including Shocker.*

For more than two years Shocker had suffered from intestinal problems which prevented him from sleeping in a prone position and would cause his death in September 1928, at the age of thirty-eight.

Shocker's overall record, in the eyes of some objective observers, is better than that of several pitchers who have gained admittance into baseball's Hall of Fame, including Don Drysdale. Shocker and Drysdale each spent thirteen years in the major leagues. Shocker had 188 victories and 117 losses for a percentage of .616. Drysdale won 204 games and lost 162 for a percentage of .557.]

Bill Slocum, New York *American*

Monday, March 14

St. Petersburg—Romance has stalked into the camp of the Yankees. And Mr. Elias Funk [*a rookie outfielder*] is the victim. Mr. Funk, youthful and handsome, has fallen for Hilda, the beautiful waffle queen, and his affair of the heart was the chief topic of conversation yesterday.

Late last night Mr. Funk was discovered in the shoppe, in the throes of gazing into Hilda's eyes, the while he inhaled a double ham and egg sandwich. Mr. Funk ate and gazed enraptured. The proprietor stood near by.

"You have beautiful eyes," murmured Mr. Funk.

"What'll you have?" said the proprietor.

"Give me another ham," quote Elias, and that's how it went.

Finally Mr. Funk gave up.

He emerged swearing. "I've spent $2.10 in that shop already," he muttered, "and I haven't got around to making a date. Every time I start to tell her what a beauty she is that guy who owns the place comes around and I have to order more sandwiches."

Truly the life of the rookie ballplayer is tough.

[*Although he would have a couple of moderately good years in the American League, only once, in 1929, would Funk appear in a regular season game with the Yankees.*]

Ford C. Frick, New York *Evening Journal*

St. Petersburg—Recruit outfielders received a shock yesterday when Bob Meusel strolled into the lobby of the hotel and declared himself ready for work. A look of further dismay crept over the faces of the young hopefuls when the tallest player on the roster announced that he was ready to sign and expected no trouble in decorating a Yankee contract.

Thus the outfield becomes an open book, for Earle Combs is expected. With Ruth, Combs, Meusel, and reserve outfielder Ben Paschal here and fit, it looks as though there is slim chance of any rookies being kept on.

Meusel, when asked if he had signed, replied, "No."

When asked if he anticipated any trouble, he answered, "No."

He thus said twice as much as on any previous occasion, for his vocabulary consists chiefly of "No's," and he seldom employs more than one at a time. He appeared to be in excellent shape, carrying a California sunburn and tan that rivals anything ever obtained in Florida. It might be added that he is still quite as handsome as he was last year and in previous seasons.

[*A lifelong Californian, and for years a resident of Los Angeles, the six-foot three-inch, twenty-eight-year-old Bob Meusel had been a regular in the Yankee outfield for the past six seasons. In five of these years, he had batted over .300, and in 1925, when Ruth had had his troubles, Meusel led the American League in home runs (33) and runs batted in (138). A fine hitter, Meusel was even more highly regarded for his throwing arm, which was probably the best among all major league outfielders. Swift and accurate in throwing to any base or home plate, Meusel could whip the ball like an infielder, and Casey Stengel, among others, called his throwing arm the best he had ever seen on an outfielder.*

Personally, Meusel was the most incommunicative member of the Yankee club. He was a man of such few words that a singly uttered "good morning" coming from him was almost akin to garrulousness. He was sometimes called Languid Bob, not only because he rarely spoke to anyone but because on the field he moved with a deceptive nonchalance that was sometimes interpreted as laziness. Although he managed to cover a great deal of ground in the outfield, because he was tall he often gave the impression of only half trying. This was, of course, a false impression, for no one who was lazy would have been tolerated for ten years by Miller Huggins. Also it should be noted that Meusel uncomplainingly performed in the sun field in order to protect the eyes of Babe Ruth. In Yankee Stadium and in two visiting ballparks, where the sun shone upon left field, Babe Ruth played right field, whereas in the remaining five parks, where right field received the sun, Ruth's playing position was left field. Thus, when Bob Meusel went to the outfield, he could always count on facing the sun.]

New York *Morning Telegraph*

Tuesday, March 15

St. Petersburg—As Bob Meusel figures it, a trip across the continent is just a train ride. The important thing is to see Jake.

Having read that Babe Ruth journeyed from California to the Eastern seaboard, saw Jake, and drew himself a raise of $18,000, Bob is marking time until he, too, can see Jake. [*Ruppert was expected in St. Petersburg on Wednesday.*]

Meusel is not looking for any raise of $18,000, but he is angling for an upward revision on the figures in the contract sent to him.

Bill Slocum, New York *American*

Thursday, March 17

St. Petersburg—Jake Ruppert, owner of the Yankees, arrived yesterday morning. He was greeted with the news that two men were still unsigned, Bob Meusel, who is here, and Herb Pennock, whereabouts unknown.

Ruppert asked Meusel to enter Manager Huggins's private office at Crescent Lake Park. Just two minutes were needed for Ruppert to make another offer to Meusel. Col. Jake, it is believed, offered Bob a two-year contract calling for $35,000, or $17,500 a season.

At the end of the two minutes, Ruppert reappeared on the field, rubbing his hands and smilingly announcing that Meusel had signed for two years.

Charles Segar, New York *Daily Mirror*

St. Petersburg—Earle Combs checked in at the Yankee camp today, leaving Herb Pennock the only absentee. Pennock, in the quiet of his family circle in silver foxes at Kennett Square, Pennsylvania, has communicated with several of his player friends that he will remain firm in his demands, and the next move will have to come from the club.

He is well fixed financially. He has plenty of the money saved that he has earned. Besides, his family has money, and his wife is said to have ample funds in her own right.

So it looks as if the silver fox breeding business may get a southpaw, which would leave the Yanks in a deuce of a pickle. There is only one Pennock, the brainiest portsider in the business. [*Known as the Squire of Kennett Square, Pennock had resided all of his life in the small town twenty-five miles west of Philadelphia. He lived on a large fox farm, where he spent each winter breeding valuable fur-bearing silver foxes. Not only did he breed foxes, he enjoyed riding to the hounds in search of them. He once said that he had three hobbies— raising foxes, hunting them, and spending the winter with his wife and two children, a daughter and a son. A man without financial worries who had won twenty-three games in 1926, Pennock was in a good bargaining position.*]

Will Wedge, New York Sun

St. Petersburg—Babe Ruth is out there every day working harder than anybody on the team. Although his bad leg is still too sore to do any running, he insists on putting a strain on it by pitching to the batters. The Babe has asked Huggins to let him pitch in exhibition games, but little Miller is sure to refuse as he has in other years. It strikes us that the daddy of all hitters is still a pitcher at heart.

When the Babe is not pitching, he can be found in a heavy sweat shirt warming up other pitchers on the sidelines.

Pat Robinson, New York Telegram

Friday, March 18

St. Petersburg—Col. Jake Ruppert is aroused over the attitude taken by Herb Pennock, who wants $20,000 a year in exchange for his highly expert left-handed playing service.

The Yanks' boss does not blame his men for wanting more money, but he is opposed to methods which he declares are unethical and unreasonable.

"Some day," he said, "the players who are holdouts will wake up and discover they are making a big mistake. The owners are realizing they must reach a turning point soon. I believe that in a few years this unethical method of demanding more salary will be wiped out. We will develop the young players. When these youngsters reach that stage in their development when they can be used for regular service, we can face the holdout situation without fearing the results."

Charles Segar, New York *Daily Mirror*

If Herb Pennock persuades Colonel Ruppert to yield to his demand for $20,000, he will be the highest salaried left-handed pitcher in the history of the national pastime.

Joe Vila, New York *Sun*

Saturday, March 19

The Yankees can get along without Herb Pennock like an automobile without its gasoline, like a hunk of liver without its rasher of bacon, like a mud-turtle without its shell.

Pennock is the best left-hander in the business, not excluding the phenomenal Lefty Grove, who is not yet matured. [*For five years (1920–24), Grove had pitched spectacularly for Baltimore in the International League, but then he had two rather ordinary seasons with the Philadelphia Athletics (twenty-three wins and twenty-five losses). Grove's great achievements lay in the future.*] If Col. Ruppert thinks the Yanks can get along without Herbie, he is kidding himself. Herbie wants $20,000, and he's cheap at that price.

Jack Conway, New York *Daily Mirror*

Tuesday, March 22

St. Petersburg, March 21—Anyone seeking information regarding the possibilities, probabilities, and potentialities of the Yankees may leave their disguises at home. Arriving at the stronghold of the American League champions, this writer [*who had been covering the Giants*] began investigating, holding a pair of false whiskers and dark glasses in readiness lest he be accused of being a Giant spy. Such fears were unfounded. Everyone was quite open and candid.

"It's the same team to a man," they admitted.

"What man?" we asked.

"Babe Ruth," was the immediate response.

"Are there any good prospects?"

"Yes, Ruth."

"How good does the team look this year?"

"Just as good as Ruth looks."

"Are the Yanks working hard?

"Ruth is."

A little more conversation and your correspondent quickly caught on to the fact that the belief prevails here that Ruth is the Yankees and the Yankees are Ruth.

Richards Vidmer, *The New York Times*

Wednesday, March 23

St. Petersburg—Columbia Lou Gehrig's work is flashier and speedier than it was last year. His physical reactions are much quicker than his mental ones. He is not a second Hal Chase [*who played for the Yankees (1905–12) and four other major league teams and is generally regarded as baseball's best fielding first baseman*], but he is improving, and as Miller Huggins says, "He's going to make a helluva fine ballplayer for me."

Every so often Lou is subject to a mental lapse. He realizes this himself and tries to improve. He is not as bad, though, as he painted himself the other day when he said, "Every time I think the ball club suffers."

Pat Robinson, New York *Telegram*

St. Petersburg—Tony Lazzeri is the key man of the Yankee infield—and a good one. No man in camp is hitting the ball harder than Tony—or holding up in the field with quite the same brilliance. A budding star last season, this year Lazzeri gives promise of full bloom to stardom. And in his own steady brilliance, he carries inspiration to shortstop Mark Koenig as well. If Huggins worried about the second base combination last season, he need have no worries now. The Yankee infield will be capably guarded. And mark this down for future reference! The names of Koenig and Lazzeri will appear frequently this season in the records that tell of base hits and runs batted in. They've both arrived.

[*Born and raised in San Francisco, Tony Lazzeri was the son of an immigrant boilermaker and was prepared to follow in his father's footsteps; indeed, in 1927, he retained his membership in the Boiler-makers Union, Local No. 6, San Francisco, and practiced this trade during the winter months. Along with boilermaking, Lazzeri played baseball, first in San Francisco's Golden Gate Park, then with lower-level minor league teams, and finally in the Pacific Coast League, where, at the age of twenty-one, he gained national acclaim when he played shortstop for Salt Lake City in 1925. Assisted by the altitude and by a 200-game schedule, Lazzeri batted .355, scored 202 runs, became the first man in organized baseball to hit 60 home runs in a season, and rolled up an astonishing 222 RBIs. Among those who were impressed by these figures was Colonel Jacob Ruppert, who outbid other interested teams and purchased Lazzeri's contract for the then extremely high price of $50,000 and five players. In 1926, playing second base, Lazzeri had an excellent rookie season. Along with Gehrig, he was one of only two Yankees to play in every one of his team's 155 games. He batted .275, hit 18 home runs, and drove in 114 runs, a figure that was surpassed by only one player in the American League, Babe Ruth. In the field he was outstanding and was considered to be one of baseball's best in executing a double play. Lazzeri's only possible source of embarrassment lay in his frequent inability as a batter to make contact with the pitched ball. He led all American Leaguers in strikeouts, with 96 whiffs, and, as already* *noted, he became baseball's most famous strikeout victim in the seventh inning of the seventh game of the World Series.*

One matter about Lazzeri was rarely discussed in print: he suffered from epilepsy. Although they never occurred on the field, he had several seizures during the 1927 season. On a couple of occasions, Mark Koenig, his roommate on the road, was forced to dash out of his hotel room in the middle of the night to seek help from "Doc" Woods. Lazzeri would never shave in a bathroom for fear of falling over backward and cracking his head on the tile floor. It is strangely coincidental that Grover Cleveland Alexander, Lazzeri's opponent in their celebrated confrontation, was also an epileptic.

A year and a half older than Lazzeri, Mark Koenig (pronounced Kay´ -nig) also grew up in San Francisco and served his apprenticeship in Golden Gate Park. After competing in four different minor leagues, Koenig was bought by Colonel Ruppert toward the end of the 1925 season while he was a member of the St. Paul club in the American Association, and he finished the year by playing twenty-eight games at shortstop with the Yankees. In 1926, he was the team's regular shortstop and appeared in 147 games, providing the Yankees with an all–San Francisco second-base combination. He batted a respectable .271, but he had his troubles in the field, and many observers said that Koenig would never make it as a major leaguer, but the old second baseman Miller Huggins never wavered in his support of his young shortstop. Whenever in 1926 and the spring of 1927 he was asked about the shortstop position, Huggins would reply, "My shortstop is Mark Koenig." Obviously, in 1927, Koenig was eager to prove that his manager's faith in him had not been misplaced.]

Ford C. Frick, New York *Evening Journal*

Team work, cooperation, understanding, esprit de corps, or whatever you want to call it, generally is found when a group of men make a success at anything. But the Yankees are individualists. Most clubs are clannish, but not the Yankees.

The Yankees go their own separate ways singly or in pairs. A cluster of three Yanks in their leisure moments would be worthy of Luther Burbank [*the famous California plant breeder who had created and improved numerous varieties of flowers and fruits, and had died in 1926*].

It starts at the top with Manager Miller Huggins. Here at the training camp the Mite Manager does not even live in the same hotel with his players, and about the only time he sees them is during business hours. [*The writer of this article, a visiting journalist who was not one of the "regulars" covering the Yankees, was apparently not aware of the simple explanation for Huggins's living apart from the others. Huggins had invested in Florida real estate, and his holdings included a home in St. Petersburg, which was maintained by his sister Myrtle. While the club was quartered in St. Petersburg, Huggins resided with his sister, but everywhere else he stayed in the team hotel.*]

Babe Ruth is another who travels alone. The great Bambino is never in evidence at the Princess Martha [*the club's hotel*], and visitors are beginning to wonder if he really stays there. The Babe has all his meals sent to his room and never uses the public thoroughfares of the hotel lobby. When he departs for practice or returns after a game, he steals silently and unnoticed through a side entrance. [*Ruth's meals were sent to his room for the same reason that they were usually sent back to his sleeping car when the Yankees were traveling—to prevent them from becoming public spectacles.*]

The rest of the players are no different. Bob Meusel, the tall and silent man from the West, always seems going or coming from some very important place, but where he goes or where he comes from no one seems to know. As he swings his tall, erect figure through the lobby, heads turn and murmur, "Hello, Bob." But nine times out of ten he is so engrossed in his own private thoughts that he doesn't even hear.

The keystone combination of Tony Lazzeri and Mark Koenig is inseparable on or off the field, but seldom are they seen with a third party. So go the Yanks. They are not the hard, disciplined troops found under Giant Manager John McGraw; nor are they the close family found under Dodger Manager Wilbert Robinson, but the Yanks evidently need no ties. Through sheer power they get there.

Richards Vidmer, The New York Times

Thursday, March 24

St. Petersburg—"Come on, Babe, give us a homer," cried a small youth seated behind the Yankees' bench as Ruth cantered to the plate to face Larry Benton in the sixth inning of yesterday's burlesque game with the Boston Braves [*which the Yankees won, 16–7*].

"Sure, kid, I'll sock a couple," the Babe answered.

Just to keep faith with that small younster, Ruth went out and not only socked a homer in the sixth inning, but he made another in the eighth.

[*This shows that not all of the stories about Babe Ruth hitting home runs for kids are apocryphal. The most famous such incident was a tear-jerker involving a young lad named Johnny Sylvester. It has been repeatedly said that on the morning of October 6, 1926, the day of the fourth World Series game, Ruth visited this poverty-stricken, dying boy in his hospital room and promised to hit a home run for him. That afternoon, Babe Ruth became the first person to hit three home runs in one World Series game. Actually, Johnny Sylvester, the son of a vice-president of the National City Bank of New York, was in a Montclair, New Jersey, hospital suffering from blood poisoning, and on October 1, when the Yankees were still in New York, Mr. Sylvester sent a letter to Ruth and asked for his autograph to boost the morale of his son. An answer arrived on October 6, air mailed from St. Louis, in which Ruth promised Johnny to "knock a home run for you." Then came the three-home-run game in Sportsman's Park. Newspapers highly publicized the episode, and physicians were quoted as saying that Johnny's fever began to abate as he listened to the game on the radio and that his recovery was initiated by the Babe's home runs. On October 11, after the last game of the World Series, Ruth was taken to the hospital for a brief meeting with Johnny in the presence of numerous photographers.*]

Charles Segar, New York *Daily Mirror*

St. Petersburg—The Babe displayed some canny base running in the fourth inning [*when he was a base runner on first base.*] By acting like a man who was tired of running, he fooled center fielder Jack Smith into pegging the ball to second while he put on speed and went to third [*on a single to center field*].

Rud Rennie, New York *Herald-Tribune*

Once Babe Ruth's contract is signed, he doesn't play for money. Ruth is one man who really loves the game. Moreover, the big fellow knows that the fans turn out to see him, and he takes a serious pride in trying to give them the best he has.

Walter Trumbull, *New York Post*

Saturday, March 26

St. Petersburg—Herb Pennock, lone Yankee holdout, arrived at camp today and failed to agree with Manager Huggins on contract terms after an hour's session in the clubhouse. Huggins and Pennock then went in to consult with Colonel Ruppert at the latter's hotel. Neither showed any enthusiasm about the conference with Ruppert.

Ford C. Frick, New York *Evening Journal*

Were it not for a few players, the stolen base, once a flashing, brilliant part of every game, would be as extinct as the dodo. As ballplayers say, "We're not running any more."

A few, like Cobb, Ruth, Meusel, and Sam Rice will run, but the overwhelming majority stick glued to a base until they are driven around.

The stolen base is passing because there is little cause to try to steal. Why run, with everybody hitting, is the attitude. When hitting came in, base stealing went out.

To a certain extent Babe Ruth is to blame for this condition. When the Babe started on his home-run rampage, others began taking a toe hold at the plate, and free hitting became the rage. And yet the Babe himself is a good runner; he stole eleven bases last year. Ruth runs bases as well as he does everything else on a ball field. He has the intuitive knack of getting the jump on a pitcher. He knows when and how to run, and he can hook a bag as well as anybody in the game. He runs hard and hits the dirt hard, and even masters of the art of tagging a runner find it difficult to put the ball on him.

[*This piece raises an important point. Because the modern conception of Babe Ruth seems to be that of someone who was big, slow, and awkward, it should be noted that he could outsprint many of his teammates and opponents. He ended his career with 123 stolen bases, and twice he stole 17 bases in one season. (By way of contrast, Joe DiMaggio had a career total of 30 stolen bases, Ted Williams had 24, and Roger Maris had 21.) Interestingly, Ruth stole home ten times; in all of baseball history only twenty-four players have performed this feat more often than he. The art of base stealing, incidentally, was conspicuously revived when blacks entered organized baseball. Since 1947, when Jackie Robinson broke the major league color line, only twice has a white player led the National League in stolen bases (Richie Ashburn in 1948 and Pee Wee Reese in 1952). In the admission of blacks to the game, the American League lagged behind the National League, but even so only once since 1968 has its base-stealing leader been a white player (Freddie Patek in 1977).]*

Pat Robinson, New York *Telegram*

Sunday, March 27

St. Petersburg—Following a conference with Col. Jacob Ruppert yesterday, Herb Pennock, Yankee pitching ace, signed a contract for three years. The terms were not announced.

By signing a three-year agreement, Pennock joins the elite few of baseball composed of New York Giant outfielder Eddie Roush, Babe Ruth, and Brooklyn Dodger pitcher Dazzy Vance. [*Pennock reportedly received almost what he asked for, $60,000 for three years.*]

New York *World*

Wednesday, March 30

St. Petersburg—A year ago, when the Yankees generally were assigned to the second division, I boldly picked them to win the pennant.

Were the Yankee champions of 1926 a one-year team? I rather think so. The 1927 Yankees should be dangerous, but it is doubtful if their pitching strength is sufficient to send the club into another World Series.

[*Fred Lieb had recently moved from the* Telegram *to the* Post.]

Fred Lieb, *New York Post*

Thursday, March 31

[*On the preceding evening, the Yankees had left St. Petersburg. They would travel slowly northward, playing exhibition games along the way with the St. Louis Cardinals, and would arrive in New York on Friday night, April 8.*]

Jacksonville—Only Babe Ruth is indifferent to what is going on around him. It's all the same to him whether he is here or somewhere else. Even his thumb doesn't bother him. One would think it was an everyday occurrence to be bitten by a fish. [*A couple of days earlier, Babe Ruth had been bitten by a large fish.*]

"It's all right," he said. "When I play, I'll wrap some tape around it. What the hell."

A lot of guys would run to a doctor to have that thumb cauterized. Ruth can't be bothered with little things like that. What a man!

Rud Rennie, New York *Herald-Tribune*

Friday, April 1

Jacksonville—Mr. Miller Huggins has gone in for training rules in a serious way. Mr. Huggins isn't yet a John McGraw in his demands—but he has ideas. And means to enforce them. [*McGraw, of the Giants, was noted for being the strictest of all managers in formulating and in enforcing rules of conduct for his players.*]

The latest edict includes the following:

No card playing for more than a 25 cent limit.

No smoking while in uniform.

No staying out after midnight.

No golfing except on Sunday and off days.

Number one is the rule which hurts worst. When young men like Mr. Ruth and Mr. Meusel get around a card table, they are accustomed to deal in sums that would make an ordinary individual gasp for breath. And the new methods cramp their style. No longer ago than last evening Mr. Ruth frittered away some

40 dollars in small dribbles before he learned that even a duffer won't let you bluff a sizable pot on a 25 cent wager. And Mr. Meusel, who has ever been willing to risk a ten case note on his chances of making "21" in a black jack game, found himself considerably handicapped when he collected only 50 cents on an ace-jack combination.

The result is that cards have lost some of their lure, and the wily poker game is being rapidly supplanted by the more intellectual bridge party. Among the recent converts to bridge is Mr. Ruth himself. Last night when a foursome was organized the Babe sat in.

"What will we play for?" inquired utility infielder Mike Gazella [*a graduate of Lafayette College*].

"Oh," replied the Babe, "let's make it the limit. Fifty cents."

The Babe lost something like $67 on the first rubber before he discovered that fifty cent bridge is a bit of a millionaire pastime, and hereafter has avowed his intentions of holding his stakes to a quarter of a cent.

Ford C. Frick, New York *Evening Journal*

Saturday, April 2

I learn from Mr. Christy Walsh that his trained seal has a new and unusual worry.

People are writing in to the home-run merchant and asking for money. This is what reformation and a surrender to economy have done for him. In days gone by, the Babe's spendthrift ways stamped him as a constant bankrupt, and nobody bothered to solicit him for funds.

Now it is different. The Babe is known to have a bank account. Wide publicity was given to the fact that he put $50,000 in one fund and, more recently, that he made a deposit of $33,000 in another.

The reaction has started to set in. The gimmies are on his trail. Mr. Walsh now fears that the Babe, having thrown one fortune away, may be moved by his big, noble, charitable impulse to give this new one away.

Joe Williams, New York *Telegram*

Any team with the batting power of the Yankees is bound to be a factor in a pennant race. Huggins's outfit is likely to go on a rampage at any given moment and blast the best pitchers in the business off the mound. With the homeric Mr. Ruth, Meusel, Gehrig, Lazzeri, and Combs chasing each other down the batting order, no pitcher knows when his life is safe.

Because of the questionable character of their own pitching, I scarcely expect the New York representatives to repeat their 1926 victory. But so long as they continue to try, they will give the team that does win some bad afternoons.

Here is the one great danger with the Ruppert Rifles. They are a temperamental team.

It has often been said that as Ruth goes, so go the Yankees. That is only partially true. It would be more accurate to say that as they want to go, so go the Yankees. Huggins has said repeatedly that lanky Bob Meusel can be just as good a ballplayer as he wants. I believe that this is true of the entire team.

The power is there. All that's needed is to use it. Much depends on the start they get. If they get off winging, as they did last year, it is going to be a man's-sized job to head them. But will the pitching be good enough to give them a flying start?

Herb Pennock, the Squire of Kennett Square, is the most dependable pitcher on the staff, and he had to be left behind in St. Petersburg to nurse a sore arm. He might not be ready for the opening game.

Outside the Pennsylvania portsider, there is not a thoroughly reliable pitcher on the Yankee roster. "Dutch" Ruether is an uncertain quantity. Waite Hoyt pitches in streaks. Bob Shawkey is old [*he was thirty-six*]. Walter Beall is wild.

If only two of them, in addition to Pennock, prove consistent winners, the champs may still be champs when the numbers go up next fall. Otherwise I can't see them beating the Athletics, and they might even finish back of the Tigers and Senators.

Bill Corum, New York *Evening Journal*

Sunday, April 3

[*Playing extremely sloppily, the Yankees lost the preceding day's exhibition game to the Cardinals, 20–10.*]

Savannah—The Yankees were weak enough at bat and bad enough in the field to interrupt any thoughts that one might have had concerning the possibilities of the club winning another pennant.

Richards Vidmer, *The New York Times*

How do the players in the American League figure their race? Well, if Mr. McGillicuddy's Athletics don't breeze in, they will be astonished. [*Philadelphia manager Connie Mack's name at birth was Cornelius McGillicuddy.*]

A straw vote among 100 American Leaguers placed the Macks on top, with the Yanks second and Washington third.

Save this grouping until October, and see what the players know about their own racket:

1. Philadelphia	5. Detroit
2. New York	6. Chicago
3. Washington	7. St. Louis
4. Cleveland	8. Boston

New York *Telegram*

Monday, April 4

Atlanta—Babe Ruth, the Peck's Bad Boy of baseball, and Dutch Ruether, veteran southpaw, had the riot act read to them by Manager Miller Huggins, and both drew a strong warning as to behavior.

Huggins called Ruether out of a card game on the train and laid down the law in no uncertain terms. Huggins warned the southpaw that if he didn't watch his step, he would find a slice cut off one of his paychecks, and pointed out the danger in having two left-handers setting a social pace for each other. Ruth also was called to order.

Many a left-hander working alone, along what might be called sociable lines, has turned a manager's hair white overnight, but two of them acting in concert is too much for even such a patient individual as Huggins.

Ruether is a smart ballplayer and intelligent off the field. It is therefore likely that Huggins's warning will bear fruit. If it doesn't, it is certain that the manager will take drastic action.

[*For many years, the stereotypical view of left-handed pitchers was that they were wild and unpredictable in their behavior on and off the field. Among the southpaw hurlers who lived up to the stereotype were George "Rube" Waddell, Vernon "Goofy" Gomez, and Walter "Dutch" Ruether.*

The thirty-three-year-old Ruether began his major league career in 1917, and he had had three excellent seasons, winning nineteen games for Cincinnati in 1919, twenty-one games for Brooklyn in 1922, and eighteen games for Washington in 1925. It should be noted that in each of these seasons Ruether pitched for a different team, and that the Yankees, who acquired him from the Senators in August 1926, were his fifth big league club. One reason for the frequency with which he moved from one team to another was that he loved his fun off the field, especially alcoholic fun. It was indeed interesting that when the Yankees were on the road Ruether's roommate was Babe Ruth.]

Pat Robinson, New York *Telegram*

Tuesday, April 5

Atlanta—Besides hitting, Babe Ruth did the best pitching of the day, but not from the box. [*In a game won by the Yankees over the Cardinals, 15–8, Ruth hit two doubles.*] He had perfect control from left field and twice cut down runners with strikes that split the plate and bounced into catcher Pat Collins's waiting mitt as the runner slid in.

Richards Vidmer, *The New York Times*

Speculation as to which teams will win the pennants is becoming lively, according to Kemp & Co., betting commissioners, of 515

Seventh Avenue. In the American League the Athletics are favored, while in the National the Giants are the choice.

These are the odds quoted for American League teams:

Philadelphia	9 to 5	Cleveland	8 to 1
New York	3 to 1	Chicago	20 to 1
Washington	3½ to 1	St. Louis	30 to 1
Detroit	5 to 1	Boston	50 to 1

New York *Telegram*

Wednesday, April 6

Knoxville, Tenn., April 5—All morning long the rain beat down in silver sheets. The little hamlet of Etowah, Tenn., was drenched and dripping, but the special train bearing the Yankees and Cardinals was somewhere along the tracks. And on that train was Babe Ruth.

In scheduling the little world series [*a reference to the exhibition games between the two teams that had played in the 1926 World Series*] the officials of the two clubs somehow had overlooked Etowah, but Etowah wasn't going to overlook the opportunity of seeing Ruth. The citizens searched the attic and closets, clothed themselves in garments best suited for the weather, and flocked to the station.

The train was an hour late, but when it finally arrived and paused, the platform contained all but four of the hamlet's inhabitants. Three were still looking for their rubbers, and the other had pneumonia already. Through the Babe's sweet, charitable nature they weren't disappointed.

The train reached Etowah just a few seconds after the Babe had bid four spades and had been doubled. He was in a precarious position. Beads of perspiration broke out on the forehead of Dutch Ruether, his partner. Ed Phillips, the rookie catcher, and your correspondent leaned forward in eager anticipation of a killing. And then the train stopped.

Everyone knew why the crowd had gathered. There was no idea that they had splashed through mud up to their shoe tops just to bring the engineer his lunch. It wasn't Alexander or Frank Frisch or Meusel or Bob O'Farrell or Miller Huggins they had come to greet. They wanted the Babe, and they made no effort to conceal their desires.

So the Babe left his four-spade bid doubled, left Ruether on the verge of a nervous collapse, and left Ed Phillips and the writer in high anticipation, and went out on the platform.

The township of Etowah came to worship at the shrine of the king and left with a feeling of friendship. When the Babe grins, awe vanishes and he makes a pal.

It was the same way when the special reached Knoxville later. A crowd was at the station to catch a glimpse of the home-run king. There was another mob swarming in the lobby of the Farragut Hotel, and at this very moment the corridors are well populated with high school boys wandering about seeking Ruth.

Richards Vidmer, *The New York Times*

Saturday, April 9

The Athletics should cross the line in front in the American League this season because Connie Mack has been getting up headway for several years and now looks to be under full steam.

Walter Trumbull, *New York Post*

Connie Mack's Athletics loom as American League champions chiefly because their batting order will include famous stars who are on the verge of retirement. Ty Cobb, Eddie Collins, and Zack Wheat are expected to play the kind of baseball that has kept them in the limelight for many years. [*This would be the twenty-third major league season for the forty-year-old outfielder Ty Cobb, the twenty-second season for the forty-year-old second baseman Eddie Collins, and the twenty-third season for the thirty-nine-year-old outfielder Zack Wheat. Cobb and Wheat would be playing for the first time with the Athletics, and Collins was returning to the team after an absence of thirteen years. All three men would be early inductees in baseball's Hall of Fame.*]

Joe Vila, New York *Sun*

Sunday, April 10

From present indications, the American League race figures as follows: Philadelphia, New York, Washington, Cleveland, Detroit, Chicago, St. Louis, Boston.

Grantland Rice, New York *Herald-Tribune*

After waiting twelve years, the "dope" points to a pennant this season for the Athletics of Connie Mack, baseball's oldest leader. [*Philadelphia had won its last pennant in 1914. Connie Mack was now sixty-five years old; he would continue to manage the Athletics until 1950, for a total of fifty consecutive years as the manager of one team, surely a record that will never be equaled.*] Mack has been building while other managers slept and "stood pat." His team figures to nose out the Cleveland Indians, with the Yankees finishing in third place.

Monitor, New York *World*

Chicago (AP)—Ban Johnson, president of the American League, believes the race for championship honors will find five clubs battling it out.

"My opinion that a splendid race is in prospect is borne out by reports from umpires who have been with the teams in the training period, and from newswriters of accepted good judgment who have added their confirmation," Johnson said.

"It seems to be the collective impression that five clubs at least will be in a pennant fight in which the winner is a toss up, so well matched in ability are they estimated to be.

"All in all, we look forward to a contest this year that should make its mark in the annals of the national game."

New York *American*

Tuesday, April 12

The major league baseball season opens today. If the weather permits, 16 teams will go to bat in 8 cities, and the 154-game struggle will be on.

The Yankees open at home at the capacious Yankee Stadium against the Philadelphia Athletics. Already, all reserved seats have been disposed of. Thirty thousand unreserved grandstand and bleacher seats will be available at the park. If the weather is fine, there ought to be the biggest first-game crowd in the history of baseball, probably 65,000 or more.

The great demand for ducats is largely due to a popular desire to see Babe Ruth, Ty Cobb, Eddie Collins, and Zack Wheat. In addition, the fans will watch two of the best teams in the league.

Miller Huggins will employ his regular lineup: Earle Combs, in center, leading off; followed by Mark Koenig, shortstop; Babe Ruth, right field; Lou Gehrig, first base; Bob Meusel, left field; Tony Lazzeri, second base; Joe Dugan, third base; and John Grabowski, catching. [*The Yankees had two men who would do most of the catching, Grabowski and Collins. Had he not been hampered by a sore arm, the first-string catcher would have been Bengough.*]

Rud Rennie, New York *Herald-Tribune*

Graphic play-by-play description of the opening Yankee-Athletic game will be broadcast through WEAF and WJZ, beginning at 2:45, direct from Yankee Stadium. [*The game itself would start at 3:30.*] Graham McNamee will officiate at the microphone.

[*McNamee was easily the nation's most famous sports broadcaster. Now thirty-eight years old, his voice was known to millions through his broadcasts of important events in ten different sports, ranging from football to auto racing. He began his career, with the National Broadcasting Company, with the Greb-Wilson fight on August 23, 1923, and he stayed with NBC until his last broadcast, in April 1942, a month before his death.*

This would be the only regular-season broadcast from the stadium in 1927. The Yankees would be one of the last clubs to provide its fans with broadcasting for an entire season. At 3 P.M. on April 20, 1939, WABC began its broadcast of the opening-day game from Yankee Stadium, with the Red Sox providing the opposition, and from that day Yankee games have been reported uninterruptedly on the radio.]

New York *American*

Wednesday, April 13

[*On April 12, opening day, in New York, the Yankees defeated Philadelphia, 8–3. Winning pitcher, Waite Hoyt.*]

The big parade toward Yankee Stadium started before noon yesterday. Subways brought ever-increasing crowds into the Bronx. Taxicabs arrived by the hundreds. Busses came jammed to the doors. The parade never stopped. At three o'clock the unreserved seats were filled, and the police formed lines at River Avenue in the back of the park and along the approaches in front. Only those with tickets clutched in their hands were allowed to pass.

By game time the vast structure was packed solid. Rows of men were standing in back of the seats and along the runways. Such a crowd had never before seen a baseball game or any other kind of game in New York.

"No question, it was the greatest crowd that ever saw a baseball game," said Ed Barrow, the Yankee general manager. "We had to be careful about overloading the runways to comply with fire and police rules or we could have sold more tickets to persons willing to stand up, but I think a conservative estimate is that we had more than 70,000 in the park." [*In fact, 72,000 people were in attendance, including 62,000 paid admissions, 9,000 invited guests, and 1,000 who had passes. The crowd, as Barrow said, was the largest in the history of baseball, and it still has not been surpassed for an opening-day game in New York City.*]

There was a circus atmosphere about the whole performance. Men, women, and children in high good humor moved restlessly and excitedly and shouted in shrill voices. Ushers in scarlet coats tried to get people to sit down. Vendors sold peanuts and hot dogs and pop. The Seventh Regiment Band, in natty gray, played loudly.

Shortly before 3:30 Miller Huggins went to the Athletics' dugout. A brigade of photographers, with cameras of all sorts and sizes, followed in his wake, and as he approached, a long, lean, funereal-looking man in black came out to meet him. He was Connie Mack, manager of the Athletics, who once more sees visions of a championship. [*With the Athletics, Mack had led six teams to a pennant and three to a world championship; in the near future, he would manage three more pennant winners and two world champions.*] They were photographed in a hundred poses, even with their arms around each other, looking for all the world like Mutt and Jeff.

The band tuned up. At least the umpah could be heard and the majordomo began to twirl his war club and look very important. The Yankees began to form in a column of fours, very seriously. The Athletics put on blue silk blouses, quite snappy, and formed a column of fours just as if that were done every morning before breakfast.

A solemn parade began. Band, Athletics, Yankees, all in line. Then a huge baseball, about four feet in diameter, pushed by a mysterious left-handed gentleman in a brown coat and hat, who acted as if he were doing something very foolish. Probably he was.

On to center field went this small army and there the band played "The Star-Spangled Banner." The crowd arose and hats went off. Perspiring workers dropped their rakes and tampers. The American flag was raised and then the American League pennant, a bit of muslin twice the size of Old Glory.

The ceremonies concluded, a long conference was held at the plate between three umpires led by Billy Evans and the rival captains. What they talked about nobody seemed to know, but Evans was apparently pointing out which was right field and which left.

Meanwhile Mayor Jimmy Walker, sitting in Colonel Ruppert's box, had risen to throw the first ball out to little Eddie Bennett, the Yankee mascot. He did it like a veteran, repeating the performance twice to make sure that every photographer had a record of the event.

An announcer:

"Laaa-deeeez and gen-tul-mun! Batteries for today's game. [*All announcements on the field were by a man speaking through a megaphone. An electronic public address system* would be installed in the mid-1930's]

Waite Hoyt, the perennial boy wonder from Brooklyn, No. 16 on the program [*in the program, players were numbered, but not until*

1929 *would the Yankees have numbers on their uniforms*] was pitching for the Yankees with G'bo'ski [*as his name usually appeared in the box score*] catching. [*Hoyt, now twenty-seven years old, had signed his first professional baseball contract while he was still a student at Brooklyn's Erasmus Hall High School. He was now in his tenth major league season, his seventh with the Yankees, for whom he had won 100 regular season games and 3 in the World Series. Grabowski was starting his first season with New York, having been acquired in the winter from the White Sox. Never at any time in his seven-year career in the major leagues would he appear behind the plate in more than seventy-five games.*] Grove was in the box for the Athletics, with Mickey Cochrane catching. Eddie Collins stepped to the plate, spat on his hands, rapped each shoe in turn with his bat, and the game was on.

Only a single unusual event interrupted the more or less uneven tenor of the game. It occurred when Babe Ruth stepped to bat for the first time, with Combs dancing excitedly off third base. Apparently from nowhere a bare-headed man [*at a time when almost all men wore hats*] appeared on the field bearing a huge silvery punch-bowl. He approached the plate, while the Babe looked at him quizzically, and the crowd began to boo.

Mayor Walker saved the situation. With three nimble jumps, the Mayor was at the plate. He took off a jauntily cocked derby with a left hand encased in a bright yellow glove. With his right, similarly covered, he shook hands with the great Bam. Quicker than you could have said William G. McAdoo, the Mayor had finished an address and presented Babe with the trophy. [*William Gibbs McAdoo had been a candidate for the Democratic presidential nomination in 1924, and his name was currently being mentioned for the 1928 nomination.*] Three more jumps and Mayor Walker was back in his box, and the Babe was eyeing Grove. The man and his silverware disappeared as they had come.

[*Probably no one typified the spirit of Broadway in the twenties more than the forty-five-year-old man who, since January 1, 1926, had been the mayor of New York, James J. "Jimmy" Walker. Charming, dapper, urbane, witty, he was the quintessential New York sophisticate in the era of the speakeasy. He was even a successful songwriter, and one of his songs, "Will You Love Me in December as You Do in May?" achieved lasting popularity. In 1929, he would win re-election by a plurality of nearly five hundred thousand votes over an opponent who himself one day would be an extraordinarily colorful mayor of New York, Fiorello H.*]

LaGuardia. As the result of the investigation and uncovering of corruption in his regime by the so-called Seabury Commission, Jimmy Walker, on September 1, 1932, would resign as mayor to forestall his certain removal from office.]

Things proceeded like an every-day ball game until the Yankees put everything on ice with four runs each in the fifth and sixth innings. Then the immense crowd began to unwind, like a ball of thread, and long lines started out of the stadium. Getting out was far worse than getting in, for the streets were soon jammed to suffocation, and the subway platforms were plainly dangerous.

Two hours of pulling and tugging, a fair bit of which was contributed by policemen and special officers, and New York returned to normal. Yankee Stadium was once more an empty park, with nothing but bits of paper, a few overturned chairs, and cleat marks in the dirt to indicate that anything had happened.

Peter Vischer, New York *World*

Waite Hoyt, the Brooklyn mortician, made a neat job of burying the opening day hopes of the Athletics. [*Baseball writers in the twenties frequently referred to Waite Hoyt as the Brooklyn mortician, and several later chroniclers of Yankee activities have dutifully reported that he was a licensed mortician. In point of fact, Hoyt was never a mortician, licensed or otherwise. The father of Dorothy Hoyt, the first of his three wives, was a mortician, and on several occasions Hoyt was photographed while standing alongside a hearse. Before long some people began to think that it was Hoyt, not his father-in-law, who was the mortician.*] Waite was on the mound last October when the Yankees lost that heartbreaking seventh game to the Cardinals. It was no fault of Waite's that that one was tossed away.

Six months elapsed, and when a new season dawned, Waite again was on the Yankee firing line.

"That fellow (Hoyt) should win 20 or more games for me every season," said Huggins in St. Petersburg last month. "He should be as good a pitcher as there is in the league."

Waite's best record has been 19 wins [*in 1921 and 1922*]. There is no time like the present to go after that 20-victory season mark.

We regret to say that our good friend, the Bambino, was the "bust" of the opening day party.

Usually George Herman rises to the big moments. The bigger
the crowds, the higher Ruth rises. But yesterday he was a flop.

With Combs on third base in the first, "Lefty" Grove fanned
George on four pitches. With Koenig on third base in the fourth,
your Hon. Babe hit a high infield pop to second baseman Eddie
Collins. With Hoyt on third and Combs on second in the fifth,
Ruth again expired on strikes.

It was Ruth's turn to bat during the sixth inning fusillade.
Koenig was on third. What's that? Ben Paschal batting for Ruth.
For whom? Yes, for Ruth. Ben slung a single to right, scoring
Koenig.

Yes, there is an explanation. Miller Huggins says that Babe
had a bilious attack. Something he had eaten, and he couldn't
see the ball. Yet I saw him hook three of Herb Pennock's batting
practice pitches into the right field bleachers. When Yankee
rookie pitcher Wilcy Moore went in, the bombardment of the
right field bleachers continued. Perhaps it was Grove's left-
handed speed ball which made "Big Bam" bilious.

Well, better luck today, Babe!

Fred Lieb, *New York Post*

Viewed from the press coop, George Herman Ruth appears to
have what is referred to as a bay window. In spite of the fact that
Artie McGovern, his trainer, will cut me dead if he sees this,
something seemed to quiver and shake as the Babe jogged in
from the outfield.

Paul Gallico, New York *Daily News*

Attendance figures for the 7 major league opening games yesterday [*with a rained-out game in St. Louis*] show that 241,000 persons
saw the contests, 18,000 more than witnessed 8 games last year.
Following are the figures:

AMERICAN LEAGUE		NATIONAL LEAGUE	
New York	72,000	Philadelphia	22,000
Washington	30,000	Boston	15,000
Cleveland	22,000	Chicago	45,000
		Cincinnati	35,000

The New York Times

Thursday, April 14

[*On April 13, in New York, the Yankees beat Philadelphia, 10–4. Winning pitcher, Dutch Ruether.*]

Although there is an admirable precept to the effect that old age should be treated with respect, the boisterous Yankees again spanked the Athletics. The gray locks of the ancient visitors awoke not a spark of pity in Miller Huggins's young men; on the contrary, the Yanks comported themselves in a brutal and unfeeling manner.

Murderers' Row broke out anew and flogged three Philadelphia pitchers for 16 hits. Mark Koenig, for whom the experts have been feeling more pity than scorn, turned the laugh on his severest critics by hitting 5 singles in a row.

Dutch Ruether, our twirler, was no great shakes, but he outlasted four members of Cornelius McGillicuddy's pitching staff.

The season is young yet, but so far the apathetic Athletics have displayed nothing that should cause a Yankee fan to walk the floor restlessly at night. Connie Mack, at first blush, appears to have an interesting but not highly valuable collection of antiques. Collins and Cobb are not covering half the ground that they did ten years ago, and Zack Wheat has not even made the varsity nine.

[*The Yankees acquired their popular nickname "Murderers' Row" in 1921, not only because Babe Ruth hit fifty-nine home runs that year, but because for the first time in baseball history every member of the starting lineup hit at least four home runs during the season. Also for the first time, at least eight home runs were credited to five members of one team: Ruth, Bob Meusel, Frank "Home Run" Baker, Wally Pipp, and Roger Peckinpaugh. To put this in proper perspective, it should be noted that four years earlier Pipp had led the American League with nine home runs, and six years earlier Bob "Braggo" Roth's league-leading total was seven.*]

James R. Harrison, *The New York Times*

The two-ply announcer system is something new at the Stadium this season. Heretofore a single megaphone man has sufficed.

The big crowd opening day required the services of two town criers, and the idea proved so popular that the pair were used again yesterday and may be continued.

Mr. Jack Lentz is the announcer with the derby hat and the large speaking trumpet. Mr. George Levy is the announcer with the soft hat and the small megaphone.

It would seem that if these two gentlemen are to be used in duet they should have similar costumes and the same sized megaphones. It would add zest to the scenery if they were dressed like old-fashioned heralds, or at least outfitted with scarlet coats, such as the Stadium ushers wear. Also they could stand a little drill in marching formations. [*Lentz had been a longtime field announcer at Yankee Stadium, and Levy had worked mainly in the Polo Grounds. Lentz was a colorful character who didn't exactly speak the king's English. When a doubleheader was to be played on the next day, he would announce, "There will be two games for the price of one omission." No one bothered to correct him.*]

The Yanks gave the announcers no work at all after the game started, as there was not a single substitution. Dutch Ruether went the full pitching route, and the regulars batted so well that no pinch hitter was needed. [*The announcers would give the name of each batter on his first trip to the plate; thereafter they would be used only for pinch hitters, pinch runners, and other changes in the lineup. On this afternoon, the Athletics kept them busy, however, with three relief pitchers and three pinch hitters.*]

Will Wedge, New York *Sun*

This is a little human interest story about Mark Anthony Koenig and Cleopatra. It might be subtitled "Partners Again." The story would have lain buried but for the fact that while the Yankees were slaughtering the Athletics again yesterday, Mark Anthony Koenig, of Telegraph Hill, San Francisco, stopped the show with five hits in as many times at bat.

As Mark Anthony got two hits in three trips to the plate on Tuesday he leads the American League with a batting average of .875. But we seem to be digressing from the little human interest story about Mark Anthony and Cleopatra.

Last month when Koenig started training with the Yankees, he got a shipment of bats from a well-known stick mill in Louisville [*Hillerich & Bradsby Company, manufacturers of Louisville Slugger bats, used by most players*], and one in particular struck his eye, a sleek, greenish black thing, fine of grain and dangerous and vampire looking. Mark Anthony picked it out for a pet and named it Cleopatra.

Koenig polished that new bat with a hambone. He steeped it in cottonseed oil. Then Mark took that sleek weapon out to the ball park—and couldn't make any hits.

Mark steeped that bat in more oil. He polished it anew. But still there wasn't a hit in greenish black Cleopatra.

So Mark Anthony hurled Cleopatra into his locker and forgot all about his hickory pet.

The training season proceeded. Mark tried other bats—light ones and heavy ones, brown ones and yellow ones. But none seemed to have any hits for Mark Anthony. He came through the exhibition season with an average of .243. The boys began to wonder how long it would be before Miller Huggins shifted Tony Lazzeri to short and sent Ray Morehart to second. [*A highly regarded infielder, Morehart had come to the Yankees from the White Sox, along with John Grabowski, in a trade for longtime Yankee second baseman Aaron Ward.*]

On Tuesday morning Mark Anthony began to cogitate. Sweet sentiment seeped into his soul. Mark Anthony decided to appeal to Cleopatra again. So when the Yankees opened their battle with the Athletics a greenish black bat once more lay in that robust collection of clouting claymores in front of the New York dugout.

You already know how Koenig got a single and triple on Tuesday.

Yesterday morning Mark Anthony gave Cleopatra another bath, this time in olive oil, and in five trips to the plate against four pitchers, Mark came up with five bingles.

As the burghers were leaving the Stadium they were wondering what had happened to Koenig. Some opined that he had got a consignment of homemade knockwurst from mommy in San Francisco. Others said that the sight of Morehart on the bench had roused Mark to action.

Still others laid the rise of Mark Anthony to [*the famous English yachtsman and tea magnate*] Sir Thomas Lipton's opinion, expressed on Tuesday, that Koenig was a great ballplayer. Little did they know about sleek Cleopatra.

Dan Daniel, New York *Telegram*

Friday, April 15

[*On April 14, in New York, the Yankees and Philadelphia played a 9–9 tie, in a game that was halted at the end of 10 innings because of darkness.*]

The infant two-game winning streak of your Yankees still is intact after yesterday's game was stopped by darkness and a descending freezing spell.

When hostilities ceased a full moon was climbing ambitiously over the vast Yankee cavern, already gripped by the gloom of a chill April evening. Lights were twinkling on the adjacent subway platform, and the clients, nearly 12,000 of them, sat huddled in their chairs, blowing on their withered hands and stamping their feet lustily.

Pitchers came and went. The Yankees managed to get an even break by employing the ancient Robert Shawkey; the young Mister Wilcy Moore; Urban Shocker, discovering that his saliva congealed on the ball as soon as it was applied; and Waite Hoyt. The same number was used by the attenuated and thin-blooded Cornelius McGillicuddy, shaking miserably from the cold in the Philadelphia hutch. They were Eddie Rommel, Lefty Walberg, Joe Pate, and Robert Grove.

Hoyt and Grove were the only two who suffered no humiliation.

The Yankees' biggest hit came in the fifth, when Long Robert Meusel whaled a ball far over center fielder Al Simmons's head for a most delectable triple with the bases full.

A long afternoon.

A cold afternoon.

A dull afternoon.

And it didn't mean a blessed thing.

Marshall Hunt, New York *Daily News*

Babe Ruth has a heavy cold. He contracted it in Brooklyn last Sunday [*when the Yankees played their final exhibition game*] and he has hardly been able to see. It is a little better now, but even so, he is playing under difficulties which would be sufficient excuse for a man to ask for a rest.

Rud Rennie, New York Herald-Tribune

The sensational fielding and heavy hitting of Mark Koenig in the first two games probably delighted Miller Huggins more than any other feature of the Yankees' triumphs. Koenig played the kind of ball of which Huggins knew he was capable when he first came here.

Huggins tabbed the young shortstop as a natural infielder possessing a wonderful throwing arm. The fact that Koenig wasn't afraid to "go after everything," regardless of errors, made him solid with the mite manager.

He was quite a hitter, too. So the Yankees' leader stuck to him and now is about to receive his reward.

In my opinion, Koenig has few superiors at shortstop and will bat with more successful results than last season [*when his batting average was .271, with 62 RBIs*]. Hooked up with Tony Lazzeri, Koenig is developing speed and steadiness.

Lazzeri, another youngster, already is one of the leading second basemen, thanks to the determination of Huggins to keep him on the beam, no matter what might happen.

Like Koenig, Lazzeri came out of the minors to make his mark in fast company early last year and Huggins quickly decided that he was made of the right stuff. The Italian, properly encouraged, learned how to cover second base, although he had always played shortstop, and soon displayed unusual batting skill [*batting .275, with 18 home runs and 114 RBIs*].

The success of Koenig and Lazzeri is attributed entirely to the judgment of Huggins. He has handled them perfectly. The same can be said of Lou Gehrig, the burly first baseman with the big wagon tongue. Huggins knew what he was doing when he benched the veteran Wally Pipp in favor of the former Columbia University player.

Gehrig today is first class in his position. He is faster on his feet and thinks quickly. As a hitter he ought to lead all of the first basemen in the American League. Huggins alone is responsible for the development of Columbia Lou.

It is worthy of note that in Gehrig, Lazzeri, and Koenig, the Yankees have young infielders who are destined to play in baseball for at least ten years. [*In fact, Gehrig would be a major leaguer for another twelve full seasons, all with the Yankees; Lazzeri for another twelve seasons, eleven with the Yankees; and Koenig for another ten seasons, three with the Yankees.*]

Huggins has the right idea. He is preparing for the future and isn't wasting time with old players.

Joe Vila, New York *Sun*

Saturday, April 16

[*On April 15, in New York, the Yankees beat Philadelphia, 6–3. Winning pitcher, Herb Pennock. Yankee home run, Babe Ruth (1).*]

Just when the venerable Cornelius McGillicuddy's venerable Athletics had figured after holding the Yankees to a tie score, they were due for a victory, Babe Ruth rose from the ashes of a poor hitting streak and smashed his first home run in the first inning yesterday. [*In ten times at bat in the first three games, Ruth had had three singles, no extra base hits, no RBIs, and three strikeouts.*]

More than 20,000 [*on Good Friday, when many workers had a half-day holiday*], most of whom had been waiting since Tuesday to see him turn the trick, joined in the biggest demonstration the big hitter ever had had since he began hitting home runs. The blow and the bellowing so softened up Athletics' starting pitcher Howard Ehmke, the Silver Creek sapling [*Ehmke was born and raised in the small New York town of Silver Creek*], that he was easy for the other Yanks until extracted for a pinch hitter.

You may say the game was won in the fourth with the fourth Yankee run, or in the seventh, when two men crossed across the plate on a lusty hit by Tony Lazzeri, but in reality it was won in the first by Mr. Ruth's ponderous blow. He took all the spirit, aplomb, finesse out of the crafty arm of Brother Ehmke. [*Ehmke was thirty-three years old and had been pitching in the major leagues since 1915. His greatest victory would come in the first game of the 1929 World Series, when, as Connie Mack's surprise starting pitcher, he would defeat the Cubs and set a Series record with thirteen strikeouts.*]

Howard had started with a world of stuff, gathering in Combs and Marcus Koenig for easy infield taps, and he threw a ball, then a strike, and then another ball to the Babe. He tried to curve another ball on the outside of the plate for a second strike, but it was met by all the steam which has been gathering in the Ruthian war club since April 9 at Ebbets Field [*when, in the exhibition game against Brooklyn, he had last hit a home run*]. The ball went a couple of dozen rows up into the right field bleachers [*which at this time had no upper tier of seats*] quicker than you can say Cornelius McGillicuddy—or even Connie Mack—and after that Master Ehmke was a changed man.

Not that he hasn't been hit for home runs by Ruth before. He has, according to the statisticians, yielded ten of the Babe's homers in his pitching lifetime in Detroit, Boston, and Philadelphia, but none was as welcome as this one to New York or as unwelcome to the Ehmke family.

Monitor, New York *World*

George Herman's first three days were miserable, but nobody had him on the griddle. No tragic yarns bemoaned the fact that at last he was through, and much to my surprise not a single story was printed to the effect that the Klieg lights at last had taken their toll. It was just as well, because before yesterday's game was two innings old, George Herman had belted a home run and cut off a tying run at the plate by one of his marvelous throws. Personally, I get a bigger thrill from those wonderful heaves Ruth makes to the plate than from his home runs. Greater skill and accuracy is required. Pat Collins didn't have to budge an inch yesterday. The ball hit his glove on the fly and Simmons was actually out before he hit the dirt. Wotta man!

Paul Gallico, New York *Daily News*

Sunday, April 17

[*On April 16, in New York, the Yankees defeated Boston, 5–2. Winning pitcher, Urban Shocker.*]

Not being able to push the [*eighth-place*] Red Sox any lower than they are without shoving them out of the league, the Yankees had to be content yesterday to keep them in the state of absolute nothingness which they seem to enjoy. Approximately 30,000 fans watched the Yanks win their fourth straight game.

The Red Sox are not a bad-looking team. They outbatted the Yankees, ten hits to six. They did not make any errors, and some of their fielding was snappy as you please. The trouble with them was that neither starting pitcher Charlie Ruffing [*who in 1930 would begin a fine fifteen-year career with the Yankees, which would lead him into the Hall of Fame*] nor relief pitcher Tony Welzer could keep the Yankees off the bases or keep them from bunching their hits.

For their part, the Yankees continued to play a splendid defensive game. It was so good that it saved Urban Shocker more than once when he was being touched rather lively. But it must be said that Shocker went to his own defense as ably as any one and was most effective in the pinch. [*Shocker was considered by many to be the best fielding pitcher in baseball; during the preceding three seasons he had been charged with only one error.*]

Rud Rennie, New York *Herald-Tribune*

Mark Koenig is rivalling Mr. Ruth for April popularity. The Frisco boy gets a big cheer every time he wiggles his little finger. Keep it up Mark, say we.

James B. Harrison, *The New York Times*

Once again the baseball boys have forgotten that a good label may hide a damaged can. The Pennant-Picking society took a frightful pasting at the Yankee Stadium last week.

It appears the horsehide sophisticates were sadly mistaken in their appraisal of Messrs. Ty Cobb, Eddie Collins, and Zack Wheat. They were good goods in their day, but they have been on the shelf too long.

In a word, they're shot. One series does not make a season, but this particular series gave unmistakable evidence that the grand old men are ready for the pension board.

Poor Connie Mack waited 13 years to purchase an art gallery and then discovered his old masters have swollen feet.

Ed Frayne, New York *American*

Monday, April 18

[*On Sunday, in New York, the Yankees defeated Boston, 14–2. Winning pitcher, Waite Hoyt (2–0). Yankee home runs: Lou Gehrig 2(2).*]

The extremely horizontal Red Sox were knocked for another row of base hits yesterday; in terms of the turf, the Ruppert entry was off fast, piled up a long lead, and won going away.

Henry Louis Gehrig, the Morningside scholar [*Columbia University is located in Morningside Heights, in upper Manhattan*], whiled away the golden hours by slapping two home runs into the right field bleachers. Henry drove in six runs—three with the first homer, two with the second, and another with a sacrifice fly which center fielder Ira Flagstead surrounded a few feet southwest of the Grand Concourse. [*The 180-foot wide Grand Boulevard and Concourse, popularly called the Grand Concourse, is the principal thoroughfare in the Bronx, and it crosses 161st Street just beyond Yankee Stadium.*]

The major efforts of the Red Sox were devoted to getting Mr. Gehrig out. In the first inning, with two mates on base, the ex-Columbian stung a line drive that cleared the wire fence and landed with a joyful plop a few feet inside the right field foul line. Lou's second attempt was not worth a letter home, but on his third try he almost removed the right ear of Mr. Phil Todt, the first baseman, with a savage grounder down the first-base line [*a single*].

That was two hits. In the sixth, with men on second and third, Mr. Gehrig hammered the longest fly of the season. On grasping the situation Flagstead turned his back on the crowd of 35,000 and began running in the direction of Hunt's Point [*a once-fashionable section of the East Bronx, near Riker's Island and far from the stadium*]. When he caught the ball Ira had one foot in the center field bleachers.

Gehrig's last bid for fame and fortune came in the eighth when he established the old toehold and brushed another homer into the right field pavilion. Mr. Ruth, who had just walked, was so lost in admiration that he was almost trampled upon by the home run hitter.

The game was strongly suggestive of one of those spring exhibition tilts between the Yanks and the Oscaloosa club of the
Grape Fruit League. Just as if the situation were not one-sided
enough, Waite Hoyt pitched a beautiful brand of ball, holding
the foe to eight hits.

James R. Harrison, *The New York Times*

Cries of "Look who's here" during the Yankees' fourth inning
took the attention of 35,000 cool and collected fans off the old
ball game, as none cared to miss another Easter parade [*it was
Easter Sunday*], down the left field runway. It was a small parade,
under a broad-brimmed yellow hat, and it drew quite a welcome.

Tammany Young, sitting up in the press box, volunteered to
relieve the curiosity concerning the late arrival, but his efforts to
select the identity were a dismal failure.

Returning from his journey to the box occupied by the girl in
yellow, Tammany reported, "She begged me not to let her name
get in the papers. She said to tell you that she is a night club
hostess, whose nom de cafe is the same as a great Southern State
near the Rio Grande. But be sure not to mention the name. The
confidence must be respected, boys. I done my best, I did."

After the game the girl under the yellow sombrero attempted
to cross the field but the crowd surged as closely as possible
around the broad brim, and she finally escaped through the
grandstand.

[*This entry introduces two of Broadway's most celebrated personalities
of the twenties, Texas Guinan (the lady in the yellow hat) and Tammany
Young.*

*Mary Louise Cecilia "Texas" Guinan went from Waco to New York,
where she became, successively, a chorus girl, a vaudeville performer,
and the most celebrated nightclub hostess of the Prohibition era. She was
noted for greeting patrons with a loud, cheerful "Hello, sucker!" and for
introducing performers by saying, "Let's give her (him, them) a great big
hand." When, a few months earlier, her club was raided by government
agents, they were welcomed with the familiar "Hello, suckers!" whereupon one arresting officer replied, "We're going to give you a great big
handcuff." Beginning in May, she would star in a Broadway review,
appropriately titled* The Padlocks of 1927, *for which she would be paid
$5,000 a week.*

As for her companion, rarely has anyone gained so much mileage on so little talent as did Tammany Young. A short, florid, extremely genial man, he knew everybody who was anybody in the theatrical world, to which he seems to have contributed nothing except to perform walk-on roles in a number of plays. Perhaps his most famous accomplishments came about as the result of his being high society's most eminent and most successful gate-crasher. Among the noteworthy events where he had sat in a box seat without a ticket were the World Series, the Army–Notre Dame football game, and, for five consecutive years, the opening night of the Metropolitan Opera Company's season. Because of this talent, Tammany Young was called a "reverse Houdini," a man who could get into any kind of a box.]

Bill Slocum, New York *American*

In the first five games of the young season, Marcus Aurelius Koenig has been the outstanding player of the Yankees. He has delivered 12 hits for a batting average close to .600, and he had handled 25 chances in the field without a slip. Some of his stops have been brilliant, and he has topped them all with throws of deadly accuracy to first base, or force plays at second.

One might say that Koenig is answering in the most impressive way the charge so often made, as a result of his erratic play, that he never would make the grade. If he finally does shake his erratic tendencies and become a first class shortstop he can thank a manager who never wavered in his rating, even when Koenig was doing everything wrong.

Bill Slocum, New York *American*

AMERICAN LEAGUE STANDINGS

	W	L	PCT	GB		W	L	PCT	GB
New York	5	0	1.000	—	St. Louis	1	1	.500	2½
Detroit	1	0	1.000	2	Philadelphia	2	3	.400	3
Washington	3	2	.600	2	Cleveland	2	3	.400	3
Chicago	3	3	.500	2½	Boston	0	5	.000	5

Tuesday, April 19

[On April 18, in New York, the Yankees defeated Boston, 3–0. Winning pitcher, Dutch Ruether (2–0).]

Colonel Jacob Ruppert rolled up to the Yankee Stadium at 5 o'clock yesterday in the leisurely manner of a man who owns the ball park and thinks he will take in the last five innings. At 5 o'clock, a man is usually in plenty of time to see five innings of an American League baseball game.

But yesterday when the Colonel stepped out of his motorcar he looked and rubbed his eyes, and the hair on his head stood on end. Thousands of persons were coming out of the gates. Coming out, mind you, not going in. He tore past them and made his way to the locker room.

"Huggins! Huggins!" he shouted. "What's the matter? Everybody's going home."

"Nothin's the matter, Colonel," said Huggins quietly. "Calm yourself. The game's over."

"Impossible, Huggins. Impossible. In an hour and a half, the game's over. Don't joke. The ball game was no good, huh?"

"The ball game was O.K.," snapped Huggins. "We won, three to zero."

"In nine innings? You played nine innings, Huggins? In an hour and a half? That's something new, isn't it?"

"It is," agreed Huggins. And the Colonel went back to his motor, shaking his head in bewilderment. *[The usual time of games was about two hours and a half, and sometimes they ran even longer.]*

As a matter of fact yesterday's game was over in one hour and 29 minutes. If for no other reason, it was a delightful game.

It was the Yankees' first shut-out of the season. Dutch Ruether was the pitcher. He allowed only three hits and walked one. It was a neat pitching exhibition.

[It has never been clear that fans object to long games, but sportswriters, then as now, have often complained about having to spend too much time in a ball park doing that for which they are paid. Thus on April 16, Joe Vila, of the New York Sun, *wrote, "Can't something be done to make the Yankees and visiting teams avoid unnecessary delays while trying to*

entertain indulgent fans in Col. Ruppert's ball park? Mr. Ban Johnson's umpires made no effort to hasten the Mackmen and Hugmen during the series that ended yesterday. They allowed players to waste valuable time on the way between their positions and the benches. Changes in lineups were made with undue deliberation, and the pitchers often consumed more than two minutes before delivering the ball. If it is impossible to reduce the playing time, the games should begin at 3:15 instead of 3:30."]

Rud Rennie, New York Herald-Tribune

In the first inning yesterday with Ruth on second, Meusel caromed a single off third baseman Topper Rigney's glove, and when the ball rolled toward second base Ruth dashed in, taking a daring chance and making a beautiful slide over a corner of the plate.

James R. Harrison, The New York Times

Have a most interesting communication on a Brooklyn fan's idea of the Yankee opening last week.

The letter follows:

"Dear Mr. Lieb: I went up to the Yankee opening, which was the first I ever saw. I went thinking I would see our old friend Zack Wheat play. [*Former Dodger Wheat did not play.*]

"Did not get any kick out of the game and walked out at the end of the sixth inning (ten minutes after five). It was the first time I ever walked out on a ball game before it was over. During all the time I had been sitting there there was not a fight, not a bottle thrown nor a player razzed. I get more excitement for four bits out in Flatbush than I get at the Stadium for a dollar ten.

"All those people up there seemed to know was Babe Ruth. They wanted to see Babe sock one, and that's all. There was not a real fan around me. Yes sir, you writers can knock us Brooklyn fans, but as the wise cracker says, "We are the boys who know our onions.""

Fred Lieb, New York Post

The Yanks closed their first week's business yesterday, and some 200,000 paid to see the seven games. As the Yankees average something like 48 cents for themselves on every admission, their share of the swag was somewhere about $96,000. That takes care of Babe Ruth and Bob Meusel for 1927.

Fred Lieb, *New York Post*

Wednesday, April 20

[*On April 19, in New York, the Yankees lost to Boston, 6–3. Losing pitcher, Bob Shawkey (0–1).*]

The worm turned at the Yankee Stadium and, in turning, it caused a lot of upsets. Primarily it upset the Yankees' winning streak and gave the Red Sox their first victory of the season.

Mark Koenig's errorless streak came to an end and, with that first miscue by Mark, came the end of Yanks' streak along the same lines. Mark had gone seven games without an error, and the Yankees had played four straight without a bungle.

The hitting streak of Koenig also suffered. He went to bat four times without making the semblance of a base hit.

All this upsetting, mates, was the result of a plea by Bill Carrigan, leader of the Boston Tribe, to a pint size southpaw who answers to the name of Harold "Pinky" Wiltse. [*For ten years early in the century, Carrigan had been a fine catcher for the Red Sox, a team that he managed for four years (1913–16). After winning two pennants and two world championships, when one of his pitchers was Babe Ruth, Carrigan retired from baseball after the 1916 season, although he was only thirty-three years old. Perhaps the major leagues' wealthiest player, he left the game to become a banker and a theatrical magnate. He received numerous offers to return to baseball, including one from Jacob Ruppert before he hired Miller Huggins, but Carrigan remained out of the game until he returned to manage the Red Sox in 1927.*]

"Please, Harold, go out and stop those Yanks. We must return to Boston with a victory," Carrigan appealingly asked Wiltse.

"O.K. with me, Chief, just tell the boys to give me some support," the portsider replied.

Wiltse got the support, and he showed your Yankees that they can be beaten.

Charles Segar, New York *Daily Mirror*

Yesterday Babe Ruth was a liability. Twice he gummed up rallies by tapping the ball to the pitcher's box for double plays.

Monitor, New York World

Thursday, April 21

[*On April 20, in Philadelphia, the Yankees lost, 8–5. Losing pitcher, Urban Shocker (0–1).*]

It will be many moons before the Yankees forget the anguish of the 1927 opening day in Philadelphia. They were not only wiped out before this city's record crowd of 38,000, but an injury to Herb Pennock, their willowy and classy southpaw, may deprive the Hugmen of his services for a week or longer.

Connie Mack's so-called Antiques rared up on their hind legs, flourished in two dashing late inning rallies, pummelled two pitchers, and gained their first triumph over the champions.

Pennock's injury occurred in batting practice and was kept secret [*so that the Athletics would prepare to face a left-handed pitcher when, in fact, his replacement would be right-handed*].

While batting, a foul from Pennock's bat glanced down his leg, struck a small bone in his left ankle, and the Kennett Square fox hunter danced in pain. Retiring to the bench, Pennock took first aid treatment from trainer Woods and limping slightly returned to practice.

The 38,000 massed in the stands settled back expecting a pitching duel between two brilliant left handers—Pennock and Mose Grove [*Grove's middle name was Moses*]. Pennock stopped pitching and hobbled to the bench.

The A's coaches held a consultation, decided Pennock intended to pitch, and paid little attention to Urban Shocker, who took a short warming up setto. The fans howled for Pennock, and the A's were surprised when Shocker stepped to the pitcher's box.

Last night at his home in Kennett Square, Pennock said he feared a broken bone. An x-ray will be taken today and Pennock is hopeful it is only an injured nerve.

As for yesterday's game, twelve lusty belts ripped off the A's bats, three for extra bases, against Shocker's "spitters" and the curving of Wilcy Moore, 29-year-old recruit right hander from Greenville, N.C. The A's had a great punch and were helped by the ability of Lefty Grove and Jack Quinn to keep Babe Ruth from making any long distance swats. Ruth, in four official appearances, failed to drive the ball out of the infield. [*For part of this game, the pitching opponents, Shocker and the forty-two-year-old Quinn, were two of the American League's four spitball pitchers. The only other spitballer to last the season had, coincidentally, the same first name as Shocker, Urban "Red" Faber, of the White Sox. The fourth spitball pitcher, Stanley Coveleski, would soon be released by the Senators.*]

From all angles it was a perfect day for Philadelphia's outpouring of fans. They packed every nook and corner an hour before game time, and Shibe Park officials stated that more than 10,000 were turned away. The crowd was the largest ever to attend a baseball game in Philadelphia.

John J. Nolan, Philadelphia *Evening Bulletin*

Billy Evans, Emmet "Red" Ormsby, and George Hildebrand, the umpires, looked positively collegiate in the blue jackets and gray pants the American League umpires wear on festive occasions.

Rud Rennie, New York *Herald-Tribune*

Men who darn their own socks have been complaining that Shibe Park [*home of the Athletics*] tickets have been advanced in price. "Isn't it terrible!" "Let's write to the papers," etc. As a matter of fact the ticket schedule is the same as last year, 50 cents for the bleachers, $1.10 for grandstand, and $2.20 for box seats.

James C. Isaminger, Philadelphia *Inquirer*

Colonel Jacob Ruppert has reduced the price of bleacher tickets at Yankee Stadium from 75 cents to 50 cents. The move has proved popular as the seats are filled to capacity nearly every day.

[*In Yankee Stadium, 22,000 seats were priced at 50 cents, the largest number of such seats in any major league park. Until 1928, the bleachers extended from foul pole to foul pole across the outfield, and there were no other seats in this area. During the off-season between*]

1927 and 1928, the triple-decked grandstands were extended beyond the left-field foul pole, and later they would stretch beyond the pole in right field.]

The Sporting News

Friday, April 22

[On April 21, in Philadelphia, the Yankees won, 13–6. Winning pitcher, Wilcy Moore (1–0). Yankee home runs: Lou Gehrig (3), Tony Lazzeri (1).]

The ambitious pupils of Professor Cornelius McGillicuddy received a slight setback in their pennant parading when the Yankees threw them for a rolling fall. It was all very wild and boisterous and not to the liking of Shibe Park fans, who rose up almost in a body in the eighth and walked out on the party.

Some of the Yanks' ringing blows were interesting, important, and influential. Lou Gehrig, the Columbia savant, smacked a long and rakish home run against the left field stand in the sixth with two on base. Moved by this noble precedent, Signor Lazzeri repeated the performance in the eighth with a similar number of runners on the lines.

Earlier in the game the Signor had slapped a three-bagger to the scoreboard in deep center, and to show his versatility, had dumped a safe bunt in still an earlier trip to the plate. The lad from Telegraph Hill knocked in a net total of five runs, but so did the lad from Morningside Hill, Mr. Gehrig.

Between the hefty clouting of our young men from New York and San Francisco, existence was just a dog's life for Samuel Gray and Edwin Rommel, two of McGillicuddy's most estimable throwers.

The trenchant power that flows from Yankee bats was never in better evidence than when eight singles, two doubles, two three-baggers, and two homers left the Athletics looking very abject, bedraggled, and careworn.

James R. Harrison, *The New York Times*

Gehrig has driven in 19 runs, Meusel 14, Lazzeri 13, and the honorable Babe—1. Outside of his one homer, George's season

has been a blank. [*In Thursday's game, Ruth was walked four times.
As Ruth himself had often said, a batter cannot hit the ball if pitchers
won't pitch to him.*]

James R. Harrison, The New York Times

Babe Ruth is not hitting. From a terror the Bambino has become
an empty spot in a lively batting order. But still a menace. Yesterday he drew four bases on balls, probably because he drove
six new baseballs over the fence in batting practice.

But in the game he hit the ball twice without driving it out of
the infield. In the eighth, he actually stooped to bunt, and by
hitting skillfully toward third he rang up his first hit in this city
this year.

Bill Brandt, Philadelphia Public Ledger

According to New York experts, Wilcy Moore is the only pitcher
who tosses a dry "spitter." His curve spins off the outside corner
of the plate with such zip the Athletics and umpires continually
examined the ball to determine if the rookie was tampering with
the stitches or using resin, tobacco juice, slippery elm, etc.

Moore passed all tests and appears to be the best rookie the
Yanks have landed in years. Huggins trusts him entirely with the
tough relief assignments.

[*A twenty-nine-year-old Oklahoman, Wilcy Moore was rather old for a
rookie. He had been pitching in various low-rated minor leagues since
1921, playing on teams representing towns like Paris, Texas, and Ok-
mulgee, Oklahoma, and not until 1926 did he attract any attention. In
that year, he was with Greenville in the South Atlantic (Sally) League,
where he appeared in 305 innings, had an ERA of 1.80, and won an
astonishing 30 games while losing but 4. When Ed Barrow learned
about this record, he immediately telephoned the Greenville club, and,
without ever having seen or spoken with Moore, purchased his contract.
Explaining his action afterward, Barrow said, "A man who can win
thirty games while losing only four is a good pitcher even if he does it in
the Epworth League. If a pitcher isn't selected on that record, there's no
use in trying."*

*Barrow's move proved to be, indeed, a wise one, for Moore was just the
man Huggins needed whenever a starting pitcher got into trouble. As
noted earlier, most writers had had preseason doubts about the Yankees*

because of their pitching staff; with the addition of Moore these doubts at once evaporated. Moore's most effective pitch was known as a sinker.]

John J. Nolan, Philadelphia *Evening Bulletin*

Saturday, April 23

[*On April 22, in Philadelphia, the Yankees' scheduled game was post-poned because of rain.*]

Philadelphia—Mr. George Herman Ruth, yclept Sultan of Swat, borrowed your correspondent's score book and sat down in the lobby of the Yankee hostelry to do some heavy figuring.

Mr. Ruth has had a hitting slump of gigantic proportions. No kidding, when Mr. Ruth goes in for anything he goes in "all over." His hitting slumps are as gargantuan as his home runs—and his strike-outs are as ponderous and enthusiastic as his line drives.

"Seems as though I can't get hold of those doggone balls these days," Mr. Ruth complained as he thumbed the score book. "They come up there big as balloons, and then I top 'em into the ground or miss 'em a mile. But I'll get going one of these days—and when I do some poor pitcher will suffer plenty."

Mr. Ruth grinned in anticipation. [*In the 10 games played thus far, Ruth had had 8 hits—7 of them singles—in 32 times at bat for a batting average of .250. As yet his only run batted in of the season came with his home run on April 15.*]

"Anyhow," he added, "I can afford to save a few wallops until we need 'em. The other boys are going pretty well right now."

Again Mr. Ruth delved into the story of the score book.

"Well, I'm a son of a gun," he exploded. "Look at these figures. I'm the worst hitter on this whole ball club. The way the boys are going now they ought to have me hitting down below the catchers." [*At this time, most catchers batted in the eighth position, just before the pitcher.*]

If the figures provided no joy for George Herman, they were more or less satisfactory to the other members of the cast. And to Miller Huggins, for Miller loves nothing else quite so much as the lethal explosion of base hits. So long as the hitting continues, Mr. Huggins is able to forget his serious pitching worries which threaten, even now, to give him a severe attack of vertigo.

Ford C. Frick, New York *Evening Journal*

Sunday, April 24

[*On April 23, in Philadelphia, the Yankees were beaten, 4–3. Losing pitcher, Wilcy Moore (1–1). Yankee Home runs, Babe Ruth (2), Lou Gehrig (4).*]

Two were out in the ninth inning yesterday when shortstop Joe Boley slid across home plate with the run that made the Mackmen victors in the game, and in the series.

It was the visiting shortstop's desperate effort to lay low the third man that upset the cause of last year's champions. The second out was a force play, Lazzeri to Koenig. Trying for a double play, Koenig undid a sensational day's work by launching the ball high and wide to first base.

Gehrig stuck up his glove. The burly first-sacker should have jumped and used both hands. But he depended on his mitt. The ball skidded off the side of his glove. Boley, who advanced from second to third on the force play, scampered home while Gehrig scrambled toward the grandstand in pursuit of the fatal spheroid.

The weather man looked at the wrong schedule and provided a perfect football day for the first at-home Saturday of the House of Mack. It was no place for a baseball game.

But Macks and Yanks went through with the scheduled setto, defying the climate. Fandom pledged allegiance about 35,000 strong, a capacity house, though not as many aisles were choked nor as many ushers as on Opening Day.

The concourse saw Babe Ruth come out of his trance. A bunt was his only hit here until yesterday. He stepped to the plate in the first inning and slambanged his second home run of the season, a line drive that dipped into 20th Street and bounced up on a porch front. [*The right-field fence in Shibe Park ran along Twentieth Street.*]

Hardly had the applauding died when Ruth's disciple, Lou Gehrig, outdid the maestro himself. Ruth hit George "Rube" Walberg's first pitch. Gehrig looked at one before he swung.

Then the Columbia gem knocked the ball into the wind, and it blew across a 20th Street housetop, the first time this year the 19th Street kids have had the laugh on the 20th streeters.

But that was the end. These resounding blasts were the sum total of dreadnaught offensive. George Walberg, left-handed, won the hero's garland by collecting himself and becoming a nine-inning ace.

Walberg was chargeable with those two tremendous thumps, but no more. Ruth whaled two loud drives to left his next two times at bat, but in later pinches he topped weak grounders to the right side of the infield. Gehrig hit the ball out of the infield no more after he lifted that first one into infinity.

Bill Brandt, Philadelphia Public Ledger

Monday, April 25

[*On April 24, in Washington, the Yankees won, 6–2. Winning pitcher, Urban Shocker (2–1). Yankee home runs, Bob Meusel (1), Babe Ruth (3).*]

Washington—Our Mr. Ruth gave the ball another buggy ride over the right-field fence, and in the wake of this festive tap the Yanks waded into pitcher Hollis Thurston and his fellow Senators before a gathering of 20,000.

It was not entirely the Ruthian drive that featured, as Cedric Durst [*a reserve outfielder obtained in the off-season from the Browns*], inserted as a pinch hitter in the sixth inning with the bases full, accommodated by slamming a full-grown triple to the edge of the green in right center.

While Durst pedaled furiously around to third, his three comrades scored with all the runs that were needed to win. On the bench, Miller Huggins dislocated his left elbow trying to pat himself on the back for the excellent judgment he showed in selecting a pinch hitter.

The Durst clean-up—the most joyous event of the season thus

far—and homers by Ruth and Bob Meusel were the blows that struck the Senators down. This trio of sturdy wallops fetched five of the six runs, Urban Shocker sending in the other one on a squeeze play. [*Shocker was regarded as the major leagues' best sacrifice bunter, someone who never hesitated to bunt on a count of two strikes.*]

Shocker was the Yankee pitcher, and a right good pitcher he was, too. He limited the hard-driving Senators to eight widely scattered hits.

Ruth's homer softened up Thurston for the other boys in the sixth. George's four-bagger [*while leading off the sixth inning*] was a high, mammoth affair which cleared a 45-foot wall 328 feet distant from the plate. The figure experts got out pen and paper and calculated that the ball had travelled some 400 feet before it disappeared over the top of a tree, which is only a mashie pitch for the Bambino. [*A medium-range golf iron was once known as a mashie; it is now called a five-iron.*]

James R. Harrison, *The New York Times*

AMERICAN LEAGUE STANDINGS

	W	L	PCT	GB		W	L	PCT	GB
New York	8	3	.727	—	Philadelphia	5	5	.500	2½
St. Louis	5	2	.714	1	Cleveland	4	6	.400	3½
Detroit	4	2	.667	1½	Chicago	4	7	.364	4
Washington	6	5	.545	2	Boston	2	8	.200	5½

Tuesday, April 26

[*On April 25, in New York, the Yankees lost, 5–4. Losing pitcher, Waite Hoyt (2–1).*]

It's a good thing daylight saving came when it did [*on the preceding Sunday*]. Without that precious hour the Yankees and Senators might have battled till moonlight yesterday. After nine slow, stalling, dragging, beefing, battling innings, the Senators won with the help of Goose Goslin's big bat and his flapping wings in fielding a couple of long drives.

The game never should have been given to Bucky Harris and his gang. [*Harris was the Senator's second baseman and, although only thirty years old, he was in his fourth season as the team's manager. In his initial two years at the helm, Washington won its first pennants, and in 1924, it became the only baseball team representing the nation's capital ever to win a world championship. When his career ended in 1956, Harris had managed in five major league cities for a total of twenty-nine years.*] Waite Hoyt had a three-run lead which he dissipated in the seventh by careless pitching. He wasn't alone to blame. Babe Ruth fanned twice when any kind of a hit would have meant victory. Goslin out-batted Ruth and grabbed all of the glory. His home run in the seventh was a crusher for Hoyt. Why he wasn't passed in that ticklish situation, no one but the Yankee Board of Strategy can tell. [*Hall of Fame outfielder Goose Goslin, a regular with the Senators since 1922, was his team's only slugger. He would hit thirteen home runs in 1927, but none of his fellow Senators would have more than two.*]

Harris used three pitchers, and Rookie Horace Lisenbee, who closed the ·book and gets credit for winning, was the best and luckiest. He was pulled out of trouble in the eighth by three nice plays by Goslin. Goose dragged down a line drive by Combs, held a long drive by Gehrig to a double and a man in position to score on third base, and then closed the frame with a brilliant catch of Meusel's long fly.

The Yanks paraded on the bases, but the Senators paraded off the field. Twenty of them were banished by Umpire Brick Owens in the second inning.

Washington pitcher George Murray was at bat and seemed to have reached for a wide ball in the second, but Owens said he hadn't. Hoyt kicked, Huggins kicked, and finally Owens called in his colleagues Red Ormsby and George Hildebrand. They must have outvoted Brick in the caucus on the diamond, for he now told Murray he was out, whereupon the Senators had a few hundred words in rebuttal.

Mr. Owens couldn't detect which of the reserves made some trifling remark about his eyesight, so to make sure he got his man he swept the dugout clean. All told, 20 reserves filed out into the gloom under the stands. Whenever a pinch hitter or a substitute runner was needed a messenger had to be dispatched, and that added to the many delays of the afternoon.

[*On August 19, 1923, Owens had had a notable altercation with Waite Hoyt. In a game with the White Sox, Hoyt tagged a runner sliding home, and when Owens called him safe, Hoyt tore into the umpire and punched him on his chest protector, for which action he received a ten-day suspension from the league president, Ban Johnson.*]

Monitor, New York World

Mr. George Herman Ruth, back from a five-day trip in which he showed signs of re-discovering the batting power which has been strangely absent, was in a jovial and mellow mood as he donned his spangles in the Yankee club house.

Mr. Ruth whistled merrily as he "boned" his favorite bat and gossiped freely as he rubbed oil in his glove. [*"Boning" the bat by rubbing it with a bottle was a common practice among hitters. This prevented the bat from chipping or splintering and hardened its surface.*]

"Hitting is a funny business," he remarked. "Some days they can't get you out and the next day you can't hit the side of a barn with a bass fiddle. All the time I was in a slump the pitches looked big as balloons. It looked as though a blind man ought to hit 'em with a toothpick, then I'd swing and top 'em into the ground. Slumps are like that.

"Maybe a guy is off his stride, maybe he's dropping his shoulder when he swings, or pulling, or doing something else that he shouldn't do, and it may take ten days or two weeks to get out of it. Then some day you suddenly start hitting again."

"What pitchers are the toughest for you, Babe?" asked "Dutch" Ruether.

"All of 'em," George Herman replied. "If I'm hitting I'll hit any of 'em. When I'm in a slump, I'm a sucker for everybody."

The conversation turned to home runs, and Mr. Ruth grew pensive.

"I don't suppose I'll ever break that 1921 record," he said. "To do that you've got to start early, and the pitchers have got to pitch to you. I don't start early, and the pitchers haven't really pitched to me in four seasons. I get more bad balls to hit than any other six men—and fewer good ones."

Babe has one big ambition.

He'd like to round out a total of 500 home runs before he puts aside his uniform, and that's a pretty big assignment. Right now he has 359 to his credit, which leaves 141 to go. [*Ruth would hit his five hundredth home run on August 11, 1929, against Willis Hudlin of Cleveland, and he would retire with a total of 714. Henry Aaron would hit 755 career home runs; Aaron would also have 3,967 more*

*times at bat than Ruth had. Aaron thus had the equivalent of seven
seasons in which to hit 41 home runs.*]

New York *Evening Journal*

The pivot is a big part of the golf swing. Babe Ruth has carried
the pivoting idea into baseball beyond any player.

Only the Babe doesn't pivot with the swing as the golfer does.
He puts on the pivot act as he takes his place at the plate. His
right shoulder is turned from the pitcher. His left foot is well
back of the right. His body is well around, and he is therefore set
to swing without having to turn. As a result his somewhat vast
body is in position to back up the big punch. There is no other
hitter who uses his shoulders and his body with better effect. It
makes good timing a trifle more complicated, but it adds 40 per
cent to the mule power of the ensuing wallop when it lands.

Grantland Rice, New York *Herald-Tribune*

It is said that no man is a hero to his valet. G. Herman Ruth has
no valet, but those who have been closest to him are the ones
who vote him superman of the diamond. He is a hero to the
"hard-boiled" ballplayers.

When Ruth goes to bat in practice the other players stop their
bunting games and warm-up exercises to watch him swing. They
peer out of the dugout to follow the flight of the ball and discuss
its relative length as a drive compared to the one he hit in Jacksonville in 1921 or the one he hit in Detroit in 1922.

Ruth is popular because he is always worth the price of admission. He is a picturesque figure whether he strikes out or knocks
a home run. He has the emotions of a boy and a heart as big as
the Yankee Stadium. Ballplayers are reputed to be "tight," but
G. H. Ruth can be crossed off that list. He has to be guarded to
keep from throwing away every dollar he makes.

It's easy to see why he is a favorite with the rising generation.
He always has time to say "Hello!" to the little lads and to autograph baseballs, score cards, and torn bits of paper.

It is sometimes as much as an hour before he can break away
from the horde of ragged admirers who waylay him after the
game in all the cities on the circuit. Few popular heroes have
been as deserving of their popularity as G. H. Ruth.

John Kieran, *The New York Times*

Wednesday, April 27

[*On April 26, in New York, the Yankees' scheduled game with Washington was postponed because of cold weather.*]

This is a story of wasted opportunity!

It's the only really sad feature of Yankee performance.

Since the season started, the Yankees have had 83 men left on base, and most of them in close games that the Yankees have lost.

In this little matter of failing in the pinch, the greatest offender has been our own George Herman Ruth. Since the season opened the Babe has had no less than 21 chances to drive in runs. He has failed every time. Our Babe has driven in exactly three—all of them personally conducted home runs [*which were hit with the bases empty.*]

Of course it isn't always the Babe's fault. Thirteen times when he had a chance to strike a blow for liberty and the Yankees he was given bases on balls. But nonetheless the fact remains that our Herman hasn't yet found himself, and until he does the Yankees will continue to have innumerable scoring chances wasted.

The fine bludgeon of a Ruth is needed—and Gehrig, Meusel, et al., even at their best, cannot take his place.

During Ruth's slump Gehrig has assumed the hero role, with Meusel a close second. Lou is not only slamming the ball for a percentage of well over .400, but he is hitting 'em when they count. He has driven no less than 21 runs over the plate, and on at least 3 occasions his drives have been directly responsible for Yankee victory.

Tony Lazzeri rates second in runs driven in, with 15, and Bob Meusel is running a close third with 14. These three have been responsible for more than half of the total runs scored.

But the boys need Ruth in there to make their attack 100 per cent.

Ford C. Frick, New York *Evening Journal*

Mr. Babe Ruth is in a truculent mood, and deplores the enforced tameness of the life and demeanor of the modern athlete. "They should let us fight," Mr. Ruth says. "Every time there is a fight the park is packed the next day."

W. O. McGeehan, New York *Herald-Tribune*

Fortunately, the Bambino does not have to step out of character to be what he is—an appealing, swashbuckling, roistering, boisterous figure who is as natural a showman as the late Phineas T. Barnum [*the most famous American showman, who had died in 1891*].

John Kieran, *The New York Times*

Friday, April 29

[*On April 27, in New York, the Yankees' scheduled game with Washington was postponed because of rain, and on April 28, in Boston, the Yankees' scheduled game was postponed because of cold weather.*]

"Every time I look over the situation, the American League pennant race looks tougher and tougher," declared Manager Miller Huggins of the Yankees yesterday in his suite at the Brunswick Hotel.

"Yes, sir," mused Huggins, "the league has a better balance than ever before in my memory. There are more tough teams in sight. And you can paste it right inside your old brown derby that this will not be a runaway race for the Yankees or any other club."

Burt Whitman, Boston *Herald*

If Miller Huggins were asked to name his most valuable player this year, he would have to place the blame on Lou Gehrig. The hustling alumnus of Columbia is leading the club in everything of note, except in hits and errors. Those honors go to Mark Koenig.

This giant of a youth is heading fast for a prominent place among baseball's great players. Day by day his work at first base is improving and so is his batting. Soon he will tower above his teammates and will be ready to take the place of Babe Ruth as the man who can "do anything on a ball field and do it well."

Of the Yankees' 86 runs to date Gehrig has driven in 21. He has scored 15 runs himself, 4 of which were homers. Subtract these 4, which are included in the runs driven in, and you find that Columbia Lou has been responsible for 32 runs.

This percentage is amazing in view of the fact that Gehrig is in only his second year as a regular. Despite his consistent hitting, he is still studying a short, chopped hit into left field, which, when perfected, will be one of the best in baseball.

No one on the team has more of a chance of playing all 154 games than Gehrig. Columbia Lou, by the way, is the only Yankee who has no substitute.

In fielding Gehrig has some distance to cover before he can become a Hal Chase, but he is improving faster than any young player in the majors today. When you watch Gehrig day after day pulling them high out of the air, off to the side, and so very frequently digging throws out of the dirt, you realize his tremendous value to the Yankees.

At 23, Gehrig is almost a finished player. He is a tower of strength, with no apparent physical weakness. It looks as though the Yankees' first base troubles have been settled for at least ten years. In that time there is no telling what unscaled heights Gehrig may attain.

[*Virtually all baseball fans know about Gehrig's durability. He would not be absent from the Yankee lineup until May 2, 1939, after playing in 2,130 consecutive games, a record that almost surely will never be broken.*]

Arthur Mann, New York *Evening World*

Saturday, April 30

[*On April 29, in Boston, the Yankees won, 9–0. Winning pitcher, Dutch Ruether (3–0). Yankee home run, Babe Ruth (4).*]

Boston—Our George Herman Ruth and the Yankees came back together. And what they had to say, they said with base hits. It was plenty.

Mr. Ruth started things by hoisting one of Slim Harris's best fast balls far over the right field stands. And thereafter the panic was on. Meusel tripled, Gehrig tripled, Collins tripled, and everybody hit. [*In 1926, Gehrig had hit twenty triples, to lead the American League in that category.*]

Some weeks ago Mr. Ruth remarked that the day would come when he would suddenly recover his batting eye and then some poor pitcher would suffer. He was right. Yesterday he not only hit a home run, but he got a double, a single, and a base on balls as well. The double was a near homer. It hit on top of the wall in left field, but with the perversity of baseball, bounded back into the field instead of into the street.

"Dutch" Ruether pitched for our boys and did a very admirable job of it, thank you. The Boston hits were as scattered as the Czar's family. [*The last of the Russian czars, Nicholas II, abdicated in 1917 and was killed in 1918. The surviving members of his family were living in exile.*] It was the third victory for "Dutch" and his second corking job of pitching.

Ford C. Frick, New York *Evening Journal*

Boston—Most Bostonians go to Yankee–Red Sox games to give the glad hand to Babe Ruth. The local fans hold the Babe in more affectionate esteem than those of any other city, not excluding New York. It was here that the Bambino started his unique career, and he always will be considered a home town product.

Herbert S. Allen, *New York Post*

Miller Huggins believes firmly that psychology is an all-important factor in baseball and says that at lesst 15 per cent of a team's power depends on how well it reacts to meet situations on the field; its ability to recover from disappointment; its response to emergencies, etc.

"Some people call it luck," says Huggins, "but I call it psychology, which in our business is largely a matter of building and maintaining confidence. Of course it is of no earthly importance unless a team has the mechanical requisites. The players who can hit, run, and field must be had first. Upon their ability a manager has to build morale or confidence. And when a fellow is dealing with 20 or more types and temperaments this is not the simplest thing in the world."

Huggins finds that today's players are less serious than those of 15 and more years ago. "This doesn't reflect on the player," explains "Hug." "It is a trend of the time. Serious people are at a premium everywhere. Baseball has become almost entirely a mechanical affair, in which the old-time inspiration that caused players to carry on with broken fingers and strained muscles is a thing of the past. Big salaries are partly to blame, for whenever you make a man too comfortable you decrease his efficiency. Incentive is a synonym for ambition on or off the ball field.

"And too much of the spirit has been legislated out of the major leagues by the process of refining the game. But of course what we have lost in playing ardor we have gained in other ways. The game has had the roughness eliminated, and the public has responded by supporting it more generously. And the game, although more mechanical, is better played than before.

"The old-time tooth and nail type of player is gone, never to return. With him went much that was picturesque and much that was useful. It was the grim seriousness with which he played baseball that put the game on its feet. Today the players regard the game in a different light. It is a means rather than the end. It has become a business with the boys, who play for the income. Can you blame them? Well, no. But an old-timer like myself can't help but regret the passing of the hip and thigh boys of a generation ago. It was a rough school and one in which the survival of the fittest was the rule.

"For example, in the old days if a young third baseman broke in with a team his life was not pleasant. He was after the older player's job, and they were hostile to him. Now players are either indifferent to recruits or anxious to aid them develop. That's a good sign. But we miss the old flare of 'go get 'em' play that used to lift an average player into a star when the occasion demanded."

[*Miller Huggins was born and raised in Cincinnati's famous Fourth Ward, where one almost had to be a fighter to survive, and so even though he was one of the smallest men in the major leagues, and one of the most highly educated, he was noted for being a tough, battling player.*]

Austen Lake, Boston *Evening Transcript*

Sunday, May 1

[*On April 30, in Boston, the Yankees lost, 3–2. Losing pitcher, Urban Shocker (2–2).*]

Boston—Urban Shocker tossed a venerable spitball at the Red Sox. For eight innings he had the Carrigans hog tied and hamstrung. He went into the ninth with a two-run lead and looked like the greatest pitcher that ever lived. Then in the final chapter he was blasted off the mound in a quick and furious rally that hauled hysteric applause from a great crowd that had turned out to see Babe Ruth try to hit homers.

The finish of the game will linger in the memory of every fan who was lucky enough to be present. Mayor Jimmy Walker of New York, who was one of the guests, was observed to faint, while his cane rolled into the Yankee dugout as Jack Rothrock was pushed across with the winning run. [*Walker's ever-present cane was carried only for the sake of appearance.*]

That last round was an inning to tell your grandchildren about. Flagstead opened with a torrid blow to left. "Baby Doll" Jacobson masseused a single off Joe Dugan's bag [*third base*]. Todt tried to commit suicide [*by laying down a sacrifice bunt to advance the base runners*], and the corners were crowded [*that is, the bases were loaded*] when Shocker had a brainstorm and heaved the ball to third [*too late to force the runner*].

Rothrock, sent in to pinch hit, flailed a double to right, and the score was tied. Urban was taken out, and Wilcy Moore sent in. He passed Grover Hartley with malice aforethought [*an intentional walk*], and three were on with nobody out.

Victory for Carrigan seemed a cinch, so he let pitcher Wiltse hit, and he fanned. "Pee Wee" Wanninger [*who had played with the Yankees in 1925*] hit to Lazzeri, whose throw to the plate forced Todt, and it looked like extra innings. It was up to Fred Haney and Wilcy. The count worked down to three and two. The next ball was a yard from the plate, and Rothrock, a brief but real hero, came over with the victory marker.

Marshall Hunt, New York *Daily News*

Monday, May 2

[On May 1, in New York, the Yankees defeated Philadelphia, 7–3. Winning pitcher, Herb Pennock (2–0). Yankee home runs, Babe Ruth 2 (6), Lou Gehrig (5).]

The Yankees provided 70,000 fans with their money's worth with three home runs.

The first two homers would have been enough to beat the Athletics. After Babe Ruth drove in one runner with a mighty clout into the right field bleachers and Lou Gehrig duplicated the feat, the Yankees could have let it go at that, but the Babe hit another homer to the same section just to show that the first one wasn't a mistake.

Old John Quinn, who was pitching in the American League when Babe Ruth was hitting homers for nothing, allowed the Yankees just two hits, but they were enough to drive Old John from the box before he had pitched six full innings. *[Quinn, a forty-two-year-old spitball pitcher, began his major league career with the Yankees in 1909, five years before Ruth entered organized baseball.]*

The victory came in the first "crucial" game of the year and left the Yankees unaccompanied as leaders in the league. *[Before the start of the game, the Yankees and Athletics were tied for first place, with nine victories and five losses. For every day during the remainder of the season the Yankees would be alone at the top.]* The crowd created a new record for receipts, according to Ed Barrow, who announced that 65,000 had paid admissions.

Ruth's two homers put him ahead of the schedule he created in 1921, when he hit his sixth homer on May 2.

The game showed that it doesn't matter how often you hit 'em if you just hit 'em far enough. The Yankees made only 5 safeties all afternoon, but they were good for a total of 15 bases and proved more than enough to offset the dozen hits the Athletics made off Herb Pennock.

Ruth's first inning homer happened after Koenig had walked. It was a thing of beauty and a joy to watch as it sailed almost on a line to the exit gap in the bleacher section. There was never any question as to where it finally would come to rest, and right fielder Ty Cobb didn't even bother to turn to see if it killed anybody when it landed. He raised a resigned eye skyward as it sailed over his head, shrugged his shoulders, and let it go at that.

Just three men reached first between Ruth's homer in the first inning and Gehrig's homer in the sixth. One got on through an error, and the other two landed there with free transportation.

But the important part is that one of them was on when Lou outdid the Babe's drive. Again it was Koenig, who had walked. He romped in ahead of Gehrig and the Yankees were ahead to stay. Quinn walked Meusel as the next act of the drama and then was yanked out of the box.

The Babe's second home run was made off Walberg in the eighth, and it was the biggest and best of the day. There was nobody on, but then it wasn't important whether there was or not.

Richards Vidmer, *The New York Times*

At least 65,000 fans jammed the Stadium yesterday, the biggest crowd to see a game in the regular run of the season. The gates were closed before 3 o'clock, and perhaps 20,000 who were looking for general admission tickets were turned away.

Monitor, New York *World*

All forenoon trains from Philadelphia were loaded with fans, who, denied Sunday baseball at home, leave thousands of dollars elsewhere to see it.

[*Sunday baseball played by professional teams would not be permitted in Philadelphia or Pittsburgh until 1934; they were the last major league cities to be hampered by this particular blue law. In 1927, Sunday professional games were also prohibited in Boston.*]

James C. Isaminger, Philadelphia *Inquirer*

Tony the Wop [*Lazzeri*] handled 4 chances cleanly yesterday, and in so doing he brought his total to 79 chances without an error.

Rud Rennie, New York *Herald-Tribune*

Bob Meusel always has the assignment of guarding the sun sector of the outfield. Yesterday in the fourth inning Meusel did not put on his smoked goggles as it was cloudy when he went to left field. Two men got on base via singles, and then up came old John Quinn who hit a high fly to left. Meusel ran in and suddenly stopped short, covering his head with his arms like a boxer guarding himself from a rain of blows. There were groans from the packed stands as Quinn's hit dropped safely for a double and two runs scored. The reason for Meusel's actions was that the sun just peeped out a trifle from behind a cloud when he was about to make the catch and he lost the ball. Hereafter he will always wear his "specs," sun or no sun, when he trots out to his position.

[*Although Babe Ruth is generally known as a right fielder because that was his position in Yankee Stadium, actually, in the majority of ballparks he played in left field.*]

New York *Sun*

One of Quinn's moist tosses got out of control in the second inning and arched a path into one of the field boxes near the Yankee dugout, striking a woman fan.

[*The spitball pitch was easy to throw but notoriously difficult to control. This was one of the reasons for declaring the pitch illegal—it was potentially dangerous—and helps to explain why among all of the inductees to baseball's Hall of Fame there are only four spitballers—Stanley Coveleski, Burleigh Grimes, Ed Walsh, and Urban "Red" Faber.*]

Bill Slocum, New York *American*

Babe Ruth never stood in higher favor with his club and with the public. Thousands waited for a peep at him after yesterday's game. There was such a mob of admirers on hand that the police had difficulty clearing the way for the armored truck which drew up to cart the cash taken in at the overworked box office to the bank.

Will Wedge, New York *Sun*

Although Babe Ruth has been unusually slow in getting into his batting form, the Yankee regulars as a group are outhitting those of each of the other major league teams. The Yankee team average of .369 is produced by the following individual records: Gehrig, .447; Koenig, .429; Collins, .421; Meusel, .415; Gazella, .361 [filling in for the injured Dugan]; Combs, .357; Ruth, .275; Lazzeri, .250.

Joe Vila, New York *Sun*

AMERICAN LEAGUE STANDINGS

	W	L	PCT	GB		W	L	PCT	GB
New York	10	5	.667	—	Washington	8	7	.533	2
Philadelphia	9	6	.600	1	St. Louis	6	7	.462	3
Chicago	10	7	.588	1	Cleveland	7	10	.412	4
Detroit	7	6	.538	2	Boston	3	12	.200	7

Tuesday, May 3

[*On May 2, in Washington, the Yankees won, 9–6. Winning pitcher, Waite Hoyt (3–1). Yankee home run, Tony Lazzeri (2).*]

It seems flirting with Fate to mention Tony Lazzeri's errorless fielding. One hates to be even indirectly instrumental in getting a bobble to bobb up in the young Italian's record. Yet some mention ought to be made of the fine work he has been doing.

While six errors scattered their vexatious presence through the blue Monday box score, three by each team, Mr. Lazzeri continued to perform in smooth and faultless style. He had four chances and handled all cleanly. That made 83 total chances in the 17 Yankee games to date without a slip for the 'Frisco boy.

Not only have Tony's fingers clutched in a very businesslike way around all the balls driven or thrown into his territory, but he has grasped his bat as a warrior of old might have grasped a broadsword and belabored his way among the American League pitching in right knightly fashion.

Tony yesterday looked after the Yanks' almost daily home run chore. He poked one of Alvin Crowder's slants into the center field bleachers in the eighth inning, and he also got a pair of singles. Meusel and Dugan also got 3 hits, helping swell the Yanks' total to 17.

Such batting as that simplified things for Hoyt, though the doughty Wilcy Moore was called on to retire the Senators in the ninth after they had made some rallying overtures.

Will Wedge, New York *Sun*

The Bambino hit four long ones into the catcher's mitt—two strikeouts and two high fouls.

The New York Times

Dutch Ruether and Babe Ruth are roommates. They are cronies, inseparable on road trips.

They are always partners at bridge, and they are always tying up in every other game which calls for a team. On the trip north during the spring a story was started to the effect that Miller Huggins had "warned" Ruether not to get too much in the company for fear he might be led astray.

The yarn made no hit with Ruether, who asked Huggins to issue a denial which was done. But it made a great hit with Ruth.

"ME lead Dutch astray," he said. "That's a laugh. He has a record so much better than mine ever will be that I feel sort of honored."

[*Ruth and Ruether enjoyed their nocturnal fun, but as Waite Hoyt observed in the Foreword to this book, so did most of their teammates. In any event, because Ruth was a loner, Ruether was only his nominal roommate, like everyone else who had ever occupied that role. Ruth's very first roommate on the Yankees, in 1920, was Ping Bodie, who, when asked about it, retorted, "Roomin' with Babe? Hell, no! I'm roomin' with his suitcase." Incidentally, it came to be considered bad luck to be Babe Ruth's roommate. Ping Bodie, Braggo Roth, Chick Fewster, Fred Hofmann, and Steve O'Neill were all released by the Yankees after rooming with Ruth for one season. At the end of the 1927 season, Dutch Ruether would receive his release. Actually, by mid-season 1927, the Yankees ceased to assign Ruth a road roommate and provided him with a suite of rooms for himself on the road, in the hope that this might keep him from straying away from the team hotel.*]

Monitor, New York World

Wednesday, May 4

[*On May 3, in Washington, the Yankees won, 6–4. Winning pitcher, Wilcy Moore (2–1).*]

Your Yankees yesterday continued their winning ways, and Wilcy Moore saved the game. It's getting so that a box score without Wilcy's name in it is as rare as a roc's egg. The big tobacco grower certainly is earning his ham and wheat cakes—and how. [*Moore owned a fair amount of land—160 acres near Hollis,*

Oklahoma and 177 acres in western Texas—upon which he raised grain and cotton, but he does not seem to have been a tobacco farmer.]

Yesterday Moore supplanted George Pipgras, youthful Dane from Slayton, Minnesota, making his first start of the season. [*Twenty-seven-year-old Pipgras was pitching in his first full season in the major leagues.*] George was a whiz for six innings. But in the seventh he began to fade, and Huggins gave Wilcy the office.

Wilcy did the rest. With the score tied, he bore down. All he needed was runs—and got them in the eighth when three singles and a pair of bases on balls netted two markers.

The Yankees' hitting continues vicious. There were no homers yesterday, but among the 13 safeties were triples by Combs and Lazzeri. Incidentally, all six Yankee runs were scored by Combs and Koenig, each of whom scored three and each of whom got three hits. [*In his third season as the Yankees' center fielder, Combs was regarded as baseball's best leadoff man because of the frequency with which he got on base.*]

Mr. Ruth had another bad day. He got one single, walked once, and struck out twice with a great clattering of bats and a great deal of commotion.

Ford C. Frick, New York *Evening Journal*

"Battering" Babe Ruth wielded the baton for 150 musicians last night in a joint concert by the St. Mary's Industrial School Band and the Evening Star Newsboys' Band, both of Baltimore, in the Catholic University gymnasium. He thoroughly enjoyed the "big brother" role with the youngsters from the school that was his home for years and in which he yearned to be a tailor. And the "Swat King" made an impressive heart-to-heart speech in appreciation of St. Mary's School and what it had done for him. The concert was a benefit for St. Mary's.

A new song called "Batterin' Babe" was distributed as a souvenir. It was sung by members of the Catholic University Glee Club as the Babe made his exit.

[*For the first seven years of his life, Babe Ruth lived over his father's Baltimore saloon, and then he was placed by his parents in St. Mary's school. (Contrary to popular belief, he was not an orphan: his mother died when he was thirteen, and his father lived until his second year in the major leagues.) The school was intended for orphans, boys from broken homes, boys from poor families, delinquents, and incorrigibles; young*

George Herman was classified as an incorrigible. At St. Mary's, where he remained, on and off, until he was twenty, he studied vocational subjects such as tailoring and shirtmaking, and he played on the school's baseball team. He played so well that when he left the institution, in February 1914, he signed a contract with Baltimore, in the International League. Before the end of that first season, he was sold to the Boston Red Sox.]

Washington *Evening Star*

Thursday, May 5

[*On May 4, in Washington, the Yankees lost, 7–4. Losing pitcher, Dutch Ruether (3–1). Yankee home run, Lou Gehrig (6).*]

Washington—Mark Koenig and Tony Lazzeri, buddies off and on the field, came out of the clubhouse arm and arm. Tony was a symphony in gray from his snappy fedora to his snappier gray top shoes. Mark was a riot in a light brown hat, a salmon colored suit, a tan shirt, salmon tie with blue dots, and light tan shoes.

"Rather snappy, what?" said Mark as he flicked an imaginary dust spot off the glad raiment. We assured Mark that he was a riot but unfortunately put too much emphasis on the riot. He replied, "Cut out the comedy and tell me if they gave me an error on that one Ruel hit." [*In these pre-electronic days, scorers' rulings were not announced at the ballpark.*] We told him that the official scorer had called it a hit.

"That's a shame," said Mark. "That was a real boot. What did they give Tony?" A look at the scorebook showed that Tony had run his accepted chances to 104 without an error, and both agreed that Tony should have had at least 2 errors charged against him. [*Thanks to the scorer's generosity, Lazzeri's string of errorless games had reached nineteen.*]

Mark and Tony had other reasons for being happy, even if the Senators won, because Mark got three hits and Tony two.

It was just one of those games. The Senators made all their seven runs in the first inning by hitting everything Ruether and Shawkey threw up to them. Myles Thomas then made his first appearance of the season, and for the rest of the game the Senators never even had a chance to score. Thomas turned in a beautiful seven innings, and Huggins again found solace in the work of a second string pitcher. [*A graduate of Pennsylvania State University, the twenty-nine-old Myles Thomas was pitching in his second season for the Yankees. In 1926, his rookie season as a major leaguer, Thomas had a record of six victories and six losses.*]

Pat Robinson, New York *Telegram*

To my way of thinking there is no better lead-off man in the majors than Earle Combs, the Yankees' brilliant center fielder.

In the old days, lead-off men as a rule were short of stature. The dope is that small men are much harder to pitch to. In this respect Combs is a radical departure, for he is six feet tall. However, he has a peculiar crouch style at bat that probably lowers his sights about six inches, making him a hard man to pitch to.

Combs also has a keen eye, seldom offers at a bad ball, hence gets many walks. Fleet of foot, he forces the rival infielder to hurry every ball to get him at first. He is adept at bunting and skillful in dragging the ball past the pitcher.

In other words, Combs has all the stuff needed for a lead-off man. In addition, he is a .300 hitter, which adds to the troubles of opposing pitchers.

The fact that Combs gets on often is a very important factor in the Yankees' success, since such sluggers as Ruth, Gehrig, Meusel, and Lazzeri follow in the lineup. With him on, the Yanks profit well when some slugger comes through with an extra base wallop.

While you don't hear much about Earle Combs, since he's a member of a colorful team noted for its slugging, which isn't part of his repertoire, he's one of the Yankees' most valuable assets.

[*A lifelong Kentuckian known as the "Kentucky Colonel," Combs began his professional career with two fine seasons with Louisville in the American Association (in the second of which, 1923, he finished with a batting average of .380, 241 hits, and 145 RBIs). In January 1924, the Yankees bought his contract for what was then a substantial price, $50,000. He missed most of the 1924 season because of a broken leg, but in 1925, he became the team's established center fielder. Combs did not hit many home runs, nor did he have a strong throwing arm, but in every other aspect of the game he was outstanding. Off the field, he was widely respected as one of baseball's finest gentlemen. Along with Ruth, Gehrig,*]

Pennock, Hoyt, Huggins, and Ed Barrow, Earle Combs is one of seven
Yankees of 1927 in baseball's Hall of Fame.

For twenty years an American League umpire, the author of this entry,
Billy Evans, was a regular contributor to the sports pages of the Telegram.]

Billy Evans, New York *Telegram*

Friday, May 6

[*On May 5, in Washington, the Yankees lost, 6–1. Losing pitcher, Ur-*
ban Shocker (2–3).]

A peculiar fast ball and a well-controlled curve stopped the Yankees yesterday. Never before this year have they looked more
hopeless than in trying to hit the youthful Horace Lisenbee.

He fanned eight Yankees, and, after the first inning, no one
reached second base. Meusel struck out his first three times and
Collins the last three times. Dugan and Lazzeri were the other
victims. Of the six scattered hits, Shocker and Lazzeri got two
each, and Combs and Ruth one apiece.

The Yankees were plainly puzzled after the game in trying to
analyze Mr. Lisenbee's fast ball, which, instead of hopping, sinks
much in the manner of Wilcy Moore's sinker ball.

Bob Meusel's trouble, as it almost always is, was in trying to hit
Lisenbee's curve ball. Meusel grips his bat half way up the handle, making it practically impossible for him to hit an outside
curve. Bob got nothing but sweeping curves which, when they
broke, looked as though they were coming in from left field.

In these days of heavy hitting, it is good to see a pitcher, especially a youngster, stand a bunch of clouters like the Yankees on
their heads, although it is a hard pill to swallow.

Arthur Mann, New York *Evening World*

Babe Ruth was almost a total loss in the Washington series, with
4 singles in 16 times at bat. It is to be hoped this is the calm
before the storm.

Herbert S. Allan, *New York Post*

Saturday, May 7

[*On May 6, the Yankees began their first road trip to the western cities, and they arrived in Chicago that night.*]

The Babe, the Babe, the colorful Babe is here. The White Sox tangle with the Yankees out at Comiskey Park, and the acknowledged lover of kids, hamburgers, and long-distance shots is expected to draw the largest crowd that ever attended a ball game hereabouts.

The Mauling Monarch is bound to pack the park. All around the circuit the Babe has drawn almost capacity crowds. In fact, the statistical boys have figured that in the first two New York games alone he drew enough cash into the Yank strong boxes to pay his salary.

'Twould be most fitting if the tubby Babe could lift one out of the park this afternoon, for the field is the largest in the league, and no one has yet managed to connect with one for four sacks. [*Comiskey Park had been renovated and enlarged for the 1927 season; for the first time it had double-decked stands that nearly surrounded the stadium.*]

Red Marberry, Chicago *Evening Post*

The kids who crawl forth at peep of day to carry water to the circus elephants had their big town prototype today in the Hyde Park boys who flanked the hotel where Babe Ruth passed the night. [*Hyde Park is a section bordering Lake Michigan about five miles from the Loop on the South Side of Chicago. The University of Chicago lies within its boundaries.*]

Shortly before 9 A.M. an elevator door slid open in the Cooper-Carlton Hotel, and a bulky person in a loose-fitting brown suit stepped into the lobby.

Instantly a hush fell athwart groups of youngsters skirmishing behind potted palms and marble pillars. The big man paced rapidly to the desk, seized a big handful of telegrams and letters, and went into the dining room, where he ordered breakfast in solitary dignity. The conclave of kid admirers rubbed their eyes, not from sleepiness but because their vigilance had been re-warded by a close-up of the great Bambino.

Other noted athletes of the Yankees came and went, and fi-nally Babe Ruth finished breakfast and returned to the lobby, where a telephone call, seven more telegrams, and agents for this and that awaited his urgent attention.

"Please autograph this baseball," pleaded a boy, holding forth an official sand-lot pellet.

The boy didn't have a pen, nor did any of his gaping compan-ions who were now edging out of the security of the potted palms. An agent for one of the Babe's numerous profit-sharing interests wanted to talk business. Babe wanted only a fountain pen. This he finally secured and scrawled the signature that rivals John Hancock's on the sand-lot sphere.

Then while the agent chafed and the sheaf of telegrams al-most burned from inattention, Babe consented to have his pic-ture taken with the kids outdoors.

Gene Morgan, Chicago *Daily News*

Sunday, May 8

[On May 7, in Chicago, the Yankees won, 8–0. Winning pitcher, Herb Pennock (3–0). Yankee home run, Lou Gehrig (7).]

Chicago—There was still some doubt about yesterday's ball game when Lou Gehrig stepped to the plate in the ninth inning with a Yankee perched on every base. After young Mr. Gehrig had taken his full swing there was no further doubt. Gehrig's bit in that closing burst of the Hugmen was a home run that landed well up in the right field pavilion of Comiskey Park's revamped ball yard. During the winter they added a lot more seats, and until yesterday no batted ball had touched the new green seats.

As Gehrig trotted around the paths behind Combs, Koenig, and Ruth, he drew a noisy greeting from some 35,000 fans who had shivered through a chilly afternoon in the hope of seeing the Babe knock one into the new section. *[The crowd was rather smaller than had been anticipated, held down by the cold weather.]*

The blow, by the way, pushed Lou out in front of the Bam-bino in the home run statistics for 1927, seven to six.

Gehrig also clouted a double and drove another close to the left field wall for a sacrifice. If Mr. Ruth is going to show the way this season, he is not going to have it all to himself.

In the excitement over the long homer, some fancy pitching by Herb Pennock was overshadowed. It wasn't showy, but it was high-class all the way.

[*Gehrig's bases-loaded home run was the second of his career. The first was hit on July 23, 1925. He would retire from baseball with twenty-three grand-slam home runs, which is still an unapproached record.*]

Bill Slocum, New York American

Anyone skeptical of the drawing power of George Herman Ruth must have been convinced yesterday. The presence of the mighty slugger and his pace-setting colleagues was sufficient to lure 35,000 customers into the rebuilt stands of Comiskey Park. Ruth failed to live up to his reputation as a home run hitter, but in batting practice the Bambino lifted a ball clear of the second tier of bleachers in right field. The crowd cheered. The architects had said no one could ever hit a ball out of the park. But they hadn't counted on Mr. Ruth.

[*This is the caption beneath an eight-column picture of Comiskey Park as it appeared on the afternoon of the Yankees' first visit of the year to the stadium.*]

Chicago Tribune

There was just as much noise when Ruth struck out in the fifth as there was when Gehrig hit his home run with the bases full in the ninth. They don't pay to see Gehrig hit 'em.

Rud Rennie, New York Herald-Tribune

Monday, May 9

[*On May 8, in Chicago, the Yankees won, 9–0. Winning pitcher, Waite Hoyt (4–1). Yankee home run, Pat Collins (1).*]

It didn't make a bit of difference to those big bullies, the New York Yankees, that the White Sox wanted gloriously to show some class yesterday at the new Comiskey Park before 52,000 fans—the largest crowd that ever saw a baseball game in Chicago [*or, indeed, in any other city but New York*].

By displaying an uncanny genius for doing the right thing at the right time and frightening Mr. Comiskey's athletes stiff with their big town manners, Babe Ruth and the rest of the heartless crowd thoroughly humiliated the south siders. [*"Mr. Comiskey" was sixty-seven-year-old Charles A. Comiskey, a nineteenth-century player and manager who had been president of the White Sox since the formation of the team in 1901 and would remain in that position until his death in October 1931.*]

Babe didn't make a homer, but he was decidedly in the game, and most of the fans were pulling for the big boy to sock one out. While Babe didn't satisfy the home run fiends personally, Catcher Pat Collins laid one in the left field grandstand, adequately fulfilling the homer-a-day clause in the Yankee contract. [*Collins was playing in his seventh major league season, his second with the Yankees. He had always been a reserve catcher who mostly sat on the bench until 1926, when, because of Benny Bengough's sore arm, he appeared behind the plate in one hundred games.*] Lou Gehrig got two triples, and Ruth made a single and a double.

Big hearted official scorers held the Sox errors down to four, although less technical observers thought the count should have been six. Added to the Sox booting and throwing spectacles was Meusel's theft of home while Bert Cole was winding up to pitch to Dugan in the ninth. [*Meusel must have especially relished this steal of home when Cole committed the most flagrant of pitching faux pas—winding up with a runner on third base. On June 13, 1924, when Cole was with Detroit, he hit Meusel with a pitch that Meusel thought had been deliberate. Meusel made a dash for the mound, and players from both dugouts poured onto the field. The result was an old-fashioned brawl followed by ten-day suspensions for both Cole and Meusel.*]

Edward Burns, Chicago *Tribune*

Ball games in New York have been taking entirely too much time. Games under two hours have been the exception. The Yankee games, especially, have dragged out, some games going as long as two hours and a half. [*Today, three-hour games are commonplace.*] I have heard a lot of fans voice displeasure over these long drawn-out contests. I suppose their wives do more than just voice displeasure, especially if the Mrs. keeps dinner waiting.

Fred Lieb, *New York Post*

AMERICAN LEAGUE STANDINGS

	W	L	PCT	GB		W	L	PCT	GB
New York	14	7	.667	—	Chicago	12	11	.522	3
Philadelphia	11	9	.550	2½	St. Louis	9	9	.500	3½
Detroit	10	9	.526	3	Cleveland	10	12	.455	4½
Washington	11	10	.524	3	Boston	5	15	.250	8½

Tuesday, May 10

[On May 9, in Chicago, the Yankees lost, in 10 innings, 2–1. Losing pitcher, Wilcy Moore (2–2).]

Chicago—Tony Lazzeri went through 22 games without a fielding blunder. While he was making this brilliant record he played baseball that smacked of brilliance. Yesterday the mighty son of Old Italy not only made his first error in the field, but he made a mental bungle in the tenth inning which gave the White Sox a victory.

Wilcy Moore was on the hill when the break came. Alex Metzler, the White Sox center fielder, the first batter to face the tall Oklahoma farmer, plastered a hit into center. Combs fumbled momentarily, but then made an accurate toss for second base. Mark Koenig was prepared to take the throw, and it looked like Metzler would be nicked.

Instead of letting the ball go through to Koenig, Lazzeri interfered with the throw, and Metzler made the bag. To add to the unpleasant situation, Moore tossed third baseman Bill Kamm's attempted sacrifice over Lazzeri's head when Tony romped over to first to take the throw [*because, as is usual in this situation, Gehrig had run in to cover the expected bunt*], and the deciding run scored.

Until Lazzeri and Moore had their lapses in the tenth, the game was the best hurling duel the Yankees have engaged in this season, between Red Faber and Dutch Ruether.

Charles Segar, New York *Daily Mirror*

The Chicago series drew a total of 100,000 people, the greatest number ever to witness three consecutive games in that city.

Herbert S. Allan, *New York Post*

Babe Ruth received a letter today from a little boy in Lachen, Germany, written in German. The boy's name is Max Schmutterer. He congratulated the Babe on his success and went on to say that some day he hoped he might enter sports and make lots of money because his mother hadn't any. The Babe was touched. He answered the letter immediately, saying in effect that his mother had died when he was young and that all the money he was now earning could never make up for the fact that he had never known her. He said that Max, with his mother, was wealthier than he was with his $70,000 a year. [*Lou Gehrig translated the boy's letter for Ruth and then put Ruth's reply into German.*]

Rud Rennie, New York *Herald-Tribune*

Wednesday, May 11

[*On May 10, in St. Louis, the Yankees won, 8–7. Winning pitcher, Wilcy Moore (3–2). Yankee home runs, Babe Ruth (7), Bob Meusel (2).*]

St. Louis—"Those fellows hit too hard. They pack too much of a punch for the rest of us. They ought to penalize them one strike before they step to the plate, so as to give us a chance," said Dan Howley last night. [*The St. Louis Browns' manager, Howley, who had played in only twenty-six big league games (with the Phillies in 1913), was now in his first season as the field boss of a major league team.*]

The Yankees had to have this punch to gain a decision yesterday. The St. Louis fans, who are the prize baseball fanatics of the universe, called it a lucky victory, but there was no luck to Lou Gehrig's slashing single with the bases full in the ninth.

The goddess of chance may have been smiling on Babe Ruth when he got his first inning home run, but there was no luck attached to Meusel's homer.

Combs opened hostilities in the first with his usual hit, and Babe got hold of a curve ball which seemed good only for a long fly. A strong wind carried the ball back until it lazily dropped on top of the high wall in front of the right field stands and bounced in among the natives.

In the sixth Meusel followed Gehrig's single with a hard smash into the stands, a homer anywhere. Milton Gaston [*who had pitched for the Yankees in his rookie season, 1924*] then went along smoothly until the last frame, when he interspersed three walks with singles by Grabowski and Gehrig and Koenig's sacrifice fly. Gehrig's winning smash came on a 3 and 2 pitch with 2 outs.

The Browns wasted golden opportunities presented by some wild Yankee pitching. In the last of the ninth they packed the bases with only one out but were shut off by a lightning double play started by Koenig.

Pat Robinson, New York *Telegram*

Gehrig is a great ballplayer, but he still has much to learn about playing first base. This is apparent when one is watching George Sisler in the same game. In the matter of putting the ball on a runner, for example, George could give Lou a head start and still beat him to the touch. [*Frequently called the best first baseman of all time, Sisler had played for the Browns since 1915.*]

Rud Rennie, New York *Herald-Tribune*

Thursday, May 12

[*On May 11, in St. Louis, the Yankees won, 4–2. Winning pitcher, Urban Shocker (3–3). Yankee home run, Babe Ruth (8).*]

St. Louis—If you read the papers last October you probably remember that G. Herman Ruth knocked a baseball into the center field bleachers of the local sports arena—a feat performed by no other batter in the history of Sportsman's Park. [*This refers to the ball Ruth hit in the sixth inning of the fourth World Series game, his third home run of the game.*] Well, the big boy duplicated that resounding blow yesterday, and this festive wallop drove in the runs that beat the Browns.

Ruth's eighth homer of the season happened in the first inning with Koenig on first base. Ernie Nevers, who was once a

star half-back at Stanford, passed one to George in the well-
known groove, and George kicked a perfect field goal into the
center field seats. [*One of the most famous of all college football players, Nevers would have a distinguished career in professional football,
with the Duluth Eskimos and the Chicago Cardinals. In 1929, he would
set a still-existent record by scoring forty points in one game. Nevers
would be one of the first persons to enter both of football's halls of fame,
for college players and for professionals, but his baseball career was less
than spectacular; in three seasons as a major league pitcher he gained six
victories.*]

Ruth's hit was higher than his World Series homer, but not as
hard nor as far. It got into the center part of the pavilion only by
the matter of a foot or two, landing a few feet on the yonder side
of the wall and bounding up in the air like Old Faithful.

It was a jolly siesta for the local customers, who caught up on
their sleep. Despite the appeals of Mr. Charles O'Leary [*who was
coaching at first base for the Yankees*] for some of "the old life," the
game was very dreary. The sleep of the customers was never
seriously interrupted. [*With only about a thousand paid admissions,
the crowd was the smallest in many years to view a Yankee game. One
reason for the low attendance was the 48-degree temperature.*]

Except for one inning Urban Shocker had the Browns backing
away and swinging wildly. The Howleymen made eight hits to
the Yankees' seven, but they were widely scattered.

Halfback Nevers was bad at the kickoff and was thrown for
repeated losses in the first, second, and third periods, but after
that the Yanks had to admit that Ernie was too much for them.
Mr. Ruth clouted a double in addition to his homer.

James R. Harrison, *The New York Times*

Friday, May 13

[*On May 12, in St. Louis, the Yankees won, 4–3. Winning pitcher,
Herb Pennock (4–0).*]

St. Louis—Perhaps somewhere in this broad land of ours there
is hidden away a pitcher who is more consistently good than
Herbie Pennock.

We say perhaps—for it's doubtful. If you happen to know of

such a one grab him quick. He's worth a lot of cash in the baseball market, for he's a rare article indeed.

Herbie loses ball games occasionally. There are times even when he is driven from the mound, but they're rare. And he never pitches a bad game. Day in and day out, season in and season out, he goes on, using his head to save his arm—pitching carefully, craftily, and cleverly. And winning three times out of four.

It was Herbie yesterday who turned back the Browns and Sam Jones. It wasn't easy, for Sam was good. So good in fact that only the mastery of a Pennock could deny him victory. Yankee bats were more or less helpless against Sam. [*Jones had been Babe Ruth's teammate on the Red Sox for four years (1916–19) and, during the preceding five years, on the Yankees, for whom, in 1923, he had pitched a no-hitter and had won twenty-one games.*]

But Pennock was just a little better. Now and then he was in trouble—but he always had just enough in reserve to worm out.

Two double plays aided Herbie, along with perfect fielding. In this respect Mark Koenig and Lazzeri stood out. Mark handled 9 chances and Tony 12 without error. Some fielding that.

Ford C. Frick, New York Evening Journal

Ruth looked pretty good going after Harry Rice's liner in the fifth. The ball looked as if it was bound for China when the Babe caught up with it [*in left-center field*], took it in his bare hand on the first bounce, and held Harry to two bases.

Rud Rennie, New York Herald-Tribune

St. Louis—Pitching to the Yankee batting order, according to rival moundsmen, involves a nerve strain that makes inroads into their effectiveness and sometimes brings them down sharply near the end of a well pitched game.

"I would rather pitch a double header against any other club than one game against the Yanks," said Milton Gaston of the Browns. "There isn't a moment's mental rest for a pitcher in that batting order. I was so tired when I got through pitching to them the other day that I could hardly drag myself to my hotel."

If you think Gaston was exaggerating even slightly—and he was voicing the sentiments of practically every pitcher that faces the Yanks—take a look at that batting order.

It starts with Combs, a smart hitter, difficult to pitch to because he seldom hits at a bad ball. He can bunt, he can hit, and he can run. In 114 times at bat this season, he has got to first base 59 times, exclusive of the times he has forced a runner ahead of him. Therefore a pitcher has to figure that Earle has at least an even chance of reaching first base.

Batting second is Koenig, a sharp, sometimes heavy hitter, who is likely to advance Combs with a bunt, a long sacrifice fly, or a hit. And after Koenig comes Ruth.

There he stands, like a mountain, as a pitcher once said. Pitching to Ruth requires as much precision as juggling a case of nitro glycerine. It is a good trick if you perform it properly, but if you are a trifle off in your calculations you may have the game blown out from under your foot. Provided you have figured correctly, that your control has been perfect, and the Babe has been put out of the way, there is no time to sigh with relief. The next batter is Lou Gehrig.

"I had rather see Ruth than Gehrig in a tight place," said Dan Howley, manager of the Browns. "Sometimes you can figure what the Babe is going to do, but you never can tell about Gehrig. He is likely to hit any kind of a ball to any field."

Behind Gehrig swings Meusel. Bob hits a ball almost as far as Ruth or Gehrig. Yesterday he drove a sacrifice fly to center field that was only a few feet shorter than the Babe's poke that went into the bleachers the day before. When Meusel has come and gone, the pitcher finds himself gazing on Lazzeri.

Because "poosh 'em up" has a pair of wrists that are as iron bars and puts all the power that lies in those wrists into the end of his swing he hits a ball amazingly far for one of his slight build. Almost every ball Tony hits is hit hard. Seldom do you read, "Lazzeri was an easy out." [*Lazzeri's nickname had its genesis when he was a minor leaguer in Salt Lake City, but there are two conflicting accounts of how it came into existence. According to one frequently repeated story, Lazzeri was invited by an Italian restaurateur to his place of business, where for several successive nights plates of spaghetti were placed before him with the injunction to "Poosh 'em up, Tony." A more probable explanation was provided by Lazzeri himself when he was interviewed by Harry T. Brundidge for the December 11, 1930, issue of* The Sporting News: "*When I was playing with Salt Lake, some wop in the grandstand who wanted me to get a hit and could not express himself properly shouted, 'Poosh 'em up, Tony,' and I've been called that ever since."*]

The next hitter is Dugan. Joe isn't hitting well now, but he always has and, probably, he will again very shortly. At any rate, he is not one on whom a pitcher can take a chance. [*During his previous four seasons with the Yankees, Dugan had had quite respectable batting averages—.287, .283, .302, and .292—and earlier, with the Athletics, he had once batted .322. But even when he wasn't hitting well, Dugan was extremely valuable, for he was perhaps baseball's best fielding third baseman, and possibly the greatest of all time at coming in on a slowly hit ball.*]

After Dugan comes either Grabowski or Collins. Grabowski gives nothing to Collins in the matter of hitting the ball frequently, but Pat is the longer hitter. In either case there is no setup at the plate.

At the very end of the order comes the pitcher—and the hapless young man on the hill will have to look searchingly through the Yankee corps to find a weakling with the stick. Moore comes closest to fitting this description. Surely, there is no soft picking for a pitcher where Hoyt, Pennock, Shocker, Ruether, or Shawkey is concerned. [*The Yankees' best hitting pitcher was undoubtedly Ruether, who had a career batting average of .258 and appeared as a pinch hitter more than 150 times. With other teams less well endowed than the Yankees with hitting strength, Ruether's bat was valued highly enough for him to play occasionally at first base.*]

Frank Graham, New York *Sun*

Saturday, May 14

[*On May 13, in St. Louis, the Yankees won, 3–1. Winning pitcher, Waite Hoyt (5–1).*]

St. Louis—Another first-class pitching exhibition was turned in by Waite Hoyt, the Flatbush mortician. Hoyt was nicked for ten hits, but only in the sixth inning could the Browns push over a run. They bunched two hits in the second and third innings and three hits in the seventh frame, but Hoyt had enough stuff to stop them in the pinch.

Babe Ruth went to bat five times, but Ernie Wingard, the Browns' southpaw, walked him the first three times.

Charles Segar, New York *Daily Mirror*

The Babe's hitting in St. Louis makes one think his "slump" is over, [*The writer used quotation marks because Ruth's batting average was about .330, and he was the major leagues' leading home-run hitter with 8; most players would thoroughly enjoy such a "slump."*] Linking this thought with a recollection of the hitting he did in St. Louis during the last World Series [*when he hit four home runs*], one wondered if he likes to hit here.

"Yes," he said, "it's a good ball park to hit in. All the parks are good except the Stadium. There is no background there at all. But the best of them all is the Polo Grounds. Boy, how I used to sock 'em in there. I cried when they took me out of the Polo Grounds." [*While playing his home games in the Polo Grounds in 1920 and 1921, Ruth had hit 54 and 59 home runs, but since the Yankees had moved to the stadium in 1923, his highest season total, in 1926, had been 47.*]

The Babe has a new goal in mind. This time it is ten World Series.

"I've been in seven," he said. "Three more and I'll be ready to quit." [*In 1932, Ruth would attain this goal.*]

Frank Graham, New York *Sun*

Monday, May 16

[*On May 14 and 15, in Detroit, the Yankees' scheduled games were postponed because of rain.*]

Babe Ruth has arrived on the screen [*at the State Theater*] with his first starring feature picture "Babe Comes Home," but there is no particular reason for John Barrymore or any other noted thespian to become agitated about the matter. Mr. Ruth is a solid, healthy appearing actor, not especially attractive in comparison to some of our male idols, but probably much better than you ever hoped for. Possibly his long experience with newsreel cameramen is responsible for his ability to keep his eyes out of the camera lens—something few movie beginners are able to do.

The Bambino is the whole show in *Babe Comes Home*. Everything is built around him, over him, and under him. The story is rather slim and is liberally padded, but for this type of picture is much better than the average. It hinges about Babe Dugan, slugging outfielder of the Los Angeles Angels, who is so filthy and careless about his tobacco chewing that even the laundry girl [*Anna Q. Nilsson*] who cleans his uniform rebels. [*The Los Angeles team in the Pacific Coast League was known as the Angels until major league baseball arrived in 1958.*] There is some note-changing and finally a meeting, which leads to love. Just before the wedding the girl becomes incensed over a wedding gift of hand-painted cuspidors and a huge box of plug tobacco. She goes back to the laundry and—well, you know the rest. There is the big game for the pennant . . . the Babe is in a slump because he has sworn off tobacco chewing . . . the ninth-inning crisis . . . the girl leans over the box into the playing field and hands Babe a plug of the old stuff . . . bang goes the ball game!

Harold Heffernan, Detroit *News*

AMERICAN LEAGUE STANDINGS

	W	L	PCT	GB		W	L	PCT	GB
New York	18	8	.692	—	Cleveland	12	14	.462	6
Chicago	16	12	.571	3	St. Louis	11	13	.458	6
Philadelphia	14	13	.519	4½	Washington	11	14	.440	6½
Detroit	12	12	.500	5	Boston	8	16	.333	9

Tuesday, May 17

[*On May 16, in Detroit, the Yankees won, 6–2. Winning pitcher, Dutch Ruether (4–1). Yankee home run, Lou Gehrig (8).*]

Detroit—Those cannon-like bats which Lou Gehrig, Babe Ruth, and Bob Meusel wield were turned on the Tigers yesterday with splendid results. The Yankees "Big Three" got in blows at opportune moments and brought Col. Ruppert's Rough Riders their fifth straight victory. [*Ruth, Gehrig, and Meusel acquired the title Big Three on September 10, 1925, in a game against the Philadelphia Athletics, when they hit three consecutive home runs.*]

Leading the attack was that mother's boy from the Bronx, Lou Gehrig. [*Gehrig lived with his parents, and writers frequently mentioned his attachment to his mother.*] "Columbia Lou" made three hits, one of them a third inning home run which gave Lou equal standing with Ruth for home run honors. Gehrig's other two blows were doubles. His first was wasted, but his second, in the seventh inning, scored Mark Koenig.

Ruth was not capable of knocking out more than one single, but this blow came in the ninth inning and scored Pat Collins and Earle Combs, who had walked. George Herman also contributed a sacrifice fly.

Now for Meusel. The tall Californian upset all Yankee tradition by stealing three bases in the third inning. Happened this way. Bob followed Gehrig's homer with a single and then stole second. Tony Lazzeri walked and, with Joe Dugan at bat, Tony strayed too far off first and pitcher Ken Holloway tried to nick him off the bag. Tony forgot Meusel was on second and set sail for that station. Bob started for third, made this without trouble, and, while Lazzeri was occupying the Tiger infielders by moving from first to second and back again, Bob let out for the plate and beat shortstop Marty McManus's throw. [*On only one other occasion has a Yankee player stolen second, third, and home in one game, Fritz Maisel, on August 17, 1915.*]

Charles Segar, New York Daily Mirror

Wednesday, May 18

[*On May 17, in Detroit, the Yankees won, 9–2. Winning pitcher, Herb Pennock (5–0). Yankee home run, Babe Ruth (9).*]

Detroit—Mr. Herman Ruth, the eminent thespian, demonstrated again the versatility that has endeared him to the hearts of his countrymen. In the eighth inning he knocked a baseball out of the lot, and those who had come to jeer remained to cheer.

Ruth's opus which sailed over the scoreboard in left center and bounced into the front yard of one of his screen admirers, was his ninth of the season, putting him ahead of the dusty parade and clinching the afternoon's argument. [*The ball was estimated to have traveled 470 feet.*]

The Yanks, however, could have won without the Ruthian rap. They made runs on the slightest provocation and at the least encouragement, and hammered out 15 blows of various kinds and sizes.

The activity of the Manhattan bats saved Herbert Pennock from a cruel fate. Herbert was in trouble so often that Miller Huggins developed a permanent wave between his eyebrows. Herb's control was bad, and when he did manage to locate the plate the Tigers hit with ferocity and fury. [*Pennock's wildness was most unusual, for he was one of baseball's best control pitchers. In 1926, for example, he issued only 43 bases on balls in 266 innings pitched.*] The Tigers had two men left on base in the second, two in the third, three in the fourth, two in the fifth, and two in the sixth. Only because Pennock was Pennock and the Yanks were ahead was Mr. Huggins moved to be patient and long-suffering.

A catch by Earle Combs was one thing that kept Pennock on the firing line. To open the fifth, Bob "Fats" Fothergill whaled a terrific drive toward deep center. Crash, not to say, wham! But Combs dashed back, stuck his glove up beyond his right shoulder, and made one of the dizziest catches ever seen in these or any parts. [*No outfielder covered ground faster and better than Combs, who was sometimes called "the Kentucky greyhound" and could run a hundred yards while wearing a baseball uniform in ten seconds flat.*]

And so Pennock stayed, and the Yanks won their eighth game in nine starts on Western fields.

James R. Harrison, *The New York Times*

Detroit—Bob Meusel broke a blood vessel in his right leg while stealing a base Monday [*the day on which he stole three bases in one inning*]. He saw a physician this morning. The Doc said that while it was nothing serious, the patient had better stop stealing bases for a day and charged him $5.

Rud Rennie, New York *Herald-Tribune*

Friday, May 20

[On May 18, in Cleveland, the Yankees' scheduled game was postponed because of rain, and on May 19, in Cleveland, the Yankees won, 4–3. Winning pitcher, Wilcy Moore (4–2). Yankee home run, Lou Gehrig (9).]

Cleveland—Perhaps you don't believe in good fairies.

If not, this is no story for you—for this is the story of a good fairy who brought Yankee victory out of defeat—a burly, awkward, raw-boned sort of fairy; a fairy of broad shoulders and bulging muscle; a fairy that chews tobacco—and swears occasionally.

And the name is Wilcy Moore.

Yesterday Wilcy Moore stood out there in the rain and mist and cold, pitching baseball. When the game started he was sitting on the bench. He watched Shocker start, and he sat while Shock was pounded and battered and sunk before his eyes.

Then with the score tied and the Indians threatening to run riot, he caught Huggins' nod and gathered up his glove. Carefully he adjusted his belt and deliberately he bit off a chew of black plug. Then he hitched his trousers, scratched his head, and pitched baseball.

Inning came and went. Rain came faster and faster. It soaked the diamond to a morass; it left the ball wet and slippery and hard to handle.

But Moore said nothing—just chewed and tossed 'em.

The fifth and sixth innings passed into history. The eighth came and went. Still the score was tied.

Then in the ninth, with one out Dugan singled. Collins found one to his liking and hit for one base, Dugan pulling up at third. Up from the Yankee dugout lumbered the awkward figure of Moore. He paused to take another bite of tobacco, then he knocked the mud from his cleats and hitched his belt.

A hit would win, but Moore can't hit, and he knows it.

But he can sacrifice—and he did.

With the adeptness of a master he laid the ball down the first base line, then lumbered after it, obstructing first baseman

George Burns's line of vision to the plate. Down the base paths thundered Dugan with the winning run. Burns made a despairing stab for the ball, took one look, and then tagged Moore out.

Cy grinned and took another chew.

His squeeze play had won the game his pitching had saved.

This was just good, hard baseball. That's the sort of chap Moore is—just plain and awkward and dependable.

He was the whole show yesterday, and he will be the whole show again, many times. But he'll never be a hero. No man can who grins and chews tobacco in a crisis.

Aside from Wilcy's pitching, Lou Gehrig was the outstanding figure. In the first inning, with one man on, Lou hit a line drive to the deepest point in center. Then, with the fans urging him on, with legs working like the drivers on engines and arms flailing wildly, he ran it out—on and on and on past second and third and into the plate in a frenzy of dust and excitement for his ninth homer of the season.

Once more he is tied up with the Babe for big league honors.

And the first guy to shake his hand and wish him luck, the first chap to help him out of the dirt where he slid was George Herman himself. A great pair these two.

Ford C. Frick, New York *Evening Journal*

Cleveland—By taking the mound against Cleveland, Wilcy Moore attained a distinction gained by few pitchers during their first year in the majors. Moore, making his first swing over the circuit, already has pitched against every rival club. He has been in the majors only since April 12, and on May 19 he had met them all, and, furthermore, had fooled them all.

Bill Slocum, New York *American*

Saturday, May 21

[*On May 20, in Cleveland, the Yankees lost, 2–1. Losing pitcher, Waite Hoyt (5–2).*]

George Uhle's mastery over the Yankees still holds. There is no way of accounting for the Indian victory except to say that Uhle pitched.

This is a simple statement of fact. One could be more verbose and dramatic, but Uhle's mastery over the greatest hitting ball club of recent years has been so emphatic that his victories almost become commonplace. [*Right-hander Uhle, now in his ninth season with Cleveland, the first person to master the pitch known as the slider, had won six of seven decisions against the pennant-winning Yankees in 1926. But he was also rather effective against other teams, leading all major league pitchers with twenty-seven victories. Uhle was perhaps even better known for his excellent hitting: his career batting average of .288 was second to that of only one other pitcher in the history of the big leagues, Babe Ruth.*]

If there was one thing that stood out in the game it was Uhle's pitching to Gehrig.

In two innings Gehrig had opportunities to break up the game. In the first inning, with Combs on first and two out, he fanned. In the fifth inning, with Koenig on second, Ruth on first and two out, he fanned again.

The fact that Uhle fanned the Columbia slugger twice in crucial situations isn't the proof of superb pitching. The fact that Uhle employed different methods each time seemed the supreme evidence of his greatness.

In the first inning, Uhle fanned Gehrig on three curve balls, the slugging batter swinging to miss the third strike. In the fifth, Gehrig fanned again but not on curve balls. He swung at two fast balls for his last two strikes and missed connection. Uhle's mental processes told him that Gehrig would be looking for curve balls, so he switched to speed.

Gehrig is a fast-ball hitter. Pitching to his strength was daring, and the successful result of daring strategy always appeals to the imagination.

Stuart Bell, *Cleveland Press*

Sunday, May 22

[*On May 21, in Cleveland, in 12 innings, the Yankees lost, 5—4. Losing pitcher, Wilcy Moore (4—3).*]

LINDBERGH DOES IT! TO PARIS IN 33 ½ HOURS;
FLIES 1,000 MILES THROUGH SLEET AND SNOW;
CHEERING FRENCH CARRY HIM OFF FIELD

[*Every word in every news column on the first five pages of* The Times *was devoted to one event, Charles Lindbergh's nonstop flight across the Atlantic Ocean. Stimulated by a $25,000 prize offered by French industrialist Raymond Orteig to the first person to make a non-stop, solo flight from New York to Paris, Lindbergh had departed from Roosevelt Field, Long Island, at 7:52 A.M. on May 20 in a Ryan mono-plane,* The Spirit of St. Louis. *The 3,600-mile flight ended at 10:24 P.M. Paris time (5:24 in New York) on May 21 at Le Bourget Field, where Lindbergh was greeted by a crowd of 100,000. But baseball went on, not quite as usual.*]

Eight-column, front-page headline, *The New York Times*

Cleveland, May 21—Charles Lindbergh landing outside the gates of Paris at the completion of his trans-Atlantic flight stopped the ball game between the Yankees at Dunn Field this warm, sunny afternoon.

Word of his arrival came over the wires in the last half of the seventh inning and spread like a breeze through the stands. The national pastime came to a pause. Fifteen thousand persons bared their heads and stood silent, but proud, while the band played "The Star Spangled Banner." It was a simple tribute to a great deed.

The game went on. Luke Sewell was advised to "sock one on the nose," and the Indians made one run and tied the score at 4 to 4 in the eighth. It required four more closely fought innings to decide the contest.

Wilcy Moore and Willis Hudlin pitched against each other in those later innings, Hudlin having pitched 11 ⅔ innings of beautiful baseball and Moore having worked 5 only to weaken in the

twelfth. With the bases loaded and 2 outs, and the count 3 and 2
on Charley Jamieson, Moore walked the batter, forcing in the
winning run.

Popular interest was divided between the game and the progress of the trans-Atlantic flier.

It was announced in the first inning that Lindbergh was approaching France. The Yankees celebrated by knocking Emil
Levsen out of the box and scoring three runs on singles by
Combs, Durst [*filling in for the sidelined Meusel*], and Dugan and a
double by Ruth. The Babe hit Hudlin, Levsen's successor, in an
unprotected part of left field for two bases in the third, took
third on an infield fly, and came home on Durst's long fly.

Dutch Ruether was working for the Yankees then, and
Hudlin's double and a low throw by Dugan in the third gave the
Indians their first run. Lindbergh was approaching Paris about
that time. He was over the flying field when Ruether weakened
in the sixth and yielded two runs. Lindbergh had landed when
Dutch was removed in the eighth and was replaced by old dependable Wilcy Moore.

Rud Rennie, New York *Herald-Tribune*

Ruth crossed the enemy defense by doubling to left in the third.
Jamieson was miles away from the ball.

James R. Harrison, *The New York Times*

Monday, May 23

[*On May 22, in Cleveland, the Yankees won, 7–2. Winning pitcher,
Urban Shocker (4–3). Home run, Babe Ruth (10).*]

Cleveland—The amiable Yankees closed out the accounts for the
Western jaunt by tanning the Indians before an overflow crowd
of 23,000. The local taxpayers were deeply pained by the atro-
cious antics of their pets, but G. H. Ruth brought balm to the
Cleveland wounds by elevating Homer No. 10 over the right
field fence in the sixth with a playmate on base.

It is not possible to wax enthusiastic over Mr. Ruth's home
run. The less said about it the better. It was neither a titanic

thump nor a wild wallop. On a field less tiny than the Cleveland enclosure the right fielder could have camped under this blow and had plenty of time for a ham sandwich and a bottle of pop.

The ball went 600 feet—300 feet up and 300 feet down. It cleared the high right field screen with almost six inches to spare. George actually blushed as he loped around the sacks.

In honor of the prestige of Mr. Ruth, the biggest local crowd of the year crashed the gates at Dunn Field. When all the seats had been filled, the customers were allowed to park along the foul lines and on fair ground in left field.

[*Dunn Field, which was surrounded by East Sixty-sixth Street, Lexington Avenue, East Seventieth Street, and Linwood Avenue, and was later called League Park, could accommodate fewer fans than any other major league stadium. It had only 21,414 seats, although sometimes, as on this occasion, the crowd would overflow onto the field. All of the Indians' home games were played in Dunn Field until 1933, when the Municipal Stadium, on the lakefront, was opened. From 1933 until 1946, Cleveland was the only big league city with two home parks. Ordinary games continued to be played at Dunn Field, and special games (those played on Sundays, holidays, and, after 1939, at night) would be moved to Municipal Stadium. Finally, in 1947, when Bill Veeck took over the club, Dunn Field was abandoned. Dunn Field had a very short right-field fence, only 290 feet from home plate at the foul line, but it was also the tallest major league fence, 60 feet, and so, as is true of left field in Fenway Park, pop flies hit into right field that would be caught in any other park might be home runs in Dunn Field. On the other hand, hard line drives that would be home runs elsewhere might be singles in Cleveland.*]

James R. Harrison, *The New York Times*

A band of colorful Oklahoma Indians attended the game, and their Chief Gorgonzola presented Jack McCallister with a blanket. [*The forty-eight-year-old Cleveland manager, Jack Mc-Callister, had never played in a major league game, and 1927 was his first and only season as a big league pilot. He would be discharged at the end of the season.*]

After Ruth flied to left fielder Jamieson in the fifth, he took everyone's attention off the game by sitting with the Indians and donning one of their feathered head dresses.

Rud Rennie, New York *Herald-Tribune*

Cy [*Wilcy*] Moore, the Yankee find, throws a sinker that is almost impossible to hit. It sinks so rapidly the Yankee catchers have to get closer to the plate to keep from picking the ball from the dirt and to prevent the umpires from misjudging the pitches.

Moore's sinker may pass the batter above the knee but drops so fast before the catcher gets it as to be only ankle high, thus creating an optical illusion. By crowding the plate, the Yankee catchers get the ball when it is almost knee high.

Stuart Bell, Cleveland *Press*

AMERICAN LEAGUE STANDINGS

	W	L	PCT	GB		W	L	PCT	GB
New York	22	10	.688	—	Washington	14	15	.483	6½
Chicago	19	15	.559	4	Cleveland	14	17	.452	7½
St. Louis	16	14	.533	5	Detroit	13	16	.448	7½
Philadelphia	17	16	.515	5½	Boston	9	21	.300	12

Tuesday, May 24

[*On May 23, in Washington, the Yankees lost, 3–2. Losing pitcher, Myles Thomas (0–1). Yankee home runs, Babe Ruth (11), Lou Gehrig (10).*]

Washington—Poor judgment on the part of Babe Ruth and a pitiable bungle by Mark Koenig robbed your Yankees of a victory. Ruth's mistake and Koenig's error came in the seventh inning.

With the Yankees in front, 2 to 1, Goose Goslin opened the seventh by banging Myles Thomas for a long drive into right field. The Babe was playing deep and tore in for the ball. It was apparent he couldn't make it, but rather than play the drive safely, Ruth tried to make a circus catch. The sphere got away from him and Goslin made three bases on the blow.

Joe Judge's sacrifice fly brought Goslin over with the tying run. Muddy Ruel continued the assault with a single to Koenig. Then Topper Rigney hit a grounder to Mark, and with a sure two-ply killing in sight, Koenig fumbled the ball and both runners were safe. Then two successive walks brought over the deciding marker.

Thomas did not pitch a bad game. Had he been given good support, he would probably have registered his first victory of the season.

The Yankee runs were scored in the opening inning when Ruth and Gehrig smacked their eleventh and tenth homers respectively. The Babe planted one into the stands in center field [*over four hundred feet from home plate*], and Lou followed with a long clout over the high right field wall.

Charles Segar, New York *Daily Mirror*

Washington—Yesterday Miller Huggins appeared on the coaching lines for the first time this season. [*Only rarely did Huggins appear on a coaching line. Almost always Art Fletcher coached at third base, Charley O'Leary at first.*] In the ninth, after Lazzeri had popped out, Dugan doubled to left center, and Huggins went into a delirious frenzy on the third base line. Waving his arms and jabbering in several languages at one time, the Yankee boss presented an inspiring picture.

James R. Harrison, *The New York Times*

Wednesday, May 25

[*On May 24, in New York, the Yankees' scheduled game with Philadelphia was postponed because of rain.*]

Babe Ruth has not been hitting the ball as frequently as he generally does and may be said to be in a slump, though his batting average is well over .300. [*In fact, he was batting .331, with 39 hits in 118 times at bat.*] In an effort to end this slump the Babe has trimmed his batting style. He isn't as footloose at the plate as he usually is, he grips his bat a trifle higher, and he doesn't take the long swing that makes him spin when he misses. He digs himself in with his cleats and starts his swing shoulder high, his aim being rather to meet the ball than to nail it with a sweep of his bat that, it sometimes seems, starts from his heels.

Hitting in this fashion, he doesn't get the tremendous power into his drives that he does with the true Ruthian swing, but even so, he hits the ball harder than anyone else. Also, he is able to pull hits into center and left, which is impossible when he is swinging naturally. His double to left field in Cleveland the other day [*May 21,*] his home run into the center field bleachers in Washington, and his blazing double against the right field fence, also in Washington, all were produced with the modified stroke.

Pegging away as he is now, the Babe is likely to make many singles and doubles, and these, with an occasional home run, will pull him out of his slump. When this comes to pass, his mind will be easier and his home runs more numerous. Thus the Babe will be happy, the fans will be happier, and all will be right with the world again.

Arthur Fletcher, who is having his first opportunity to study Ruth at close range over a protracted period, has been very much impressed by the Babe. [*Until 1927, the forty-two-year-old Fletcher had been a National Leaguer, primarily as a shortstop for the Giants (1909–20). Midway in the 1920 season, he was traded to the Phillies, a team that he managed from 1923 until the end of the 1926 season, when he became a Yankee coach. Fletcher would remain with the Yankees until he suffered a heart attack on September 10, 1945; he would participate in ten World Series and would become the highest paid coach of all time (until the recent inflation of all baseball salaries). As a player, Fletcher had been a fighter and a hustler—a "McGraw type"— and now, with the Yankees, he displayed this same temperament in the third-base coaching box.*]

"I never realized until this season what a really great player he is," said Fletcher. "I had regarded Ruth only as a phenomenal hitter. Now I know he deserves to be rated among the greatest outfielders of all time. He covers a wide territory, is sure death on fly balls and all the line drives he can get his hands on, plays ground balls that come to him as well as an infielder, and throws amazingly. I have seen a lot of accurate throwing by outfielders, but I never saw a man who had even a slight edge on the Babe in pegging." [*Sometimes during fielding practice a towel would be laid down near home plate, and from deep right field Babe Ruth would throw in baseballs that more often than not would hit the towel.*]

Frank Graham, New York *Sun*

Thursday, May 26

[*On May 25, in New York, the Yankees' scheduled game with Philadelphia was postponed because of rain.*]

There are hitters and hitters in this jolly old game of baseball.

And your Yankees have more than their share.

The sensational Ruth, the powerful Gehrig, the lackadaisical Meusel, nowhere will you find more potential destructive power than in this trio.

But—

With the winning run on second base, two out, and victory hanging in the balance, it isn't Ruth that opposing pitchers dread most to see at the plate.

It isn't Gehrig that gladdens most Yankee hearts or brings fear to the heart of opponents. Nor is it Meusel, though Lanky Bob is a tough, tough man in a pinch.

There's another one more dangerous—another one whose record shows a greater penchant for hitting when hits count.

And the middle initial of his first name is Earle Combs.

For three seasons the lanky Kentuckian has gone about his business quietly and carefully and has left the cheer and the hullabaloo to the others. He lacks the showmanship which characterizes Ruth; his trim figure lacks the suggestion of awkward power which symbolizes Gehrig.

But he's all there.

And if the fans fail to appreciate his work, that lack is more than made up in the appreciation of his team-mates—and his opponents.

This year Huggins sent Combs to the lead-up position. It was a good move. In 158 possible chances to reach first base Combs has succeeded 77 times. [*When the 1926 season began, Koenig batted first, followed by Combs, but in June they changed positions, and Combs led off for the rest of the season and would do so for all of 1927.*]

When you've got a man who reaches first base safely once out of every two times he faces a pitcher, you've got a chap who, in his own way, is more valuable than Ruth or Gehrig or Meusel or any of the sluggers.

American League pitchers know this.

George Uhle was punching the bag with a few correspondents a few days ago, and conversation turned to Yankee hitting.

"You guys are overlooking the toughest man on the Yankee club," George said. "Ruth and Gehrig and the rest of them are tough enough. They hit a ball hard and they're apt to break up a ball game any time they get hold of one. But, inning in and inning out, game in and game out, the toughest man on the Yankee line-up to pitch to is Combs. He's apt to hit anything you toss up."

Combs has most of the attributes of a great player. He can hit; he's fast; he thinks quickly; he can go get 'em—and he loves to play. He has two weaknesses. He is a bit bad on ground balls, and his throwing arm is erratic.

He never fails to run out a hit. He never fails to back up the other outfielders. He's always on the job.

And when a winning run is on second, with two men down, let someone else have their Ruths and Gehrigs. What's needed in a spot like that is a man who will hit the ball, and that man is Earle Combs.

[*Several times during this season writers paid tribute to the generally underpublicized Yankee center fielder, and they usually took note not only of the ballplayer but also the human being. Here, for example, is an excerpt from Fred Lieb's* New York Post *column of September 16: "He is quite an interesting chap, Earle Combs. If you visit Earle in his hotel room some night after a game you are likely to find him reading his Bible. And he doesn't try to hide it when anyone comes into the room, nor does he show any embarrassment that he should be reading this book.*

"This does not mean that Earle Combs is a gloomy, praying Colonel. There isn't a player on this club who is more full of life, joy, and good nature. He loves his pranks and his jokes; he loves his hits and winning ball games."

In 1970, Earle Combs would receive lasting recognition of his greatness as a ballplayer by being named to baseball's Hall of Fame, an honor that thus far has eluded his more highly acclaimed teammates Bob Meusel and Tony Lazzeri.]

Ford C. Frick, New York *Evening Journal*

Saturday, May 28

[*On May 26, the Yankees were not scheduled to play. On May 27, in New York, the Yankees split a doubleheader with Washington, 2–7 and 5–0. Losing pitcher, Herb Pennock (5–1); winning pitcher, Waite Hoyt (6–2). Yankee home run, Lou Gehrig (11).*]

Back in the era of 1908, the Cubs employed a southpaw pitcher, Jack Pfiester, known far and wide as "Jack, the Giant killer." Several years later (1910–13), the Cubs had a right-hander, Louis Richie, who wasn't particularly effective against anyone else, but at the Polo Grounds he was "Lou, the Giant killer." [*Jack Pfiester became the original "Giant killer" after winning three consecutive decisions against New York late in 1908, when the Cubs captured the pennant from the Giants on the last day of the season.*]

Now the Washington Senators have "Lizzie, the Yankee tamer," Horace Lisenbee, who tamed the Yankees for the third time this spring yesterday.

After "Lizzie" Lisenbee attended to his taming, Waite Hoyt won the Yanks an even break in a double header.

We must refer our readers to our dispatches from the Grapefruit front last March. Remember all the nice things we said about the great Lisenbee. Well, isn't he?

Herb Pennock dashed his five-game winning streak against the Yankee tamer. Herb met his first defeat of the season and was bombarded out of the yard in less than four innings. On the other side of the picture, the great Lisenbee held the Yanks to four hits, one an infield scratch by Combs.

It looked as though the home gang might put on a rally against Lisenbee in the ninth, when Ruth singled for his only hit of the double header and Gehrig walked. But "Lizzie" induced Meusel to pop a gentle lift to first baseman Judge and then curved a third strike past Tony Lazzeri's hip pocket. [*Lisenbee, who would defeat the Yankees again before losing to them, would turn out to be a one-season pitcher. In his rookie season of 1927, his record would be 18 wins, 6 losses, and 4 shutouts. He would remain in the major leagues for an additional 7 years, during which time he would have 19 wins, 49 losses, and no shutouts.*]

Every so often Herb Pennock has an off day, and yesterday was one of them. It was evident early that the clever boy from Kennett Square, Pa., was not himself. He hadn't enough speed to break a goose-egg. In 3 ⅔ innings he yielded 9 hits, walked a man, and hit another, which was ample proof that it wasn't the real Herb Pennock pitching.

George Pipgras did well after relieving Pennock, yielding only one hit. [*Pipgras had not been the pitcher of record in any game yet this season.*]

Waite Hoyt made a tidy job of bringing in the victory in the second game. The Brooklyn mortician was never better. It takes good pitching to shut out that Washington batting order with such thumpers as Goslin, Speaker, and Judge. Waite yielded only three hits, and they were about as useful as a cat's whiskers when it tries to get into a bottle of cream. Goslin hit the first, and Ruth's good peg nailed him by several Yonkers blocks when he tried for a double.

This looks like one of Hoyt's best seasons. In the last four games he has yielded three runs, two of them earned. He shut out both the White Sox and Senators, held the clubbing Browns to one run and Cleveland to two.

Our frolicsome Columbia alumnus, Lou Gehrig, again caught up with the biffing Bambino in that private home-run war. Lou birched his eleventh four-bagger among the happy four-bit customers in the right-field bleachers. They scrambled cheerfully for the souvenir.

Fred Lieb, *New York Post*

Looking over the record of runs driven in by the Yankees, one again sees the muscle-gnarled form of Mr. Lou Gehrig, who has pounded over more runs than any other man in either league. So far as the Yankees are concerned, Mr. Gehrig rates win, place, and show. No one else is even in the money.

Lou has smacked 46 runs over the plate thus far. Long Bob Meusel, despite his absence from the game for more than a week [*because of the burst blood vessel in his leg*], rates second. Mr. Meusel, in his slow, deliberate fashion, has accounted for 28 scores, and is a stride ahead of Tony Lazzeri, who has pounded in 26. The more or less famous George Herman Ruth is running a close fourth with 24 to his credit. The rest of the field is scattered, as the boys say at the track.

Ford C. Frick, New York *Evening Journal*

Sunday, May 29

[*On May 28, in New York, the Yankees split a doubleheader with Washington, 8–2 and 2–3. Winning pitcher, Urban Shocker (5–3); losing pitcher, Wilcy Moore (4–4). Yankee home runs, Babe Ruth (12), Bob Meusel (3).*]

The most the amiable Yankees could pry loose from the tenacious Senators yesterday was a fifty-fifty division of the swag. After George H. Ruth had set the example with his twelfth homer in the first game, the visiting firemen rushed back to capture the other warm argument.

Forty thousand customers were thrilled as the Hugmen made a gallant rally in the second affair, only to be thrown back by Fred Marberry with the tying run on second base and two out.

[*At a time when relief pitching was not nearly as specialized and highly regarded as it is today, Fred "Firpo" Marberry and Wilcy Moore were regarded as baseball's two best relief pitchers. For the preceding three consecutive years, Marberry had led American League pitchers in games saved, and in 1924 and 1925, he had appeared in relief more than any other man.*]

G. Ruth had one of his most succulent days in the earlier soiree. He collected a homer, a triple, and a single in four times at bat. The three-bagger and single were just a grand economic waste, but the homer provided the biggest moment of the day when it went soaring into the right-center field bleachers with two on in the seventh.

This modest tap, which again put the Babe ahead of his classmate, Louis Gehrig, in the home-run sweepstakes, barely cleared the chicken wire, but it was a long-flung drive, hurdling the barrier about 50 feet to the right of the scoreboard [*about 430 feet from home plate*].

In the second game Miller Huggins sent Wilcy Moore to the

hill [*his first major league start*], and Bucky Harris retorted with Fred Marberry, which made it a fight to the death between the two greatest relief pitchers of this day and age. [*This was the only time that they faced each other as starting pitchers.*] They both lasted nine innings, and for seven of these it was as pretty a duel as ever graced a ball field.

At the start of the eighth the match was all square, 1 to 1, but the Yanks couldn't keep up the mad pace. With one out, Marberry singled to right and went to second on Earl McNeely's single. Then Harris rolled to Koenig, who tossed him out. Bucky stepped on Gehrig's ankle crossing first and Lou fell forward on his face and went into such violent convulsions that the customers feared his leg had been broken or cut off at the ankle. While Louis writhed agonizedly, Marberry scored unmolested from third.

After all these goings-on, Gehrig finally got up and resumed play. Apparently he was so stunned by a blow on the ankle that he could not get up and head off Marberry at the plate.

James R. Harrison, *The New York Times*

Ruth provided all the action in the first inning of the first game. He crashed into the right field stands to catch what looked like a home run for Bucky Harris. Then he crossed the Senators by cracking a ball into left field and taking three bases by dint of some smart base running. It was the first triple for the Babe this year.

Rud Rennie, New York *Herald-Tribune*

Monday, May 30

[*On May 29, in New York, the Yankees defeated Boston, 15–7. Winning pitcher, Myles Thomas (1–1). Yankee home run, Babe Ruth (13).*]

Yesterday 40,000 watched a battle that from start to finish was one of turmoil, strife, murderous slugging of young and hopeful pitchers and gaudy bits of fielding.

None of the Yankee fans would have given a perforated dime for the chances of the Huggins crowd at the close of the third

Boston time at bat. "Dutch" Ruether had been flattened by two runs in the first, a home run by your old friend Grover Hartley [*the Red Sox catcher, who had played for six years with the Giants*] in the second, and another homer by Fred Haney in the third. Myles Thomas took Ruether's place after the Haney incident and proceeded to allow a double, make an error, and distribute another single and a pass, so that the Red Sox had a five-run lead.

That was seeing the Yanks at their worst. But then they dragged themselves aloft by their shoelaces. They went after Harold Wiltse, a left-hander who has always given them trouble, and disposed of him in a seething fourth inning, when they tied the score and then eased ahead. After disposing of Wiltse, they dropped Fred Wingfield over the side. He pitched to four batters and got only the illustrious Ruth out. Dan MacFayden of the Holy Cross MacFaydens came in and stopped the trouble and pitched good ball. [*MacFayden, a rookie, was one of the first major league players to wear glasses while in uniform. He and Joe Dugan had both studied at Holy Cross College.*]

In the eighth inning, with two strikes on Ruth, MacFayden grew careless and shot a ball over the plate just on the outside. The Babe lashed out in desperation and made one of his very unusual homers, a drive into the left field stands. [*In* The New York Times, *James R. Harrison said that the ball "drifted out into the left field stand—out in the end section where the box seats curve out toward the lawn and then suddenly end."*]

That seemed to discourage MacFayden. He retired Gehrig, but Meusel and Lazzeri shot doubles to left, and a newcomer, Herbert Bradley, came on and was as complete a bust as Mark Roth would have been if Huggins had elected to have him pitch. [*Formerly a baseball writer for the old New York* Globe, *which had become defunct by 1927, since 1915, the forty-five-year-old Mark Roth had been the Yankees' traveling secretary.*] Bradley was clipped for two hits, hit a man, gave two passes, and when Ruth, up for the second time in the inning, slapped a single to right for Runs Nos. 6 and 7 of the frame, Bradley left. Jack Russell made Gehrig hit into a double play to end the festivities.

Talking of Gehrig, he hit on hard luck. Bill Jacobson was lying in wait with the wire of the left field screen in his back when Lou socked one in the first inning, and he went over to the running track in left center for a great catch. [*This was not a warning track such as is found in all ballparks today, but a cinder track used for athletic meets.*] THAT would have been a triple. But wait.

In the sixth Lou smacked a drive dead into center and HIT like a pile driver. Ira Flagstead started back with the crack of the bat, and as he was nearing the flagpole beyond the running track he flung up his gloved hand and speared the ball. That was a homer filched from the Gehrig record. Flagstead was cheered for three minutes.

In this game the hitting hero was Jack Grabowski, who made four hits and drew a pass in five trips to the plate. Brother Mark Koenig had three hits in a row, all doing damage.

Monitor, New York *World*

Why Babe Ruth doesn't hit oftener to left field is one of those mysteries that only George himself can solve. His triple Saturday and homer yesterday would seem to indicate that if Herman wants to hit about .500 all he has to do is to shift his line of attack. When Ruth comes to bat the left fielder moves over to center, the center fielder takes up a position in right, and the right fielder leans against the grandstand. A slap down the left field foul line in this setting is practically ruinous.

The Bambino is a victim of his own home run record. If he but said the word he could compile a batting average that would make Hornsby's efforts look ill.

[*Rogers Hornsby, who began his major league career late in 1915, retired with a career batting average of .358, which was second only to that of Ty Cobb. He set the record for a single season average (.424 in 1924), and during one five-year stretch, he compiled this incredible record: 1921, .397; 1922, .401; 1923, .384; 1924, .424; 1925, .403. But Ruth was no slouch when it came to acquiring base hits. He led his league in batting in 1924 with an average of .378, and, in 1923, although he was nosed out for the title by Harry Heilmann, his average was .393. His career average of .342 is the ninth highest of all time and compares rather favorably with that of such recent superstars as Willie Mays (.302), Henry Aaron (.305), and Mickey Mantle (.298).*]

James R. Harrison, *The New York Times*

AMERICAN LEAGUE STANDINGS

	W	L	PCT	GB		W	L	PCT	GB
New York	25	13	.658	—	Cleveland	19	21	.475	7
Chicago	25	16	.610	1½	St. Louis	18	20	.474	7
Philadelphia	21	17	.553	4	Detroit	16	21	.432	8½
Washington	17	18	.486	6½	Boston	10	25	.286	13½

Tuesday, May 31

[*On May 30, in Philadelphia, the Yankees split a doubleheader, 8–9 and 6–5, in 11 innings. Losing pitcher, Bob Shawkey (0–2); winning pitcher, Wilcy Moore (5–4). Yankee home run, Babe Ruth (14).*]

Philadelphia—Babe Ruth transformed the jeers of 40,000 fans into cheers when he hit his fourteenth home run of the season in the afternoon game yesterday. The circuit blow came in the eleventh and was the deciding run. The triumph gave the Ruppert Rough Riders an even break, the morning battle going to the enemy. [*For the morning game, there were also 40,000 fans. This Memorial Day crowd of 80,000 was the largest number of persons ever to watch baseball in one day in Philadelphia. Playing two separate games instead of a doubleheader permitted the home club to sell tickets for each game. Although unheard-of today, this was not then an extraordinary practice either in the major or the minor leagues.*]

For three hours and five minutes the teams battled on; then the illustrious Bambino came to bat in the eleventh. Rube Walberg got a count of two and two on him. The next one was to Babe's liking and he socked it into the upper stands in left field.

One of the most unusual plays ever seen happened in the fourth. With one out, Eddie Collins and Ty Cobb were on second and first. Al Simmons raised a pop foul fly near the Mackmen's dugout. Johnny Grabowski went after it and caught it while leaning over a railing. After the catch, Grabby fell over the railing and into the Athletics' dugout. Before he could come out with the ball, Collins and Cobb scored.

These runs would have tied the score. Huggins and his Rough Riders protested vehemently. Umpire in Chief Roy Van Graftan declared the catch was similar to a sacrifice fly and that both runners were entitled to score. Huggins appealed to the other

umpires, Clarence Rowland and Thomas Connolly, and the arbiters held a lengthy conference. First they decided that the runners were within their rights to score. Then, after Hug and the
Yanks continued arguing, the arbiters compromised and permitted only Collins to score and sent Cobb back to third base. Veteran baseball men say that they have never seen a play like it
before. [*This may have been the only time in baseball history that a
runner scored from second base on a sacrifice fly to the catcher.*]

Charles Segar, New York *Daily Mirror*

While the attendance yesterday was estimated at 40,000 for each
game, that did not represent all the people that shouldered and
fought through the streets around the park. Lehigh Avenue
[*which ran along the first-base line*] was impassable, and so were
many of the small streets nearby. Cars were parked two abreast,
and conditions were that of an army suddenly swooping down
on a locality. John Shibe declared that if he had a capacity for
80,000 he could have sold out for each game.

It was a remarkable tribute to the popularity of baseball. All
parks are too small and antiquated. The owners must build them
larger. [*Philadelphia would have its new ballpark, Veterans Stadium,
which accommodates a crowd of 60,000, in 1971.*]

[*John Shibe, a lifelong Philadelphian then fifty-five years old, was the
younger of two sons of Benjamin F. Shibe, who had become the first
president of the Athletics when the club was founded in 1901. When
Benjamin Shibe died in 1924, his elder son, Thomas, became president,
and John, the club secretary, replaced Thomas as vice-president. Although John Shibe would not become the Athletics' president until his
brother's death in 1936, he actually had been in charge of conducting the
club's front-office operations for years, long before he became vice-president. Like Jacob Ruppert, the Shibes never interfered with the conduct of
their manager; on the field and in the clubhouse at Shibe Park there was
only one man of authority, Connie Mack.*]

James C. Isaminger, Philadelphia *Inquirer*

Philadelphia—At last George Herman Ruth has done it. He has
broken a ball with the force of his blow.

Before the second game yesterday, with Mike Gazella pitching,
the Babe caught one on the end of his bat. So terrific was his

swing that he broke the horsehide cover for a space of more than two inches, or half the circumference of the ball.

The broken ball is now carefully cached away in John Shibe's office as mute testimony of the force of a Ruthian swing.

New York *Evening Journal*

Wednesday, June 1

[*On May 31, in Philadelphia, the Yankees won a doubleheader, 10–3 and 18–5. Winning pitchers, Waite Hoyt (7–2), Urban Shocker (6–3). Yankee home runs, Babe Ruth 2 (16), Lou Gehrig (12), Tony Lazzeri (3), Pat Collins (2), Mark Koenig (1).*]

Philadelphia—If you don't believe the Yankees can hit, ask Cornelius McGillicuddy, the lean leader of the Athletics. Mr. McGillicuddy's valiant lads were drawn, quartered, cooked in boiling oil, massacred, and otherwise slaughtered by the champions before 25,000 chagrined fans, and what was left of the Athletics' pitching staff looked like something that the family feline had dragged in.

The Babe went crazy and ran amuck. He clouted homer No. 15 in the first game and No. 16 in the second, making 5 round-trippers in 4 days. You should have seen the second one. It cleared the right field fence a foot inside the foul line, soared over a two-story house across the street, and when last seen it was headed for the North Philadelphia Station—out on a spree to see life.

These two festive bunts were only part of the general attack. Crash, zam, and zowie went the New York bats. Ruth, Gehrig, and Collins slammed out four-baggers in the opener. Ruth, Lazzeri, and Koenig did likewise in the second massacre.

The figure jugglers announced that the champs had made 37 hits in the 2 affrays—6 homers, 4 triples, 4 doubles, and a scattering of singles.

Earle Combs helped himself to two doubles, a three-bagger, and two singles in the night cap; Lazzeri got a homer, double, and two singles, and believe this one or not, Urban Shocker produced three dashing singles.

Bringing out another batch of statistics, Lou Gehrig's mite in the first assault was only a homer, a triple, and a double. Pat Collins got sore and patted the ball clear over the double-decked stand in left—the second time this trick has been turned at Mr. Shibe's park.

James R. Harrison, *The New York Times*

The games yesterday were not without comedy. The Babe batted right-handed his final appearance, and Simmons, tired of chasing to the fence for batted balls, finally climbed the ladder at the scoreboard [*in center field*] and sat down to watch the drives soar over the fence.

Ford C. Frick, New York *Evening Journal*

For no particular reason the obstreperous Hugmen quiet down amazingly at the Stadium. Time and again they have laid waste enemy territory and later have been plundered of all their spoils in battles on the east bank of the Harlem. Home cooking doesn't seem to agree with the Huggins heavy artillery. It takes the boos and jeers of enemy rooters to spur them to deeds of derring-do.

There's Waite Hoyt, the singing undertaker of Flatbush, for instance. [*Although Hoyt, whose father performed in vaudeville, was not a "singing undertaker," he did indeed have a good singing voice, good enough to earn him $1,500 a week on the stage of New York's famed Palace Theater when he was on tour during the winter months after the seasons of 1928 and 1929.*] He's of the type of the famous Lord Marmion who dared "to beard the lion in his den, the Douglas in his hall." [*The reference is to Sir Walter Scott's romantic narrative poem* Marmion.]

Before the home fans at the Stadium Waite has pitched some listless games, but put him on the firing step in an enemy town and he fairly revels in the tough going. He's a bit sluggish in defending the Yankee trenches, but he's a brilliant battler on a raiding party through the enemy lines.

It was Master Hoyt, by the way, who made the sage observation that, in spite of all the wet weather the ball clubs encounter, he had never seen a player carrying an umbrella on a road trip.

Bob Meusel and G. Herman Ruth are at their best on the road. Meusel takes added interest in life when roaring bleacherites are crying for his scalp. Ruth, of course, is a favorite all around the circuit. He probably hits better on the road than at home because it's contrary to the general order of things. The Babe always does the unexpected.

The Yanks are a peculiar club viewed from any angle. They give away games after they have won them, and they grab back others after they seem lost beyond recall.

Huggins uses about three signs in running his club, one for the hit and run, one for a pitch-out, and one for a postponement on account of rain.

The best feature of this system is that it works.

John Kieran, *The New York Times*

Thursday, June 2

[*On June 1, in Philadelphia, the Yankees won, 2–1. Winning pitcher, Myles Thomas (2–1).*]

"I wanna go home!" the ten-year-old razzberry customarily cast at Joe Dugan by Shibe Park's comical crackers, bounced back and hit the crackers between the horns yesterday.

Joseph usually grins at them and runs his finger along the inscription he wears across his uniform's chest. Yesterday his retort knocked the comical crackers for a complete double back somersault. Joe's reverberating rebuttal was the ninth-inning break-up of a tight twirling tiff betwixt George Walberg and Myles Thomas.

Dugan limps with his left foot ever since he slid too hard to third on Monday [*and was replaced in the lineup by Ray Morehart*]. He watched yesterday's pitchers' battle from the bench.

Came the ninth inning and the score tied 1 to 1. Some poor infielding placed a pair of Yanks on the bases after Walberg had turned back Ruth for the fourth time. Two were out when Miller Huggins poked Dugan's ribs and handed him a bat. Joe limped to the plate as pinch-hitter for Ray Morehart.

From all sectors the comical crackers sang the old, old song, dating from the time when Joe was a young shortstop just out of college and so easily discouraged that when the bleacherites of 1917 yelled "Pop-up Dugan" he climbed on a train and retired from baseball into private life at New Haven.

"I wanna go home!" wailed the comical crackers, and echo answered, "Go ho-o-o-ome."

Dugan did not answer with words. Walberg, a great pitcher yesterday, had been turning down the big-fisted sphere-smashers all afternoon. They had three hits off him up to the ninth.

So the comical crackers gloated over the tasty morsel served in the ninth inning by the mite manager.

"Strike one," brought a louder chorus of "I wannas." The second strike unloaded a chorus that was deafening. It took just another strike to put Dugan back on his cushion by the water cooler.

But instead of a third strike Dugan hit the ball squarely. A line drive smashed into center field, taking a long hop to center field. Ben Paschal [*filling in for Meusel*] was the man Dugan sent home, and when Ben scored from second base on the pinch single he scored the rubber run of the tight-waged battle.

[*The cry "I wanna go home," which Dugan regularly heard when he played in Philadelphia, harks back to the time when he played for the Athletics. Dugan grew up in the coal-mining town of Mahanoy City, Pennsylvania, and from high school he went to Holy Cross College, and from there, in 1917, he went directly to the Athletics. Dugan had a rather miserable five years in the City of Brotherly Love, which is notorious for being the only place where Santa Claus was booed. For various reasons—one of which was to care for an invalid mother—Dugan periodically left the team to go home. From these trips developed the cry "I wanna go home" and also his lifelong nickname, "Jumping Joe." Because of this verbal chastisement, Dugan pleaded with Mack to trade him, and on July 23, 1922, he was sent to the Yankees. There was much criticism of this trade, which helped the Yankees to retain their pennant, by the margin of a single game, and this led Commissioner Landis to formulate the rule that prohibits trades after June 15. Dugan performed well for the Yankees, and in 1922 and 1923, he was outstanding in the World Series.*]

Bill Brandt, Philadelphia *Public Ledger*

Babe Ruth is getting the ingredient he needs to set a new home run record—competition.

Lou Gehrig has blossomed forth as a formidable rival for the Babe's slugging crown, and the threatened invasion of his sacred precinct has aroused in Babe the urge to do bigger things—an urge that has not moved him since his record season of 1921.

If Gehrig does not falter he may be the means of forcing the Bam to break his own record this season.

Jack Conway, New York *Daily Mirror*

Friday, June 3

[On June 2, in New York, the Yankees defeated Detroit, 2 to 0. Winning pitcher, Dutch Ruether, (5–1).]

When the Yankees picked "Dutch" Ruether out of the waiver grab-bag in the latter part of last season, they picked up one of the biggest bargains since Colonel Ruppert snared Babe Ruth from Harry Frazee seven years ago.

In his present form the California Dutchman is likely to help pitch the Yankees into another profitable World Series. *[Ruether was born in Alameda.]* He never looked better than he did yesterday when he held the Tigers to two hits and pitched as neat a shutout as has been turned in this year.

Ruether had an abdominal operation after the last World Series, and then he spent the fall and winter resting up. Gradually Ruether's strength returned, and today he is as strong as when he first came into the league. *[In 1917, Ruether began his major league career, and in 1925, he came to the American League.]* The ball curved over the plate yesterday from so many angles that the Tigers couldn't tell whether it was coming or going. In seven of the innings only three men faced Ruether. He had the Michigan boys hitting into the air, and 15 went out on flies.

There was something even more out of the ordinary yesterday than the two-hit shutout. The game was reeled off in 1 hour 31 minutes. No, not 2 hours 31 minutes. The 1 hour 31 minutes is correct.

[Ruether was an especially graceful, picturesque pitcher. Here is Will Wedge's description of Ruether's windup as it appeared on April 30 in the New York Sun *and written when the Yankees were in Boston: "Ruether has a wind up that appeals to the intelligenstia. He stands on*

the rubber and ponders deeply, corrugating his high and alabaster brow into meditative wrinkles. He faces sideways and extends both his hands as if plucking a volume from a library shelf and then draws his hands inward as if holding the volume under his nose for research work. Naturally such high-brow hocus pocus impresses Bostonians, and the Back Bay athletes are as but freshmen, open mouthed and gullible in the presence of a master."]

Fred Lieb, *New York Post*

There's a lad out there in Yankee uniform, doing his stuff and doing it nobly—a chap seldom heard of and seldom lauded.

He's Johnny Grabowski, blond haired Viking who, along with Pat Collins, has done the catching for the Huggins troupe. A quiet, soft-spoken, easy going chap, you don't hear much of Johnny. When he plunged into the runway under the Philadelphia stand a few days ago he got his first "press notice" of the season.

But talk to the players and you'll hear plenty about Johnny— and all of it good! Working in alternate games with Pat Collins, he has delivered day after day. He is a good receiver, he has a corking arm, a good head, and he's a fair hitter.

There's no faster man in the league than little Stuffy Stewart [*a reserve second baseman*] over at Washington. He has tried stealing on Grabowski just once this season—and Johnny tossed him out by a city block. In Philly the other day Eddie Collins got on first and tried to steal. He never had a chance. Ty Cobb was up next and walked. Ty tried to make second, and Lazzeri put the ball on him six feet from the bag. [*Until Lou Brock recently passed them, Ty Cobb was baseball's all-time leading base stealer, and Eddie Collins was in second place; in 1927, however, Cobb and Collins were both forty years old. Apropos of Brock, it should be remembered that he played in seasons with 162 games while Cobb and Collins had only 154 games a year in which to do their running.*]

After that, when A's got on base, they stayed there until someone hit 'em around. They took no chances with Grabowski's arm.

Early this spring, with Benny Bengough laid up, Miller Huggins was a bit worried about his catching. He isn't now. Pat Collins and Grabowski have done a mighty workmanlike job of a rather difficult assignment. [*As a catcher, Bengough was clearly the best of the three.*]

Like Grabowski, Pat is no seeker after limelight, no colorful sensation. But he's a plugger. And he has the physique to go day in and day out and do the things expected of him.

Ford C. Frick, New York *Evening Journal*

Saturday, June 4

[*On June 3, in New York, the Yankees lost to Detroit, 3–1. Losing pitcher, Herb Pennock (5–2). Yankee home run, Lou Gehrig (13).*]

Somehow or other, little Jackie Tavener, mite of a Tiger short-stop, thinks he might be in that Ruth-Gehrig home run competition if he had his mail sent to Yankee Stadium. Prior to last summer, home runs were something which Jackie read about in the papers. And then one day at the Stadium Jackie took a good swipe at a ball, and wonders will never cease—that ball described a beautiful arc and landed among the four-bit sun-worshippers in the right field stands. At first Jackie had to pinch himself to find out if he was dreaming. But no, the coach on third base waved him around. It was a real, honest-to-goodness homer, the first in Jackie's career [*which had begun in 1925*].

After that little Tavener was like a golfer who had made a hole in one. He knew it was possible and he had a commendable ambition to do it again.

Things were going rather badly with the Tigers yesterday. Herb Pennock had blanked them in the first six innings. Then in the seventh Heilmann was safe on Koenig's fumble, and Charlie Gehringer whipped a single through the box. That brought up little Jackie.

"I did it once, and I can do it again. I did it once, and I can do it again," cooed Jackie to himself in his best Coué style. [*Philip Emile Coué, who died in 1926, was an internationally famous French psychotherapist who preached that many ailments and illnesses are psychologically induced, and can be cured by methods of autosuggestion. His most famous statement was, "Every day, in every way, I am getting better and better."*]

Zing! Jackie did it again. For the second time in his big league career he felt the thrill of a free merry-go-round ride around the bases while several dozen bleacher fans scrambled for the ball.

Heinrich Lou Gehrig also whistled a homer into those right field bleachers, but he was unfortunate enough to hit it when no tenants were on base.

Fred Lieb, New York Post

Sunday, June 5

[On June 4, in New York, the Yankees' scheduled game with Detroit was postponed because of rain.]

In the face of expected denials, players in both major leagues are reporting almost daily the reappearance of the jackrabbit ball, and pitchers are complaining of a particularly heavy fire from the batters. Within the past ten days three or four pitchers have had the wind knocked out of them by quickly rebounding liners that struck them amidships before they could even see the ball. Others have been hit on the shins and knees and knocked out of the game for a week or so. Herb Pennock of the Yanks has been wounded so frequently that he declares it an open question as to whether he or the jackrabbit will last longer.

The increasing number of home runs in the American League started talk of the jackrabbit's reappearance some time ago, but now the infielders are ducking and dodging in the National League.

"No matter what we say," one player remarked, "the officials will deny the existence of the lively ball and nothing will be done. Just the same, somebody will get his head knocked off one of these days if they don't stop putting dynamite in those balls."

Bozeman Bulger, New York Evening World

Monday, June 6

[On June 5, in New York, the Yankees defeated Detroit, 5–3. Winning pitcher, Myles Thomas (3–1). Yankee home run, Babe Ruth (17).]

The Yankees and Tigers played the longest game of the rain-ridden spring yesterday, taking close to four hours. One hour and twenty minutes was waiting time in the third inning when the battle was held up by showers. A crowd of almost 40,000 wouldn't go home, and the battle was resumed at 5 o'clock and the game was finished in the shadows of night.

The Yankees won, thanks to a timely single by your playmate, George Herman Ruth, who also smacked his seventeenth homer of the year. His hit in the eighth was most timely, for Combs had walked and Koenig had been hit by a pitched ball when the moment arrived. Combs scored what proved to be the winning run.

It was a great game for the crowd. The first flinging of 1927 straw hats followed Ruth's homer and also the first kisses of the year for the Babe. He was hugged out on the field in full sight of thousands as he came in after catching the ball which ended the struggle.

The Babe's "No. 17" came in the sixth, and it was a most convincing wallop. Earl Whitehill, ace of the Tiger staff, served three bad balls and then drifted over a perfect strike which the Babe let pass unnoticed. [*At this time, when the count was three balls and no strikes, a batter rarely swung at a pitch, which was often called an automatic strike.*] Then Whitehill essayed to put another in the same place, and this time it was hit—hit so hard that it was still going up when it landed far across the right field screen and well up among the bleacherites.

Monitor, New York *World*

Baseball statisticians are inviting attention to the fact that Babe Ruth is on his way to beating his own record of 59 home runs in a single season. In the roll of meritorious deeds this may mean comparatively little, but in the aggregate box office of professional baseball it means considerable work for the cash register.

With the stout Mr. Ruth chasing his record through the various big league cities, this ought to be the most profitable season in the history of the national pastime. If Mr. Ruth is within a home run or so of his 1921 record toward the end of the season there will be such a rush of customers that Colonel Ruppert will have to call out the reserves to keep them from tearing down the barriers.

While the breaking of a home run record will be of no extensive benefit to humanity, I hope that it will be achieved.

Ever since the good-natured Babe started to bask in the limelight a number of mediocre minded ones have predicted each year that "Ruth was all through." There always was an earnest note in this prediction. The resentment has grown because the Babe systematically has crossed up the prophets just as they saw hope for the best, which meant the worst for the Babe.

All in all, the Babe has done very little harm to anybody except himself and has provided a considerable amount of entertainment for persons of the male gender of all ages. There is an admirable sincerity in his manner of taking a cut at a baseball. His regard for his "public" is boyishly genuine and good natured. Certainly he has made the game of baseball more enjoyable for his presence.

Outside of Charles Chaplin, I do not know of an entertainer who has provided more enjoyment than the Babe, and if there were any way of appraising the drawing power of the Babe I think that he would be shown to be the greatest money maker as an entertainer for all time.

Another reason why I am cheering for the Babe is that I am quite sure that Mr. Wayne B. Wheeler will not point him out as an example of what total abstinence will do. I notice recently that Mr. William Tilden 2d was pointed out by Mr. Wheeler as an example of what water will do for an athlete. I am happy in the conviction that they will never place the Babe on the same pedestal with Mr. William Tilden 2d.

This insistence on "clean living" and what it will do in the way of bringing about success becomes a bit boresome. Besides, all successful men have not been "clean livers" according to the standards of the Anti-Saloon League. The notion of this organization is that anyone who ever has drunk intoxicating liquor automatically becomes a dirty liver.

The opponents of the Anti-Saloon League show a considerate

frame of mind when they abstain from pointing out the successes scored by persons who have not abstained from intoxicating liquors—Washington and General Grant, for instance.

The boys who talk "clean living" have been rubbing it in and have made themselves monotonous. Therefore it caused me no little personal enjoyment when old Grover Cleveland Alexander, after having his usual number of nightcaps rose with a clear head and firm step to win the last game of the World Series.

Mr. Wheeler could not place him on the Tilden pedestal and hurl at him the reproach, "Clean living did it."

[*Grover Cleveland Alexander was one of baseball's most notable drinking pitchers. After he had won the sixth game of the 1926 World Series for the Cardinals, and had pitched the full nine innings, he assumed, especially since he was thirty-nine years old, that he would not be needed on the next day. And so he had a fine liquid celebration that night. He was nevertheless called on by manager Rogers Hornsby in the seventh inning of the seventh game with two outs and the bases loaded. Then came the celebrated strikeout of Lazzeri followed by two scoreless innings.*

The Anti-Saloon League, founded on May 24, 1893, at Oberlin College, was the most prominent organization in the Prohibition movement, culminating in the Eighteenth Amendment. As of January 1, 1920, the manufacture, sale, importation, or exportation of alcoholic beverages in the United States was prohibited. Wayne B. Wheeler, a student at Oberlin, joined the league soon after its formation and stayed with it as he earned a law degree and then became the league's general counsel and national legislative superintendent. A true zealot, Wheeler argued many cases for the league before the Supreme Court, and he was highly influential in bringing about the Prohibition amendment.

Bill Tilden was the world's best tennis player in the 1920's, and some people rank him as the number-one performer of all time. Tilden had indeed been cited by Wayne Wheeler as a conspicuous example of moral rectitude. Some years later, Tilden would be sent to prison for sexual offenses involving young boys.]

W. O. McGeehan, New York *Herald-Tribune*

AMERICAN LEAGUE STANDINGS

	W	L	PCT	GB		W	L	PCT	GB
New York	31	15	.674	—	Cleveland	22	24	.478	9
Chicago	30	17	.638	1½	Washington	20	23	.465	9½
Philadelphia	23	22	.511	7½	Detroit	19	25	.432	11
St. Louis	22	23	.489	8½	Boston	12	30	.286	17

Tuesday, June 7

[*On June 6, the Yankees were not scheduled to play.*]

We commend the following to the attention of our good friend,
Cousin Egbert Barrow:

"Dear Mr. Conway,

"May I call your attention to a disgraceful occurrence at the
Yankee Stadium Sunday. When it started to rain, the bleacher
fans started for cover, and, of course, as there was a large crowd,
it caused some confusion. But, not satisfied with that, the Keystone Kops ordered those fans who tried to stay under the stands
to move on and, after being shoved and pushed like a herd of
cattle, they were put out in the rain, a few of the policemen
using strong arm methods. I hope that those in charge can learn
to use that knob on top of their shoulders and not treat people
like a lot of sheep.

"Yours truly, Edward Quigley."

Jack Conway, New York *Daily Mirror*

The business of catering to the tastes of baseball fans has gradually developed into one of the big enterprises of the country.
One of the ball parks out West had gross sales two years ago of
nearly half a million dollars.

The man at Forbes Field [*the home of the Pittsburgh Pirates at this
time*] in charge of the refreshment stand says that the favorite
foods of Pittsburgh fans are small hamburger steaks stuck in a
round roll and the regulation hot dog. [*Note that the writer found it
necessary to describe a hamburger sandwich; for some people it was still a
novelty.*] In the spring and fall the hamburger leads, while the
hot dog scores heavily during the hot months. The peanut
doesn't go nearly so well in Pittsburgh as in New York, but pop
corn goes much better. The New York fan positively declines to
eat pop corn. There hasn't been a package of pop corn sold at
the Polo Grounds or the Yankee Stadium in years.

The Pittsburgh fan goes in rather strong for soda pop, buttermilk, and sweet milk. The New Yorker, Harry Stevens informs me, will not drink soda pop. No attempt has ever been made to sell him milk. His staple drink is charged mineral water, ginger ale, and occasionally sarsaparilla. Before every game at Forbes Field there is a line of fans to get milk, hot dogs, and hamburgers. The temper of the crowd, they tell me, reflects the way the fans have been fed. When they have time to eat well they are easy on the umpires and much more tolerant to visiting players.

A student of psychology, though he doesn't know it, explained to me that most of the rabid outbursts of fans in Cincinnati and St. Louis are due to a sparsity of refreshment stands. His theory is that if fans could be kept occupied in eating their anger would not be so easily aroused over "one of them close decisions at the plate."

St. Louis fans will not eat a boiled sausage. The dogs must be broiled and taken directly off the griddle. That interferes with distribution through the stands. This impatience over inability to get the dogs served hot while watching the game, explains our psychologist, is largely responsible for the outbursts of temper so distressing to umpires. The road to peace and tranquillity is more and better hot dog stands.

In Pittsburgh Barney Dreyfuss has arranged his refreshment layout so that it is the first thing seen by incoming fans. His is the only stand where the customer has to buy hot dog and hamburger tickets in advance. [*Dreyfuss had owned the Pirates since he bought the club late in 1899. He was the principal founder of the World Series in 1903, and he was probably baseball's most highly regarded club owner.*]

This arrangement works nicely ordinarily, but one day last summer it resulted in the first hot dog panic in history. A heavy rain caused suspension of play, and there was a great rush for hamburgers and hot dogs. The ticket sellers sold their little checks by the yard—they look like subway tickets—and then the hot dogs ran out! The only thing that stopped the clamoring was resumption of play.

Barney Dreyfuss declares very gravely that he has taken such precautions that there can never be a hot dog scandal in his park.

Johnny Seys, who is in charge of refreshments for the Cubs, has discovered that the baseball fan is rapidly becoming a candy eater. He attributes this to the lack of beer. Thousands of pounds of candy are now consumed by fans in Chicago, and it was not even sold a few years ago [*before Prohibition*].

The Cubs, by the way, have a quaint custom of serving the press box that is not known in any other park. Promptly at 4:30 old Walter, a colored man, brings in his trays and serves every writer tea, coffee, or lemonade (according to the weather) and sandwiches. Walter has performed this ceremony for 15 years. [*Nowadays, complimentary press box refreshments are commonplace.*]

An object in this treatise on fan foods is to encourage the introduction of the little Pittsburgh hamburgers in other parks. It's almost impossible after leaving that town for a baseball scribe to be able to take his hamburgers or leave them alone. They are the cat's mee-ow.

[*The creator of the sports concessions industry was Harry M. Stevens, mentioned in the above article, often called the "hot dog king." Born in London, he came to the United States in 1882 and settled in Niles, Ohio. While watching a baseball game, he had the idea of printing and selling scorecards, and he did so, not only in Niles, but eventually in ballparks, racetracks, hockey arenas, and other sports facilities throughout the country. But it was concessions that made Stevens famous. After he had brought various types of food and drink into ballparks in Milwaukee and several other localities, he went, in 1894, to New York City. His major league career began in the Polo Grounds, where he became an extremely familiar figure, and he also obtained full concessions privileges in Yankee Stadium, Ebbets Field, and Braves Field (in Boston), as well as many of the large racetracks and other athletic arenas.*]

Bozeman Bulger, New York *Evening World*

Wednesday, June 8

[*On June 7, in New York, the Yankees defeated Chicago, 4–1. Winning pitcher, Waite Hoyt (8–2). Yankee home runs, Lou Gehrig (14), Babe Ruth (18), Pat Collins (3).*]

Alphonse Thomas, crack White Sox youngster, was the first major league pitcher to hang up ten victories, but he still has to beat the Yankees. [*In his rookie season, 1926, Thomas won fifteen games,* but he lost all four of his decisions against the Yankees.] For three innings yesterday, Alphonse did not yield a hit or run, and he saw visions of hanging up his first Yankee scalp.

Then came the fourth, as they say in the movies. George Herman Ruth, swinging a powerful cudgel, took his place at the plate. His little boy friend, Heinrich Lou Gehrig, stood a few feet away in the offing.

George Herman swung from the hips and a towering fly dropped deep into the bleachers in right center. Then Heinrich Lou took his wallop. This time a wicked liner flew into the bleachers about ten feet fair.

With Waite Hoyt on the mound, those two runs were enough, though Pat Collins rammed a lengthy four-bagger into the left field bleachers later in the game.

This promises to be Hoyt's best year [a prediction that would be fulfilled]. He had speed to burn, and Chicago's only run was scored by a homer [inside the park] by young John Clancy. This run might have been nipped at the plate had Koenig not stopped the relay at the plate long enough to give Ban Johnson's signature on the ball a minute examination. It was the only run scored by these Chicago upstarts on Hoyt in 18 innings. [Hoyt, it may be remembered, had shut out the White Sox in Chicago on May 8. As for Clancy, this was his first major league home run.]

All told, the opening fray between the two top American League contenders was a pretty snappy affair. Both sides did some fancy outfielding. A lot of balls were "kissed," as the boys in the dugout put it, but some outfielder always was in the way to stop the "kissed ball" in flight.

Fred Lieb, New York Post

In Yankee Stadium a crucial series is under way. [Because the White Sox were in second place, only one game behind the Yankees, some writers were referring to the four games between the two teams as the first crucial series of the season.] The notion persists that the visiting firemen amount to shucks, and this typewriter now rests on the desk in the press box, where observations will be taken on exactly how crucial this series is.

Waite Hoyt is pitching for us, and the crowd went "OOOOO ooooo," as a man by the name of Alex Metzler bunked one in the Babe's hip pocket. Well, I don't see anything exciting about that.

It was a sort of a now you see it, now you don't. [*The next two batters were also easy outs.*] Waita minute, we come to bat now.

Who's this egg batting against Thomas? It's Earle Combs, and see how he bends almost double and hunches over his bat? How he waves his bat at Master Thomas, and he hits it? Are we about to become crucial? We are not. Center fielder Metzler steps here, he steps there, he runs, he stops, he gobbles the fly. Pfui! Koenig next. Mark has a case of foulitis before he rolls one at shortstop Bill Hunnefield. Funny, that ball streaked across the turf, and he never had to move.

It is now Crucial. Master Ruth is up, and Thomas cannot find the plate. Does Thomas fear him? No, he does not, because Ruth swings and misses and walks, and the crowd shrieks with glee as Buster Gehrig comes up with two out. [*Increasingly, as the season progressed, Gehrig came to be called by certain sportswriters "Buster," a nickname by which he was not known to his teammates.*] Another streaker into Hunnefield's hands. So that's the kind of game it's going to be.

What do fielders do when they are not fielding? Well, Lazzeri leans forward and rests his hands on his knees, teetering a little on his toes, follows the line of the pitched ball with his eyes, and his body moves as the batter swings and always in the direction of the ball, which distinguishes the good player from the indifferent.

The Bambino swings his arm, pounds his glove, and, too, takes that characteristic pose of hands on knees. He, too, moves with the batter. Watch him now—Hoyt winds up, Thomas swings at it, and the arc of his bat pulls Babe forward and to the left. Now again—the ball flashes, and Ruth is already trotting in. Even before the White Sox pitcher had completed his whiffy, the Babe knew the inning was over. Whatta man!

These players from Chicago seem to be a very orderly crew, and so far have done no shooting whatsoever. [*In this era of Prohibition, Chicago was noted for its gangsters, men like Al Capone and Bugs Moran.*] They do not seem to be typical Chicagoans, but a ball team is cosmopolitan and most of the members come from other places. Ow! I wish you could have seen that one!

Metzler belts one and it has that hollow home-run sound. Who is that twinkling figure speeding in the field? Ruth? Yes, Ruth! See him go! See those legs work! How can a man so bulky run so fast? Up the embankment he goes. He turns. He reaches. He hauls it down. He holds it. Hear the crowd cheer. Whatta man!

Folks, the existence of Santa Claus cannot be denied. With his own eyes your reporter saw G. H. Ruth and L. Gehrig line two baseballs in succession in the right field stands. Boy, am I glad I came!

Paul Gallico, New York *Daily News*

It seems likely that Babe Ruth gets his tremendous hitting power from the fact that his weight is above the waistline. The Babe is built like a top, and when he slashes at a ball he spins like a top. That is how his bat gets its tremendous velocity.

Walter Trumbull, *New York Post*

Thursday, June 9

[On June 8, in New York, in 11 innings, the Yankees defeated Chicago, 12–11. Winning pitcher, Myles Thomas (4–1). Yankee home runs, Tony Lazzeri 3 (6).]

Come you Fascist and anti-Fascist, unite for just a few moments, and, with all the enthusiasm you can muster, let us acclaim Tony Lazzeri with three rousing cheers. For Tony, favorite son of Italy, was the hero of the Yankees' victory in 11 hair-raising innings.

"Push 'em up" hit three home runs. Imagine that! Tony's first four-bagger came in the second inning, with Cedric Durst [*filling in for the injured Bob Meusel*] on first. It was a long fly that just dropped into the right field stands. His second, in the eighth, was terrifically hit into center field and rolled to the stands [*an inside-the-park home run*].

The Yankees, due to inferior hurling on the part of Dutch Ruether, Wilcy Moore, and Joe Giard, entered the ninth inning five runs behind. [*Giard had come to the Yankees from the Browns, but he would not be of much help to his new team. He would have no decisions in 1927, while posting an ERA of 8.00, and after this season he would never appear in a major league game.*] Then came the rally that knotted the score. Earle Combs led off with a single. Dugan was out, but Ruth, Gehrig, and Durst connected for hits.

Three runs were over, and up strode Tony again. Once more he put his strength behind his wallop. The ball sailed into the right field stands, just fair by a hair, and Durst counted ahead of him.

Three homers in a game. What a feat! [*Lazzeri was only the sixth player in the American League, and the first Yankee, to hit three home runs in one game. In the National League the feat had been performed five times in the twentieth century. Nine years later, on May 24, 1936, Lazzeri would have an even more noteworthy day at bat, when he would become the first player in major league history to hit two bases-loaded home runs in one game and would set a still-standing American League record of eleven runs batted in one game.*]

Myles Thomas, who is credited with the victory, pitched the tenth and eleventh, and not a ball was hit out of the infield. [*The game was won when Morehart hit a sacrifice fly.*]

Charles Segar, New York Daily Mirror

[*Occasionally, Frank Graham would sit on the Yankee bench before a game listening to, and taking notes of, what was said. The following selection is the first of five of his transcripts of dugout conversations contained in this book. Yankee players praised Graham for the accuracy of his reports.*]

The scene is the Yankees' dugout at the Stadium. The time, less than an hour before yesterday's game.

Dugan—Look at Gehrig hit the ball. Every time he swings it's a base hit.

Durst—He'll hit one in the center field bleachers yet.

Morehart—Did anybody ever hit one in there?

Lazzeri—Ask the Babe.

Morehart—Hey, Jedge, did anybody ever hit one in the center field bleachers? [*"Jedge" should be "Jidge," a contracted form of George. To his teammates, Ruth was less often "Babe" than "Jidge."*]

Ruth—Sure. I did.

Morehart—Who was pitching?

Ruth—Ask Dugan.

Dugan—Sam Gray, of the Athletics.

Bib Falk [*the White Sox left fielder*] emerges from the tunnel leading from the dressing rooms.

Falk—Hello, bums.

Combs—Hey, Falk, know what Gehrig says about you?

Falk—What?

Combs—He says your hair is marceled.

Falk—His ain't so straight.

Ruth—Hey, Eddie, hand me that bat.

Koenig takes the bat from Eddie Bennett, the team mascot, and hefts it before relaying it to Ruth. [*Eddie Bennett was the official Yankee mascot and full-time batboy, but he was no longer a boy. He was twenty-four years old and had been the Chicago White Sox mascot from 1917 to 1919. A New Yorker, he served in the same capacity with the Brooklyn Dodgers in the pennant-winning year of 1920. He was hired by the Yankees for the 1921 season and remained with the club until he was seriously injured in an automobile accident in mid-season 1933. The hunchbacked Bennett was a great favorite with the Yankee players, some of whom thought that he brought them good luck; during his period of service, the club won seven pennants and four world championships. He died from alcoholism in January 1935. His furnished room on West Eighty-fourth Street contained four pictures on the walls: autographed photographs of Babe Ruth, Lou Gehrig, Herb Pennock, and Waite Hoyt.*]

Koenig—Why don't you use the heavy bat now?

Ruth—I'm getting old.

Red Faber [*the White Sox spitball pitcher*] comes through the tunnel.

Faber—Hello, Dutch. You and I today?

Ruether—Yes.

Faber—Well, the boys ought to get some hits.

This proves to be prophetic.

Frank Graham, New York *Sun*

One thing I noted at the Stadium seemed a study in futility, and maybe Babe Ruth could do something about it. At the far exit gate back of left center, a gang of eight or ten urchins wait patiently for the game to end and the gates to open. No sooner is the last putout made, the players duck for the dugout, and the crowd swarms over the field, when these tiny figures come down from the exit, scuttling as fast as their little legs will take them. Now begins some of the finest broken field running that you ever saw. The objective of the youngsters is the dugout, where they hope to catch sight of a ballplayer before the last one has vanished into the tunnel that takes him into the showers. Into the teeth of the crowd they run, twisting and squirming, dodging, plunging, stepping on the feet of homeward hurrying citizens, always converging on the promised land. One by one the ballplayers vanish into the dugout. You hope that just one will be left for the youngsters to see, but by the time they reach their objective, a semi-circle of curious fans has formed around it, and they cannot get through or look over. The quest fails.

Perhaps one day Ruth or Gehrig or some other hero can drag his feet a bit as he comes in, stop to look around for a friend, or kneel to tie his shoe, or do something to give the flying brigade a fighting chance. As it stands they're licked before they start, but they never stop trying.

Paul Gallico, New York Daily News

With the ever-increasing toll of home runs, the conviction grows that the big leagues are using the rabbit ball.

Every time there is an insinuation that the baseballs have been made livelier there is a tearful protest from the manufacturers, who insist that the specifications for league baseballs have not been changed. Any increase of speed in the ball is because the grade of horsehide, yarn, rubber, and cork has improved.

But when Signor Lazzeri gets himself three home runs in one game, it must be that the baseball has—to put it mildly—greater resilience than the baseball of a few years ago.

Understand, I do not think there is anything criminal in having livelier baseballs. This may improve the game in the eyes of the customers. But I insist that the magnates and manufacturers should be frank. They should admit that the new baseball has a lot more speed than the old one, and that this is for the improvement of the national pastime. When they try to convince the customers that there has been no change, they intimate that the customers are dumber and blinder than they actually are.

W. O. McGeehan, New York Herald-Tribune

Friday, June 10

[*On June 9, in New York, the Yankees defeated Chicago, 8–3. Winning pitcher, Herb Pennock (6–2). Yankee home run, Ray Morehart (1).*]

The Yankees play with the White Sox as a cat plays with a mouse. They let the Sox get so far ahead and then pounce on them. Ray Schalk's lads thought they had a game tucked away yesterday, but there is no telling when or where the Yankee batting order will break out. [*Hall of Fame catcher Ray Schalk's playing days had virtually come to an end in 1926, and he was now serving his first year as a manager. His managerial career would end with his removal during the 1928 season.*]

The Sox led in the first half of the sixth inning by three runs. Ted Blankenship had limited New York to a pair of singles. The Yanks woke up in their half of the sixth when Cedric Durst poked in two runs with a triple but was out trying to run it into a homer.

The real explosion came in the following frame, when Blankenship was cuffed out of the box. Bert Cole tried his hand as a rescuer with rather dubious results. Ray Morehart [*replacing the injured Joe Dugan*] gave the left-handed Mr. Cole a warm greeting. He slashed the first pitch out to the left-field boxes for a homer, the lick being good for three runs. [*The only home run in Morehart's three-year major league career, a career that would end with the 1927 season, clearly was a fluke. Here is how Rud Rennie described it in the* Herald-Tribune: *"Morehart rapped the ball between third baseman Willie Kamm and the bag, whence it rolled rapidly toward the left field stands and bounded off them with left fielder Falk chasing it this way and that as if it were alive. Pennock scored. Combs scored. And Morehart went pounding around the bags and came in standing up."*]

After that Ruth hit one so far out that Bib Falk couldn't hold it and it went for one of the Babe's infrequent triples. Just to cash full value on the hit our Bambino immediately proceeded to steal home. When the inning was over the Hugmen had six runs.

Fred Lieb, *New York Post*

Saturday, June 11

[*On June 10, in New York, the Yankees lost to the White Sox, 4–2.
Losing pitcher, Urban Shocker (6–4).*]

Playing the title role in the stirring tableau, "The Worm Will
Turn," the White Sox laid the Yankees over their knees yesterday and gave them a sound spanking as Ted Lyons hung up his
eighth straight victory. [*Ted Lyons went directly from Baylor University to the White Sox, for whom he would pitch for 21 years and win 260
games. He would never play a game for any other major or minor league
team, and he would be elected to the Hall of Fame.*]

Many a ball team would have been discouraged by the situation in which the White Sox found themselves at 3:29 P.M.
yesterday. Three of their best pitchers had been thrown by the
Yanks for lengthy losses. The local larrupers had smacked Chicago twirling to practically every corner of the lot. What had
started out to be a very crucial series had become a rout.

Were the Chicago athletes downhearted? No. In his younger
days Manager Ray Schalk had been a devoted follower of
Horatio Alger, Burt L. Standish, and Ralph Henry Barbour. He
had read that if at first you don't succeed, try, try again. He was
aware that it is a long lane which has no turning, and he was not
ignorant of the fact that it is darkest before dawn.

Consequently, Mr. Schalk's White Sox tore into Urban
Shocker and knocked him slightly lop-sided while Ted Lyons
held the Yanks to five, as they say, scattered hits.

[*Horatio Alger, Burt L. Standish, and Ralph Henry Barbour were
enormously prolific authors of novels and stories for boys. Alger wrote
about poor but honest boys who struggled against insurmountable odds to
achieve fame and fortune. "Burt L. Standish," the pen name of George
W. Patten, wrote hundreds of stories about the phenomenal Frank Mer-
riwell, the Yale University athlete who was famous for last-minute hero-
ics. Barbour wrote more than eighty books on deeds of valor performed on
schoolboy athletic fields.*]

James R. Harrison, *The New York Times*

Yesterday the ace of the White Sox pitching staff [*Ted Lyons*] bewildered the powerful Yankee hitters with his several wind-ups. He'd swing his arms back and forth maybe twice, maybe three or four times, before delivering the ball. On one occasion he annoyed Ruth so much that the Babe twice stepped out of the box, saying finally in exasperation:

"Listen. If you're going to jump, jump. If you're not, for heaven's sake throw the ball." [*One may be certain that Ruth did not say "for heaven's sake."*]

That was all Lyons needed to be sure he had our hitters buffaloed. He didn't allow a hit after the forth inning.

[*In this instance, exasperation drove Ruth out of the batter's box. The current practice of stepping out of the box because of whim or a desire to disconcert the pitcher would not have been tolerated in 1927. If for no legitimate reason a batter left the box, the home plate umpire would call for a pitch, even a quick pitch, which if it were anywhere near the plate would be declared a strike. This was one reason for games being more quickly played than they are today.*]

Rud Rennie, New York *Herald-Tribune*

Sunday, June 12

[*On June 11, in New York, the Yankees defeated Cleveland, 6–4. Winning pitcher, Myles Thomas (5–1). Yankee home runs, Babe Ruth 2 (20), Lazzeri (7).*]

Babe Ruth hit two more homers yesterday, one of them so long that Luke Sewell, the Indian catcher, demanded an inspection of Ruth's bat.

"Lemme see that club," demanded Mr. Sewell, after Mr. Herman had hit the ball into the center-field bleachers in front of the score board. "Lemme see that stick. Nobody could hit one like that without having a slug of lead of something in the end of his bat."

Mr. Sewell took the Ruth bludgeon and peered at it suspiciously. He scrutinized the end of it, balanced it in one hand, and even sniffed at the unoffensive shillalah. Though he found nothing illegal, Mr. Sewell was still dubious and unconvinced and he shook his head skeptically.

National Baseball Hall of Fame

The Greatest of All Teams, the New York Yan-
kees of 1927—**Top Row** Gehrig, Pennock,
Lazzeri, Moore, Ruth, Miller, Meusel, Shawkey,
Hoyt, Giard, Paschal, Styborski, Woods,
Trainer. **Middle Row** Shocker, Dugan, Combs,
Coach; O'Leary, Coach; Huggins, Manager;
Fletcher, Coach; Koenig, Ruether, Grabowski,
Pipgras. **Bottom Row** Wera, Gazella, Collins,
Bennett, Bengough, Morehart, Thomas, Durst

(upper) Babe Ruth and Yankee owner Jacob Ruppert have just agreed on salary terms for 1927 as General Manager Ed Barrow looks on. (lower) The "mighty mite" manager, Miller Huggins, with four men, each of whom served under him for at least ten years: Waite Hoyt, Babe Ruth, Bob Meusel, and Bob Shawkey

United Press International Photo

Miller Huggins shakes hands
with the Babe and peers out
from the dugout.

The one and only Sultan of Swat, the Bambino, Babe Ruth himself

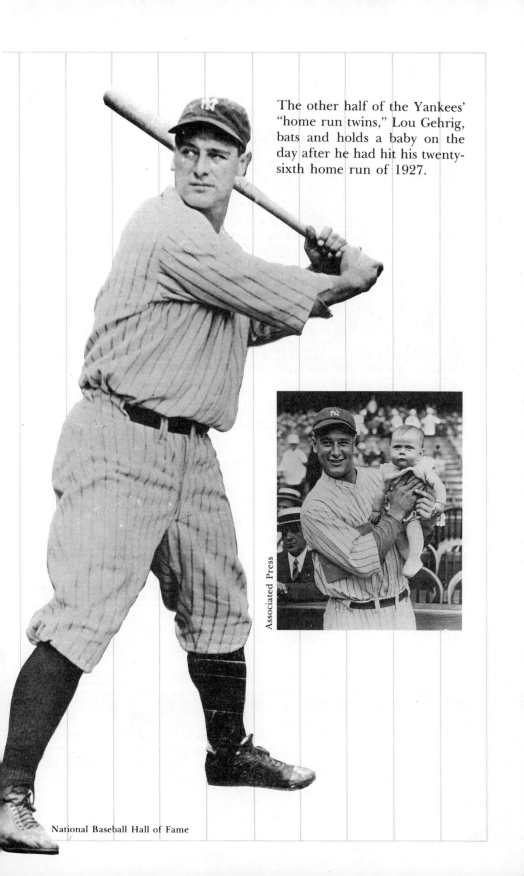

The other half of the Yankees' "home run twins," Lou Gehrig, bats and holds a baby on the day after he had hit his twenty-sixth home run of 1927.

Associated Press

National Baseball Hall of Fame

Lou joins Babe to greet local townspeople from the rear platform of the team train returning from spring training and, later in the year, "listens" to his teammate "play" the saxophone he received from Paul Whiteman.

Two of the most prominent members of "Murderers' Row," (left) outfielder Bob Meusel and (above) second baseman Tony Lazzeri

They helped to guard the middle of the diamond: (below) center fielder Earle Combs and (right) shortstop Mark Koenig.

National Baseball Hall of Fame

National Baseball Hall of Fame

The great fielding third baseman Joe Dugan and the superb
relief pitching ace of 1927,
Wilcy Moore

Three shots of Hall of Fame pitcher Waite Hoyt: showing his hurling form on the golf course, getting a rub-down from trainer "Doc" Woods, and relaxing at home

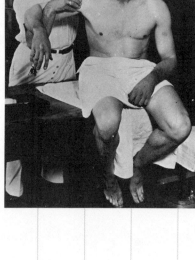

The pitching staff's left-handed member of the Hall of Fame, Herb Pennock

Three productive members of
the club: pitchers Dutch Ruether
and George Pipgras and catcher
Pat Collins

National Baseball Hall of Fame

National Baseball Hall of Fame

National Baseball Hall of Fame

With Muddy Ruel catching, Babe Ruth hits the ball that would become his sixtieth home run and a few seconds later is congratulated by Lou Gehrig as he crosses the plate.

EARLE BRYAN COMBS
NEW YORK YANKEES 1924-1935

LEAD-OFF HITTER AND CENTER FIELDER OF
YANKEE CHAMPIONS OF 1926-27-28-32.
LIFETIME BATTING AVERAGE .325, 200 OR
MORE HITS THREE SEASONS. LED LEAGUE
WITH 231 HITS IN 1927 WHILE BATTING .356.
PACED A.L. IN TRIPLES THREE TIMES AND
TWICE LED OUTFIELDERS IN PUTOUTS.
BATTED .350 IN FOUR WORLD SERIES

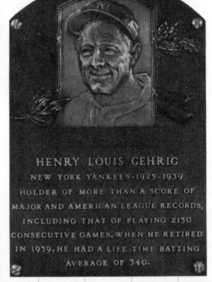

HENRY LOUIS GEHRIG
NEW YORK YANKEES-1923-1939
HOLDER OF MORE THAN A SCORE OF
MAJOR AND AMERICAN LEAGUE RECORDS,
INCLUDING THAT OF PLAYING 2130
CONSECUTIVE GAMES. WHEN HE RETIRED
IN 1939, HE HAD A LIFE-TIME BATTING
AVERAGE OF .340.

WAITE CHARLES HOYT
"SCHOOLBOY"

NEW YORK YANKEE PITCHER 1921-1930.
LIFETIME RECORD: 237 GAMES WON, 182
GAMES LOST, .566 AVERAGE, EARNED RUN
AVERAGE 3.59. PITCHED 3 GAMES IN 1921
WORLD SERIES AND GAVE NO EARNED RUNS.
ALSO PITCHED FOR BOSTON, DETROIT AND
PHILADELPHIA A.L. AND BROOKLYN,
NEW YORK AND PITTSBURGH N.L.

The plaques in the National Baseball Hall of Fame, Cooperstown, honoring Earle Combs, Lou Gehrig, and Waite Hoyt

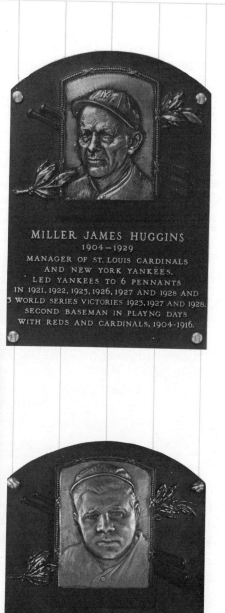

MILLER JAMES HUGGINS
1904–1929
MANAGER OF ST. LOUIS CARDINALS
AND NEW YORK YANKEES.
LED YANKEES TO 6 PENNANTS
IN 1921, 1922, 1923, 1926, 1927 AND 1928 AND
3 WORLD SERIES VICTORIES 1923, 1927 AND 1928.
SECOND BASEMAN IN PLAYNG DAYS
WITH REDS AND CARDINALS, 1904-1916.

HERBERT J. (HERB) PENNOCK
OUTSTANDING LEFT HANDED PITCHER IN
THE A.L. AND EXECUTIVE OF PHILADELPHIA
N.L. CLUB. AMONG RARE FEW WHO MADE
JUMP FROM PREP SCHOOL TO MAJORS. SAW
22 YEARS SERVICE WITH PHILADELPHIA,
BOSTON AND NEW YORK TEAMS IN A.L.
RECORDED 240 VICTORIES, 161 DEFEATS.
NEVER LOST A WORLD SERIES GAME,
WINNING FIVE. IN 1927, PITCHED 7 $\frac{1}{3}$
INNINGS WITHOUT ALLOWING HIT IN
THIRD GAME OF SERIES.

GEORGE HERMAN (BABE) RUTH
BOSTON—NEW YORK, A.L.; BOSTON, N.L.
1915–1935
GREATEST DRAWING CARD IN HISTORY OF
BASEBALL. HOLDER OF MANY HOME RUN
AND OTHER BATTING RECORDS. GATHERED
714 HOME RUNS IN ADDITION TO FIFTEEN
IN WORLD SERIES.

The plaques for Miller Huggins, Herb Pennock, and Babe Ruth. A seventh Yankee of 1927 who is a member of the Hall of Fame is a man who did not wear a uniform, General Manager Ed Barrow.

The blow which provoked this search into Mr. Ruth's arma-
ment was probably the second longest he has hit at the Stadium.
Caught by a favoring wind and traveling with great momentum,
the ball leaped the fence in front of the scoreboard, landing a
half dozen rows up. It put the 30,000 customers in mind of an
even longer drive by the master driver two years ago, a punch
further to the left, and higher up in the stands.

After Ruth's nineteenth chip shot of the year came No. 20 on
his next turn at bat. Garland Buckeye was simply Mr. Ruth's
dish. The mammoth southpaw [*he weighed 257 pounds*] tossed
one up in the fifth round and the Babe put it into the bleachers a
few rows from the top, no fragile bunt this one, either. It would
have cleared most fences.

Ruth's homer and one by Tony Lazzeri inside the grounds
gave the Yankees an opulent lead. When the ninth opened Myles
Thomas had a five-run margin to play with—and he did, fast
and loose.

A double, two walks, and a single made it 6–3, filled the bases
with one out, and brought old Deacon Moore on the run from
the bull pen.

Leave it to the Deacon. He nailed Jamieson on a grounder to
Gehrig. A run scored and a hit now meant a tie score, but Cy
fanned Fred Eichrodt on three pitched balls. Good enough.

James R. Harrison, *The New York Times*

Ruth said before the game that he felt a home run coming on
and refused to participate in batting practice. "I have an idea,"
he said, "that I'm about to sock one and I'm not going to waste
any time hitting 'em now when they don't count."

Rud Rennie, New York *Herald-Tribune*

George Burns [*Cleveland first baseman*] opened the third with a
single through the box and hurried around the sacks when Joey
Sewell blasted one high and far toward the right field bleachers.
It looked like a homer to the crowd, to Burns, and to Sewell, but
not to Ruth. The Babe ran up the bank in front of the screen
and, leaping in the air, nipped the ball as it was passing over the
wire. It was only a lazy throw then to double up Burns.

Monitor, New York *World*

Monday, June 13

[On June 12, in New York, the Yankees lost to Cleveland, 8–7. Losing pitcher, Waite Hoyt (8–3). Yankee home run, Babe Ruth (21), George Pipgras (1).]

The sailor who scattered largess with a reckless hand was a prudent and economical citizen compared to the Yankees yesterday. Our extravagant champions gave the Indians a seven-run start and then spent the remainder of the afternoon in fruitless attempts to catch up. It was a lot of fun, but expensive.

Not even G. Ruth's twenty-first homer could loosen the Indian stranglehold. Herman the Great larruped the ball midway up the right-field slope in the seventh and tickled 45,000 fans mightily, but the Yanks were too heavily in arrears.

The Yankees' repentance came too late. So did their good pitching. Waite Hoyt tarried in our midst one and a fraction innings and pulled the Yankee house down in ruins about his mangled form. Then came George Pipgras, and the Indians made only one run in seven frames, but that was one too many.

The Babe hit a homer when it didn't mean much and fanned twice when just one-fourth of a homer, or a plain, garden variety single, would have meant the game. He slowed up two blossoming rallies, did George, one in the fifth and the other in the ninth.

The homer, then, was merely icing on the cake. It was pretty icing at that. George Uhle was pitching when the seventh round started, and George Uhle is a mean hombre as far as George Ruth is concerned. He has fanned him many a time and oft, as he did later in the ninth, but this time Ruth caught hold of the ball and gave it a buggy ride high, far, and handsome. It bounced into the laps of the customers in the middle of the right field bleachers.

The Yanks were still battling when the ninth chukker came around. "Up and at 'em, my brave lads," said Miller Huggins. "Remember that the game isn't over until the last man is out." Or words to that effect. *[Or, as the then two-year-old Yogi Berra would one day say, "A game isn't over until it's over."]*

Morehart punctuated the oration with a single, and the Babe came up to get a raucous reception. The citizens wanted a home run. But did George hit a homer or even a single? He did not. He took three swings—one, two, three—and went back and sat down.

James R. Harrison, *The New York Times*

Sunday baseball in this state and town have been vindicated. For eight years it has provided clean, wholesome, healthful recreation for teeming millions. Yet before the war there were gloomy forebodings that Sunday ball would lead to disturbances, organized roughhouse, and what not.

Yesterday I watched 45,000 fans file out after the game. It was a refreshing sight. The game was so close that no one stirred until two were out in the ninth and Uhle had two strikes on Mark Koenig, the last batsman.

Leisurely, good-natured, without any unnecessary pushing or shoving, the big throng dispersed. It was entirely different from the rush-hour jam in the subway, when it is a case of every man for himself.

The lady fans grow more numerous with each passing year. Never is this more noticeable than in the Sunday crowds. At least a quarter of that crowd yesterday were women.

When Cy Young was in New York recently he spoke of the appeal the game now had for women folk. He considered that one of the best signs of the upward tendencies of the present day game. Cy regretted to say that when he was a player the conversation on the field frequently was of such a nature that if a man brought his wife or sweetheart once he usually did not bring her a second time. [*Cy Young's 509 major league victories, tops among all pitchers, were gained from 1890 until 1911.*

In 1907, the only major league cities that permitted Sunday baseball were Chicago, St. Louis, and Cincinnati. Soon thereafter, it became legal in Cleveland and Detroit, and, in 1917, in Washington, the first eastern city to rescind this blue law. (It was considered important to provide Sunday recreation for the many wartime workers in Washington.) Sunday baseball finally came to New York and Brooklyn in 1919; to Boston in 1929; and, last of all, to Philadelphia and Pittsburgh in 1934.]

Fred Lieb, *New York Post*

AMERICAN LEAGUE STANDINGS

	W	L	PCT	GB		W	L	PCT	GB
New York	35	17	.673	—	Detroit	24	26	.480	10
Chicago	32	22	.653	4	St. Louis	23	27	.460	11
Philadelphia	28	23	.549	6½	Cleveland	24	29	.453	11½
Washington	25	24	.510	8½	Boston	12	36	.265	20½

Tuesday, June 14

[*On June 13, in New York, the Yankees defeated Cleveland, 14–6. Winning pitcher, Herb Pennock (7–2). Yankee home runs, Ben Paschal 2 (2), Tony Lazzeri (8), Joe Dugan (1), Pat Collins (4).*]

Millions saw Lindbergh yesterday, and 20,000 watched the Yankees defeat the Indians. [*This was the day of the Lindbergh parade through Manhattan, the biggest reception and celebration in the history of New York City.*] One might ask, "Why weren't the 20,000 down at the reception?"

It would be easier if Lindbergh's name could be worked in with the ball game, but that's out of the question. He wasn't there, and the cheer that greeted Ben Paschal's two home runs was but a whisper compared with the bedlam which greeted this young man along the line of his triumphal march.

There won't be a story in any paper today into which the name of Lindbergh will not be woven in some fashion. It is customary to poach upon fame and public interest in this manner. If tradespeople and advertising "master minds" may couple up the name of this young man with their products and bargains, why cannot the desperate newspaper worker, shamed at the inferiority of his story, link up the fame and publicity of Lindbergh with his own drab product? [*In the days since Lindbergh's flight, dozens of newspaper advertisements had appeared with his name and picture, for products ranging from the petroleum his airplane used to the candy bars he carried with him.*]

This particular talebearer was at the game yesterday and has a neat and accurate score card to prove it. But coming to the Yankee Stadium after seeing that demonstration downtown left his mind almost as blurred as people say it is. And while he would much rather write about Lindbergh and the reception, he realizes that a sports writer is at his best only when attending to his own business.

Yet how are you going to tell about home runs and timid pitching when nothing remains in your mind but the picture of that sunburned face and the unconquerable blond hair above it? Between the vague thoughts of singles, triples, and sacrifice hits, there looms the one regret that you, too, didn't become an air mail pilot and pull the stunt before anyone thought of it!

There was a perfectly good game yesterday, and upon deciphering the hieroglyphics in my score card, it is learned that Herb Pennock pitched an excellent game, and, inasmuch as the Indians made 9 of their 10 hits in the last 4 innings, he must have eased up after being handed a 13-run lead. The score card shows that Ben Paschal made Bob Meusel wince by getting four hits—two homers, a double, and a triple—and by scoring five runs in five trips to the plate. He was subbing for Meusel in left field.

Pat Collins hit a homer, a triple, and a single in four times up, while Lazzeri and Dugan each hit a homer and a single.

Arthur Mann, New York *Evening World*

Ben Paschal emerged from obscurity to be king of batsmen for a day. And but for a few feet of wire netting on the right field bleachers his name would have gone into the book along with those of Robert L. Lowe and Ed Delehanty as the third man to have hit four home runs in one game. [*Since 1927, three American League players and five from the National League have hit four home runs in one game. One of the eight was Lou Gehrig, who on June 3, 1932, in Philadelphia, hit home runs on his first four times at bat. On his fifth trip to the plate, Gehrig hit what many observers insisted was his hardest and longest drive of the afternoon, caught by Al Simmons against the fence in deep center field. Had the ball been pulled but a few feet, Gehrig would have become the only major leaguer in history with five home runs in one game.*]

As it was, Ben poled two home runs into the left field stands. It sounds silly to say he batted in hard luck, but he did. The two home runs were hit in succession. On his third trip to the plate he hit a double against the right field screen, which was potentially a home run, and would have been if it had been three feet higher. Then he hit a triple which was harder hit than the double and missed being a homer by less than a foot.

[*Ben Paschal, who came within an eyelash of having a four–home run game, ended the season with just two home runs, the pair he hit on this day. During his career, he would play in 364 games and would hit 24 home runs.*]

Rud Rennie, New York *Herald-Tribune*

Wednesday, June 15

[*On June 14, in New York, the Yankees' scheduled game with Cleveland was postponed because of rain.*]

With the season a fraction more than one-third finished, G. Herman Ruth is running neck and neck with his home run record of 1921.

At that time all hands were agreed that the record would stand until the bleachers were moved into the base lines.

Asked if he thought he would equal the mark this year—or better it—Ruth said, "I dunno, but I'll be in there swinging."

G. H. Ruth is modest. If he talked about his batting as Jack Sharkey [*a principal challenger to Gene Tunney's heavyweight championship, at the time training for a bout with Jack Dempsey in Yankee Stadium on July 21*] does about his fighting we would have the Colossus of Clout addressing bleacherites through a megaphone as follows: "That pitcher gives me a laugh. Boys, what I won't do to him will be nobody's business. He'll throw me a curve maybe. I love curves. Or he'll toss me a fast one if he's crazy, and I think he is crazy. Or a change of pace if he's smart. That means I'll only get a triple. Watch me murder him."

The Yankee home run hitter extraordinary has no such notions. He thinks most pitchers are fairly capable workmen, which is in direct contrast to many weaker batsmen who bat five times without a hit and then announce, "The lucky stiff is out there with a glove and a prayer."

Not so Mr. Ruth. He has almost as much respect for a pitcher's arm as a pitcher has for Mr. Ruth's bat.

Ruth, by the way, introduced the slogan "Keep cool with cab-bage" to the Yankee dugout. A succulent head of cabbage is dis-sected and the leaves are spread upon ice in the water cooler. Baseball is warm work, and any cooling system is appreciated.

Ruth showed the boys how to take an iced cabbage leaf out of the cooler, trim it so that it wouldn't fall down over a man's shoulders, place it on the head, and conceal the whole plot by pulling the cap down over the cabbage.

One medium leaf keeps the top of the head cool for approx-imately three innings. Ruth, having a slightly larger than average cranial expanse, changes his refrigerating plant every two in-nings. Sometimes he puts two leaves under his cap at once.

Ruth always removed the cabbage from his hat before he went to bat, but one fatal day last summer he forgot about the vegeta-ble matter. He knocked a home run, and the multitude cheered him to the echo.

In his usual courtly way Signor Ruth took off his cap with a sweeping gesture of thanks—and two large, greenish-white leaves of cabbage were exposed to view.

"My word! What a place for a garden" was the comment of one astonished spectator.

Ruth hastily clapped his cap back on his head whereupon a small boy shouted, "Take it off again, Babe, maybe there's a white rabbit under it." [*Or, if he were Casey Stengel, a bird might fly out.*]

John Kieran, *The New York Times*

From Sunday, June 4, to Monday, June 13, approximately 275,000 people attended nine games at the Yankee Stadium. This is an average of 30,555 per day, far more than the individ-ual capacity of Ebbets Field, Dunn Field in Cleveland, Fenway Park in Boston, or Baker Field in Philadelphia.

This nine-day record eclipses anything in the record books, and stands as a monument to something. Maybe the Yankees have "it!" [*In the twenties, "it" was commonly used to denote someone's charisma or sexiness, deriving from the 1925 film* It, *starring Clara Bow, who was thereafter known everywhere as the "It Girl."*]

Arthur Mann, New York *Evening World*

Thursday, June 16

[*On June 15, the Yankees were not scheduled to play.*]

Will aviation change the makeup of big league circuits and bring the great cities of the Pacific Coast into friendly baseball rivalry with the metropolises of the East? This is no idle dream but is within the realm of possibilities within the next few years.

By 1937 do not be surprised to see the San Francisco Seals alight somewhere in the rear of Coogan's Bluff [*a hill immediately to the west of the Polo Grounds*] for a series with Giants, or have the Los Angeles Angels fold their wings near the Concourse Plaza and prepare for a joust with the Yankees.

The development of commercial aviation within the next ten years should bring New York and Los Angeles as close together as New York and St. Louis are today, probably closer. And only the fact that Los Angeles and San Francisco have been too far removed from the other major league cities has prevented them from getting big league franchises. [*Los Angeles and San Francisco would join the National League when the Brooklyn Dodgers and New York Giants moved to these cities for the season of 1958.*]

Fred Lieb, *New York Post*

Friday, June 17

[*On June 16, in New York, the Yankees defeated St. Louis, 8–1. Winning pitcher, Waite Hoyt (9–3). Yankee home runs, Babe Ruth (22), Lou Gehrig (15).*]

Three freshly painted field boxes, looking strangely incongruous against the background of a crowd that passed close around them, stood vacant at the Yankee Stadium yesterday.

Five hundred policemen, white-gloved and sturdy, stood at attention through the stands, waiting and waiting.

"Lindy's coming!"

Word went through the stands like magic.

"Lindy's coming!"

Interest in the ball game disappeared entirely under the spell of that magic promise.

Babe Ruth smacked a home run in the first inning. But no one paid much attention. They saw the ball settle into the right field stands and raised a perfunctory cheer.

They began, once more, watching the exit in left field.

Gehrig hit one, too, immediately after.

A few people applauded.

Up by the press box a youngster turned to his dad.

"Gee, Dad, that was a peach," he said. "Did you see it?"

"Yes, son, I saw it," the father replied. "But keep watching. Lindy will be here any minute."

Yankee base hits rumbled and muttered; Yankee runs came acrashing over the plate. The game continued, fast and furious. One inning, then two, then three. Still the three field boxes yawned vacantly. Still the cops stood at attention.

Came the sixth inning, then the seventh. Colonel Ruppert entered and took a seat in the boxes of honor. A few policemen, tired from their long vigil, followed suit.

Hoyt was going beautifully. Gaston was performing wonders for St. Louis. Nobody cared. For those three field boxes were still vacant.

Finally the game ended.

There was a rush for the exits.

"Gee, Daddy," remarked the kid by the press box, "he isn't coming, after all."

And then.

A sudden commotion at the left field exit. A yell, and like one man the 20,000 fans, who a moment before had been making for the exit, turned and stormed the gate. An automobile nosed through the gate, the siren blowing madly. Alongside six motorcycle cops pushed and shoved and pushed again into a human wall that gave but refused to break.

In the back seat a smiling kid grinned and grinned again.

"Lindy! Lindy! Lindy!"

The crowd took up the cry, and as one man turned again to the field they had just vacated. Around the official "Lindy" car they swarmed—hundreds of them, thousands of them.

And "Lindy" came. With 500 cops, forming a flying wedge to break a path through the throng.

Pushing slowly through the crowd the official car made its way to the vacant boxes. There was a pause. Colonel Ruppert, blushing and shy, was pushed forward. Lindy rose to greet him. He smiled the golden Lindy smile; they shook hands.

Then a whirl of the motor and the car started forward again, only to be stopped by the human wall that demanded more and more. Lindy rose to his feet in the back seat. He waved. He bowed. He smiled.

The cops worked frantically. They cleared a small path, and the waiting chauffeur saw it. Zip! He was away and clear and quickly was gone from view.

As the car dashed from sight there was the final glimpse of a tall slender figure smiling a good-bye; the fleeting sight of blond hair that waved in the breeze.

That's the way Lindy came to a ball game.

Oh, yes, the Yankees won rather handily. But nobody cares.

Out of that game there's but one memory to carry away.

That's a beribboned automobile, a cordon of fighting, pushing, gesticulating cops, a narrow path cleared by main force through a throng of excited humans.

And above that the trim figure of a mere stripling of a youth, his hair waving in the breeze, his face wreathed in a glorious smile as he rose to bow appreciation to the roaring thousands who knew only one cry: "Lindy! Lindy! Lindy!"

Ford C. Frick, New York *Evening Journal*

The scene is the Yankees' dugout. The time, less than an hour before yesterday's game. The Browns are taking hitting practice.

Wally Schang [*a Browns catcher, in the big leagues since 1913*] comes up the steps from under the stand.

Schang—Hello, boys.

Combs—Hello, Wally. Where's Lindbergh?

Schang—I couldn't wait for him, so I left a couple of passes on the gate.

Hoyt—He's coming to see me pitch. I think I'll ask him for an autographed airplane.

Pipgras—Let me see that bat, Wally.

Combs—Show us how you hold it to make home runs, George. [*On the preceding Sunday, Pipgras had hit the first of his two career home runs.*]

Pipgras obliges, holding the bat close to the end of the handle.

Pipgras—See? Why shouldn't a big, strong fellow like me hit home runs when he can hit with a bat like that? That shows power.

Durst—The writers said it proved the ball was lively.

Browns second baseman Oscar Melillo comes through.

Ruth—Hello, Dago.

Melillo thinks it was Lazzeri who spoke.

Melillo—Hello, Wop.

Fletcher—There's center fielder Bing Miller hitting. Better watch him. He's leading the league.

Combs—How will we pitch to him?

Hoyt—Play him deep and throw him an easy one.

Pennock—He hits slow balls.

Morehart—He hits curves, too.

Fletcher—He must be a pretty good hitter. [*At the end of the season, Bing Miller would bat .325; at the end of his career, .312.*]

Gaston comes through. He was reported to have taken a punch at an abusive spectator in Philadelphia earlier in the week.

Huggins—Hello, champ.

Gaston—Hello, Hug. [*During his rookie season, 1924, Gaston had pitched for the Yankees, and Huggins.*]

Ruth—Did you hit that guy, Milt?

Gaston—No. I tried to, but he covered up too well.

Manager Dan Howley comes through.

Howley—Well, you murderers, how are you?

A bounding ball skips into the dugout, narrowly missing Howley.

Howley—I know where that came from without looking. Every time I turn my back that [Coach Bill] Killefer hits me with a ball. He's got me black and blue.

Frank Graham, New York *Sun*

Lazzeri to Morehart to Gehrig. Morehart to Lazzeri to Gehrig. Lazzeri to Gehrig. Morehart to Gehrig—game after game these combinations reap a fielding harvest for the Yankees, and promise to carry the club to a degree of steadiness it has not known since Scott, Ward, and Pipp functioned so faultlessly four years ago. [*For three years, 1922–24, the Yankees' infield consisted of Wally Pipp, first base; Aaron Ward, second base; Everett Scott, shortstop; and Joe Dugan, third base. In 1922, each of the first three men played in at least 152 games. Scott, the first to leave, was traded to Washington in the winter of 1924–25; on June 2, 1925, Gehrig made his celebrated replacement of Pipp, and in 1926, Pipp was the first baseman for the Cincinnati Reds; and, finally, Ward, after sitting on the bench for most of 1926 watching Lazzeri play second base, was traded at the end of the season to the White Sox. Scott established a major league record by playing in 1,307 consecutive games, a mark that has been surpassed by only one player, Lou Gehrig.*]

The substitution of Morehart for Koenig, who was injured by a thrown ball almost two weeks ago, has improved the Yankees' infield to a marked degree. Morehart is playing as well at second base as Lazzeri did, while Tony is a stonewall as a shortstop. [*After Koenig's injury, Lazzeri moved from second base to shortstop, and Morehart took over at second base.*] Tony is giving daily thrills with his remarkable playing on territory that extends from second to third base. It is astonishing.

Yet when you pay $50,000 for a player, as Huggins did for Koenig, you must use him else explain to the man who signed the check the reason for his idleness. But unless Morehart or Lazzeri slumps it is probable that Musical Mark [*who was an accomplished pianist*] will have a difficult time getting back his job.

Huggins may take it into his head to put Koenig back into the line-up, but he may be breaking up one of the most promising combinations the Yankees have had the good fortune in possessing, especially since Morehart has developed into an unusually valuable hitter, being able to hit and sacrifice and uphold the honors that fall to the second place position [*in the lineup*].

[*Upon recovering from his injury, Koenig would return to his regular position and would not retire from the big leagues until 1937. Morehart, on the other hand, would be dropped by the Yankees after the 1927 season and would never again appear in a major league game.*]

Arthur Mann, New York *Evening World*

Saturday, June 18

[On June 17, in New York, the Yankees defeated St. Louis, 3–2. Winning pitcher, Urban Shocker (7–4).]

The crack of the two-bagger and the thunderous smash of the home run were sadly absent at Yankee Stadium yesterday.

It was a pitcher's day instead 'neath murky leaden skies that were made to order for pitchers. It was a day for fielders too, flashing their stuff across the spongy turf and breaking into brilliance with stops and catches that turned three baggers into easy outs and two baggers into double plays.

The Yanks won because the crafty knowledge of Urban Shocker was a mite more effective than the youthful arms of Walter Stewart and Ernie Nevers, who opposed him. And because the calibre of Yankee support was steadier, if not more brilliant, than that accorded the Brownie hurlers.

Yesterday was Earle Combs day. Six times Earle chased far into the distance to pull down long drives and turn seeming runs into putouts. His shoe-string catch of Bing Miller's drive to center in the seventh was the greatest fielding bit of the day. And proved again that Earle is in a class by himself when it comes to riding the wide ranges of center field.

Tony Lazzeri did nearly as well when he chased to the left field boxes to pluck Sisler's high foul out of the very lap of a cash customer who already had visions of a souvenir. And a moment later Joe Dugan electrified the fans by a flashing one-hand stop of Melillo's grounder—a stop of the sort that Joe used to make in the good old days.

Quite a game, and a good one to win.

But not without its sad note. For Mr. George Herman Ruth pulled up lame in the first inning and had to leave. Babe pulled a tendon or wrenched his knee or something in Thursday's game. Yesterday the knee was so badly swollen and painful that play was impossible. Perhaps he'll be out for three or four days, thereby taking a decided sock on the chin in his quest for a new home run record.

Ford C. Frick, New York *Evening Journal*

Babe Ruth retired from yesterday's game as a result of an injury that is perhaps unique. He sustained his injury striking out.

During the fourth inning on Thursday, Milt Gaston set the home run king down on three pitched balls—two called strikes and then a swing such as only George Herman can make at a speeding baseball.

The third strike did the trick. Babe put so much energy into it that he strained his right knee badly and yesterday limped through practice and out to right field. When he grounded out to Melillo in the first inning, he limped a few steps, then returned to the dugout, and Cedric Durst replaced him in right field.

New York *American*

Professor Urban Shocker enjoyed his best game of the season yesterday, allowing only four hits, all singles. How the professor continues to do it remains a mystery. After 13 years in the big leagues, Shocker hasn't the varied assortment of deliveries that he once had, but it has leaked out that his arm has passed by a studious and diligent process into his head. Professor Shocker is nobody's straight man, though he makes the batters look like a very droll lot of comedians. [*Shocker was called professor because he was regarded by many to be baseball's smartest pitcher.*]

James M. Kahn, New York *Graphic*

Sunday, June 19

[*On June 18, in New York, the Yankees defeated St. Louis, 8–4. Winning pitcher, Myles Thomas (6–1). Yankee home runs, Lou Gehrig 2 (17).*]

Sturdy as an oak, this Henri Louis Gehrig, powerful legs supporting a robust body and huge arms rippling with their sinews. A New York boy this Henri Louis Gehrig, alumnus of Columbia, who swapped his graduation certificate for a first baseman's heavy mitt. [*Although Gehrig spent only two years at Columbia and never received a "graduation certificate," he was repeatedly referred to as an alumnus of the institution.*]

This Henri Louis Gehrig yesterday fashioned two superb home runs, and those two masculine socks into the right field bleachers defeated the Browns.

Yet that was not the full measure of Gehrig's hitting because he also pelted a triple to left which resulted in a run.

Columbia Lou was directly involved in the patterning of six of the Yankees' eight runs. A laurel then for Henry Lou!

Lou's sixteenth came in the first inning after Earle Combs had singled and Ray Morehart was safe on Melillo's error.

His triple came in the fifth, and he scored on Cedric Durst's poke to left.

And in the eighth Ray Morehart had just beat out a hit when Larruping Lou trudged to the plate and projected a missile into the bleachers again.

Myles Thomas did passably well until the sixth, when a home run by your old friend Wally Schang [*who had been a Yankee catcher for five years, 1921–25, and a member of three pennant-winning clubs*] and subsequent disturbing activities prompted Manager Huggins to send for ever ready Wilcy Moore.

Babe Ruth, still suffering a strained knee, played eight innings, and his only hit was a wasted single in the sixth.

Marshall Hunt, New York *Daily News*

The Yankees went through 56 games without having a player thrown out by the umpire, but this distinction faded yesterday when Joe Dugan became so demonstrative in expressing disgust for a decision by Umpire Bill McGowan. Joe didn't have to travel far to the showers as his position is so close to the Yankee dugout.

New York *American*

Babe Ruth has often been asked, "Do you think you'll ever better your home run record of 1921?" His answer is, "If they pitch to me, I will."

Unfortunately, the Babe couldn't figure out a way of making pitchers pitch to him, and if all the bases on balls he has received in the last five years were laid end to end he could take a non-stop walk to China. There didn't seem to be any way of making pitchers pitch to Ruth. Then along came Lou.

Lou, that is Gehrig, solved Ruth's problem quite unintentionally by stepping out this year and pounding out more hits than any one else on the team for a batting average close to .400. He also exhibited an ability to knock the ball out of the park. And strange as it may seem, the harder Lou hits, the better chance Ruth has of breaking his record this year.

Lou Gehrig has made it inadvisable to walk Ruth. There is no percentage in walking Ruth, when Gehrig, the next man up, is hitting 50 points or so better than Ruth and is just as likely to place the ball in the stands.

With Gehrig in back of him as a warning to pitchers, Ruth has the best chance he has had in years of setting a new home run record. If he avoids injuries, and if nothing happens to Gehrig, he ought to give his own record a terrible tussle.

Rud Rennie, New York Herald-Tribune

Monday, June 20

[On June 19, in New York, the Yankees' scheduled game with St. Louis was postponed because of wet grounds.]

The most remarkable feature of the Yankee winning streak [*fifteen of the last nineteen games*] has been the frequent changes of line-up Miller Huggins has introduced [*because of injuries*] without any effect on his team. Besides using Durst and Paschal in the outfield, he has introduced an interchangeable infield, with Tony Lazzeri playing at all positions but first base.

Huggins has been minus his shortstop and third baseman at times and had to fill in at second base with a substitute, Ray Morehart. Yet no matter what the infield line-up, the Yanks have gone on winning. It is a striking tribute to their versatility.

James R. Harrison, The New York Times

AMERICAN LEAGUE STANDINGS

	W	L	PCT	GB		W	L	PCT	GB
New York	39	17	.693	—	Detroit	26	29	.473	12½
Chicago	34	26	.567	7	Cleveland	27	32	.458	13½
Philadelphia	31	25	.554	8	St. Louis	24	30	.444	14
Washington	28	26	.519	10	Boston	15	39	.278	23

Tuesday, June 21

[On June 20, in Boston, the Yankees' scheduled game was postponed because of rain.]

Some of the habituees of Yankee Stadium have fallen into the habit of taking fielders' gloves with them to the games, hoping thus to make sure of not missing the catch if Ruth, Gehrig, Lazzeri, or some other Yankee slugger gives the ball a ride into the seats near them.

"Sportsman," Boston *Globe*

Wednesday, June 22

[On June 21, in Boston, the Yankees won a doubleheader, 7–3 and 7–2. Winning pitchers, Herb Pennock (8–2) and Waite Hoyt (10–3). Yankee home run, Lou Gehrig (18).]

Boston—It was not only Signor Antonio Lazzeri day in the Province of the Prudes, but Yankee day as well yesterday. The Fascists of Boston gathered and presented the good Signor with a diamond ring, breaking precedent by omitting a travelling bag, a pair of blue suspenders, and a replica of Paulie Revere's alfalfa mangler [*the usual gifts when a baseball player was given a "day"*].

The good Signor responded with four hits in the doubleheader.

Forget not Master Waite Hoyt in the second encounter, who threw easily and effectively, nor Henri Louis Gehrig, who urged a baseball to take flight over the left field boards.

The Red Stockings suffered their embarrassment stoically. They have been rehearsing this act long enough to go through with it uncomplainingly.

Marshall Hunt, New York *Daily News*

Boston—The Babe, still regarded as one of Boston's own, limped through two games and disappointed fans who came to see his home run record grow. He hit the fence in left field for a double, his longest hit of the day. Late in the second game, Ben Paschal went to left field, and Babe gave his injured knee a rest. [*When evaluating Babe Ruth's record for 1927, one should keep in mind the games in which he played in an obviously weakened condition.*]

Bill Slocum, New York *American*

That the Red Sox were beaten in both games was nothing to their discredit. They were up against Herb Pennock and Waite Hoyt, who right now are the best pitchers in the League, and are, in a large measure, responsible for the New York club's present position in the race, although they have a bunch of sluggers and fine fielding players behind them that would make ordinary pitchers look good.

James C. O'Leary, Boston *Globe*

Thursday, June 23

[*On June 22, in Boston, the Yankees won a doubleheader, 7–4 and 3–2. Winning pitchers, Wilcy Moore (6–4) and Urban Shocker (8–4). Yankee home runs, Babe Ruth 2 (24).*]

Boston—When a pitcher holds the Yankees to three hits, two of them rank, raw flukes, and still loses, what's the use?

That is what Mr. Charles Ruffing of the local slab staff probably asked himself today at the end of another disastrous afternoon for the Red Sox. Although Charles pitched what the ancient Medes would have called a lullapolosa of a game, he lost 3 to 2. [*When, in later years, Ruffing was a star pitcher for the Yankees, he was always called Red.*]

The double header was a compromise. The Yanks won the first game, and the Red Sox lost the second. This arrangement satisfied everybody except the Red Sox.

George Herman Ruth cut two more notches in the handle of his trusty rifle during the earlier proceedings. The Babe biffed one over the garden wall in left center in the fifth inning, and on his next time at bat, in the seventh, he socked a venomous blow into an open space between the right field and center field bleachers.

No. 23 was long, but 24 was longer. The drive went between the two stands, rolled across a vacant lot, and brought up smartly against the wall of a garage where six men and two boys fell on it and engaged in a battle royal. [*At this time, before Tom Yawkey's 1934 reconstruction, Fenway Park had wooden bleachers in center field and in right field, and there was a space between them.*]

George is now slightly ahead of his 1921 record, despite a crippled leg that interferes with his stance. And now that Mr. Ruth's achievements have been properly recorded, let us bend a knee in the direction of Signor Tony Lazzeri, who heard himself being compared with Columbus, Marconi, and Mussolini at a dinner last night. [*sponsored by Boston's Italian-American Society*]. Tony didn't discover America, but, on the other hand, Columbus never went back of third [*Lazzeri was still playing shortstop*] for an overthrow and killed the tying run off at the plate in the ninth inning. That is what Tony did in the second scrimmage.

James R. Harrison, *The New York Times*

The amiable Mr. George Ruth rapped a couple of home runs onto the railroad tracks yesterday, and thereby, as they say, hangs a tale.

It seems that a kid named Billy Kennedy had come all the way from Manchester, N.H., the previous day to watch George do his stuff, and George had failed him. Now, Babe Ruth is no ordinary figure in the life of Billy Kennedy, because the Bambino helped to save his life.

A year ago an automobile whizzed around the corner and into the street where Billy was running out a base hit and beat him to the curb. He was so seriously hurt that the doctors despaired. Four operations were performed, and finally the head surgeon told Billy's father that if the little fellow's strength held out he might pull through.

"If only we can get him to want to live badly enough, he may do it," he said.

That made Billy's father think of Babe, for Babe was Billy's idol. So he sat down and wrote a letter to Mr. Babe Ruth, New York City, enclosing a check and asking for an autographed baseball, "From Babe to Bill."

The ball came right back. So did a telegram, which read: "Tell

Billy for me that he must get well and strong and come to Boston to see me play." It was signed Babe Ruth.

Billy was there long before the first game of Tuesday's double header to fulfill his part of the bargain. He wanted to see his hero hit a homer. His hero tried—and didn't.

"Come back tomorrow and I'll hit two to make up for it," Babe promised.

This time he didn't fail. He rarely does when something big depends upon him.

Quite a fellow, Babe Ruth!

Bill Corum, New York *Evening Journal*

Those who have studied Babe Ruth with an eye to discovering the secret of his hitting power are struck by the manner in which he handles his bat. He does not wave it, as other players do when addressing the pitcher. He flicks it with a switching motion, and in is hands it becomes as responsive as a baton in the hand of a symphony conductor. But that is not all, for there are a host of other mighty men in major league baseball. Ruth's secret does not lie in sheer muscle power.

What the student of batting might next note is the co-ordination which Ruth applies to his swing. His combined leg, shoulder, arms, and wrist motion is almost 100 per cent efficient as far as it concerns getting weight behind the swing. Ruth's bat on a missed strike usually fills a full circle and three-quarters of another. Ruth, when he misses such a mighty swipe, is not insensible to its effect on the crowd. "Oh-O-O-O-ooooo" groans the crowd, expelling breath that was held when Ruth started his swipe. Ruth shakes his shoulders with the motion of a Hercules knocking out fungoes with apples of the Hesperides, and he is twice as deliberate about getting back into the batter's box as any ordinary batsman would dare to be. [*A fungo is a ball hit to an outfielder during pregame practice. The last of Hercules' twelve labors was to obtain golden apples guarded by the three sisters of the Hesperides.*]

Ruth also has that famous "brown eye" which oculists say is unrivalled for sharpness of vision. Served as he is with fewer good pitches than any other hitter, he relies on sight that is several times as rapid as that of the average human in picking up the flying ball. [*Two of the handful of players who have batted .400 in a season, Rogers Hornsby and Ted Williams, were also noted for their extraordinary eyesight.*] There is also Ruth's judgment on batting matters, which is the result of long experience and a mental action so automatic that it is faster than the flight of actual thought. And lastly comes his co-ordination of eye, mind, and muscle, an action that is so synchronized as to be instant and accurate.

Austen Lake, Boston *Evening Transcript*

Friday, June 24

[*On June 23, in Boston, the Yankees won, 11–4. Winning pitcher, Dutch Ruether (6–1). Home runs, Lou Gehrig 3 (21).*]

Boston—On a balmy summer afternoon in Boston, Henry Louis Gehrig, son of Columbia, scaled the dizzy heights by hitting three home runs in one game, the second Yankee to turn the trick this season.

He is now only three homers behind Ruth, is Mr. Gehrig, and the race between them is furnishing the greatest slugging competition in the history of baseball. Gehrig is travelling fast enough to give point to the words of Ruth the other night [at a dinner honoring Tony Lazzeri], when he said that Columbia Lou is the only man that would beat the Babe's record.

That's the Babe's prediction, and he's sticking to it, and the way Gehrig smacked them today it looked as if G. Herman is the seventh son of a seventh son. One drive went over the fence in left center. The second was a mammoth liner that landed in the right center field seats. The third was the gem, high, mammoth, and powerfully stroked, arching its way a quarter of the way up the stand in right center.

Take them blow by blow, and they were three homers as handsome and as far as any man ever hit in one game. Nearly every one was as far flung as Ruth's second homer in the first game Wednesday.

[*There were numerous "firsts" in this game. When Gehrig hit his initial home run, it was the first ever for him in Fenway Park. His third marked the first time that anyone had hit three home runs in one game in this ballpark and also the first time that anyone had ever hit two balls in one game into the distant right-field bleachers. Naturally, this was the first time that Gehrig had chalked up three homers in a game. (Twice in the future, on May 4, 1929, and on May 22, 1930, he would duplicate the feat, and then, as already noted on June 3, 1932, he would become the first American Leaguer to hit four home runs in one game.) Finally, for the first time in modern major league history two players from one team (Lazzeri and Gehrig) had three–home-run games in the same season. Incidentally, although Ruth had hit three home runs in the fourth game of the 1926 World Series, and would repeat the feat in the fourth game of the 1928 World Series, only once in his entire career, on May 21, 1930, did he perform this exploit in a regular-season game. Some of Gehrig's greatest accomplishments, unfortunately for him, did not have the proper timing. Thus, when he hit three home runs on May 22, 1930, his action was completely overshadowed by what Babe Ruth had done on the preceding day. And a couple of hours before he hit four home runs in one game, sports departments received the startling news that after thirty years John J. McGraw had resigned as manager of the New York Giants.]*

James R. Harrison, *The New York Times*

Saturday, June 25

[On June 24, the Yankees were not scheduled to play.]

Lou Gehrig isn't another Babe Ruth because there will never be another Ruth. No one else ever has hit a baseball as far as the Bambino hits it when he truly leans on it, and doubtless no one else ever will, nor has any other player ever had quite the color of the Babe. Yet Gehrig is the nearest approach to Ruth in modern baseball.

Lou is a college man, but doesn't look it—which is no knock at either Lou or college men. There simply isn't anything "collegiate" about him. He's burly, broad shouldered, deep chested, long waisted, stout legged, and muscled like a wrestler. He walks with a rolling gait, chews tobacco, reads the funny papers, and plays pinochle. He would rather play ball than eat, though he has a tremendous appetite, and thinks he's lucky to be permitted to play every day. His home-run hitting has added to the zest which the game has for him, but hasn't added a sixteenth of an inch to the size of his cranium.

[*In addition to Miller Huggins, there were six other former college men on the Yankees: Joe Dugan (Holy Cross), Benny Bengough (Niagara University), Earle Combs (Eastern Kentucky State Teachers College), Mike Gazella (Lafayette, where he was a star halfback), Ray Morehart (Stephen Austin College, Texas), and Myles Thomas (Penn State).*]

He's a good first baseman, too. No Hal Chase maybe, but, just as there never will be another Babe Ruth, so there never will be another Chase. [*Hal Chase has always been used as the standard against which to measure fielding first basemen. His absence from baseball's Hall of Fame stems from several unsavory episodes in his career.*] Gehrig's improvement as a first baseman may have been slow, but it has been steady.

"I never have tried to force Gehrig's development as a first baseman," said Miller Huggins. "Almost all he knows he has learned in the best way—by experience. He's a pretty darn good first baseman right now, and as he gets better all the time I guess I won't have to worry about him for a while."

Frank Graham, New York *Sun*

Lynn, Mass., June 24—The long line of miracles evolved by electricity was added to tonight when more than 5,000 persons watched a full nine inning baseball game played under the rays of flood lights on the athletic field of the General Electric Company. [*An experiment arranged by General Electric engineers, this was the first game of professional baseball ever played at night.*]

In the grandstand were the entire Washington team, the Red Sox, and college instructors, as well as lighting experts from various parts of the United States. They were unanimous in the opinion that the game was played equally as good as many produced on big league diamonds under the sun rays.

Players on the Lynn and Salem clubs of the New England League had no difficulty in following the ball on pitches, hits, or throws, the ball being plainly seen as it passed through the rays of 26,300,000 beam candle power, supplied from 72 projectors mounted on 50-foot poles.

There were the usual daylight scenes—the candy and pop

butchers and scorecard vendors, and the usual cries of encouragement of brilliant plays.

Representatives of big league clubs declared they could follow the course of the ball at all times as plainly as in day time. They predicted that before long night ball would be added to the card of the American and National League.

[*During the next few years, night baseball would spread throughout the minor leagues, some of which could not have survived the Depression without it. The first major league night game would be played in Cincinnati on May 24, 1935. Yankee Stadium would have its first night game on May 28, 1946, after Ed Barrow had retired.*]

New York *World*

The Pennsylvania Supreme Court today banned professional Sunday baseball in Philadelphia.

The State's highest tribunal fully sustained the Dauphin County Court, which previously had declared Sunday baseball "a worldly employment," in violation of the Sunday law of 1794.

A game between the Athletics and the Chicago White Sox, played Sunday, August 22, of last year, was the basis of the legal proceedings.

The Supreme Court, in the majority opinion [*by a vote of seven to two*], says, "We cannot imagine anything more worldly or unreligious than professional baseball as it is played today."

[*As noted earlier, Sunday baseball would become legal in Pennsylvania in 1934.*]

Philadelphia *Evening Bulletin*

Sunday, June 26

[*On June 24, in New York, the Yankees lost a doubleheader to Philadelphia, 7–6 and 4–2. Losing pitchers, Herb Pennock (8–3) and Waite Hoyt (10–4)*].

Connie's White Elephants, for the first time this year, are flapping their ears joyfully and curling their trunks with pride again. [*The insignia upon the Philadelphia Athletics uniform was that of a white elephant.*] Yesterday the Mackmen gained two hard-fought victories, their first wins in the Metropolis this season and sweeter than any triumphs they have tasted since the schedule turned the teams loose.

They conquered Pennock and Hoyt, paladin pitchers of the run-away pace-makers, and they smashed the Yankee winning streak of nine straight.

In each game the closing passages spotlighted the royal rescuer of 1926, Joe Pate. The plump southpaw knuckle-baller from Fort Worth made kittens out of Murderers' Row as the mighty fence-breakers sweated and strained to redeem their lost cause by last-ditch rallies.

Grove in the first game and Walberg in the second achieved manful moundsmanship through the heat of the battle, even though Pate had to hurry to the hill at the finish of each contest.

The last dramatic moment staged a Pate knuckleball gliding across home plate for the third strike of the last out. The tying run stood on third and the winning run teetered on first. The batter was no less than Buster Gehrig. Each pitch by Pate had the high-tension sobs of 60,000 spectators for accompaniment. When it stood three and two, Pate flipped a neat knuckler over the outside corner of the plate.

A vast groan welled up to the brim of the three-tier bowl as Umpire Clarence Rowland's right hand was elevated on high. The multitude yammered, but Gehrig and his brother Yanks made no bleat.

[*In 1926 Joe Pate broke into the major leagues at the age of thirty-four, and his rookie season was extraordinary. He had 9 victories without a loss, to go with an earned run average of 2.71, and all of his wins came in relief. But he was a one-season phenomenon. Never again would he be the winning pitcher in a major league game, and after 1927 he faded forever from big league baseball.*]

Bill Brandt, Philadelphia *Public Ledger*

Babe Ruth's bad leg, which he hurt again in Friday's exhibition game at Springfield, gave way in the ninth inning of the first game yesterday, and Durst ran for him. The Babe played one inning of the second affair and then retired. He could hardly walk. A wrenched knee is the official diagnosis.

James R. Harrison, *The New York Times*

Washington (AP)—Although fame is fleeting, Babe Ruth seems determined that it will not flit away from him while he sits idly by.

In a tax appeal filed at the Treasury Department, the baseball celebrity has disclosed that during 1924 he "expended the sum of $9,000 for the purpose of establishing and maintaining good-will to the extent of entertaining sports writers, press agents, and others similarly situated in order to constantly keep himself before the public."

This item, more than most baseball players receive in a year, Ruth wants deducted from the deficiency assessment placed on his earnings of 1924, which were given as $66,215.34. [*His salary was then $52,000.*]

The New York Times

Monday, June 27

[*On June 26, in New York, the Yankees split a doubleheader with Phila-delphia, 2–4 and 7–3. Losing pitcher, Myles Thomas (6–2); winning pitcher, Wilcy Moore (7–4). Home run, Lou Gehrig (22).*]

Mr. Connie Mack's Athletics and Mons. Miller Huggins's Yankees neatly divided the best attended double header of the year. The A's took the first battle before 61,000 onlookers, and the Yanks swept up the second. Master Henri Louis Gehrig's twenty-second homer of the year was part of the show. It was a sadly misplaced wallop. If it had come in the ninth inning of the first game the Yanks might have cleaned up both battles. As it happened, it was just excess baggage.

It was a day for veteran experience, the craft of age, the steadiness of the old timer. Jack Quinn, a quarter of a century in the pitching business and still going strong, held the Yanks to six hits in the first game. [*In four trips to the plate in this game, Gehrig struck out three times and bounced out weakly to the second baseman.*] Wilcy Moore, the 29-year-old minute man of the Yanks, started his second game of the year in the closing encounter and broke the [*three-game*] losing streak of the Hugmen by holding the Mack clouters to five hits. [*This was Moore's first complete game as a*

major leaguer.] The old fellows were smooth and brilliant performers. If Jack and Wilcy had been only hooked up together,
what a battle!

The 61,000 roared and laughed and swore at times, with all
their regular fervor, but the lad who provokes the biggest cheers
wasn't there. Babe Ruth couldn't play. His bad right knee will
keep him off the field for about four days. Gehrig, meanwhile,
improved his time with his second game homer. He is only two
behind the Babe now.

Old Mr. Quinn had far too many tricks in his flapping sleeves
for young Mr. Thomas in the first game. [*At this time, pitchers
would tear the sleeves of their long undershirts, causing them to flap in
the air and distract the batters. "Dazzy" Vance, of the Dodgers, was noted
for doing this, and, later, "Dizzy" Dean would not be a stranger to this
practice. Nowadays, pitchers are prohibited from having their sleeves torn
or of unequal lengths.*] The 44-year-old marvel was hit safely only
six times, and only two of these counted—a three-bagger by
Earle Combs and another three-bagger by Jumping Joe Dugan.

Monitor, New York *World*

AMERICAN LEAGUE STANDINGS

	W	L	PCT	GB		W	L	PCT	GB
New York	45	20	.692	—	Detroit	29	30	.492	13
Philadelphia	37	28	.569	8	Cleveland	29	34	.460	15
Chicago	36	30	.545	9½	St. Louis	27	33	.450	15½
Washington	33	29	.532	10½	Boston	15	47	.242	28½

Tuesday, June 28

[*On June 27, in New York, the Yankees won, 6–2. Winning pitcher,
Dutch Ruether (7–1). Home runs, Earle Combs (1), Tony Lazzeri (9).*]

Walter Ruether doesn't start as many games as some of the other
New York pitchers, nor does he finish so many, but when
"Dutch" pitches, the Yanks seldom lose. Yesterday his fast left-
handed curves proved too much for Connie Mack's host of left-
handed batsmen.

"Dutch" came close to pitching his fourth shutout of the season, but got into a little trouble in the ninth. Two infield hits and two passes forced in a run and left the bases full with one out. The Yanks led by five runs, but Miller Huggins got fidgety and called in Herb Pennock, who seldom does rescue work. Herb squashed Eddie Collins, appearing as pinch-hitter, and Joe Boley, and the Yankee lead again sprouted to nine full games.

Howard Ehmke, a Yankee jinx several years ago, also turned in a pretty neat pitching job, but Ehmke couldn't stop pitching the "home run" ball. Earle Combs slapped him for one in the first, the Kentuckian's first of the season, and Tony Lazzeri hit his ninth with Meusel on board in the fourth.

The Big Bambino still is out of commission.

Fred Lieb, *New York Post*

Bill Brandt, called "Doc" out of consideration for his early try at horse doctoring, is one of the veteran writers travelling with the Philadelphia Athletics. Bill, like most veterinarians, has horse sense, and he has developed plenty of baseball savvy. I was interested in what he had to say yesterday.

"It is against all the legends of baseball," said he hoarsely, "for a team to hit over a stretch the way the Yankees have been slugging. If their hitting falls off, the Yankees are licked.

"That infield will cost them the pennant if Ruth, Gehrig, and Lazzeri go into any considerable slump. Gehrig is not a high-class defensive player, Dugan is old enough to play on the Athletics, and Gazella is below championship team caliber. Morehart, Lazzeri, and Koenig are good defensive man, but first base and third base are in and out. If the Yanks lose their punch and have to depend on tight defensive play, that infield will crack."

Inasmuch as the Doc is travelling with the Athletics, it might be suspected that the wish is father to the thought.

[*The writer of this piece is the same person who later wrote the widely read Broadway column in the New York* Daily News *and was host of the enormously popular television variety show bearing his name. A twelve-letter athlete at Port Chester, New York, High School, he began a newspaper career in 1918 with the Port Chester* Daily Item. *After serving briefly for the Hartford* Post, *the New York* Evening Mail, *the Philadelphia* Bulletin, *the New York* World, *the New York* Morning Telegraph, *and the Philadelphia* Public Ledger, *in 1927, at the age of twenty-five, he became sports editor of the New York* Graphic. *He remained at this post until 1929, when his colleague Walter Winchell moved to the* Daily Mirror *and Sullivan took over Winchell's position as the* Graphic's *Broadway columnist. In 1932, Sullivan began his Broadway column with the* Daily News, *which he retained until his death in 1974.*]

Ed Sullivan, New York *Graphic*

Henry Louis Gehrig today is the outstanding player in baseball. There is nothing to be said about his doings that has not been said before. There is room, however, for an explanation of his power.

Power is written in his every feature, while his massive muscles bulge and quiver beneath the cloth that covers them. There is not an ounce of superfluous flesh on his huge frame. Nor is there any behind his ears. He is alert from the moment he steps on the field. Many players insist that he is not smart, yet he has not made a single error of omission this year. It is assumed that the adverse criticism is the result of sour grapes.

Gehrig's hitting will undoubtedly raise him to heights never before attained by a player. His constant improvement is quite evident. Pitchers are beginning to dodge the issue, disguising their intentions by throwing wide ones.

His powerful arms which extend from his more powerful shoulders enable Gehrig to hit to all fields without extra effort. He is known as a stiff-arm swinger, in contrast to Ruth, who is the pivoting, free-swinging type. Ruth's power comes from the tremendous swing and the fact that his timing is almost perfect. Gehrig does not swing his bat much. His arms and shoulders are so strong that when the bat meets the ball it has about the same momentum as Ruth's.

Baseball occupies most of Gehrig's thoughts—baseball, his mother, and fishing. He takes his car after the games on hot summer evenings, calls for his mother, and then spins down to Rockaway for a session at the hook and line. After a satisfactory catch he whisks back into town by 11:30 P.M.

There are no girls in his life as yet. The letters he receives at the hotels on the road are all from his mother. His light blond curls, laughing eyes, and dimples, six inches deep, make him one of the Yankees' many handsome young men, but thus far he has failed to show any interest in anything but his batting, his mother, and fishing.

With his perfect health, of which he is proud, he should be guarding first base for the Yankees in 1937. No part of his huge frame has given any sign of breaking down, and he seems to be in for a long siege of fame and health, and plenty of each.

By the time another four or eight years have passed Lou should be a rich man, especially with the money he saves by not wearing vests or overcoats. Thus another tale of the poor city boy who worked his way through school and into subsequent riches will have been woven. It will be a story of perseverance, health, and strength, and clean living.

[*On June 2, 1941, seventeen days before his thirty-eighth birthday, Lou Gehrig would die, a victim of amyotrophic lateral sclerosis, a rare form of polio that is now popularly called Lou Gehrig's disease.*]

Arthur Mann, New York *Evening World*

In an income tax appeal, Babe Ruth discloses the interesting information that during the season of 1924 he spent $9,000 on "entertaining sports writers in order to constantly keep himself before the public." Ruth led the league in batting in 1924. He played in 153 games and hammered the ball for 200 hits, including 46 home runs. Yet the Bambino insists that he spent $9,000 to keep himself in the limelight.

Lou Gehrig, who is crowding Ruth for home run honors, isn't paying for publicity.

Joe Vila, New York *Sun*

Wednesday, June 29

[*On June 28, in New York, the Yankees defeated Philadelphia, 9–8. Winning pitcher, Urban Shocker (9–4). Yankee home run, Lou Gehrig (23).*]

The Athletics put on the most spectacular ninth inning rally seen in New York this season, but it wasn't quite enough to snatch the fat out of the fire. Starting the ninth with a score of 9 to 0 against them, they chased three of Huggins's pitching stars, Shocker, Moore, and Pennock, and made the final score 9 to 8 before Morehart tossed out Gordon Cochrane for the last out.

The game again proved the uncertainty of baseball. Urban Shocker waved his arm so dexterously that the Athletics got only four singles and no runs in the first eight rounds. It looked like a soft shutout.

However, Bill Lamar, Al Simmons, Cochrane, Jimmy Dykes, and Jimmie Foxx clouted Shocker for ringing hits in the ninth, all as clean as a whistle. Wilcy Moore was called in, and Joe Boley and Ty Cobb rapped him for two clean hits. Five runs and still none out.

Pennock was summoned from the bullpen. Max Bishop's sacrifice fly, scoring the sixth run, was the first out. A walk to Cy Perkins, a few gift steals ["*gifts*" *because neither pitcher nor catcher paid any attention to the base runners*], and a wild throw by Morehart put over two more runs, with Lamar on first as the tying run and only one out.

With the dangerous Simmons, a hard right-handed hitter, up, Huggins declined to gamble on Pennock [*because he was left-handed.*] He called in Myles Thomas, and the Penn Stater made quick work of the Athletic rally and got two of the toughest men on the A's, Simmons and Cochrane. [*This ninth-inning outburst foreshadowed baseball's most famous late-inning rally. In the fourth game of the 1929 World Series, on October 12 in Philadelphia's Shibe Park, the Athletics began their half of the seventh inning behind, 8–0. They thereupon scored 10 runs in that inning to win the game, 10–8.*]

While George Herman Ruth nursed his injured knee another day, biffing Lou Gehrig got within one of George's home-run total. In the third inning Heinrich Lou knocked No. 23 out to the right field sun worshippers. With the score 9 to 0 that homer looked like just an incident of an easy victory, but before the day was over that homer proved quite a factor.

Lou also knocked in a run in the ninth with a single, while Simmons robbed him of a triple with the best running backhanded catch seen at the Stadium this season.

Earle Combs also did considerable execution with his bat, thumping out a double and three singles. Bob Meusel matched the double and two of the singles.

Fred Lieb, *New York Post*

The New York Yankees of today are the greatest ball club of all time, mainly because of their terrific power.

This observation was made by Wilbert Robinson, manager-president of the Brooklyn Dodgers, today on his sixty-third birthday.

"Fifty-five years in baseball," jubiliated Robbie. "I have seen some great ball clubs, but I have no illusions about the good old days. We thought the Orioles of 1896 were a great gang. Then came the old Cubs [*of 1906–08*], then the Athletics [*of 1910–14*], and now we have the smashing Yankees, the greatest club ever got together."

"Aren't you being a traitor to the Orioles to make that statement?" we asked.

"Yes, the gang will want to hang me when they hear about this," Robbie chuckled. "The Orioles had a lot of smart players, but we did not class with the Yankees in smashing power, and our pitchers never would have stopped Hug's crew.

"The Yankees have qualities apart from their murderous habits. They have speed, and they are wiser than most folks give them credit for being. There isn't a soft spot in their batting order. Pass Ruth, and you've got Gehrig, and then you run afoul of Lazzeri, who is going to be one of the best all-round infielders baseball has seen."

[*In the mid-1890's, Robinson caught for the Orioles, the first baseball team to be called "the greatest of all time." Robinson's teammates included Hughie Jennings at shortstop, Willie Keeler in right field, and, later, John McGraw at third base. As he had expected, Robinson's observations were strongly challenged by some, including McGraw.*]

Dan Daniel, New York *Telegram*

Not since Eddie Collins sneaked away from the campus of Columbia University and took a local to Philly, there to play for Connie Mack under the disguise of "Sullivan," has a player from that college distinguished himself so notably as Lou Gehrig. The manifold successes of Collins never received intimate recognition from New Yorkers because his second-basing has always been dedicated to Philadelphia, Chicago, and then again Philadelphia. Gehrig, however, has stuck right in New York.

[*Collins, often called baseball's best second baseman, took over that position for the Athletics in 1908 immediately after graduating from Co-*

lumbia. In 1908, he used his correct name, but in the six games in which he appeared for the A's in the summer of 1906, he was known as "Sullivan," because in the eyes of some people baseball wasn't a reputable vocation, especially for a college man. In 1908, the game apparently gained a measure of respectability, for in that year, Sammy Strang of the Giants, a former student at the University of Michigan, decided that it was safe to play as "Strang" rather than "Nicklin," his baseball name for the preceding eleven years. Columbia, incidentally, is the only college or university with two former students in baseball's Hall of Fame.]

Larrupin' Lou is a typical home boy. After a game you will find him with a German police dog in some park, or you may find him home with his mother and father, lounging around the living room. I don't believe he has ever been to a night club. His tastes are those of a youngster of the nineteenth century rather than the bustling, noisy twentieth century.

Opposing pitchers have become so scared of this dynamiter that they chant to Huggins: "You can bring Babe and Tony too, but for Gawd's sake, Hug, don't bring Lou, Lou!" Huggins, however, never had an ear for music.

Ed Sullivan, New York *Graphic*

"I was hoping I would have a very good year at second base," said Tony Lazzeri, rather regretfully, one thought. Tony hasn't been at second base for a couple of weeks now.

Well, if it is any consolation to Tony, he is having a very good year all over the infield. He hasn't played first base yet, but he can. He has played second base, third base, and shortstop. He is playing shortstop now [*because of an injury to Koenig*] and playing it so well that opposing managers and players are talking about him. That is the big test of a ballplayer's worth. If the other players talk about him he's there.

"When I was a kid," continued Tony, "I played everywhere, as any kiddoes. Finally I settled down in the infield, but not in any one position. When I broke into professional baseball in Salt Lake City, I played around the infield the first year, spending most of my time at first base. Then I moved to shortstop in 1925. Last year Hug put me at second base and I've got so I'd rather play there than anywhere else. Oh, I don't mind playing shortstop, or anywhere, but I'd got to thinking of myself as a second baseman and I was after a record or two in that position."

The young Italian, who set a record for rookies by making 18 home runs in 1926, has 9 so far this year. Almost every time he hits the ball he hits it with a power one scarcely would suspect is concealed in his slender frame. This power is derived largely from his wrists, which are as two thin steel bars.

"When I was with Salt Lake," he said, "I admired the batting style of Duffy Lewis, who managed the club. Duff was a wrist hitter, and I tried to copy his style. I couldn't make it, but I developed the commoner style of wrist hitting." [*Lewis was a major leaguer for eleven years (1910–21), in six of which (1910–15) he was part of one of baseball's most famous outfields, playing with the Red Sox, along with Harry Hooper and Tris Speaker.*]

Frank Graham, New York *Sun*

Thursday, June 30

[*On June 29, in New York, the Yankees defeated Boston, 8–2. Winning pitcher, George Pipgras (1–0). Yankee home run, Lou Gehrig (24).*]

Clouting Lou Gehrig caught up with Babe Ruth by hitting his twenty-fourth home run of the season off Harold Wiltse, a young southpaw, yesterday. Ruth played but got no home runs. The big fellow, however, smashed out four solid hits which helped the Yankees to crush the lowly visitors from Boston.

Gehrig's home run came in the fifth inning with the score tied and the bases unoccupied. Wiltse broke over a curve ball that Gehrig swung at. There didn't appear to be any great effort behind the swing, but the ball sailed high and far into right field and landed well up in the bleachers. As soon as the ball left the bat, the crowd started cheering and never stopped until the first baseman disappeared under the dugout. Ruth, who was sitting on a box resting up against the right field stand, appeared to enjoy the ovation that Gehrig received. [*Ruth was sitting there because he had just grounded out, and instead of turning around and running back to the Yankee dugout behind third base, he saved energy by continuing on to right field and sitting in foul territory. Today, he would not be permitted to do this.*]

The Babe missed a home run by a few inches and also de-

stroyed a perfectly good first baseman's glove. With Morehart on
first in the third, Ruth drove a ball that hit the railing near the
top close to the left field foul line. If it had bounced a few inches
higher, the Babe would have had his twenty-fifth home run. As
it was, he got a double and Morehart scored.

The hardest drive of the game came from Ruth's bat in the
fifth inning just before Gehrig hit his home run. The Babe
smashed a terrific drive down the first base line that Phil Todt
attempted to catch back of the bag. The ball almost tore Todt's
hands off. The first baseman, however, recovered the ball and
threw out Babe, Wiltse taking the throw. There was so much
force behind Ruth's drive that it ripped open Todt's glove and
he had to send for a new one.

George Pipgras's pitching must not be overlooked. It was the
best that he has turned in since he became a member of the club
several years ago. He held the Sox to three hits and runless in all
but the second inning.

[*Although Pipgras had appeared briefly with the Yankees in 1923 and
1924, winning one game and losing four, 1927 was really his rookie
year. In 1926, he had pitched for St. Paul in the American Association,
winning twenty-two, losing nineteen, and leading the league in strikeouts. Of Danish descent—he was sometimes called "the great Dane"—he
grew up on a farm in Minnesota. Pipgras was big and strong, and his
fastball was probably the fastest of any of the Yankee pitchers.*]

                                      Monitor, New York *World*

Yankee Stadium, outside the dugout. Two o'clock. Hot sunlight.
The boys are batting grounders to the infield and fungoes to the
outfield. The stands are gradually filling with straw hats and
shirt-sleeves.

Miller Huggins is back of the batting net talking with the Red
Sox manager. Pretty soon he sways over this direction like a ban-
tam rooster.

"The boys look pretty cheerful. How do you keep 'em from
getting over-confident?" we began.

"I don't," he answers, shaking hands hospitably. [*The writer did
not cover the Yankee games and was an infrequent visitor to the dugout.*]
He perches on the edge of one of the boxes and would look like
a school boy except for that face of a pirate chieftain. "A little

over-confidence might be good for 'em. Relieves the strain this time of the season. But I don't think they have it."

He chews thoughtfully on whatever is in his mouth, and we mention the tough luck the Giants are getting.

"Luck? I never put any stock in it. The winning team always gets the breaks and the losing team the bad luck! You always hear that howl. My theory is the breaks even up in the long run. A smart team will make its own breaks."

The swarm of Yankees stroll in off the field looking hot while the Red Sox go out. They sprawl over the bench wiping their faces. Babe Ruth slumps forward with wrinkled brow, looking mournful and detached as usual. But he doesn't miss a word dropped in the dugout. When he speaks his cavernous hollow bass sounds like the growl of a grizzly. He easily dominates the dugout even when silent. His sudden answers are usually funny and nearly always unprintable.

Lou Gehrig moves about quietly, not entering in much of the banter. His position on a level with the home-run king seems to make him serious.

Twice the Babe gets up to swallow a couple of barrels of water from the fountain. At the corner of the dugout a big Italian gentleman with whiskers is telling Lazzeri how he compares with Mussolini, and Tony is having trouble concealing his pleasure at the hearty slaps on his back. Earle Combs is trying to stir up some conversation. It starts with collisions—the one in the World Series last year. [*In the fourth inning of the fourth game, in St. Louis, Cardinal outfielders Taylor Douthit and Chick Hafey collided while going after a fly ball hit by Joe Dugan, which became a run-scoring double.*] The Babe waits his turn and bellows, "Collisions— you never saw one if you didn't see Speaker and a guy come together when I was playing with Boston. They carted both them babies to the hospital." [*This collision occurred in 1915 and involved Tris Speaker and Harry Hooper, neither of whom spent much time in the hospital.*]

Benny Bengough remarks that in all collisions the big fellow gets the worst of it. Everybody agrees, including Ruth. He tells of running into a little shortstop and nearly getting killed. "His head sunk right in here," and he places a paw over his famous stomach. "I like to died. Never hurt him much."

Combs, with his pleasant, mischievous smile, keeps trying to stir up something, until finally the Babe soars at him, "Earle, you're getting to be a blankety-blank barber." [*The term "barber" was then regularly applied to talkative players, especially catchers.*] This quieted things for a while. In the lull Styborsky, a sub pitcher [*who never appeared in a regular season game*], says, "Babe, get a homer today, I need a new straw hat." (The crowd always gets excited and throws their hats on the diamond.) The Babe looks out at the stands and answers, "You won't get anything but derbies from this crowd."

"Well, get a homer for the Governor of Texas, then—he's here!" The Babe thinks he's being kidded and answers, "To hell with the Governor of Texas!" He would have said the same if it was George Washington.

"Now, don't call 'em too fast today, will you?" Babe calls out to the umpires, who are just arriving. Even the umpires smile and take the Babe's banter when he bellows at 'em. As they started out to take their positions, I asked Huggins if there's any jealousy between Ruth and Gehrig.

"Not a bit," answered Huggins smiling. "Ruth doesn't mind a bit. The Babe and I got over that sort of thing a long time ago. It's all new to Gehrig, and he gets a kick out of it. But after a while it won't mean anything at all—that hero-worship stuff. Just playing ball games and doing your best—that's all that counts, and that's what the Babe thinks."

Burris Jenkins, Jr., New York *Evening World*

Friday, July 1

[*On June 30, in New York, the Yankees defeated Boston, 13–6. Winning pitcher, Wilcy Moore (8–4). Yankee home runs, Lou Gehrig (25), Babe Ruth (25).*]

There was a ball game at the Yankee Stadium yesterday, but nobody paid the slightest attention to it. Everybody knew that the Yankees would beat the Red Sox. It wasn't the ball game that drew the customers to the ball yard; they had come to see the great home run derby between G. Herman Ruth and H. Louis Gehrig.

Mr. Gehrig, the favorite son of Morningside Heights, smacked his twenty-fifth home run of the season in the first inning and chuckled sardonically as he circled the bases. "Laugh that one off, you big stiff," he said to G. Herman Ruth. [*This remark is highly apocryphal.*]

Mr. Ruth, now the ex-home run king of the American League, looked slightly depressed as he jogged in ahead of Columbia Lou. His brow was furrowed, and his shoulders drooped. It was the first time in many years that anyone had had the effrontery to challenge the monarch's title to his throne. [*In 1922, when he was sidelined for six weeks because of a suspension, and in the disastrous year of 1925, when he appeared in only ninety-eight games, Ruth lost out in the battle for the home-run leadership. Otherwise, however, not since 1920 had anyone led Ruth in home runs after the first week of the season.*]

In the fourth Mr. Ruth decided to rally around the flag and get back his laurels. Mr. Slim Harriss, the Boston pitcher, was thoroughly impartial in the Yankees' internal quarrel. Having served Gehrig an easy one with the count two and nothing, Slim did the same with Ruth. Babe took a toe hold and swung; there was a loud, ringing crash, and the ball leaped through the murky air and made a non-stop hop into the right field bleachers.

"Take your change out of that one and see how you like it," remarked Mr. Ruth as he touched off at the plate and found Mr. Gehrig waiting as a reception committee of one.

You can't beat the Babe when it comes to rising to the occasion.

Of the two homers, Ruth's was the longer and higher, but Gehrig's was by far the sharper and harder hit.

Oh, yes, the ball game. It was a very nice game. The Yanks won their fifth straight and the Red Sox lost their twelfth straight. The Sox are due to win one any week now.

James R. Harrison, *The New York Times*

"If Lou Gehrig outhits Babe Ruth this season and leads Ruth in home runs, will he take Ruth's position as the outstanding figure in baseball?" The question is asked by a reader of this column, and recently I heard a number of persons discussing the subject.

It simmers down to this: Can Lou Gehrig develop into another Babe Ruth?

One must answer with that rather evasive "Yes and no."

As Gehrig passed his twenty-fourth birthday a few days ago [*on June 19*] and Ruth is 33, it is only a question of time when "Biffing Lou" of Columbia passes the illustrious Babe of Baltimore. If he doesn't catch Ruth this year he'll surely do it next year or the year after that. Even before Gehrig went on his present home run spree, ballplayers recognized Gehrig as Ruth's logical successor.

Whether Gehrig can become the drawing card that Ruth is and have the same hold on American youth, and for that matter on all America, is an open question. Only time can answer it.

Baseball always will have its idol, whether it is a Mathewson, a Cobb, or a Ruth. As a college man, Gehrig might develop into an even greater sports character for American youth to pattern after than Ruth, a product of a Baltimore reform school.

However, Lou doesn't have the Babe's color. He is a good-natured type, gets into an occasional argument with an umpire, but otherwise he is a peaceably inclined citizen. He believes in going to bed early, his habits are of the very best, and his only dissipation is to go fishing. His conduct card will show nothing but good marks, whereas the Babe's cards frequently have been marked pretty low.

That is the paradoxical thing about hero worship. They loved, admired, and respected Matty because of his virtues and sterling character, and Cobb for his aggressiveness, dynamic energy, and indefatigable spirit.

But with Ruth they often loved him for his naughtiness. They were amused at the Babe's scrapes and antics, his troubles with umpires and fans, with Ban Johnson, with Judge Landis, with Miller Huggins. He would go off the reservation and then try to regain popular favor by knocking a few more over fences which never had been cleared. And the regaining never was difficult.

Of course I do not recommend the Ruth procedure for Lou Gehrig. Color sometimes is obtained at a sacrifice of the best in a man. Earle Combs never has been put out of a game; no one ever heard him swear; and his good nature and kindly philosophy no doubt will prove an asset in the journey through life. Earle never will get any color by threatening an umpire or drawing a suspension for insubordination or breaking training rules.

So it is with Gehrig. He is more aggressive than Combs, and his language frequently is more vigorous. He plays the game as hard as Ruth, loves to play it just as much, yet Lou will get all of his publicity on the ball field.

Then Ruth was the first great home run monarch. When Ruth hit 54 and 59 in 1920 and 1921, he was the Lindbergh of the home run brigade. Anyone who now gets over 50 home runs will only be following the trail of the great home run pioneer. [*When Ruth hit fifty-four home runs in 1920, he broke his own record of twenty-nine, established in 1919. Prior to Ruth, the only major leaguer ever to hit more than nineteen home runs in a season was Gavvy Cravath, of the Phillies, with twenty-four in 1915.*]

　　　　　　　　　　　　　　　　Fred Lieb, *New York Post*

Not only is Lou Gehrig a model ballplayer, but off the field he is an estimable citizen. It is good to find a star athlete with all the virtues generally attributed to heroes of the field of sports but seldom found in them.

　　　　　　　　　　　　Jack Conway, New York *Daily Mirror*

Saturday, July 2

[*On July 1, in New York, the Yankees defeated Boston, 7–4. Winning pitcher, Herb Pennock (9–3). Yankee home runs, Lou Gehrig (26), Earle Combs (2).*]

Just one Colossus straddles the baseball world this pleasant morning, Mr. Henri Louis Gehrig, named for two kings and a king in his own right. [*The Colossus of Rhodes was one of the seven ancient Wonders of the World. According to unsubstantiated legend, the 105-foot statue straddled the harbor so that arriving and departing ships passed between its legs.*] He celebrated the close of the fiscal year by dethroning George Herman Ruth, who has been emperor, king, potentate, sultan, tsar, and absolute ruler for the last seven years, by lifting a ball outside the confines of the Yankee Stadium.

Few paid attention to the game. The crowd watched the duel between Ruth and Gehrig, and other happenings meant nothing. It may be mentioned that the Yankees won their sixth straight game while inflicting a tenth straight defeat on the Red Sox.

Gehrig is king, but on a teetering throne. The Babe is hitting. He slapped two singles, hard-hit balls which just didn't rise to the height needed to sail into the stands. They were ground-gouging vicious drives. Gehrig was hitting, too. He drove a double which would have been another four-bagger with ten more feet of carry.

The fact that Herb Pennock was hit by a liner and forced out of the game and that Bob Shawkey finished in creditable style made little impression on the crowd. The folks were there to see the battle of bats between Ruth and Gehrig.

Ruth singled in the first and came home on Gehrig's homer. He died on a drive to the box in the second, and Gehrig fanned to open the third. Ruth singled in the fourth, and Gehrig was out on a grounder to the first baseman in the fifth. Both were trying too hard.

They came along together in the seventh. Ruth scored a run with a furious drive which first baseman Phil Todt handled, but which allowed Combs to skip in from third. Gehrig slammed a two-bagger. They rested absolutely even on the day, four times at bat and two hits apiece.

Monitor, New York *World*

In from the broad acres of Iowa a letter comes to this writer's desk this morning.

"Tell me," asks E.C.W., "something of Ruth and Gehrig. What are they like off the field? How do they stand with the other players? Can they do anything besides hit?"

Ruth is big and jovial and smiling. So is Lou. Lou is good natured. So is the Babe.

But there resemblance ends. In characteristic, in habit, in aim, and in desire they are as opposite as the two poles.

Ruth has been accused of clannishness. He has been pictured as disagreeable, selfish, and inimical to the other players. Stories have been written of his dumbness on the field, and off.

They're bunk.

Like you and I, the Babe is only human. He has shortcomings and weaknesses. But he is and ever will be a big-hearted, smiling, generous kid. A boy who never grew up.

The Babe isn't a dumb ballplayer. Far from it. In all the years that this writer watched him performing his duties, he has never seen him make a bad play. His is true baseball instinct. To him never came the bitterness of learning by experience. He was born to baseball—and knows it as thoroughly as Paderewski knows his keyboard or Kreisler his violin.

Time was when the Babe was intolerant of mediocrity. That's true of every genius. But passing years have tempered his enthusiasm and increased his judgment. He may chide a fellow player, he may arouse enmity with "kidding" that is brutal in its frankness. But put to the test, every man knows that Ruth would go the limit for a friend or an acquaintance. He would give his shirt to a man in distress, growling like a bear all the time with growls that mean nothing.

Babe has no idea of thrift. Money to him is a plaything, to be tossed about as whim dictates. Money has come easy to him. It has given him everything he wants, but it has not spoiled him. He loves the spotlight and the glamor of fame, but amid the greatest adulation he has balance enough to realize that it's a flitting public fancy at best.

And kids? There is the Babe's weakness. Attention of youngsters is no pose with the Babe. He likes them. And one child can influence him more than a dozen grown men of affairs. Of course, there's a reason. The Babe is still a kid at heart—a kid who has never grown up and never will. That's his greatest charm.

Gehrig is quite the opposite. Stolid and plodding by nature, his baseball has come to him through hard work. His is not the true baseball instinct. He learns by experience. On the field he doesn't think rapidly. He must master each lesson as it comes— but with true German tenacity he stays with the job. And once a fact has been mastered he never forgets.

Unlike the Babe, too, Gehrig is imbued with real thrift. Money, to Lou, is something to be saved and kept. He picks his friends from among his acquaintances—boys like himself who are thrifty and patient. Lou's whole life centers about his family, his home, and his mother. His keenest excitement is an evening with the boys at the corner drugstore or the movie. His greatest thrill is a spin in his car with his mother or a fishing trip for eels down Long Island way.

Lou is pleasant and good natured and kindly with friends he has known. But he doesn't make new acquaintances easily. He's too shy and too retiring. Reports have gone out that recent success has made Gehrig a bit chesty, that his hat size has increased with his batting average.

The writer hasn't noticed it.

To me, Gehrig is still the smiling, good natured, somewhat dazed kid he was when he first donned a Yankee uniform. Chances are he doesn't even appreciate how good he is. He still feels that he's lucky to be permitted to stick around, and he's worried for fear some youngster is going to bob up and beat him out of his job.

Being naturally slow, Lou is frequently panned by his team-mates for making poor plays or for failing to cover his position properly. He takes it all without a comeback. He's pathetically eager to learn, and he thinks Babe Ruth and Miller Huggins are the two greatest men in the world.

Oh, yes, the attitude of the men toward each other.

"There'll never be another guy like the Babe," says Lou. "I get more kick out of seeing him hit one than I do from hitting one myself."

"There's only one man who will ever have a chance of break-ing my record," countered the Babe, "and that's Lou Gehrig. He's a great kid."

Ford C. Frick, New York Evening Journal

Sunday, July 3

[*On July 2, in New York, the Yankees defeated Boston, 3–2. Winning pitcher, Dutch Ruether (8–1).*]

Bitter disappointment came to 18,000 fans who braved watching the Red Sox in the hope of seeing G. Herman Ruth and Lou Gehrig continue their home run duel.

Boston manager Bill Carrigan shattered hopes for four-bag-gers and fence-clearing drives by sending to the box a young man with instructions to throw nothing but curves. The change from fast balls to twists and hooks ruined the day for home runs, and Lou and Babe were able to collect only a single apiece.

The young man with the armful of curves was Jack Russell. He was opposed by "Dutch" Ruether, a considerable curve baller and cross-firer himself. Russell did well, but Ruether did better. But for overanxious fielding by the Yankees it's doubtful if the Red Sox would have scored at all. Ruether had good support too. Lazzeri and Morehart made some spanking plays around second base.

Monitor, New York *World*

As the Yankees speed toward the half-way mark in their dash for another pennant, they are so far ahead of the field that the American League race has become a laughing matter. But compare them man for man with other great teams of the past, and you may wonder what the secret of their success is.

Hitting—that's the answer. The big punch carried Jack Dempsey and Bill Tilden to the top, and it is carrying the Yanks to their second pennant in two years. It's the old sock that counts.

Wham, zam, and crash, a couple of long hits and the Yanks have broken up a ball game. One home run can cover up a multitude of minor weaknesses.

James R. Harrison, *The New York Times*

Monday, July 4

[*On July 3, in Washington, the Yankees lost, 6–5. Losing pitcher, Myles Thomas (6–3). Yankee home runs, Babe Ruth (26), Tony Lazzeri (10).*]

Washington—Though our Mr. Ruth came out with his twenty-sixth home run, tying Louis Gehrig, the Yankees failed to halt the mad pace of the Senators, who won their tenth straight game before a wildly cheering crowd of 30,000.

Signor Lazzeri emulated the noble example of the Babe and poled a homer into the left field stand, but it was not enough. Ruth's smack was the longest ever hit into the center field bleachers at Griffith Field, landing at the very edge of the stand, a little to the right of dead center and a dozen rows from the top. [*The ball traveled at least 450 feet.*]

Urban Shocker hurt his ankle in the third and the whole course of the game was altered. His successor, Myles Thomas, was knocked out in the fifth when the Senators scored three times—just enough to win.

After Speaker had doubled in the fifth with one out and Goslin had walked, Judge smacked a double down the first base line, scoring Speaker. Goslin also crossed the plate but was sent back to third because the ball had hit a pop salesman in fair territory.

The merchant was nearly frightened to death when he saw the ball coming. He made nimble efforts to dodge but was hit squarely amidships. Then there was a fine how-de-do. The umpires dashed hither and yon and rounded up all the pop boys in sight, shooing them back into the stands. [*Vendors were supposed to remain in the stands, but when a large crowd was in attendance, clogging the aisles, they often walked onto the field to sell their wares.*]

At this psychological moment an inebriated citizen [*in the midst of the era of Prohibition!*] opened a gate in deep center field and calmly sat down on the grass to enjoy the game. The umpires waved sternly at him, and he courteously waved back. When Ruth bade him begone he turned his back on George and pawed with his feet, yelling "Hee-haw!" seemingly in imitation of a donkey. The gendarmes finally led the disturber out, and the game went on.

Ruel singled sharply to left, and two runs hoofed home, putting the locals three to the good.

James R. Harrison, *The New York Times*

I do not wish to borrow trouble for my good friend Colonel Jacob Ruppert while the customers are hammering on the gates of Yankee Stadium to see the neck-and-neck home run race between Babe Ruth and Lou Gehrig. But Mr. Gehrig is said to be of a thoughtful disposition. Naturally, Mr. Gehrig will be thinking along the lines of his business. The fact that Babe Ruth is being paid $70,000 yearly will furnish considerable nutriment for thought to Mr. Gehrig [*whose salary was $7,500*]. Mr. Gehrig might pass Mr. Ruth in home runs. Then at the end of the season such a contingency might cause Mr. Gehrig to think about asking for a considerable raise.

Baseball players think along these lines. When you see them sitting in the corridors of hotels, they are sometimes even brooding over such matters. I do not wish to erase the beatific smile on the face of Colonel Ruppert at this time, but all of the joys of a baseball magnate must be tempered with a little sorrow, and that usually is of a financial nature.

[*On January 4, 1928, Gehrig would sign a three-year contract for $25,000 a year, making him one of baseball's highest paid players. Immediately after signing the contract, he made a down payment on a handsome home in New Rochelle for his parents and himself.*]

W. O. McGeehan, New York *Herald-Tribune*

Dwellers in apartments which fringe Wrigley Field, home of the Chicago Cubs, have learned the trick of watching a baseball game and hearing it on the radio at the same time.

They pick out a seat in the front window overlooking the park, turn on the loud speaker, and know more about what is going on than many a paying spectator. White Sox fans are less favored, for no apartments abut upon Comiskey Park.

Broadcasting home games has been tried by Chicago stations this year, and club owners say it helps attendance. Many casual fans get interested in radio accounts and come to see the teams in action. [*Almost unchanged from 1927, Wrigley Field continues to be the only major league park where games may be watched from nearby rooftops.*]

Washington *Evening Star*

AMERICAN LEAGUE STANDINGS

	W	L	PCT	GB		W	L	PCT	GB
New York	51	21	.708	—	Philadelphia	37	34	.521	13½
Washington	40	29	.580	9½	Cleveland	32	40	.444	19
Chicago	42	33	.560	10½	St. Louis	28	40	.412	21
Detroit	36	31	.537	12½	Boston	15	53	.221	34

Tuesday, July 5

[*On July 4, in New York, the Yankees won a doubleheader from Washington, 12–1 and 21–1. Winning pitchers, George Pipgras (2–0) and Wilcy Moore (9–4). Yankee home runs, Lou Gehrig 2 (28), Tony Lazzeri (11), Pat Collins (5), Julie Wera (1).*]

The biggest baseball crowd in history, more than 74,000 persons, stampeded into Yankee Stadium yesterday to watch the Yanks inflict a fearful beating on the Senators in both sections of the holiday double-header.

By this two-ply stroke the Yanks went 11½ games ahead in the so-called pennant struggle, and Henry Louis Gehrig sent the crowd into a delirium of joy by hitting a homer in each game, putting him two up on Mr. George H. Ruth.

By more than 2,000 the crowd exceeded the greatest previous baseball attendance. The paid admissions were 72,641, according to Edward G. Barrow, in themselves greater than the throng of 70,000 paid and unpaid, which set a new record at the opening game in the Stadium last April.

Add to this a total of 1,500 deadhead patrons that Mr. Barrow estimates filtered through the gates and you have figures that bewilder the mind and stagger the imagination.

There never was a World's Series crowd that approached this assemblage, for the reason that in the World's Series the management did not dare to pack the customers in as solidly as they were packed yesterday. Every available seat was filled, and the crowd ringed itself four and five deep around the back of the stand. When these vantage points had been filled, the fans overflowed into the runways and aisles, stood on tiptoes in the most uncomfortable positions, and even swarmed up the pillars and rafters of Colonel Ruppert's steel arena.

Male and female fans put up with almost every form of discomfort just to be privileged to watch Babe Ruth, Lou Gehrig, and company send the Senators staggering under a vicious bombardment of stinging blows.

Not only that, but thousands of customers streamed into the avenues surrounding the Stadium, stood in line for an hour or more, and finally were turned away when the last square foot of standing room had been disposed of.

In this setting the Yanks swept over the Senators like a Mississippi flood. The Capital athletes came to the metropolis cocky and confident, with a winning streak of ten straight. They left the Stadium after the game looking like something the cat had dragged in.

Gehrig's first homer was made off Walter Johnson with two on base in the eighth inning of the first game. [*Johnson was pitching in his twenty-first major league season, all of them with Washington. At the end of this year, with a record of five wins and six losses, he would retire from baseball.*] Gehrig's second came in round seven of the next game with the bases full, a tremendous drive into the right center field bleachers.

George Pipgras and Wilcy Moore went the full route in each game.

James R. Harrison, *The New York Times*

To the New York baseball patron, the home run is bigger than the game. At least it seemed so yesterday. Whenever a four-base knock was made, the 72,641 persons who paid their way into Yankee Stadium arose en masse and shrieked to the skies. A home run seemed to be the only thing they wanted, and every time a strong-armed athlete hammered the apple to a point that permitted him to circle the bases, the stupendous steel and concrete structure was shaken to its foundation by the roars from the customers. But nothing else aroused the crowd.

John B. Keller, Washington *Evening Star*

It seems to be slightly better than an even bet that Lou Gehrig will beat Babe Ruth in the great Home Run Derby of 1927. While it does not appear likely that Buster Lou will excel the Babe's record of 59 homers, even that is not without the pale of probability.

Gehrig has everything in his favor—power, youth, perfect physical condition, an ideal stance, and splendid coordination. Another potent ally is unbounded confidence. Just now Gehrig is hitting a harder ball than even Ruth himself, and he is making longer drives. In the home run hitting form the Babe is what is known as a dead right field hitter. Gehrig also hits to right, but he lands in a broader radius.

If Gehrig could master the trick of pulling his drives into dead right, there would be no real contest with the Babe. Lou would smack at least 65 homers this season. But for the good of the Yankees 'tis better that Gehrig bats as he does. He insists that he makes no deliberate effort to hit a home run.

Big, young, and strong, Gehrig is hitting more impressively than Ruth. The Babe finds himself confronted with a most serious challenge, and he is making savage efforts to pull away from the collegian. But Gehrig won't be left behind as the big derby swings into the second half of the season.

Dan Daniel, New York Telegram

When Babe Ruth steps out from the Yankee dressing room after a game, a wild clamor for his signature on baseballs, score cards, and autograph books comes from several hundred youngsters.

It is remarkable how good natured he is about it, since this stunt is a regular diet with him, at home and abroad. As he works his way through the crowd to his waiting car, he daily signs his name at least 50 times.

Billy Evans, New York Telegram

Wednesday, July 6

[*On July 5, in New York, the Yankees defeated Washington, 7–6. Winning pitcher, Bob Shawkey (1–2). Yankee home run, Tony Lazzeri (12).*]

"Poosh 'em opp!" And did he? He did. And how!

Recklessly, with crazy abandon, the Yankees splattered their energy over Col. Ruppert's lawn on the holiday, but yesterday there was something lacking for a while. The Yanks, apparently, had spent their sap in the holiday program.

But—

"Poosh 'em opp" batted in the last half of the ninth inning. The walloping wop, the spaghetti mangler, or whatever one chooses to call this magnificent infielder, came to the plate with the score tied and two out, and caramba!

He hoisted a masculine home run into the left field stands and won the game.

Whatta wop! whatta team! to overcome a five-run lead the Senators established in the first inning when Master Waite Hoyt and Joseph Giard failed! The boys fought on and on. And what baseball story these days is complete without the name of Henri Louis Gehrig? None, it seems! In the seventh Columbia Lou whacked a delectable triple far to center and tied the score when he came plunging home on a sacrifice by the high Robert Meusel.

"Poosh 'em opp!" And did he? He did! And how! And so the Yankees were entrained last night [*on the season's second trip to the western cities*] fortified with a 12½ game lead.

"Poosh 'em opp!"

Marshall Hunt, New York *Daily News*

To the rear and left of the plate at Yankee Stadium, in the reserved grandstand, there is always an interesting gathering when the Yanks are at home. They are the wives of the Yankee players watching the hubbies go through the motions. You can spot Mrs. Pennock, Mrs. Ruether, Mrs. Lazzeri, Mrs. Dugan, Mrs. Hoyt, on occasion. They talk of this and that and are tactful enough to talk about other things when one of the hubbies pulls a boner on the field.

Players will tell you that the cost of dressing their wives in New York and Washington is no small item. New York sets a high standard in fashions, and Washington is just as exacting. Other cities are not so tough on the bankrolls of players with wives. They say that the wife of any New York player never comes to the park in the same outfit two days running.

Ed Sullivan, New York *Graphic*

Thursday, July 7

[*On July 6, the Yankees were not scheduled to play.*]

Mr. Babe Ruth shuffled into Colonel Ruppert's office just before the team left on its Western trip.

"Say, Colonel," the Babe said, "I'd like to have a drawing room for this trip."

The Colonel hemmed a bit. It isn't usual to provide players with Pullman drawing rooms—not even the Babe.

"Why do you want a drawing room?" he asked.

Babe stammered and blushed.

"I-I-I want to practice, and I'm afraid I might disturb the boys."

"Practice what?" asked the amazed Colonel.

"I'm going in for saxophone playing," the Babe stammered. "I'm learning to toot a sax, and it takes lots of practice."

Don't laugh! It's a fact.

The home run king and champion hot dog consumer of the world has taken up music.

Some days ago Paul Whiteman presented the Babe with a saxophone and a book of instructions. Since that time the Babe has tooted himself blue in the face. And he figures, if he can get a drawing room, keep the door locked, and practice only when the train is in motion, he may master the thing before he returns.

As a matter of fact the Babe already is noted as a musician, a harmonica player.

Some years ago he carried a dozen choice harmonicas as a regular part of his baggage, and his daily concerts were a part of every road trip. Unfortunately, about that time he turned his attention to white trousers, and the necessity of carrying a dozen pairs of flannels for every occasion forced the harmonicas out of his grip into discard.

But now he's on the trail again.

The saxophone did it.

The home run champion has found new interest in Grieg and Chopin.

P.S. He got the drawing room.

[*Just as Babe Ruth was the home-run king of the 1920's so Paul Whiteman was that era's monarch of sweet, danceable, jazzlike music. Like Ruth, the three-hundred-pound jovial bandleader was a universally recognized national personality.*]

Ford C. Frick, New York *Evening Journal*

If Tony Lazzeri had as many lives as a cat, Miller Huggins would use all of them at once, for the San Francisco Wop is baseball's most versatile player.

The Yankee pilot has had Tony filling in for everybody but the catcher and pitcher, and when he gets the race sewed up, he intends to let him play an inning at every position. [*This, in fact, did not occur, perhaps because the bashful Lazzeri was disinclined to be an exhibitionist.*]

Not a few players believe Tony is a better third baseman than Dugan, a niftier shortstop than Koenig, a classier second sacker than Morehart, a steadier and flashier first baseman than Gehrig, and as good an outfielder as anybody Huggins has.

On the field Tony is a bristling, snarling battler. Off the field he is quiet and reserved with little to say on anything except baseball.

Some guy, deesa boy Tony!

New York *Telegram*

The jackrabbit ball is with us again. For the benefit of the uninformed, the jackrabbit ball is a baseball that the other side is slugging something scandalous. This felony is discovered annually by some ball team that has just been through a frightful shellacking. When the Yankees pasted the Washington Senators, 12–1 and 21–1, it was discovered suddenly that someone had sneaked the lively ball into the yard. No explanations were offered why it was that when the Yankees hit the ball it turned into a jackrabbit, while every time the Senators touched it up it was nothing but the good old-fashioned beanbag. The jackrabbitting was very onesided.

While the magnates swear that it is the same old baseball that our whiskered forefathers battled around, the inference is that at dead of night the undersecretary of the club owner sneaks to a private telephone, summons the manufacturer, and bids him pour a little strychnine or digitalis into the old apple to make its heart action quicken. The factory gets out the ball bearings, the block rubber, and the go-juice, and the home run epidemic follows. This is known as commercializing baseball and jeopardizing the lives and limbs of the players [*because they were allegedly in danger of being hit and injured by the ball as it shot across the infield*].

Paul Gallico, New York *Daily News*

Saturday, July 9

[*On July 7, the Yankees were not scheduled to play. On July 8, in Detroit, the Yankees split a doubleheader, 8–11 and 10–8. Losing pitcher, Dutch Ruether (8–2); winning pitcher, George Pipgras (3–0). Yankee home runs, Tony Lazzeri (13), Babe Ruth (27).*]

Detroit—Having done dire things to the Eastern representatives, the Yankees began wrecking the Western half of the American League, but their start wasn't as destructive as it might have been. The best they could do was break even with the untamed Tigers, to the joy of 25,000 automobile owners.

In the merry race for home run honors, a purely private affair, George Herman Ruth gained a notch on Henry Louis Gehrig when he punched his twenty-seventh round-trip ticket to deep center field in the second game. It was one of those homers he had to run for, but he made the circuit and finished standing up, driving in Combs and Morehart before him. The Babe's smash put a stamp of security on the contest, as it provided the finishing touches for a five-run rally behind the pitching of George Pipgras. [*This was Ruth's only inside-the-park home run of 1927, and the only home run of this kind that he ever hit in Detroit. He was assisted by a faulty relay throw from center fielder Heinie Manush, which was not good enough to get the ball into home plate quickly but not bad enough to be called an error.*]

Pipgras had to be relieved because of inclination to pass his opponents, but Wilcy Moore, the old faithful, stepped in before George's generosity could have any serious effect. It was no surprise when Moore stopped a budding rally, but when he drove out a single, his first hit of the season, everyone was shocked. When he hit safely again in the eighth it became a matter worthy of an investigation.

Wilcy must have been struck with the notion that no good pitcher should hit that well and immediately stopped being a good pitcher. The Tigers shook him loose from a couple of runs in the seventh, and when they filled the bases with none out in the eighth Herbie Pennock had to be summoned.

The Yankees were leading 10 to 4 when Herbie arrived, but they only had a 3 run margin when he got 3 men out. But they never got any closer. At 8:29 P.M. Eastern Daylight Saving Time, Tony Lazzeri threw out Jack Warner to finish 6 hours and 44 minutes of baseball.

Richards Vidmer, *The New York Times*

Sunday, July 10

[*On July 9, in Detroit, the Yankees split a doubleheader, 19–7 and 4–14. The second game ended after seven innings because of darkness. Winning pitcher, George Pipgras (4–0); losing pitcher, Urban Shocker (9–5). Yankee home runs, Babe Ruth 2 (29), Tony Lazzeri (14), Bob Meusel (4), Joe Dugan (2).*]

Detroit—The king is back on his throne again.

When Babe Ruth knocked out his twenty-eighth home run of the season he caught up with Lou Gehrig, pretender to the crown of clout. When he walloped his twenty-ninth he once more took his place at the head of the procession.

What matter, then, if the Yankees lost one ball game to the tempestuous Tigers? What matter if they were beaten at their own game of slug and keep on slugging, 14 to 4? What matter anything as long as the king is on his throne again?

The monarch's blows were smote in the first game while Ken Holloway [*a right-hander in his fifth year with Detroit*] was in the box. Both sailed into the center field bleachers, but the second one sailed higher and further.

While the Babe was doing these things his mates followed his lead and battered out twenty hits. They took three hours to do it, but they needed only three minutes. When Babe hit his homer in the first frame with one on he sent the Yanks into a lead which the Tigers never caught.

It was different in the second game. Sam Gibson held the Yanks to nine hits, which is something of an achievement in these days of destruction.

One of the biggest crowds that ever flocked into Navin Field watched the double header, 30,000 crowding into the grandstand, climbing into temporary bleachers in the outfield, and overflowing onto the turf. They picked a good day for it. They not only saw two mighty Ruthian smashes, but Bob Meusel, Joe Dugan, and Tony Lazzeri also hit for the circuit.

The Babe just about won the first game single-handed. In just four innings he hit safely three times for a total of ten bases, drove six runs in and one pitcher out. Before nine innings were completed he added two more hits and three more bases to his total.

[*Detroit's ballpark, which opened in 1912, was called Navin Field until 1937 and had a seating capacity of 29,000. After the 1937 season, the park underwent major alterations; the seating was increased to 50,000 and the name was changed to honor the man who had succeeded Frank Navin as president of the Tigers, Walter Briggs. In 1961, Briggs Stadium became Tiger Stadium. During the 1937–38 reconstruction, the distance from home plate to the right-field fence was considerably shortened. Until the 1938 season, the right-field fence at the foul line measured a healthy 370 feet. Dead center, where Ruth hit his two home runs during this doubleheader, was normally 467 feet away, but the distance was shortened on this occasion because of the bleachers on the field.*]

Richards Vidmer, *The New York Times*

"Sir: After looking over a few games at Yankee Stadium recently I venture an explanation of why Gehrig is threatening the supremacy of the Babe. The explanation lies in their batting positions. I noticed that on an average five balls were thrown to Ruth each time he came to bat. No ball, as far as I could see, was a good one. The pitchers, under extraordinary strain, were working carefully.

"Isn't it reasonable to suppose that a pitcher will let down after such a strain? Gehrig, in other words, profits enormously by coming to bat after Ruth.

"H.R.W. (of Boston)"

It's almost a joke to think of any pitcher "easing off" against any part of the Yankee batting order. Earle Combs leads off, and so far he has been getting to first base on an average of once in every two trips to the plate.

Mark Koenig, when he is in there, is a turn-over hitter [*a switch-hitter*] of good quality, and behind Master Koenig, the piano player, comes G. H. Ruth, owner but not player of a silver saxophone. A base on balls to the Babe is a moral victory for the pitcher.

Then comes Lou Gehrig, who hits to all directions and to great distances. Behind Gehrig is Bob Meusel, who is up in the select list of league-leading hitters.

And there's Antonio Lazzeri, who once hit a home run over

Johnny Mostil's head in dead center field at Yankee Stadium, a proof of Lazzeri's speed as well as his strength. [*Mostil, of the White Sox, was one of the all-time best center fielders. He sat out most of the 1927 season because of a severe case of depression following an attempted suicide.*]

Where can a harried pitcher find an easy spot in this array of bludgeons?

John Kieran, *The New York Times*

Monday, July 11

[*On July 10, in Detroit, the Yankees lost, 6–3. Losing pitcher, Herb Pennock (8–4).*]

Old Joe J. Slump has arrived and taken up rooms in the same hotel with your Yankees.

The boys have been dropping games with abandon since coming out here, and the worst of it is they've played like a lot of high school boys.

On Friday and Saturday they dropped two because they could not get any pitching. Yesterday they varied their performance by dropping one because they did not get base hits. Earl Whitehill had them completely tied up, and he made the biggest saps out of our Messrs. Ruth and Gehrig, the twin kleagles of klout.

Mr. Ruth in five times at bat did not get the ball out of the infield. Twice he struck out. Gehrig was a little better. Lou was up four times and got a long double. Like the Babe, he was twice a strikeout victim. As Mr. Ruth remarked this morning, "There are days you can't lay up a cent. And others when you even lose money."

Among other young men who have suffered immensely in this series might be mentioned the Yankee catchers. The slow-footed Tigers have simply run wild on the bases. Saturday, for instance, Johnny Neun annexed five stolen bases, including a steal of home. [*Neun was never noted for his base running, but only five other major leaguers have stolen five bases in one game, and just one man— Eddie Collins—has surpassed this total. (Collins twice, within the space of eleven days in September 1912, stole six bases in a game.) This was*]

*not Neun's only memorable achievement of 1927. On May 31, he be-
came one of seven players in big league history to make an unassisted
triple play. This was quite a year for a substitute first baseman who in six
major league seasons spent most of his time sitting in the dugout.*]

Yesterday little Jack Tavener took up where Neun left off.
After singling in the fourth, he stole second, third, and home on
three successive pitches. [*No record has been kept on this matter, but
this may have been the only time in major league history that three bases
were stolen by one man on three pitches.*]

The pitching showed a bit of improvement, but it was still
nothing to write home about. Our Mr. Pennock was pounded
right, left, and crooked during his tenure in office.

Ford C. Frick, New York *Evening Journal*

Babe Ruth, on his way to left field, was interrupted several times
by boys who ran out to have him autograph programs and balls.
Ruth obliged them.

H. G. Salsinger, Detroit *News*

AMERICAN LEAGUE STANDINGS

	W	L	PCT	GB		W	L	PCT	GB
New York	56	24	.700	—	Philadelphia	42	37	.532	13½
Washington	45	32	.584	9½	Cleveland	34	45	.430	21½
Detroit	42	35	.545	12½	St. Louis	31	45	.408	23
Chicago	44	37	.543	12½	Boston	19	58	.247	35½

Tuesday, July 12

[*On July 11, in Detroit, the Yankees won, 8–5. Winning pitcher, Waite
Hoyt (11–4). Yankee home runs, Lou Gehrig (29), Pat Collins (6).*]

Detroit—The Buster and the Babe are neck and neck once more
in the Great American Home Run Handicap of 1927.

Except for the fact that Buster Gehrig hit his twenty-ninth
home run of the season, putting him again on even terms with
Babe Ruth, it hardly seems worthwhile mentioning the little
game of baseball between the Yanks and Tigers.

The Yanks won. That might be an item of some interest. It also might be mentioned, casually, that Waite Hoyt and Bob Shawkey made the wild and ferocious Tigers appear like house cats. But these factors are merely incidental to the main bit of gossip.

Having done nothing more devastating than to bang out a few singles, doubles, and triples since Independence Day, Lou decided it was about time to get back into the race where hits are really worthwhile. He warmed up with a double off Lil Stoner in the sixth inning, which started a five-run rally, and he took up the main business of the afternoon as a starter to the seventh.

Stoner, through a little oversight on the part of George Moriarity, was still on the pitching premises. [*George Moriarity, who had played third base for the Yankees and Tigers for ten years (1906–15), was in his freshman year as a major league manager, a career which would end at the close of the 1928 season.*] The Yankees were far enough ahead to make a run or two of small concern. But Buster had his own personal affairs to think of and took no pity on anyone, least of all the ball.

He belted it on a line into the bleachers that nestle between right and center field and then trotted around the bases as though he hit 'em like that every day. Well, he does—almost.

Pat Collins also hit for the circuit. His drive went in the other direction, settling somewhere beyond the left field fence in the fifth inning.

Richards Vidmer, *The New York Times*

Tony Lazzeri continues to glisten at shortstop. In the fifth inning yesterday Warner poked a ball toward left field, but Tony snared it with a back twist of his gloved hand in deep short. He had the ball, but he still had to throw it a long way against a fast man, and he did it, cutting Warner down by inches.

"I haven't seen a play like that in fifteen years," said Miller Huggins. "Actually it would be hard for me to put my finger on another like it, no matter how far I might go back."

Arthur Fletcher, one of the game's greatest shortstops in his salad days with the Giants, thinks Lazzeri is on a par with any infielder he ever saw.

"You look at him at shortstop," said Fletcher, "and you are sure that's where he belongs. Then you look at him at second base, and you're sure he belongs there. The long and short of it is that he is great on either side of the bag. He goes to his right as well as to his left, he fields balls cleanly, and when he comes up with one how he whistles it over there."

                              Frank Graham, New York *Sun*

Wednesday, July 13

[*On July 12, in Cleveland, the Yankees won, 7–0. Winning pitcher, Urban Shocker (10–5). Yankee home run, Babe Ruth (30).*]

Cleveland—Ruth will out. [*Baseball writers enjoyed leading their stories with plays upon Babe Ruth's name. On June 25, 1925, the day after Babe's first Yankee Stadium bases-loaded home run had given his team a 6–5 win over Chicago, James R. Harrison thus began his account of the game in* The Times: *"Ruth is stranger than fiction." And then there was Heywood Broun's famous opening sentence in the* World *for October 12, 1923, after the Babe had hit two home runs in the second World Series game: "The Ruth is mighty and shall prevail."*]

But it's best not to count on it. After failing to hit safely in 14 consecutive times at bat, the slumbering Babe awoke in the ninth inning, measured the distance to the high right field fence with a practiced eye, and drove the ball in the general direction of Dixie. [*The right-field fence in Dunn Field fronted on Lexington Avenue, in a southerly direction from home plate.*]

It was a sock to speak of in glowing terms. It was high and hard and fine to see as it sailed through the sultry summer air, but the most remarkable thing about it was that it was the Babe's thirtieth home run of the season and broke the tie between the King of Clout and the persistent pretender to the throne, Lou Gehrig.

Morehart was on second at the time, and Joe Shaute was pitching. At least he was going through the motions. He hadn't been very successful even before that, his only claim to fame being that the Yankees' other 13 hits had stayed inside the field.

On the other hand Urban Shocker had quite a day until the game was over. He scored a shutout, and, thanks to a leaping one-hand catch by Ruth, a great stag of a line drive by Gehrig, and the general usefulness of Tony Lazzeri, allowed only seven hits. But in fielding a slow roller to retire the last man in the ninth Shocker twisted his already weakened ankle and had to be carried from the field, a tragic end of a nice afternoon.

Richards Vidmer, *The New York Times*

Babe Ruth showed some expert fielding on Charlie Jamieson in the seventh yesterday. He backed to the wall, jumped up enough to block the drive, and then caught the ball as it came down.

Bill Slocum, New York *American*

Thursday, July 14

[*On July 13, in Cleveland, the Yankees won, 5–3. Winning pitcher, Dutch Ruether (9–2).*]

Cleveland—In four official trips to the plate yesterday Mr. George Herman Ruth smacked out as many hits, the final one a double. The Babe's hitting, coupled by some very excellent pitching, was enough to heave the Indians overboard.

Mr. Ruth's case is an interesting one.

Not so many days ago he was in a slump. He made 18 consecutive trips to the plate without anything that bore the faintest resemblance to a hit. Then Paul Whiteman presented him with a saxophone.

Since getting that sax, the Babe has been pounding the ball over the lot with a vengeance. It might not be a bad idea for Colonel Ruppert to invest some of his surplus in a flock of saxophones and distribute them around to the boys.

It is well the Babe is hitting. Comrade Gehrig isn't doing so well. For several days his hits have been falling off to singles and doubles, and yesterday he had only a base on balls to show for a day's work.

Mr. Gehrig, it seems, misses his pickled eels, and he is convinced that he won't do much hitting before he gets to St. Louis. In that unique city there's a delicatessen within two blocks of the Yankees' hotel where the boys make a specialty of eels. Lou hangs out there all the time he's in the town.

The elderly Mr. Ruether, according to all reports, is not a hot weather pitcher. But it was hot here yesterday, plenty hot. And Mr. Ruether pitched as if it were zero.

Ford C. Frick, New York *Evening Journal*

Friday, July 15

[*On July 14, in Cleveland, the Yankees lost, 4–1. Losing pitcher, Wilcy Moore (8–5).*]

One of the Indians' greater intellects stopped his team's slide [*an eight-game losing streak*] by pitching well enough to defeat the Yankees. Walter Miller, a graduate of Ohio State University, held Huggins' homicide squad to ten scattered hits.

The cash customers got quite a thrill out of the way Mr. Miller interfered with the home run business operated by Mr. George Herman Ruth and Mr. Louis Gehrig. The two gentlemen faced Mr. Miller four times each, and all that was gleaned out of the eight times at bat was a base on balls to Mr. Ruth.

This pass, in the third inning, filled the bases when there were two out and nobody but Mr. Gehrig at bat. If there has been any doubt as to the superiority of Ohio State over Columbia as an institution of higher learning or vice versa it was obliterated in this inning when Mr. Gehrig watched a third strike float across home plate.

Stuart Bell, Cleveland *Press*

Saturday, July 16

[*On July 15, in Cleveland, the Yankees won, 10–9. Winning pitcher, Myles Thomas, (7–3).*]

Cleveland—You may sing of the ancient Orioles. You may chant of the glory that was the Cubs a score of years ago. You may harken back to the Athletics before the wreckage. [*The "wreckage" occurred when Connie Mack broke up his team of 1911–14 by selling most of the regulars to other teams.*] But before anyone starts making broad statements concerning those famous teams, let him consider the frolicking, rollicking, walloping Yanks of the present.

Facing the fire of George Uhle, the big righthander, the Yanks entered the eighth inning six runs behind. The Yanks knocked Uhle off the hill and picked up three runs in the eighth. They hammered Garland Buckeye into submission and tied the score in the ninth. Then Mark Koenig belted a single to center that drove in the winning run before Willis Hudlin could get the third man out.

The Yankee pitchers may fail, as Waite Hoyt, George Pipgras, and Myles Thomas failed to stop the Indians, but the hitters never—well, hardly ever.

Richards Vidmer, The New York Times

Babe Ruth is trying to disprove the statement that you cannot teach an old dog new tricks. Prior to yesterday's game, he spent ten minutes in hitting nowhere but to left field. Why? Because pitchers are feeding him balls on the outside of the plate, trying to make him hit flies to left. As a result of his practice, the only hit he made yesterday was a single to left that scored two runs. To show his versatility, Babe pitched five minutes to the batters and also caught for five minutes.

Henry P. Edwards, Cleveland Plain Dealer

Sunday, July 17

[*On July 16, in St. Louis, the Yankees won, 5–2. Winning pitcher, Herb Pennock (10–4).*]

Samuel Pond Jones, known as Sad Sam, is just a bit sadder today. [*Jones was in his first and only year with the Browns, having previously pitched for three other American League teams, including the Yankees (1922–26), for whom he had thrown a no-hitter in 1923.*]

Yesterday Jones had a chance to gain the first victory for Dan Howley's team against the Yankees this season. But Sad Sam failed, and thus the men of Huggins are 12 full laps ahead of the field.

Jones spent his greatest efforts in silencing Babe Ruth. Thus he overlooked a few of the lesser lights, who batted out the victory.

Ruth went to bat five times. Not once did he hit. Twice he slugged into double plays, once he fouled to the catcher. Then he walked, and on his final appearance he drove out a long sacrifice fly. On each of the five occasions one or more runners were on the paths.

Sad Sam also kept Columbia Lou Gehrig from hitting outside the enclosure. But Sad Sam could not keep Gehrig from swatting safely. The Yankee first sacker rapped out a single and a double which chased three runs across the plate, enough to decide the game.

Jones pitched a creditable game, but not good enough to beat Herb Pennock.

Herman Wecke, *St. Louis Post-Dispatch*

The crowd yesterday set two records. It was the smallest gathering before which the Yanks have played on this trip and the largest attendance the Browns have drawn in Sportsman's Park this year.

There is only one thing wrong with that statement. The Browns didn't draw the 10,000 who sweltered in the heat. They came to see the Babe and the Buster.

Richards Vidmer, *The New York Times*

Monday, July 18

[*On July 17, in St. Louis, the Yankees won, 5–4. Winning pitcher, Wilcy Moore (10–5). Yankee home runs, Lou Gehrig (30), Bob Meusel (5).*]

St. Louis—Bam 'Em Babe was a bust yesterday.

But Bust 'Em Lou came through with the bam.

And Dan Howley is tearing his hair and swearing vengeance against the fates that put the Yankees in the same league with the Browns. Mr. Howley has cause for complaint. In nine games thus far this season the Browns haven't been able to take a single decision.

Mr. Gehrig's home run came in the eighth inning with the Browns leading 4 to 3. Mr. Ruth had fanned, to the great glee of the assembled burghers, who were out in goodly numbers and much Sabbath enthusiasm. Mr. Gehrig swung viciously at a fast one—and parked it high up in the center field bleachers in the most distant corner of the lot.

"Try that one on your piccolo," he shouted to Milton Gaston as he lumbered around the bases.

Next came Bob Meusel, and Bob was so inspired by Lou's clout that he grabbed one for himself—not so long as Lou's nor so hard hit, but a most potent sock withal. And the winning clout of the game.

Thereafter it was the phlegmatic Wilcy Moore pitching sinkers that had the Brown hitters winging vainly through to the finish.

By and large it was a good game. Gaston, the Teaneck lothario, was on the mound for the Browns. And Milton was good. He was too durn good for the peace of mind of Miller Huggins, who, through six of the nine innings paced madly up and down muttering, "Why did I trade him? Why did I trade him?" [*In his rookie year, 1924, Gaston won five and lost three for the Yankees, after which he was traded to the Browns. In 1926, he had a league-leading total of eighteen losing games.*]

But for the long clouts of Gehrig and Meusel, Milton would have breezed through.

The mention of Meusel recalls the fact that the silent, lanky outfielder has been a tower of strength as well as altitude on this rather tiresome journey through the hinterland. Bob has been hitting and fielding like a fiend, and each succeeding game finds him getting better and better. Young men casting about for apt candidates upon whom to bestow the most valuable player award can afford to take a peek or two at Long Bob. He might not be such a bad selection. [*In the 1920's, a player could not win the Most Valuable Player Award more than once. In 1923, for the only time in his career, Babe Ruth had been voted the American League's Most Valuable Player, and he could not be chosen again. Thus, in 1926, when Ruth led the Yankees to a pennant with a batting average of .372 and league-leading totals of 47 home runs and 145 runs batted in, the MVP award*] *went to Cleveland first baseman George Burns, who batted .358, with 4 home runs and 114 RBIs.]*

Ford C. Frick, New York *Evening Journal*

Lou Gehrig has now made a home run in every American League park this year. The only park in which Babe Ruth has failed to hit a homer this year is Chicago's Comiskey Park.

New York *Telegram*

AMERICAN LEAGUE STANDINGS

	W	L	PCT	GB		W	L	PCT	GB
New York	62	25	.718	—	Chicago	47	41	.534	15½
Washington	48	35	.578	12	St. Louis	35	48	.422	25
Philadelphia	47	39	.547	14½	Cleveland	35	51	.407	26½
Detroit	45	38	.542	15	Boston	21	63	.250	39½

Tuesday, July 19

[On July 18, in St. Louis, the Yankees won, 10–6. Winning pitcher, George Pipgras (5–0). Yankee home run, Lou Gehrig (31).]

St. Louis—Mr. Lou Gehrig's special shipment of pickled eels arrived just in time.

When Lou failed to hit in Cleveland, he immediately sent his mother a telegram asking her to forward some of his special home-run food at once. And Mrs. Gehrig did it.

The eels arrived just before the game on Sunday. Lou took a bite and immediately socked one into the center field bleachers. Yesterday he devoured another section—and then, with 18,000 of St. Louis' beauty and chivalry shrieking soprano encouragement, he socked another, into the left field stands. [*In St. Louis, Monday was ladies' day.*]

Now our Mr. Gehrig leads our Mr. Ruth in the great home run sweepstakes 31 to 30. Which is just as well, perhaps. The neck and neck race between "Bam 'Em Babe" and "Bust 'Em Lou" is about the only interesting feature left in the American League race.

The game, in case you're interested, was another Yankee victory. The jovial Mr. Howley is plumb discouraged.

"They ought to organize a new league for those murderers," he declared from the cooling solace of the showers last evening.

With the fair ones present, the boys started out to make a real ball game of it. Your Yankees, with ladies present, were the most gentle little playmates you can imagine for the first six innings. Then somebody must have wise-cracked or something.

In the seventh they came out with eyes blazing and bludgeons swinging. When the dust blew away, Mr. Ernie Wingard had hied his form to the showers, and the bombardment had left Mr. Ernie Nevers bruised and bleeding as well.

Along at the finish the Browns became a bit incensed too. And many a soprano cheer split the air as George Sisler hammered the ball over the fence with the bases loaded. It was a magnificent gesture—but a worthless one. By the time George got in his shot it was all over but the shouting—and even that was dying in the fair ones' throats.

Oh yes, our Mr. Ruth went hitless. During hitting practice he sprained four fingers signing programs for the fair visitors, it is said.

Ford C. Frick, New York *Evening Journal*

St. Louis—This was a screaming day hereabouts. The quaint custom of occasionally letting ladies into Sportsman's Park gratis still obtains here, and 18,527 maids and matrons attended today's party as guests of the gallant management. [*The figure cited was actually the total attendance, about half of whom were women.*]

How they screamed!

Not even the six runs with which our side stowed away the victory in the seventh inning could quiet the thousands of soprano voices. Many a St. Louis husband was startled yesterday evening to find his good wife speechless for the first time since they marched to that tune of Mendelssohn's.

[*Ladies' day originated in 1876, in Cincinnati and Philadelphia, and soon thereafter, the practice was adopted in several other cities, including Brooklyn, but by the turn of the century it had been abandoned everywhere. In 1912, the St. Louis Browns inaugurated ladies' day in the American League, and in 1917, the St. Louis Cardinals revived the*

*custom in the National League. The Yankees would hold their first ladies'
day on Friday, April 30, 1938, with 4,903 women attending.*]

Will Murphy, New York Daily News

Wednesday, July 20

[*On July 19, in St. Louis, the Yankees won, 6–1. Winning pitcher,
Dutch Ruether (10–2).*]

St. Louis—Hardly a man is now alive who remembers when the
Browns won a ball game from the Yanks. Yesterday the Huggins
hammerers tore into the promising left-hander Walter Stewart
for a convincing cluster of long hits in the third inning, and
cleaned up the present series.

The great home run race afforded no added thrills. Lou
Gehrig blazed a three-bagger close to the top of the fence in left,
and the Babe, after making a long single and walking once,
drove a deep fly to center and then fanned on three pitches in
the ninth. He was trying too hard to raise one over the fence,
and Alvin Crowder, the third Brown pitcher, flung him three
curves and he missed all.

But the Babe made his presence felt even if he didn't hit. He
dragged down a liner hit by Bing Miller in the sixth with two
men on base, charging straight for the concrete wall. He stopped
just in time or there would have been either a marred fence or a
broken up home run star. [*Seven years later, on July 24, 1934, in
this same park, the career, and almost the life, of Earle Combs came to an
end when he ran full speed into the wall, fracturing his skull. Warning
tracks were not installed in ballpark outfields until after World II, and
padded fences first appeared in the 1960's.*] In the eighth Ruth made
two smart catches of short flies, speeding desperately for the infield. The Brown rooters actually cheered the Babe in his feats.

"Dutch" Ruether won his tenth game of the year, although he
had to be taken out because of the heat and a threatening gesture by the Brown batters in the seventh. Wilcy Moore stalked in,
quelled the uprising, and retired the rest of the Browns with no
one getting on base.

Monitor, New York World

Babe Ruth autographed everything imaginable at Sportsman's Park during his four-day stay, winding up yesterday when several hundred Boy Scouts seated in the left field stands kept him busy writing until he had to run in to take his turn at bat. [*As on numerous other occasions, Ruth signed autographs on the field while the game was in progress, a practice that would not be tolerated today.*]

Martin J. Haley, St. Louis Globe-Democrat

Poker, once the favored game of big league players to kill time, is no longer very popular. Three other games of chance, bridge, hearts, and "rhummy" have supplanted poker.

Bridge is by far the most popular of the three, played with a small limit. A number of major league managers are very strict about the gambling limits, and in some cases they have set it very low to eliminate the trouble that invariably results when one or more in the game get badly stung.

Billy Evans, New York Telegram

Thursday, July 21

[*On July 20, in St. Paul, the Yankees defeated the American Association team in an exhibition game, 9–8.*]

St. Paul, July 20—The King of Clout still reigns supreme, and the Prince is just a pretender. Buster Gehrig is a home run ahead of Babe Ruth, but the popular verdict is that Babe is mightier than the mathematicians.

The Yankees came here today to play the St. Paul club. Some 15,000 citizens braved a threatened storm to see the celebrated sockers. But that's not the point of this story. This little tale concerns the relative popularity of the Babe and the Buster.

A few days ago in St. Louis Ruth came to bat in the eighth inning with the Yanks one run behind. He ingloriously struck out. Gehrig stepped up and socked the ball over the fence. But the Babe was still the King in the eyes of the fans. After the game the Babe was besieged by the boyhood of America. They surrounded him at the exit gate and thrust baseballs, scorecards, autograph books, and bits of paper at him with demands for his signature. The Buster walked out of the gate and up the street alone and unmolested.

Last night as the special train carried the Yanks through Hannibal, Keokuk, Burlington, and other rural regions it was met at every stop by throngs who demanded a look at Babe Ruth. The Babe never failed to step out on the platform with a smile and a few words. But only when the Babe went in and dragged him out did the Buster appear.

Today it was the same. Throughout the game Ruth, who played first base, was kept busy signing baseballs. and otherwise tormented by his worshippers. One youth even rushed out to the diamond and took the Babe a bottle of pop. Gehrig was practically in seclusion in right field until the eighth inning, when he was surrounded by autograph seekers. [*The players switched positions in this game for the sake of Ruth's legs. Playing first base, he would not have to do much running, nor would he be required to travel far from the dugout to his position.*]

Two showers in the ninth inning gave the game a farcical finish. One was a shower of rain, and the other a shower of cushions hurled by the fans when Ruth went in to pitch. They seemed to think that his appearance in the box was a signal for a holiday. Perhaps they never heard that Mr. Ruth was once the leading pitcher in the American League.

Richards Vidmer, *The New York Times*

[*A guest of the Yankees on their current road trip was a seventeen-year-old left-handed pitcher from Madison High School, Brooklyn, who was rewarded by the New York* Telegram *for being chosen New York City's most valuable high school baseball player. The following is one of his reports.*]

The Yankees' visit to St. Paul was one of the most interesting and pleasant features of the whole tour for me. I had never seen anything like the reception Babe Ruth and Lou Gehrig got on the way from St. Louis to St. Paul, where crowds met them at every station, even after midnight. Nothing would do, though both had gone to bed, than that they must get into their clothes and go out on the platform and make speeches.

Babe took it all very easily because it is old stuff to him, but Lou was very much embarrassed most of the time and hardly knew what to say.

Jimmie Pattison, New York *Telegram*

Friday, July 22

[*On July 21, in Chicago, the Yankees won, 4–1. Winning pitcher, Waite Hoyt (12–4).*]

Chicago—George Connally knows now that you can fool some people some time, but you can't fool all the people all the time. Connally, a young right-handed pitcher for Ray Schalk's White Sox, had the Yankees fooled for seven innings yesterday. In the eighth the Hugmen fooled him and romped off with the game.

For seven innings Connally had given our boys one hit, a lucky two-bagger by Larrupin' Lou Gehrig. He had the champs either popping up or hitting 'em where the fielders tossed them out with ease.

Tony Lazzeri swung like an old gate until he came to bat in the eighth. He was being fed on a curve all afternoon, and he expected it again. Connally pitched him the curve, and Push 'Em Up smacked it into right center for three bases. That started our boys and before the inning was over the Hugmen had four runs.

Waite Hoyt pitched, and though in danger several times, he gave a good exhibition, allowing only seven hits.

Charles Segar, New York *Daily Mirror*

Saturday, July 23

[*On July 22, in Chicago, the Yankees lost, 7–5. Losing pitcher, Herb Pennock (10–5).*]

Chicago—Earle Combs, nursing a head injury that will keep him out of the two remaining games on the Western trip and possibly two or three at the Stadium next week, is nevertheless a very fortunate young man. If the ball that struck him in the right temple during practice before yesterday's game had been thrown with greater force he might have been killed, or at least been kept out of the lineup for the balance of the season. As it was, he was knocked senseless.

One incident that followed the mishap lightened the gloom that settled over the Yankee clubhouse as the unconscious player was carried in. A physician in attendance prescribed whisky, and it hastily was obtained from a nearby drug store. After he had gained consciousness he was propped up and a generous portion of it was offered to him. [*He was a man noted for being a strict abstainer from alcoholic drinks.*] Still in a daze, he gulped it, probably not realizing what it was until he had got it down. He never had taken a drink of whisky before, and the jolt it gave caused him to sit bolt upright and gasp, to the amusement of the other players.

Combs was removed to the Yankees' hotel shortly afterward and put to bed with an ice bag on his head. The blow may have caused a slight concussion, and for this reason, over his strident protests, he will be kept quiet at least until the team gets back to New York.

In yesterday's game Cedric Durst patrolled Combs' territory well, started the Yanks off in the first inning with a double, and had another potential hit taken away from him by a fine play on the part of first baseman Bud Clancy. There was very little to the game except the Sox. Ted Lyons was in good form, and Herb Pennock wasn't, and pitching decided the game.

                                    Frank Graham, New York *Sun*

Sunday, July 24

[*On July 23, in Chicago, the Yankees won, 5–2. Winning pitcher, Urban Shocker (11–5).*]

Chicago—Some 30,000 fans came out to Comiskey Park to see the White Sox beat the Yanks and watch Babe Ruth or Buster Gehrig hit a home run. They didn't see these things but instead witnessed a performance by Mr. Marcus Aurelius Koenig that gave the nifty New Yorkers another victory.

The score was 5 to 2, and as Mr. Koenig scored 2 tallies and drove in the other 3, it is rather obvious that he needed very little help from his mates.

When Koenig stepped to the plate in the seventh, there were three runners on the bags and the Chicagoans were leading by one run. This seemed a very propitious moment to turn the trend of events, and Koenig didn't wait for opportunity's second ring at the door-bell. He smote a lusty triple to deep left center, and three runs tip-toed across the plate.

The twin thrillers, Ruth and Gehrig, confined their clouts to singles and doubles, which disappointed the crowd not a little.

Richards Vidmer, *The New York Times*

The writer sought the expert opinion of Babe Ruth and Miller Huggins on why there are more home runs than ever before.

Ruth's reply was blunt and meagre in words. That is his way. He said, "I always used to hit the old ball as far as the new one, and they're hitting this one farther because they're all swingin' from their hips." [*In support of Ruth's statement that he could hit the old ball as well as the new, it should be remembered that as far back as 1920 Ruth had hit fifty-four home runs. In that year, Ruth alone had more home runs than were hit by fourteen of the fifteen other major league teams. Only the Phillies, with sixty-four home runs, exceeded Ruth's total.*]

A lucid explanation but not enough. Mr. Ruth didn't explore sufficiently into the whys and wherefores. He was not disposed to search and analyze, as was Huggins.

"It's the pitching for one thing," said Huggins. "The days of the shine ball, the sailer, the fingernail ball, and what not are gone. They made the ball do things that pitchers aren't allowed to do now.

"Babe tells me that when he pitched umpires came on the field with no more than four balls. Now they bring on two dozen, and a new ball is thrown in if the cover is the least scratched or marred, keeping better balls in the game to hit.

"And then there are increased opportunities for home runs. There isn't as much bunting or sacrificing as there used to be, and, consequently, there are more opportunities to hit the ball out. Further, they hit at two and none and three and one nowadays where they didn't use to do it at all." [*Batters had yet to go so far as to swing when the count was three and none.*]

W. B. Hanna, New York *Herald-Tribune*

Nothing new in baseball?
How about those Rotating Receivers?

Miller Huggins attempted something novel at the start of the season when he decided to start Pat Collins as his catcher one day and John Grabowski the next. And not since the season opened has there been a break in this scheme of rotation. Neither maskman has started two games in succession. Unless illness or injury forces it, there will be no change.

Grabowski, with more work behind the bat than in any previous year as a major leaguer, thrives on it. Collins works better when not asked to do all the work. So the system has helped both catchers and the club.

New York *American*

Monday, July 25

[*On July 24, in Chicago, the Yankees won, 3–2. Winning pitcher, George Pipgras (6–0). Yankee home run, Babe Ruth (31).*]

Chicago—His Highness Babe Ruth knotted up the great home run scramble when he gave a fast ball a faster ride into the right field stands at the new White Sox park, setting his season figure abreast of Larruping Lou Gehrig, the Crown Prince, who has been giving his old man a lot of worry.

It was a day for crashing records. The record for attendance at the park was fractured with an outpouring of close to 50,000. The Babe hit these three record breakers:

1. The longest drive ever hit inside the park, a three-bagger in the first.

2. The longest home run ever hit here, a drive into the upper stands in right, where no one had hitherto hit a ball.

3. The highest foul ball.

That was enough. He scored two of his team's runs and made a couple of galloping catches in left, but he does those things every day. He was voted a great success by the delegates from Kalamazoo, Oshkosh, Grand Rapids, and Paducah who attended.

The Hon. G. Pipgras attended to the pitching with success until the ninth, when the old steamboat man, Cy Moore, was called on to do his every-day rescue act.

Alphonse Thomas [*who would win nineteen games this season*] gave the Yanks quite a tussle, and if he could have chloroformed Ruth he might have been a winner.

In the first inning with two out the Babe hit the longest ball that ever stayed inside the White Sox park—a booming wallop dead into center. Little Alex Metzler made a gallant try, but bumped into the fence as he got his hands on the ball and it rolled away for a triple. Then Comrade Lou Gehrig pulled a low line drive into right for a single on which Ruth trotted in.

The same situation came about in the third—two out and the Babe striding to the plate. The crowd clamored and the Babe heard them. He let one ball go by and then swung, not with any great effort. But the effect was marvelous. The ball rose and climbed until it lodged among the white-shirted throng half way up in the upper stands toward right center, where no ball ever had been hit before. It would have travelled to Wentworth Avenue [*the street upon which the right-field fence ran*] but for that waiting upper deck.

Monitor, New York *World*

Every Italian restaurant in Greater New York will serve "Spaghetti a la Lazzeri" on Lazzeri Day, September 6.

Through the efforts of the Lazzeri Day committee and the *Spaghetti News* [*a trade paper*], the restaurant owners have agreed to serve Poosh 'Em Up Tony's favorite dish, spaghetti with mushrooms.

Lazzeri Day will be a half-holiday for Italian-Americans of New York and vicinity.

New York *Graphic*

AMERICAN LEAGUE STANDINGS

	W	L	PCT	GB		W	L	PCT	GB
New York	67	26	.720	—	Chicago	48	47	.505	20
Washington	53	38	.582	13	St. Louis	38	52	.422	27½
Detroit	49	39	.557	15½	Cleveland	39	54	.419	29
Philadelphia	48	43	.527	18	Boston	24	67	.264	42

Tuesday, July 26

[*On July 25, the Yankees were not scheduled to play.*]

"I ain't a pitcher," says Wilcy Moore. "I'm a day laborer." Which is no more than the truth.

Day after day, when Huggins peeks out of the dugout and sees his regular pitchers beginning to bog down a bit, he gives three blasts on his tin whistle, and Wilcy Moore appears on the scene. He belongs on the night shift. He goes to work when the other boys are through.

Instead of carrying the lantern, the umbrella, and the dinner pail of the ordinary night watchman, however, he brings with him a fast sinker that sends everybody home to supper.

He has saved more games than half the pitchers in the league will win this year. [*Along with his nineteen victories, Moore would finish the season with thirteen saves.*]

John Kieran, *The New York Times*

Babe Ruth made his debut as a film actor last night [*at the Long-acre Theater, where* Babe Comes Home *began a six-week run*], but the Babe can still play ball! As a flicker light he's in the same class with the Prince of Wales in a jockey role. He may make home runs, but he was never built for romance under the kliegs.

The picture is woefully lacking in any demonstration of the Babe's long suit and concerns itself chiefly with his tobacco chewing habits.

Ted Wilde directed the opus, which can't be blamed on any one individual. After all, a ballplayer belongs on the diamond.

Betty Colfax, New York *Graphic*

Wednesday, July 27

[*On July 26, in New York, the Yankees won a doubleheader from St. Louis, 15–1 and 12–3. Winning pitchers, Dutch Ruether (11–2) and Hoyt (13–4). Yankee home runs, Babe Ruth 2 (33), Lou Gehrig (32).*]

Babe Ruth, who hit only five home runs in the West and batted a mere .340, has emerged from his slump. Although he complains that the Stadium is not arranged to suit his fancy, it was at the Stadium the Babe emerged. The setting for his emergence was yesterday's double header in which, going to bat eight official times, he made seven hits, two of which were home runs.

To the ordinary mind 5 home runs and an average of almost .340 in 18 games scarcely constitute a slump, but the Babe's attitude on his hitting no more approaches the ordinary standard than does his hitting itself. His displeasure dates back to a time just before the Yanks went West. He was crabbing on the bench because he had not been able to make more than two hits in any one of a string of games just before that. It was suggested that if he made two hits in every game he would wind up with a very fair batting average. He agreed—but:

"Hell," he said, "a fellow likes to get out of the 'two class' once in a while."

Well, he got out of it yesterday. This, in brief, is what he did: Lifted a ball into the right field bleachers with Koenig on base in the first inning of the first game. Beat out a smack to first baseman George Sisler in the third inning. Singled to right center in the fourth. Lifted another ball into the right field bleachers in the sixth. Walked in the eighth. Singled to right in the first inning of the second game. Singled to left center in the third inning. Grounded to third baseman Frank O'Rourke in the fifth. Singled to right in the seventh.

While this was going on Lou Gehrig was doing pretty well. Lou got two singles in the first game and a home run and a double in the second.

Frank Graham, New York *Sun*

Thursday, July 28

[*On July 27, in New York, the Yankees defeated St. Louis, 4–1. Winning pitcher, Herb Pennock (11–5). Yankee home runs, Lou Gehrig (33), Tony Lazzeri (15).*]

The Crown Prince of Swat, otherwise known as Lou Gehrig, tied the King of Clout, known to millions as Babe Ruth, in home runs by parking the ball into the right field bleachers in the sixth inning yesterday.

Ruth indirectly helped Brother Lou to his latest home run. The score was tied when Babe came to the plate in the sixth. Win Ballou was pitching, and he worked hard to keep the big fellow from hitting the ball into the bleachers. With the count three and two on Babe, Ballou threw a curve ball on the outside of the plate. The umpire called it a ball, and Babe strutted down to first.

Ballou spent a lot of energy in pitching to the Babe, and the first ball that he pitched to Gehrig came sailing up to the plate about shoulder high. "This is No. 33," said Gehrig as he leaned his bat against the ball. There was plenty of power behind the swing, and the crowd jumped to its feet as soon as the ball was hit.

There was no doubt about it being a home run, for it sailed high and far and landed well up into the bleachers. Babe waited for Lou at the plate, and then they walked back to the bench.

They passed Tony Lazzeri, who shouted to them, "I'm going to show you a real home run."

"I'll buy you the biggest plate of spaghetti in town," came back the Babe.

The spaghetti is on Ruth, for after Meusel grounded out, Tony slammed the first ball pitched into the extreme corner of the left field stand, a tremendous drive and worth the price, no matter what the Babe pays for the spaghetti.

Ruth failed to get a hit although he was officially only twice at bat. He walked twice.

Herb Pennock's great pitching must not be overlooked. The slender southpaw, working in his easy, graceful way, held the Browns to three hits.

William Hennigan, New York *World*

"The greatest arm I've ever seen," said Buck Herzog of Lazzeri's wing just after Tony had made a one-handed catch of a throw from Gazella [*filling in for Dugan at third base*] and doubled a man at first with a whipping relay. [*Herzog had been a National League infielder for thirteen years (1908–20) and a member of four pennant winners with the Giants.*]

W. B. Hanna, New York *Herald-Tribune*

Friday, July 29

[On July 28, in New York, the Yankees defeated St. Louis, 9–4. Winning pitcher, Urban Shocker (12–5). Home run, Babe Ruth (34).]

Just as the strains of "Revive Us Again" floated across the stadium walls from the camp meeting tent of Uldine Utley yesterday, Babe Ruth came to bat in the eighth inning. The game needed reviving, for it was a slow, one-sided contest devoid of feature. So the Babe revived it by driving his thirty-fourth home run of the year up into the slooping terraces of seats in right center, and he took the lead in the home-run walloping contest. Lou Gehrig came next, and although the orchestra played and the choir sang "I Need Thee Every Hour," Lou couldn't do anything about it. He fanned.

The Yankees won their fifteenth straight game from the Brownies, but not without a struggle. In the first inning the young men of Howley actually looked like winners when they scored three runs. Urban Shocker was pitching, and out in the bullpen, that rock in a weary land, Wilcy Moore, was warming up. But the Browns were retired, the Yanks made five runs to overcome the three they "spotted" the visitors, and Shocker went along with no trouble.

The music from Miss Utley's tent was a great help to the boys. When the band played softly "There's Sunshine in My Soul Today," Mike Gazella hit one of the loudest three-baggers of the year, and he made a sweet single to the strains of "Shall We Gather at the River?" and Mr. Pat Collins saw that the gathering took place by socking one of the longest sacrifice flies of the current month. Ken Williams snatched this out of the left field seats. Bob Meusel snatched one on Frank O'Rourke's bid for a homer in the same manner.

[Uldine Utley was an extremely popular fifteen-year-old evangelist whose extended revival meeting had begun on July 18 in a large tent, with a seating capacity of over 5,000, on a vacant lot adjoining Yankee Stadium. The blond-haired, white-uniformed Miss Utley preached every day but Saturday, and at the end of each session she invited her listeners to step forward and dedicate their lives to the principles she had been

espousing. A goodly number always accepted her offer. The campaign had been scheduled to end on August 13, but because of the large crowds it was extended until August 20.]

Monitor, New York *World*

Someone should introduce you to Christy Walsh. He's an interesting guy. He is what you might call the literary godfather of athletes. He's the gent who entices the Ruths, the Cobbs, the Hornsbys, the McGraws, etc., to take pen in hand and distill immortal epics for the daily journals.

Until Christy Walsh came along with his persuasive initiative and soothing energy, a vast amount of literary talent in the field of professional athletics was going to waste. It was he who harnessed this Niagara of writing genius and turned it into artistically useful channels.

Other hardy pioneers had dabbled in this unique literary field, but it remained for Walsh, a tall, dark-haired Irishman in his middle thirties, to put the proposition on a sound, systematic basis, by which the reading public was assured the best thoughts of the best athletic minds in the best manner.

Walsh started with Ruth. He signed Ruth in the waiting room of Grand Central six years ago. By a magic yet simple formula he transformed the Bam from a bat swinger into a pen swinger.

The formula consisted of this—"Say, Babe, why don't you write for the papers?" "Hell, I can't write." "I know that, but why don't you write, anyway?" "All right, I'll write."

Thus was the beginning of a great author's career.

Walsh has made big money for Ruth and big money for himself. It was a lucky break for Walsh. Two days before he had lost his job in an advertising agency. He had previously tried his hand at cartooning without exactly causing a stampede of art editors to his doorstep.

On nerve and hope, Walsh opened a two-by-four office on West Fortieth Street. He hired a stenographer and installed a phone. He wrote letters to editors and told them the great news. He sat back and waited for developments. The only development was that the stenographer quit.

About this time Ruth started banging home runs for incredible distances. He began to get more publicity than any player had ever gotten. There was a live and vibrant interest in him. The editors began to buy his literary works.

Walsh has probably grossed a quarter of a million dollars on Ruth's writings. He is by far the biggest seller of authorship by proxy sports has ever known. There have been times when Ruth's returns from this source have exceeded his yearly income on the diamond.

Two weeks ago Walsh signed a new five-year contract with Ruth as his manager and adviser in all activities apart from the business of crashing the old apple. The intricate details connected with endorsing corn plasters, abdominal belts, and headache wafers, as well as movie contracts, must first be passed on by Walsh—the man who made the Ruthian bankroll what it is today.

Joe Williams, New York *Telegram*

Saturday, July 30

[*On July 29, in New York, the Yankees lost to Cleveland, 6–4. Losing pitcher, George Pipgras (6–1).*]

Jack McCallister, chief of the Cleveland Indians, has not been given credit for a great deal of managerial acumen, but he had enough yesterday to discover the weakness of the Yankee batting order and play to it. He gleaned that Robert Meusel is in a batting slump, and he maneuvered the doings of his pitcher, Willis Hudlin, so that whenever the Yankees threatened to score, Meusel was brought to bat—usually through intentional passes to Babe Ruth and Lou Gehrig. [*Jack McCallister, who had never appeared in the major leagues as a player, was serving his apprenticeship as a major league manager. At the end of the season, he would be discharged, and, as it turned out, 1927 was his first and his last managerial year.*]

So it came to pass that Meusel flopped on four occasions when a hit meant runs, with George Pipgras taking an undeserved defeat.

There were no home runs. They wouldn't let the Babe have a

fair chance, and Lou Gehrig wasn't overstrong. Whenever Ruth had a chance he hit the ball—two doubles, a single, and two passes in five times at bat tell the tale. Hudlin hadn't much difficulty with the other Yankees, except Earle Combs. The Kentucky wonder snapped out four singles in a row and was robbed of a three-bagger by a great catch by center fielder Fred Eichrodt.

Hudlin pitched well in the pinch, as the total of twelve Yankees left on base testifies. Whenever he got into a jam he passed Ruth and Gehrig, and Meusel did the rest.

Monitor, New York World

Sunday, July 31

[On July 30, in New York, the Yankees won a doubleheader from Cleveland, 7–3 and 5–0. Winning pitchers, Dutch Ruether (12–2) and Waite Hoyt (14–4). Yankee home runs, Lou Gehrig 2 (35), Bob Meusel (6), Dutch Ruether (1).]

Fortune smiled on Buster Gehrig yesterday, but had nothing but frowns for his twin-thriller, Babe Ruth.

As a result of this fickle favoritism, Louis, the Prince of Punch, sits on the home run throne, while George, the King of Clout, looks to his lost laurels with a worried expression.

Fortune not only helped Gehrig to make his second home run of the afternoon, but robbed Ruth of two. The first the Buster busted into the right field bleachers was the genuine article. It was hammered fair and square and landed high up against the sun seats, but his second barely got into the left field section and then only after taking a hop off the running track. *[Until 1931, a fair ball that bounced into the stands was a home run; since 1931, this type of hit has been a ground-rule double. All of Babe Ruth's home runs of 1927 were legitimate drives.]*

While 40,000 fans saw the persistent pretender to the throne catch up and pass the king, they also saw the Babe himself fling two mighty punches into the high heavens, only to have them gathered in by a center fielder who was playing somewhere in the next county. *[At this time, official attendance figures were an-*

nounced only on rare, highly unusual occasions, and so on this matter reporters had to speculate. Thus Monitor, in his account in the World *on this date, spoke of "a crowd of close to 50,000."*] The Babe hit those two hard enough to keep pace with Gehrig, but they were in the wrong direction.

Both of Lou's blows were made in the opener. The one homer in the second contest, by Bob Meusel, would have been sufficient to win the game, as Waite Hoyt shut out the Indians with six hits. But the Yanks did not let it go at that, and they hammered Joe Shaute for ten hits and five runs.

Hoyt was supreme in that closing affair, allowing more than one hit in only one inning, and doing his best pitching right after his worst, which was not at all bad. In the eighth, with the Yanks holding a two-run lead, singles by Johnny Hodapp and Shaute and an error by Paschal filled the bases with only one out. Hoyt faced the prospect of having the score tied right before his eyes, but he forced Burns to pop up to Gazella and then struck out Homer Summa, leaving the three runners right where they were.

This was the only time Hoyt was even threatened. No other Indian even got as far as second and only four others reached first.

And so when the auditors had checked up on the day's activities, they found that the Yankees had walloped the Indians twice and that the Buster had taken the lead in the great American Home Run Handicap.

Richards Vidmer, *The New York Times*

Monday, August 1

[*On July 31, in New York, the Yankees' scheduled game with Cleveland was postponed because of rain.*]

With the Buster leading the Babe, 35 to 34, in the great American Home Run Handicap, sentiment around the circuit seems about evenly divided. Those favoring the Babe point out that he has been a pretty good king in the past, but the other faction points out that a lot of good kings are losing their thrones, and they would like to see the Buster take over the chair.

As for the Babe and the Buster, they cheer each other's success as enthusiastically as they enjoy their own. When the Babe hits one for a non-stop flight around the bases, he always finds the Buster waiting with a merry quip and a welcoming hand at the plate. When the Buster hits one with the Babe on base they meet at the last stop and chat gayly as they walk to the dugout arm in arm. It's the greatest act in baseball.

It's all spontaneous and not at all a rehearsed routine. Every day brings this chronicler a dozen queries regarding the social state of affairs existing between the Babe and the Buster. The answer is that they're pals.

"One of the finest fellows in the game," the Babe says of the Buster.

"The only real home run hitter that ever lived. I'm fortunate to be even close to him," the Buster says of the Babe.

They disagree on only one subject, when to take your partner out of a one no trump bid. You see, the twin thrillers have joined up as a bridge team. They never play as opposites, always as partners. Which is a pretty fair tip-off on their respect for each other.

Richards Vidmer, *The New York Times*

AMERICAN LEAGUE STANDINGS

	W	L	PCT	GB		W	L	PCT	GB
New York	73	27	.730	—	Chicago	50	51	.495	23½
Washington	59	39	.602	13	Cleveland	41	59	.410	32
Detroit	52	44	.542	19	St. Louis	39	58	.402	32½
Philadelphia	51	47	.520	21	Boston	29	69	.296	43

Tuesday, August 2

[*On August 1, in New York, the Yankees lost to Cleveland, 2–1, in a game halted after six innings because of rain. Losing pitcher, Herb Pennock (11–6).*]

Score one for Umpire Dick Nallin. Single-handed and with one fell swoop, His Nibs the Umps tucked away a game for the Indians. The game was started in gloom, played for three innings in semi-darkness, and three more innings in Stygian blackness when a cloudburst swept the proceedings into the dugouts.

In the first inning the Yanks begged Nallin to call the game. He was deaf to all entreaties.

Said Ruth to Nallin: "For the love of Mike, Dick, call this thing off. I can't see what Jake Miller's throwing."

Said Nallin to Ruth: "Get up there, you big stiff, and play ball. You can't see what he's throwing even on a good day."

The press box was at a loss to know whether fielders caught the ball, dropped it, or trapped it.

The "L" trains [*elevated trains*] were all alight as they shot by in the darkness. Electric lights twinkled through the stands, and everybody was unhappy but Nallin.

In the sixth the Indians put over a couple of markers on three hits off Herb Pennock and an error by Ruth. The Babe made a perfect throw to the plate, but the ball bounced away from Bengough, and in all such cases the poor outfielder gets chalked up with a black mark. [*Fans still complain regularly about the injustice of this type of ruling. Some have suggested that in a play like this, where no one has committed an infraction, it should be called a "team error," with no individual player being penalized.*]

After the sixth inning the cloudburst came. In three minutes the field was a lake. The Indians' dugout filled and overflowed, the boards from the bottom of the pit floating up and out around the diamond. [*Today no dugouts have wooden floors.*]

The Indians took off their shoes and socks and raced through the downpour to shelter. Even then Nallin was holding the fort. That bird is first cousin to a duck. After a half hour he finally decided he had enough swimming for the day and stopped the show.

Pat Robinson, New York *Telegram*

Wednesday, August 3

[*On August 2, the Yankees were not scheduled to play.*]

There has been no more valuable player on the Yanks this season than Mr. Wilcy Moore. Without him the Yanks would not have made a joke of the American League race. Moore has come to the rescue of many a game that was about to die on the Yanks' hands.

Richards Vidmer, *The New York Times*

Thursday, August 4

[*On August 3, in New York, the Yankees split a doubleheader with Detroit, 5–6 and 8–6. Losing pitcher, Urban Shocker (12–6); winning pitcher Wilcy Moore (11–5). Yankee home runs, Lou Gehrig 2 (37).*]

With only 51 games remaining, the query fired by all hands since the season started—"Do you think Gehrig will beat out Ruth?"— seems to need revision.

It's now, "Do you think Ruth will beat out Gehrig?" The Master Mauler is now the pursuer, not the pursued. And he has been the pursuer for the last month and has put on no home run spurt to indicate that he is about to reverse the situation.

Still, as Michael Casale, the race horse man, maintains, class always asserts itself in the stretch, and as the lads go down the stretch, Mr. Gehrig leading 37 to 34, it seems wise not to compose any obituaries until the race is won.

The permanency of Gehrig's elevation to the home run nobility can no longer be questioned. He isn't hitting over his own head so much as he is hitting over the other fellow's head—usually the fellow in right center. His blows are no scientific cruises that cunningly evade the opposition. They are non-stop flights that draw their impetus from 200 pounds of socking power.

His thirty-sixth and thirty-seventh yesterday, one in each game, were clouts like the others—tremendous drives into the right field bleachers. They were delivered in the manner to which he has become accustomed, and this manner isn't one that indicates easy days ahead for the Babe. The Babe, of course, will go on hitting them, but it's the suspicion that Gehrig will go on hitting them a little bit faster that is disturbing the Ruth rooters in the right field bleachers.

James M. Kahn, New York *Graphic*

The Babe's long reign as king of the sluggers appears to be drawing to a close. Gehrig will be cock of the walk from now on until a new slugger comes along.

Jack Conway, New York *Daily Mirror*

"King Ruth" just missed a home run in the seventh inning of the second game yesterday. With Pipgras and Combs perched on base, Ruth came strutting up to the plate while the crowd cheered. Like Dempsey, the Babe is the real idol of the fans, and they cheered long and loud for a home run. [*It was fitting to compare Ruth to Jack Dempsey. Although Gene Tunney had won the heavyweight championship in September 1926, the boxing fans' overwhelmingly favorite fighter was still Dempsey; even if Gehrig were to become the home run champion, the "people's choice," by a large margin, would still be Ruth.*]

"It's your last chance, Babe," yelled many of the fans.

Ruth swung viciously at a curve ball and drove it high and far into center field. Heinie Manush scurried up the embankment, but it looked as if the ball would go into the bleachers. It hit the top of the railing and bounced back into the field. Instead of his thirty-fifth home run, all the Babe got was a double.

William Hennigan, New York *World*

With Lou Gehrig crashing along with 37 home runs, we cornered Miller Huggins for his dissection of the Gehrig rampage. Hug said it could be explained in one word—Confidence.

"Gehrig thinks he has changed his batting style," chuckled the Yankee leader. "He's wrong. His stance is the same one that he had last year. He believes that he is meeting the ball earlier. Nothing of the kind. It's just confidence. And behind that is a study of pitchers and an ability to match wits with them."

Dan Daniel, New York *Telegram*

Gehrig will be the lion and guest de luxe at a midnight supper tonight, and it is rumoured that the real instigator of the supper is Ruth. The Babe knows full well that a man can't be at his home run best under the influence of indigestion, drowsiness, or liver torpidity. Indeed, after seeing Gehrig hit yesterday he favors a late supper for him every night and the later the better.

W. B. Hanna, New York *Herald-Tribune*

Friday, August 5

[*On August 4, in New York, the Yankees lost to Detroit, 6–2. Losing pitcher, Dutch Ruether (12–3).*]

Young Owen Carroll, the best of college pitchers while at Holy Cross, pitched rings around the Yankees yesterday. "Rings" is perfectly right. He showed them more hooks, curves, loops, parabolas, and elusive and fleeting trajectories in the flight of a baseball from the pitcher's box to the plate than they have looked at in many a day. Babe Ruth could do nothing, nor could Bob Meusel. Lazzeri gave up in disgust. They were all throwing away their bats. [*Playing in his first full season with Detroit, Owen Carroll was the latest former Holy Cross student to reach the major leagues. His career record was not up to the standard of his performance on this day: in 9 years, he had 65 victories, 89 defeats, and only 2 shutouts.*]

Just two innings marred the success of the house of Carroll. Buster Lou Gehrig made two hits, one of which was ALMOST his thirty-eight home run of the year, a long drive which caromed off the right field screen and yielded two bases. The other untoward occurrence was an error of Charlie Gehringer's in the first inning which allowed the Yanks' first run. But for this and a blunder of his own, Carroll would have had a shutout. The Yankees haven't been shut out this year, and that would have been quite an honor for the youngster. [*On July 19, the Yankees had played in their eighty-ninth game of the season without being shut out and thereby broke their own year-old record of eighty-eight games. The current game extended the record to 104 games.*]

Ruth is trying too hard. He hammered into a double play, drew a pass, lined to first, and grounded to second in four appearances, to the disappointment of a big crowd. Not once did he "get hold" of a ball.

Monitor, New York *World*

Saturday, August 6

[*On August 5, in New York, the Yankees defeated Detroit, 5–2. Winning pitcher, Waite Hoyt (15–4). Yankee home run, Babe Ruth (35).*]

Mr. George Herman Ruth hit his thirty-fifth home run of the season yesterday, but that wasn't the feature of the game!

The Yankees won, but that wasn't the feature.

Waite Hoyt pitched great ball to turn in the victory, holding the Tigers scoreless through the last eight innings. That, mates, wasn't it, either.

No, sir. The feature of the game was contributed by Mr. Robert Meusel, of the California Meusels, when he scored all the way from first base on Lazzeri's single to center. It was one of the prettiest and most daring pieces of base running the old Stadium has witnessed in some time. When it comes to running bases, the lanky Californian can step with the best, and his stunt yesterday was one that few men except Ty Cobb would attempt. Mr. Cobb, of course, in his earlier days would try anything. [*No records are kept of this, but scoring from first base on a single is one of the rarest feats in baseball, occurring in the major leagues on an average of, perhaps, once in a season.*]

Mr. Ruth's home run was the only one of the day. Earlier Babe socked out a double that was about as long as three ordinary homers. The ball carried to the wall in dead center on the fly and would have been a homer almost anywhere else in the park.

Mr. Gehrig socked a triple as his contribution, bringing out Mr. Ruth home grinning.

Waite Hoyt pitched beautifully. Touched for two runs in the first inning, he settled down and thereafter the Tigers never even got close to the plate. Once or twice Hoyt was in a hole, but each time he pulled out nicely. It was a great job of pitching from a chap who has pitched nothing but great ball since the season opened.

Incidentally, the slump that the pessimists were talking of seems not to have materialized. The Yankees played bang-up baseball, smart, fast, and peppy. Their fielding was flashy at times and adequate always. Their hitting was timely, and their judgment was good.

Ford C. Frick, New York *Evening Journal*

Ruth's homer yesterday was a low-flung liner, and Red Wingo almost batted it down with his glove as it cleared the screen. If he had, it would only have added to the Babe's hard luck of the past three or four days.

Monitor, New York *World*

Sunday, August 7

[*On August 6, in New York, the Yankees lost to Chicago, 6–3. Losing pitcher, Herb Pennock (11–7). Yankee home run, Earle Combs (3).*]

When a pitcher works through nine innings without letting Babe Ruth, Lou Gehrig, and Bob Meusel get to first base, he is entitled to victory and something more. Ted Lyons performed the feat before 30,000 fans yesterday.

The Sox went to the front after combing Herb Pennock and Wilcy Moore for five straight hits in the sixth inning, and Lyons kept them there.

Lyons did his best work against the Yankees' sluggers. He registered only four strike-outs in hanging up his eighteenth victory of the season, tops in the league, and all four were rung up against heavy hitters. Ruth took two of them, while Gehrig and Meusel each fanned once. Neither Babe nor Lou hit a ball past the infield.

[*This was the third victory of the year by Hall of Famer Ted Lyons against the Yankees. Lyons was on his way to completing a season in which he would lead the league in victories (22), complete games (30), and innings pitched (308), and would have an earned run average of 2.84, second only to that of Waite Hoyt.*]

Bill Slocum, New York *American*

Catching Ted Lyons yesterday was Moe Berg, who never caught a big league game prior to yesterday. [*The twenty-five-year-old Berg was in his third season as a utility infielder with the White Sox. Until this day, he had played 84 games at shortstop, 13 games at second base, 4 games at third base, and no games at catcher. On the White Sox, as on the Yankees, two men shared the catching duties, Harry McCurdy and Buck Crouse; suddenly, at this time, both suffered minor injuries, and manager Ray Schalk, himself a catcher for sixteen years, was also temporarily disabled. Schalk asked for a volunteer, and when Berg said that he had caught a few games at Princeton he was told to put on a mask and chest protector. He did a fine a job this day and the following day as well, and a catcher was born. In his remaining 13 years in the big leagues, he would play in 533 games, once at first base and 532 times behind the plate. Berg was by no means an outstanding backstop, nor was he much of a hitter; only once, in 1929, was he a first-string player. Nevertheless, the national pastime has had few players who were more fascinating than Moe Berg. He received degrees from Princeton, Columbia Law School, and the Sorbonne, and he spoke ten languages fluently. (A teammate once said, "Berg can speak ten languages, but he can't hit in any of them.")* New York Times *Sports editor John Kieran called him "undoubtedly the most scholarly professional athlete I ever knew." However, his most exciting adventures occurred after his retirement from baseball in 1939. In 1941, he was an OSS agent posing as a businessman in Switzerland, gathering secret data. And during the war, Berg, one of whose languages was Italian, was dropped behind the lines in Italy, where he successfully performed his mission to contact an Italian scientist on the progress of German atomic weapons.]*

Edward Burns, Chicago *Tribune*

Monday, August 8

[*On August 7, in New York, the Yankees defeated Chicago, 4–3. Winning pitcher, Urban Shocker (13–6).*]

That the last shall be first [*Luke 13:30*], and that the race is not always to the swift nor the battle to the strong [*Ecclesiastes 9:11*] was the lesson taught 45,000 yesterday who had gathered to see Babe Ruth and Lou Gehrig smear the greensward with bruised baseballs. Babe and Lou had very little to do with winning a victory, but Benny Bengough clipped a three base hit in the fourth inning which scored two runs, and he counted with the winning tally himself a few seconds later. Yes, Buffalo Benny broke up the ball game which started as a pitchers' battle between Urban Shocker and Ted Blankenship. [*Benny Bengough, from Niagara Falls, who had been a Yankee since 1923, became the regular catcher in 1925 and was regarded as the best fielding backstop in the American League. After the 1925 season, he developed a sore throwing arm which baffled nerve and muscle specialists and refused to respond to treatment. In 1926, Pat Collins took over as regular catcher, but Huggins was patient with Bengough, and when, toward the end of the season, he had apparently worked out his soreness, he was restored to the lineup, only to have Cleveland pitcher George Uhle, a Yankee nemesis, throw a pitch that hit Bengough's lately sore arm and break a bone above the wrist. Only now, in August 1927, had he recovered sufficiently to return to play.*]

Bengough wasn't the only hero. When the going became too rough for Shocker in the sixth, Huggins shrilled a call for help to the bullpen, and in trudged the useful Wilcy Moore. The Oklahoman stopped the trouble in that frame, and then went through three more with only one man reaching first and smilingly held the one-run lead.

Shocker didn't do so well in the box, but he was an important personage at the plate. He upset the Sox in the fourth with a squeeze play bunt on the third strike which was responsible for the winning run.

Monitor, New York *World*

When Ruth bounced to the box with two on in the third, he hurled the bat further than he hit the ball. Judging from his form, it's lucky for a few records that the Babe never went in seriously for hammer throwing.

Richards Vidmer, *The New York Times*

AMERICAN LEAGUE STANDINGS

	W	L	PCT	GB		W	L	PCT	GB
New York	76	31	.710	—	Chicago	52	56	.481	24½
Washington	63	41	.606	11½	Cleveland	44	62	.415	31½
Detroit	55	47	.539	18½	St. Louis	41	63	.394	33½
Philadelphia	55	50	.524	20	Boston	34	70	.327	40½

Tuesday, August 9

[*On August 8, in New York, the Yankees' game with the White Sox was postponed because of wet grounds.*]
The Sultan of Swat will not have to worry when he finally has to quit the diamond. Here the Babe is signing the first $50,000 bond of his trust fund. Frank L. Hilton, vice-president of the Bank of Manhattan, is at the left. Christy Walsh, Ruth's business manager, is the other interested spectator.
  [*This is the caption beneath an illustration showing Babe Ruth, pen in hand, seated between two men.*]

New York *American*

Wednesday, August 10

[*On August 9, in Philadelphia, the Yankees lost, 8–1. Losing pitcher, Dutch Ruether (12–4). Yankee home run, Lou Gehrig (38).*]

Only Lou Gehrig, the new home run king, and his powerful bat stood between Rube Walberg and the distinction of administering a shutout to the New York Yankees in the flossiest twirling exhibition of the season. [*Left-handed Rube Walberg was pitching in the fourth of his nine seasons with the Athletics.*]
  Gehrig drove a home run over the right field fence in the ninth round, spoiling Walberg's expectations, but the A's gave the Yanks their worst trimming of the season. Had Walberg been a trifle less confident with Gehrig he would have kalsomined the Yanks with ease. [Kalsomine *is a variant spelling of* calcimine, *meaning a whitewash.*] No other hurler has set them down as handily as Walberg did.
  Stepping along with an eight run lead, Walberg flung a speedy, inside pitch to Gehrig, the first batter in the last frame. Wham! A powerful left hand swing from a pair of massive shoulders. The ball never stopped until it bounced on the roof top of a 20th Street residence and disappeared.

Gehrig now leads Babe Ruth by 3 four-base drives and is generally recognized as the uncrowned home run king.

In four official times at bat Ruth went hitless for the third straight day, and he was not the first to rush and congratulate Gehrig when he crashed the ball out of the park. Babe hit a terrific drive to center field in the sixth only to have Ty Cobb collar it against the bleachers.

John J. Nolan, Philadelphia Evening Bulletin

About 20,000 were out yesterday, a remarkable gathering for a club that has seen its pennant hopes shattered. Perhaps a big part of this crowd can be charged to the drawing power of the Yanks.

Bill Slocum, New York American

Thursday, August 11

[*On August 10, in Washington, the Yankees won, 4–3. Winning pitcher, Waite Hoyt (16–4). Yankee home run, Babe Ruth (36).*]
Washington—They haven't had such a stormy afternoon in the National Capital since the days of the big war as they had yesterday while the Yankees were plastering a most unwelcome trimming on the noble Senators.

Even into the night the rabid rooters were still roaring, and it looked as if they would have to lock up all the rope in Washington to save Clarence Rowland from dangling on the limb of an old apple tree. In fact, any kind of tree would do.

In the third inning manager Bucky Harris, after being called out on strikes, jolted the umpire and was ordered to the bench.

That's when the fun began. If you don't think the Washington fan can put a lot of sarcasm on his curve and a lot of abuse on his fast one just ask Mr. Rowland.

Came the end of the game, as they say on the screen. Also came a flock of gifts from the stands for Mr. Rowland. From the press coop one could see in the haze of wrath that was being flung plateward the following:

Four pop bottles.
One brief case.

Five straw hats.

Four containers, shedding liquid contents.

Numerous papers and score cards, twisted in various sizes.

Ice.

Mr. Rowland chose not to run. Nor did he stand still. He walked calmly and deliberately to the steps leading from the Washington dugout into the umpires' dressing room. Captain Doyle of the local police force served as escort, and players also gathered around, but the control of the throwers was so bad that the bottles hit nobody.

Rowland disappeared down the runway, but the fans wanted vengeance. They swarmed around the dugout entrance, guarded by police. Word that Rowland was at the other side had the effect of drawing a rush from the field to the main entrance of the stadium. Finally it became necessary to call out police reserves, but the fans continued to howl. What a lot of nice boys one ball game brought out. From the upper deck, where this is being written, the hooting fans can still be heard. What do they care for meals? Major league fans haven't given a party like this in years.

More noise from angry fans. Rowland must be on his way out. The noise has been repeated so often that one wonders if he keeps going in and coming out again. Yes, sir, it looks like a great series!

Besides chasing Harris, the umpire had occasion to send Coach Jack Onslow off the coaching lines, and he carried on separate and distinct arguments with various Washington players.

BULLETIN. Umpire Rowland has been allowed to escape by use of the entrance to the left field bleachers on Elm Street.

As for the game, it was quite a battle. George Herman Ruth accounted for all four New York runs with a single in the first inning and a home run in the third. The homer, Babe's thirty-sixth, came with two runners on base.

The Senators tried hard to catch up, but Wilcy Moore, the big ambulance man, stepped into the picture in the sixth inning to relieve Waite Hoyt and carried away the victory. The Senators were halted in their tracks by Mr. Moore.

Bill Slocum, New York *American*

Friday, August 12

[*On August 11, in Washington, the Yankees, in 11 innings, lost to Washington, 3–2. Losing pitcher, George Pipgras (6–2).*]

Any time a pitcher can hold Babe Ruth, Lou Gehrig, and company to 8 hits in 11 innings he should be a candidate for baseball's "Hall of Fame." [*The writer was speaking metaphorically; not until 1936 would the Hall of Fame be created in Cooperstown, New York.*] That's what Horace Lisenbee did yesterday, and that's why the 11,000 or more fans who saw him do it are willing to cast their votes for him in case he "chooses" to run. [*President Calvin Coolidge had recently issued his famous statement concerning his reelection plans: "I do not choose to run." As for Lisenbee, this was the rookie's fifth consecutive victory without a loss against the Yankees. Lisenbee would have been well advised to enjoy the fruits of victory while he could, for, in 1928, he would win a grand total of 2 games while posting an earned run average of 6.08.*]

It was a great contest, with George Pipgras performing even better than Lisenbee. A third error by Mark Koenig ended it in the second extra frame after the Yankee moundsman had hurled brilliantly.

The fans got their big thrill in round eleven. With one down, Judge sent a liner down the right field line. Ruth was hot on its trail, but it evaded him twice. Meanwhile, Joe Judge was breaking some of Charlie Paddock's sprinting records on the base paths. [*Known as "the world's fastest human," Charlie Paddock, a graduate of the University of Southern California, held many sprint records. He had competed in the two preceding Olympic Games and had been the 100-meter champion in the games of 1920.*]

The Babe retrieved the ball just as the first sacker was rounding second. Lazzeri and Koenig were lined up for the relay, the latter taking it and pegging past third as Judge slid in the bag. Here the Nats were favored by "Lady Luck," for the ball bounced into the stands. But for this Judge would not have scored, for he pulled a "charley-horse" making the slide and dragged himself home.

Earle Combs was Lisenbee's enigma, with four hits, one a triple. The "Bustin' Babe" had nothing but a walk and a stolen base, while he fanned to end the sixth with a man on base. A triple and a pass were the best Gehrig could draw.

Frank H. Young, *Washington Post*

Saturday, August 13

[*On Friday, August 12, the Yankees were not scheduled to play.*]

When Babe Ruth knocks out a home run he puts everything, from his ankles to his ears, into the clout. Babe follows through like a golfer. He uses every flexible muscle in his body, in his legs, and in his long arms.

Lou Gehrig is a shoulder hitter. He takes a short chop at the ball. He is not a long swinger like Ruth. He is a tremendously powerful man, built like a wrestler. His shoulders slope, his neck is long and thick, his arms are like an ordinary man's legs, and his wrists and hands might make him a world's champion knocker-out if he went in for boxing instead of baseball.

Gehrig looks much more the natural athlete. He doesn't have to bake off a lot of stomach every spring, as Ruth does. Ruth and Gehrig are a couple of behemoths, but Gehrig looks like a fellow who will last longer. [*When Ruth was 38, he batted .301, hit 34 home runs, and drove in 103 runs. When Gehrig was 38, he was dead.*]

The battle between these mastodonic swatters has been the most interesting thing in many years of baseball. Baseball fans used to watch their favorite teams. Now they watch their favorite individual players. A Ruth or a Gehrig is like a boxing champion, monopolizing all the ballyhoo.

Both Ruth and Gehrig started late, which makes the home run record a tough one to break. To reach record figures one of the home run kings will have to clout about three a week for the rest of the season. Ruth's record doesn't seem seriously endangered.

Robert Edgren, New York *Evening World*

Sunday, August 14

[*On August 13, in Washington, the Yankees won, 6–3. Winning pitcher, Wilcy Moore (12–5).*]

After being held to even terms through seven innings yesterday, the Yankees walked through the last two rounds to victory.

Walk to victory is just what the Yanks did. After Babe Ruth watched a third strike breeze by to start the eighth, Lou Gehrig walked and was singled to second by Bob Meusel. Another walk to Tony Lazzeri loaded the cushions. The situation was somewhat relieved when Joe Dugan forced Gehrig at the plate, and then Dutch Ruether came up to bat for Bengough. After Bump Hadley had pitched three wide, high ones to Dutch, he was replaced by Firpo Marberry, who managed to heave one strike but then threw the fourth ball which forced Meusel over.

In the ninth Marberry did a little passing on his own account. After Durst gained life on an error he was sacrificed to second by Koenig. Then came a walk to Ruth and another to Gehrig, and the corners were filled. Meusel kindly popped to Bucky Harris, but Lazzeri smote a hot one toward shortstop Bob Reeves. The wily Ruth, stopping in front of Bob as though to avoid being hit by the drive, must have balked the shortfielder. The ball went through his wickets at a mile a minute clip, and Durst and Ruth raced home.

Meanwhile, the Nationals were unable to do anything really worthwhile against the pitching of Wilcy Moore after the second round.

John B. Keller, Washington *Evening Star*

To the other members of the Yankees he is known as "Cy." It should be "Doc." For Wilcy Moore, the biggest find of the 1927 season is above all a doctor. He specializes in treating ailing ball games and putting them back in a healthy condition. He is without question the greatest relief pitcher of the year, one of the best of all time. No pitcher before him ever came up from the minors to do as much for his club in a single season.

Moore takes his place in the bullpen almost every day. When Huggins' starting pitcher is holding the enemy in check, or the sluggers are making it easy for the pitcher, Moore also takes it easy. But if a Yank pitcher wavers in a close game Huggins calls for the ambulance man, and Wilcy ambles in to save the ball game. He has it partly saved as soon as he starts his march across the field because every other club has had its lesson frequently.

Moore has a poise that few veterans have attained. He has confidence in himself. He has seldom come into a game without somebody on base, often two or three men. Nothing disturbs him. On this foundation he has a baffling low delivery, a sinker ball, and control de luxe.

Moore's record is one of repeated successes. He has halted so many clubs in their tracks, prevented scoring which would have brought about Yankee defeats, and carried his club out of troublesome situations, that his value cannot be over-emphasized. He has done his work under stress when only airtight pitching meant anything. He works when the going is toughest, and how he works!

The best play made by the Yankees all year was their pick-up of Wilcy Moore, the ambulance man. [*It will be remembered that the idea of acquiring Moore, who in 1926 had been pitching in one of the lesser minor leagues, was strictly that of Ed Barrow.*]

Bill Slocum, New York American

Monday, August 15

[*On August 14, in Washington, the Yankees won, 6–2. Winning pitcher, Waite Hoyt (17–4).*]

With his Yankee mates acting as pallbearers, Waite Hoyt, the singing mortician, yesterday buried the Nationals. About 24,000 fans attended the obsequies.

Conditions were bad for baseball, with fly-chasers splashing around in lakes in the outfield like so many Volga boatmen.

It was simply a case of too much Waite Hoyt. He was master of the Nats at all times and kept the few hits he allowed well scattered.

Neither the Babe nor Gehrig helped their home-run figures, Paschal [*filling in for Combs*] and Meusel leading the Yanks at bat with two hits each.

Frank H. Young, *Washington Post*

Two Yankee outfielders are more than slightly under the weather.

Earle Combs was forced to leave Saturday's game when he was seen staggering around in the outfield. He suffered a bad attack of ptomaine poisoning and did not play yesterday. All these setbacks to Combs are the result of being run down. He has played the game so very hard that he hasn't enough resistance to go at his usual pace. Being a thoroughbred, he was too proud to ask a respite, and played right on until he dropped.

Bob Meusel is suffering greatly from headaches and biliousness. Meusel plays all the sun fields to favor Ruth's eyes. Now lanky Bob is paying dearly for his services. He leaves ball games each night with terrific headaches and is trying to struggle along on handfuls of aspirin. Rest, not medicine, is the only remedy for this condition. Staring into the sun for two and one-half hours each day is far from a joke. [*Since the starting time of games was 3:30, Meusel would play with the sun at its worst position.*]

Arthur Mann, New York *Evening World*

"Who do you regard as the greater outfield, Duffy Lewis, Tris Speaker, and Harry Hooper of the old Red Sox [*1910–15*] or Bob Meusel, Earle Combs, and Babe Ruth of the present Yankees?" asks a reader.

I prefer the Yankee trio. Lewis, Speaker, and Hooper had a little on them in defensive play, but the Yanks make it up with their terrific slugging.

A weak arm is Combs's only drawback. Otherwise Earle hasn't a single weakness. He can run, hit, and field, and he is one of the game's best leadoff men.

If Combs's arm is not as strong as it might be, he has two wonderful sharpshooters alongside of him. I go back a quarter of a century, and in my time I never have seen a player with a stronger arm than Bob Meusel. Bob can throw and likes to throw. Nothing pleases him more than to have a hostile base runner gamble with his "whip" by attempting to score from second on a single or from third on an outfield fly.

The Babe can peg them in almost as well as Meusel. How many times do runners try to make two bases on a single to right field on Ruth? Not often, unless the hit and run play is on and the base runner has a long lead.

Ruth is such a good hitter that he has never been given full credit for his fielding ability. Few fielders cover more ground than Ruth. Like Hans Wagner, the Babe is a very fast big man. He gets over the ground in pursuit of fly balls, and before the Yanks had Combs, Huggins once told me that Ruth was the fastest man on the club going from first to third.

It is in hitting that the Yankee trio gets a decided advantage. I say that, even considering the difference in the ball. The last averages show Ruth hitting .361, Meusel, .347, and Combs .349.

[*Ruth and Combs are, of course, in baseball's Hall of Fame, but one might wonder why Meusel isn't also there. Certainly his record bears favorable comparison with that of several outfielders who have been admitted into Cooperstown. Meusel could hit, hit for power, field, throw, and run, and he performed all of these functions superlatively well. And one should not forget that he contributed to six league championship teams, and that, to protect Babe Ruth's eyes, he always played in the sun field. Perhaps the main reason for ignoring Meusel is that he was an introverted person who rarely talked to people. It is unfortunately true that, apart from the undeniable superstars, elections to the Hall of Fame, especially in recent years, have been, to a certain extent, popularity contests.*]

Fred Lieb, New York Post

AMERICAN LEAGUE STANDINGS

	W	L	PCT	GB		W	L	PCT	GB
New York	79	33	.705	—	Chicago	53	58	.477	25½
Washington	65	45	.591	13	Cleveland	47	64	.423	31½
Detroit	60	48	.556	17	St. Louis	41	68	.376	36½
Philadelphia	60	51	.541	18½	Boston	36	74	.327	42

Wednesday, August 17

[On August 16, in Chicago, the Yankees won, 8–1. Winning pitcher, Herb Pennock (12–7). Yankee home run, Babe Ruth (37).]

Chicago—When Commy Comiskey rebuilt his Sox Park this winter he took one long look and then announced proudly, "Well, nobody is going to hit a ball over those right field stands!"

Commy was wrong.

Our George Herman Ruth did that very thing yesterday—did it with a tremendous prod of his huge shoulders that not only sent the ball over the roof, but landed it well into the center of an auto-parking space beyond. [*This is how Marshall Hunt, of the* Daily News, *described the drive: "Whang! As that ball coursed its way to right the crowd rose in silence and twisted its respective necks. Higher, higher! My gosh! It disappeared over the roof!" The ball vanished at a point 360 feet from home plate, and the roof is more than 75 feet high. Some observers have called this the longest home run ever hit by Babe Ruth, and this, of course, means that it was the longest home run in the history of baseball.*]

And now Herman has 37 to his credit, only one behind Comrade Lou Gehrig, who was unable to manufacture anything more potent than a double. Some 18,000 cash customers thrilled to the might of the Babe's blow, and came near mobbing him as a sort of concert performance to the main show. As the Babe came galloping in from the outfield at the finish, it seemed as though every kid in Chicago was at his heels or swarming around his feet.

At the steps to the dugout he was entirely halted, and for a moment it looked as though he would go down under the swarming mob. But the cops came to his rescue, and he dashed down to shelter with the pack yelping at his heels. Quite a boy, this George Herman of ours.

The "boys" came out of their hitting slump in great style yesterday. Chief among the battering crew was Long Bob Meusel, who was up four times and got as many hits, including a long double.

Ford C. Frick, New York *Evening Journal*

Ruth pitched a perfect strike over the plate from deep left field and prevented the Sox from scoring in the first inning. The bases were filled with one out when Falk flied to the Babe, whose throw doubled Ray Flaskamper at the plate.

Richards Vidmer, *The New York Times*

Commissioner Keneshaw Mountain Landis announces that he intends to make his official visits to the different ball clubs in airplanes. He predicts that it will not be long before all the clubs will be making their tours in airplanes.

[*The first flight by a major league team would occur on June 8, 1934, when the Cincinnati Reds traveled from Cincinnati to Chicago. The Yankees would fly for the first time as a team in a chartered DC-4 from New York to St. Louis on May 13, 1946.*]

W. O. McGeehan, New York *Herald-Tribune*

Thursday, August 18

[*On August 17, in Chicago, the Yankees, in 11 innings, won, 3–2. Winning pitcher, Wilcy Moore (13–5). Yankee home run, Babe Ruth (38).*]

Chicago—What a figure of surprising contrasts the illustrious George Herman Ruth can make when he clutches his heavy weapon, shuffles a bit in the dust, takes a few preliminary swings, and then takes an official cut with every ounce of his vast strength thrown into the swing!

Today, in the eighth inning, G. H. Ruth clawed futilely at the gelid ambient three times when the bases were full and there was a chorus of razz-berries from the 8,000 addicts.

But in the eleventh!

Ah, in the eleventh the estimable soul accepted one ball from George Connally and one strike and then that devastating club swishing from behind his bull-like neck and there was that tell-tale sound of mighty impact.

The ball zoomed against the wind and whistled its way into the lower stands in left field. O, that ball had to grunt and strain itself to clear the wall in front of the stands, but it found haven among the empty chairs in that sector none the less.

Thirty-eight for the Bambino! He is now tied with Henry Looey Gehrig, in the greatest home run contest in all of baseball's gripping history.

Thirty-eight apiece—Babe and Lou. What a pair!

As Babe came loping home in the eleventh, Comrade Gehrig rushed toward the plate and was the first to grip his hamlike paw.

And there must be a wreath of praise for Pipgras, who pitched superbly for seven innings before being taken out for a batter. [*As usual, Moore pitched in relief, allowing no runs in four innings.*]

                              Marshall Hunt, New York *Daily News*

Chicago—The daily 100-yard dash of the Babe becomes more arduous. He is compelled to put on more speed each afternoon at about 5:30. If it continues the "King" will be a mere shadow of 215 pounds when he returns to the Stadium.

The dash is executed from right field to the steps of the dugout each day immediately after the final out. The Babe is paced by his friends and admirers, the kids.

The tipoff on this Babe-Lou thing is that the Babe must do his daily dash while Columbia Lou ambles peaceably enough through the milling populace.

Let Babe miss a step and he is lost, surrounded by eager individuals who long to pat him on the back, shake his hand, see for themselves what sort of a mouth he has or if he sings tenor or bass.

Jack Dempsey, the other "King," who moved into town today [*in advance of his attempt to regain from Gene Tunney his heavyweight title on September 22*] and was welcomed by his populace, speaks tenor. The Babe speaks a very rough and expansive, as well as expressive, bass.

The Babe must increase the speed of his dash, because the impulse to smite his back becomes stronger with each home run.

                              Fred Lieb, *New York Post*

Friday, August 19

[*On August 18, in Chicago, the Yankees, in 12 innings, won, 5–4. Winning pitcher, Wilcy Moore (14–5).*]

Life is getting tougher and tougher for your Yankees.

If the thing keeps up, there will be a strong movement to organize a players' union so the lads can cash in on all their overtime. [*The union was born twenty years later.*]

Wednesday it took eleven innings to subdue the pesky White Sox. Yesterday it took twelve. Heaven only knows how long today's fray will take, and [*traveling secretary*] Mark Roth is frantic. Overtime games are excellent stimulants for the appetite, and after taking a squint at the steak orders last night Mark Roth is out with a suggestion that all extra inning games be done away with under the heading of "unnecessary expense."

The boys won, but it was tough going. Young Mr. Ted Lyons gave them an awful tussle, and only the presence of Cy Moore saved the day. Cy replaced Shocker in the ninth and pitched with his usual finesse. It's getting so the enemy just folds up the minute Cy steps to the mound. And two-thirds of the Yankee squad already has sprained tonsils from chirruping their daily Couéism of "good work, Cy." [*This last sentence refers to infield and dugout chatter, the constant verbal encouragement given to pitchers by their teammates, which was once a universal practice in baseball.*]

In the last five games, Cy has been credited with three victories. As Miller Huggins remarked this morning, "Thank God for Cy Moore. He kept us out of a World Series in Philadelphia." [*This refers to the preseason predictions that the Athletics would win the pennant.*]

The great home-run handicap was at a standstill. Mr. Ruth got a double and struck out twice in five at bats, while Lou made a single and a double in four official trips to the plate.

Ford C. Frick, New York *Evening Journal*

Ruth took a perfect strike in the seventh and then looked surprised when Emmett "Red" Ormsby called him out. The Babe does that well. His movie training has taught him how to render any emotion.

W. B. Hanna, New York *Herald-Tribune*

Tony Lazzeri made another one of those "impossible" plays for which he is famous when he skidded over behind second base, picked up Falk's hot hopper with his bare hand, and flipped the ball to Koenig to start a double play.

Richards Vidmer, *The New York Times*

Saturday, August 20

[*On August 19, in Chicago, the Yankees lost, 3–2. Losing pitcher, Waite Hoyt (17–5). Yankee home run, Lou Gehrig (39).*]

Chicago—A chap named Theodore Blankenship stepped onto Mister Charles Comiskey's pitching rubber, and that's why your Yankees didn't sweep their series with the White Sox.

O, there was a gesture of reprisal in the ninth inning when that robust Henry Louis Gehrig stepped confidently to the plate, rubbed his hands with dirt, and, like all ballplayers, wiped it off on his pantaloons.

Wham! The ball whistled its way into the lower right field stands for Gehrig's thirty-ninth home run of the season. Once again New York's own kid leads the illustrious G. Herman Ruth in the greatest home run race of all times.

Except for Gehrig's home run and a run scored in the sixth by successive hits by Koenig, Ruth, and Gehrig, the game was one of golden opportunities missed.

Waite Hoyt, the apprentice Mortician of Brooklyn, pitched throughout for the Yanks, his eighteenth complete game. [*Hoyt would be the team's season leader in complete games pitched.*] Wilcy Moore was not summoned from the bull pen and thinks he is about to quit the Yankees, believing he was slighted.

Marshall Hunt, New York *Daily News*

A girl with a yellow slicker ran out on the field yesterday, turned her back on Babe Ruth, and insisted that he autograph her slicker. The Babe obliged and then looked around for more slickers.

W. B. Hanna, New York *Herald-Tribune*

Sunday, August 21

[On August 20, in Cleveland, the Yankees lost, 14–8. Losing pitcher, Bob Shawkey (1–3). Yankee home run, Babe Ruth (39).]

Cleveland—Cleveland batters cudgeled New York pitchers often and lengthily yesterday. Ruether, Shawkey, and Thomas all felt the weight of crescendo hitting, but, one thing to be thankful for, the willing and industrious Wilcy Moore received an afternoon off.

Babe Ruth saw to it that Lou Gehrig didn't hold his home run lead long. In the first inning Ruth belted his thirty-ninth off Miller, the southpaw, who was soon belted from the arena. It was the longest ball the Babe ever hit here. It went far down over the right field fence across the street [*Lexington Avenue*] and into a back yard without ever touching the roof.

The right-hander George Grant, who succeeded Miller, stopped the New York hitting until the ninth, when he was too far ahead to care.

W. B. Hanna, New York *Herald-Tribune*

Cleveland, August 20—The train loaded with Yankees came to a stop at the break of dawn this morning.

"Are we in?" asked Gehrig in a sleepy voice from lower 7.

"Well, practically," replied Ruth from lower 6. "We've got a 15-game lead." Which seemed like rather rapid repartee at such an early hour.

[On some clubs, some players were assigned upper berths, but on the Yankees everyone slept in a lower berth, except the manager, the coaches, and "Doc" Woods, who rode in bedrooms. Woods, incidentally, had a constant road companion, his pet poodle. Since the dog could not enter the dining car, team members would take back scraps of food, which eventually angered Woods when he saw how fat his animal had become. On its trips the club used two cars which were always placed at the end of

*the train so that other passengers would have no need to walk through.
Thus in these pre–air conditioning days, when it sometimes was insuf-
ferably hot and stuffy, especially on trips to St. Louis, some players felt
free to play cards while clad only in their underwear.*]

Richards Vidmer, *The New York Times*

Monday, August 22

[*On August 21, in Cleveland, the Yankees lost, 7–4. Losing pitcher,
George Pipgras (7–3).*]

Cleveland—Willis Hudlin, a cocky young right hander with as
big a curve ball as you will see in the major leagues and with far
greater nerve, is proving the latest Yankee killer.

Hudlin stepped on the hill in the fourth inning yesterday with
bases filled and none out. He kept the Yanks from getting more
than one of those runners in, and for the rest of the way he
breezed along, giving up only one hit in five innings. [*For the
current season, this was Hudlin's fourth victory over the Yankees in five
decisions.*]

The Bambino was unable to appear at bat more than once. He
hurt his back swinging at a ball, and he could hardly run out a
long hit to center. He made first base, but Ced Durst ran for
him, and the Babe watched the remainder of the game from a
box near the Indian dugout.

Charles Segar, New York *Daily Mirror*

AMERICAN LEAGUE STANDINGS

	W	L	PCT	GB		W	L	PCT	GB
New York	82	36	.695	—	Chicago	54	63	.462	27½
Detroit	66	48	.579	14	Cleveland	50	68	.424	32
Washington	66	50	.569	15	St. Louis	47	69	.405	34
Philadelphia	66	52	.559	16	Boston	36	81	.308	45½

Tuesday, August 23

[On August 22, in Cleveland, the Yankees lost, 9–4. Losing pitcher, Wilcy Moore (14–6). Yankee home run, Babe Ruth (40).]

Cleveland—Perhaps the Yankees started resting up for the World's Series a little too soon. Today the Tribe won again. This stretched the New Yorkers' losing streak to four straight, their longest of the season, and it was the first clean sweep of a series against them.

Joe Ben Shaute was the principal cause of the Yankees' pitiful performance, allowing them just eight hits, only one of which worth mentioning above a whisper. This particular blow was wafted over the right field fence by Babe Ruth. Even this wouldn't be worth more than casual comment except that it happened to be the Babe's fortieth homer of the year and put him one ahead of his persistent pursuer in the Great American Home Run Handicap, Louis Henry Gehrig.

Otherwise the homer was a hit that Wilcy Moore might make if he ever made one. It was of no importance as no one was on at the time. In fact, very few were on at any time.

Mr. Huggins was serious about the game, for he used three first-string pitchers. Moore started and faded in the sixth, Shocker and Pennock being his successors. Moore isn't accustomed to working before the fourth or fifth inning, and he found the habit a hard one to break when he was selected to start. He didn't seem able to feel at home during the first three innings, and the Indians took advantage of his uneasiness to gather a substantial lead.

Richards Vidmer, *The New York Times*

Thursday, August 25

[On August 23, the Yankees were not scheduled to play. On August 24, in Detroit, the Yankees won, 9–5. Winning pitcher, Wilcy Moore (15–6). Yankee home run, Tony Lazzeri (16).]

To Owen Carroll was entrusted the task of keeping the Tiger winning streak unbroken yesterday before a crowd of more than 25,000. [*Detroit had won thirteen consecutive games.*] One pitched ball beat Carroll. It was pitched to Tony Lazzeri in the ninth with the score tied and the bases filled. The man who became famous by striking out in a similar situation in the last World Series went to the other extreme on this occasion. With the count two balls and one strike, he drove the ball over the left field enclosure for a home run. The drive not only cleared the fence but also crossed Cherry Street on the fly to take its place among the longest home runs ever made at the Detroit ball yard.

There went the Tiger winning streak with one swish of the Lazzeri bludgeon.

Carroll's pitching opponent at the start was Waite Hoyt, who is still sometimes described as the "Brooklyn schoolboy" [*although he was pitching in his ninth full major league season*]. Hoyt pitched well in the face of discouraging support until removed in the seventh to allow Cedric Durst to bat for him. Wilcy Moore, taking part in his forty-second game of the season, shut out the Tigers for the rest of the game.

Sam Greene, Detroit *News*

It is nearly time for Babe Ruth to start on his round of straw hat destruction. If he will destroy his own first he will be a public benefactor. At present Mr. Ruth looks like a Rembrandt painting entitled "A Large Gentleman Under an Umbrella."

[*When the straw-hat season ended on Labor Day, Babe Ruth thoroughly enjoyed destroying other players' hats by tearing them, jumping on them, squashing them, or in other ways defacing them. The spectacle of Babe Ruth mutilating straw hats came to be an annual New York ritual. Straw hats were inexpensive, costing no more than a couple of dollars.*]

W. B. Hanna, New York *Herald-Tribune*

Detroit—When the Yankees purchased Tony Lazzeri from the Salt Lake club, they did so because he had built up an excellent reputation as an infielder and a home-run hitter in the Pacific Coast League. As a Yankee he has played the infield amazingly well and hit many a ball out of the lot, but his drawing power is based more on the fact that he is an Italian. He has been feted by Italians in Boston, he will be feted by Italians here tonight, and on the opening day of the Yankees' final stand at home, he will be feted again.

All this is a trifle embarrassing to Tony, as modest a young man as one could wish to know, yet it must warm his heart. Also it adds to his store of worldly goods. In Boston he received a silver set, a diamond ring, and a check for $1,000. Today he will receive a silver service at the ball park, and, it is whispered, other gifts will be conferred upon him at a dinner tonight.

This sustained enthusiasm for Lazzeri is perfectly understandable. He isn't the first Italian to make good in the major leagues. None of his predecessors, however, even closely approached him in all-around skill. He is, in short, one of the truly great infielders of all time, though he has been in the major leagues less than two full seasons. He stands out as the league's best second baseman only because he plays second base most of the time. He is just as good at short or third base as he is at second. He has that sixth sense, with which only great ballplayers are endowed, that takes him where he should be when the ball is hit. He handles cleanly every ball he can reach. His throwing arm is as powerful as any in either league. He never makes a wrong play. He is the bulwark of the infield.

Frank Graham, New York *Sun*

[*This piece appeared on the following day; it is included here because of the way in which it complements the preceding selection.*] Detroit—The most significant tribute a man can receive is from his fellow craftsmen. From this standard, Tony Lazzeri is the best prospect in the American League for the next ten years.

"Lazzeri is the best ballplayer I've seen come up," said Bob Shawkey, who has been in the American League since 1913.

And the other Yankees agree with their oldest inhabitant and say great things about Tony.

"Did you ever see him play shortstop?" asked Dutch Ruether. "He's the best in the game. He makes plays nobody else can."

"And he has baseball brains," chimes in Shawkey. "Just a natural born player."

The Yankees love Tony's hitting, his arm, his speed, his fielding. But what they respect and admire most in Anthony Michael is his spirit—that determined, deadly spirit of old Rome. An army of Lazzeris would be magnificent.

[*Earlier, a question was raised concerning Bob Meusel's absence from baseball's Hall of Fame. A more flagrant omission is that of Tony Lazzeri, almost indisputably one of the greatest infielders of all time. Lazzeri appeared in 1,461 games at second base, 166 at third base, and 148 at shortstop, and he was judged by his contemporaries to be the best at each of these positions. As a batter, he had a career average of .292 to go with 178 home runs and 1,191 runs batted in, and certainly these statistics would compare favorably with those of most of the infielders who have been issued plaques in Cooperstown. Even as a baserunner Lazzeri was no slouch, with 148 steals. Finally, it is perhaps not irrelevant to point out that throughout his career Lazzeri played with a physical disability: he was a lifelong epileptic. The failure to award him a place in baseball's Hall of Fame is inexplicable and indefensible.*]

Frank Wallace, *New York Post*

Friday, August 26

[*On August 25, in Detroit, the Yankees won, 8–2. Winning pitcher, Herb Pennock (13–7). Yankee home run, Lou Gehrig (40).*]

Detroit—Herbie Pennock's name has been scratched from Miller Huggins's list of things to worry about. For the past three or four weeks Herbie's name has occupied a place of prominence on the list, written in red ink. For our Mr. Pennock hasn't been doing so well, and when one's star southpaw suddenly goes to pieces one has a right to worry, even if one happens to be Miller Huggins.

But recently Herbie has shown a return of the old familiar stuff. His game against the White Sox a week ago brought a smile to Hug's somewhat wan and sour features, and when Herbie yesterday turned the Tigers back with seven hits the smile broadened into a grin.

"Looks like Pennock has found himself again," Mr. Huggins remarked. "Maybe we'll win this confounded pennant yet."

Running only a step behind Mr. Pennock yesterday was the ponderous figure of Columbia Lou Gehrig, the swatting fisherman. Mr. Gehrig started things off properly in the second inning by fashioning his fortieth home run of the season off the swinging side-arm curve of Sir Earl Whitehill. As clouts go, this one wasn't much. Just a short, loping fly. But it counted—and Lou is tied up again with our Mr. George Herman Ruth in the grand American home run handicap.

Following his home-run effort, Lou continued to thrust his ponderous frame into the thick of the affray. No less than four of the Yankees' runs were the result of his bludgeoning, and he scored twice himself. Quite a day for Henry, quite a day.

Ford C. Frick, New York *Evening Journal*

There has been nothing like the slugging race between Gehrig and Ruth in all baseball history.

Ruth and Gehrig opened their act back in April, and they have been spilling climaxes all along the route for over four months. The horsepower of their rival punch is so well matched now that the accruing climaxes may carry to the last day.

All of this may be considered destructive to team play, but it is even more destructive to the other team's defensive system.

Grantland Rice, New York *Herald-Tribune*

Detroit—The extent to which Wilcy Moore has impressed his teammates is revealed in the casual, often trivial conversation of the Yankees. Last night fire engines shrieked and banged their way past the hotel at which the club makes its headquarters, and pulled in front of a blaze two blocks down the street. Perhaps a dozen players followed the apparatus, and after they had watched the firemen at work for about ten minutes Mike Gazella remarked, "It's under control now. They must have sent Cy Moore in." [*For many years, relief pitchers, who are usually asked "to put out a fire," have been called "firemen." This is one of the earliest linkages of the two vocations.*]

Mock appeals for help by Moore are raised by the Yankees under any circumstances. Is the train late? Is the service in the dining room poor? Do workmen experience difficulty removing a huge granite block? The Yankees pipe with one accord: "Get Cy Moore in."

Moore is the mainstay of the team. Every time a pitcher gets into a jam Moore may be seen in the bull pen lobbing a ball to a catcher. He has worn a path between the Yankees' dugout and the bull pen in every city on the circuit, and the most oft-re-peated phrase among the Yanks is, "Nice work, Cy."

Frank Graham, New York *Sun*

Saturday, August 27

[*On August 26, in Detroit, the Yankees won, 8–6. Winning pitcher, Wilcy Moore (16–6).*]

"Well, it's a bet."

Mr. Babe Ruth was joshing Wilcy Moore about his hitting abil-ity, or lack of it.

"I'll bet you," said Mr. Ruth, "that you won't make three hits this season."

"What odds will you give?" asked Mr. Moore.

"I'll bet you $300 to $15," replied Mr. Ruth.

"It's a bet," said Mr. Moore, and so it was.

This conversation took place several months ago [*during spring training in Florida*] and as the months rolled by, it looked as if Mr. Ruth would have no trouble with his wager. From the way Mr. Moore handled himself at the plate, it didn't seem possible for the Babe to lose. One might have been disposed to rebuke Mr. Ruth for betting on a sure thing.

Then one day in July in Navin Field Moore made two hits off George Selby Smith, the Detroit righthander.

It didn't disturb the Babe.

"He'll never get another hit as long as he lives," said Ruth. "My money's as safe as a church."

Another month passed, and it certainly appeared as if the Babe had the right dope. From July 8 to August 26 Moore tried in vain to get his third hit.

Yesterday Moore was called as a relief pitcher in the seventh. His first turn at bat came in the next inning. Sam Gibson was pitching. Gibson struck out Pat Collins and then faced Moore confidently as all pitchers face Moore.

With a sudden stroke of genius, Mr. Moore decided to bunt. The ball rolled toward third base, and Mr. Moore hied himself hastily in the opposite direction. Jackie Warner, Tiger third baseman, disdained to pick up the ball. He was sure it would roll foul, but it came to a dead stop squarely on the chalk line.

It was a base hit, worth exactly $300 in United States currency to Mr. Moore, and it proved to be the starting point in the winning Yankee rally. Combs reached first on an error, and Koenig's fourth single drove Moore home. Combs tallied on Gehrig's high fly to center fielder Heinie Manush at the foot of the flagpole. Those two runs provided the Yankees's winning margin.

Mr. Ruth was interviewed just before he departed with the Yankees for St. Louis last night.

"I lost," said Mr. Ruth, "but it was worth it."

Mr. Ruth contributed liberally to the Yankee cause yesterday. The Babe came up in the seventh with the bases filled and the Yankees trailing by three runs. He promptly cleared the bases and tied the score with a triple to center.

Sam Greene, Detroit News

Detroit—They were still celebrating Lazzeri day when the Yanks prepared to say farewell to the Tigers. Just before the game, Tony was called to the plate, and this time he drew a platinum watch.

Bill Slocum, New York American

Sunday, August 28

[*On August 27, in St. Louis, the Yankees won, 14–4. Winning pitcher, Waite Hoyt (18–5). Yankee home runs, Babe Ruth (41), Bob Meusel (7), Earle Combs (4).*]

St. Louis—Among the Yankees' feats yesterday were Ruth's forty-first home run, homers by Combs and Meusel, the sixteenth consecutive victory over the Browns, and Waite Hoyt's eighteenth winning game this year.

The Browns never had a show to win against Hoyt, who, however, was wilder than is his wont and not in typical form. [*It was unusual for Hoyt to be wild. In 256 innings pitched in 1927, he gave up 54 walks, averaging fewer than 2 walks per 9-inning game.*]

The Babe went far and high over the right field roof with his home run and once more broke away from Lou Gehrig, who is now one behind. A double by Gehrig, and a triple and homer by Ruth, composed the day's grist for the macing monarchs.

The eighth was an old Yankee home run inning. On the heels of Koenig's hit, Ernie Nevers made so bold as to put one within reach of Ruth's loaded weapon. Then over the hills and far away. The Babe blazed a trail atop the right field stand without touching any part of it. [*This was the second time this season that Babe Ruth hit a home run on a pitch delivered by the great football player Ernie Nevers.*] The second home run of the inning was Meusel's hit into the left field seats, sending in ahead Gehrig, who had walked.

Earle Combs had infringed on the Ruth-Gehrig-Lazzeri monopoly in the fourth. Hoyt had forced Collins, and with two out Combs raised a ball to the right field roof, and from there it dropped into the outer world. Hoyt and Combs jogged home in tandem.

W. B. Hanna, New York *Herald-Tribune*

Monday, August 29

[*On August 28, in St. Louis, the Yankees won, 10–6. Winning pitcher, Urban Shocker (14–6). Yankee home runs, Babe Ruth (42), Mark Koenig (2).*]

St. Louis—The Babe leaped into a lead of two home runs over Gehrig. In the first inning, off Wingard, he rushed a long, low, swiftly driven ball over the right field roof and into some other part of St. Louis. It merely skimmed the roof. Gehrig, however, outbatted Ruth. Lou had three hits, while Ruth struck out twice.

On the mound, Urban Shocker turned up with a strong game after Dutch Ruether was batted out in the fourth. Shocker's spit ball was breaking to order, and puzzled the best St. Louis hitters.

W. B. Hanna, New York *Herald-Tribune*

St. Louis, Aug. 28—Yesterday Ruth warmed up a pitcher and threw right-handed. Today Meusel practiced in the outfield and threw left-handed [*Meusel was a right-handed thrower*]. Maybe the Yanks are going to play this way and give the Browns a chance. When they start clowning, it's a good sign that a pennant is within easy reach.

Richards Vidmer, *The New York Times*

It now appears certain that the 1927 Yankees will lay claim to another unusual distinction, that of going through the season with its batting order untouched. Combs was lead off man from the start, with Koenig, Ruth, Gehrig, and Meusel following in that order and with Lazzeri, Dugan, and the two battery players finishing up.

Injuries [*to everyone but Gehrig and Lazzeri*] have forced substitutions for regulars, but whenever these players were performing, they occupied the same batting place as on opening day.

New York *American*

AMERICAN LEAGUE STANDINGS

	W	L	PCT	GB		W	L	PCT	GB
New York	87	37	.702	—	Chicago	59	64	.480	27½
Philadelphia	71	53	.573	16	Cleveland	55	69	.444	32
Detroit	68	53	.562	17½	St. Louis	47	74	.388	38½
Washington	66	57	.537	20½	Boston	38	84	.311	48

Tuesday, August 30

[*On August 29, in St. Louis, the Yankees won, 8–3. Winning pitcher, Herb Pennock (14–7). Yankee home run, Lou Gehrig (41).*]

Even the ladies [*on ladies' day in St. Louis*] were unable to jolt the Browns loose, and the Yankees closed their season in St. Louis with a record of 18 consecutive victories over the Howley horde.

Herb Pennock was far from the Pennock of World Series fame, but he knew how to cover up in the clinches and received brilliant help on defense, especially from Babe Ruth. [*Pennock's World Series record then stood at 4 victories and no defeats. He would retire with 5 wins, no losses, and a remarkable earned run average of 1.95.*]

Ruth proved that he doesn't have to hit home runs to draw applause. The Big Bam gave as colorful an exhibition as has been seen in an outfield here in many months. Six times he devoured fly balls, and on four of these occasions he climbed to stardom to turn Brownie batters back to the bench with black words on quivering lips. Babe went to the foul line for Harry Rice's fly with the bases loaded and two gone in the fourth. In the fifth, he made successive glove-hand catches, first to pick Bing Miller's low liner off the turf, and again to spear Oscar Melillo's high liner near the left-field wall. Then to top his performance, the animated Apple King sprinted far into left center to rob Leo Dixon of a double in the sixth.

Meanwhile the Babe's shadow, Lou Gehrig, was making home-run hay while the Babe was shining. Lou hit his forty-first of the season with two mates on the runways in the third inning, placing him within one homer of Ruth's total.

[*Gehrig became the fourth person in major league history to hit more than 40 home runs in one season. Ruth had performed the feat 5 times (1920, 54 home runs; 1921, 59; 1923, 41; 1924, 46; 1926, 47; Rogers Hornsby had 42 home runs for the Cardinals in 1922, and Cy Williams had hit 41 for the Browns in 1923.*]

Martin J. Haley, St. Louis *Globe-Democrat*

Thursday, September 1

[*On August 30, the Yankees were not scheduled to play. On August 31, in New York, the Yankees defeated Boston, 8–3. Winning pitcher, George Pipgras (7–3). Yankee home runs, Babe Ruth (43), Tony Lazzeri 2 (18).*]

"Push 'Em Up Tony" Lazzeri hit two home runs yesterday, one into the left field stand and the other into the right field bleachers, and was sitting under the spotlight when along came Ruth in the eighth inning. The Babe smashed out his forty-third home run of the season and was again two up on Lou Gehrig.

Ruth's latest home run was a real clout. He swung in his characteristic way at one of Tony Welzer's curves, and the ball sailed high and far into right field. For a second or two it looked as if the ball would land outside of the park. At that it cleared the heads of the fans in the bleachers and landed near the top of the stand.

While Ruth stole some of Lazzeri's thunder, Tony played a large part in the victory. Four runs rode over the plate as the result of Tony's clouting. His first home run came in the third inning and scored Ruth and Meusel ahead of him. His second home run came in the fourth with nobody on at the time.

William Hennigan, New York *World*

Friday, September 2

[*On September 1, in New York, the Yankees' scheduled game with Boston was postponed because of rain.*]

In Ruth, Gehrig, and Lazzeri, Colonel Ruppert has so much color that the Yankees resemble a necktie designed for the trade in upper Harlem. In comparison, the other teams in the American League look particularly drab.

W. O. McGeehan, New York *Herald-Tribune*

Saturday, September 3

[*On September 2, in Philadelphia, the Yankees won, 12–2. Winning pitcher, Waite Hoyt (19–5). Yankee home runs, Babe Ruth (44), Lou Gehrig 2 (43).*]

Before the Mackmen got a base runner on the paths yesterday the Yanks held a 7 to 0 lead. Before an Elephantine pilgrim touched second base it was 10–0, and after Ruth and Gehrig took their last swings in the eighth the figures stood 12–0.

A two-base fumble by Mark Koenig in the ninth ruined a perfectly good shutout which Waite Hoyt languidly wove around the Pachyderm bat pile.

Overshadowing everything in the game were the mighty hulks of Ruth and Gehrig, the Bambino and Slambino of the Gargantuan Gotham gang.

In the first inning, with two out, came the thunder and lightning.

The Bambino flailed a long spinning liner to right-center. Cobb turned his back on second base and stood as if to play the rebound off the stone wall. But the ball cleared the wall.

"Forty-four!" shrieked the home-run accountants. "That puts him three ahead of Gehrig."

"Yes, but Gehrig hasn't been to bat yet!"

Gehrig came immediately, and slambinoed his team as neatly as at any time this beam-slamming season. Gehrig took a cut at Walberg's first pitch. Gehrig's bat likewise fired a liner, but this one aimed dead to right. Right fielder Walter French did a pivot, like Cobb, but not to play any wall-bounces.

Gehrig's liner cleared not only the fence but also the porch roof across the street and the bay windows full of pallid faces, and almost the very housetops. Last seen, that ball scooted over the back rim of somebody's cottage thatch and fetched up in someone's backyard grass.

Thus Bam and Slam showed their wares to the public.

Then a series of misfortunes hashed up the second inning, and before you could say, "The big bums," up came Bambino and Slambino again. This time the act went after the altitude record. Walberg slow-balled Ruth, and the Bambino exalted a sky-high fly to right. French retreated until his back nearly touched the wall. The ball fell into his hands, counting a sacrifice fly, scoring Combs from third.

Slam outbammed Bam again. His skyscraper scraped a higher sky. French backed up again, but this time he came away from the wall empty handed. The Gehrig fly came down beyond the farthermost concrete, though it did not put a hole in anybody's tin roof.

In all, the Yanks garnered an even 20 hits, of which Gehrig, Combs, and Koenig each bagged 4. Gehrig had two singles subsequent to his two boundary busts.

Bill Brandt, Philadelphia *Public Ledger*

The most astonishing thing that ever happened in organized baseball is the home run race between George Herman Ruth and Henry Louis Gehrig. Even as these lines are batted out of the office typewriter, youths dash out of the AP and UP ticker room every two or three minutes shouting—"Ruth just hit one! Gehrig just hit another one!" There has never been anything like it.

If anything ever looked to be permanent, say three years ago, it was Babe Ruth's record of 59 home runs in one season. You could have given any kind of odds that it would never be duplicated, certainly not within ten or fifteen years. Now Lou Gehrig is a sure thing to break the mark within a few years, and a lot of experts will be confounded again.

Gehrig, of course, cannot approach Ruth as a showman and an eccentric, but there is time even for that. Lou is only a kid. Wait until he develops a little more and runs up against the temptations that beset a popular hero. Ruth without temptations might be a pretty ordinary fellow. Part of his charm lies in the manner with which he succumbs to every temptation that comes his way. That does not mean that Henry Louis must take up sin to become a box office attraction. Rather one awaits to see his reactions to life, which same reactions make a man interesting or not. Right now he seems devoted to fishing, devouring pickled eels, and hitting home runs, of which three things the last is alone of interest to the baseball public.

For this reason it is a little more difficult to write about Henry Louis than George Herman. Ruth is either planning to cut loose, is cutting loose, or is repenting the last time he cut loose. He is a news story on legs going about looking for a place to happen. He has not lived a model life, while Henry Louis has, and if Ruth wins the home run race it will come as a great blow to the pure.

Paul Gallico, New York *Daily News*

Sunday, September 4

[*On September 3, in Philadelphia, the Yankees lost, 1–0. Losing pitcher, Wilcy Moore (15–7).*]

Sergeant York took a hundred Germans and spiked a dozen menacing machine-guns single-handed. Lefty Grove put a muz-

zle and collar on Murderers' Row and made toothpicks out of
the large lumber lugged to home plate by Ruth and Gehrig. [*On
October 10, 1918, Corporal Alvin York, the reluctant infantryman from
the Tennessee mountains, performed an action that made him a legend.
Single-handedly, he wiped out an entire German machine gun battalion.
With 18 shots he killed 18 men, and the remaining 132 men, including
3 officers, became his captives, and 132 guns were silenced. Three weeks
later, on November 1, Corporal York was promoted to Sergeant.*]

The Tennessee mountaineer pulled his miracle nearly ten
years ago. The Marylander [*from the town of Lonaconing*] did his
just yesterday, with 30,000 neighbors watching him work his
wonder. Saturday's children howled with happiness.

Saturday, September 3, served the league-leaders their first
shutout of the season. Robert Moses Grove was head waiter,
and the service was perfect. Red-hot fireballs all afternoon was
the menu, garnished with a fall-away curve which they never ordered. In giving them first taste of whitewash, Robert Mose
touched the volcanic peak of his 1927 record. He fanned nine,
and in the second inning he flattened Meusel, Lazzeri, and Dugan on strikes, on just ten pitched balls. After two strikes, Dugan
nicked a foul, preventing Grove from tying the world's record,
three strikeouts on nine pitched balls.

The decision was gained over the arch-enemy of the A's, Wilcy
Moore.

[*The Yankees had played in 127 consecutive games this season without
being shut out, a mark that then stood as a record. In 1932, the Yankees
would erase this record by going through the entire season of 156 games
without being shut out. The season provided the heart of another record,
308 consecutive games without being shut out, from August 3, 1931,
through August 2, 1933.*]

Bill Brandt, Philadelphia Public Ledger

Monday, September 5

[*On September 4, the Yankees were not scheduled to play.*]

The straw hat season has been called in so far as the Yankees are
concerned. Convinced that their summer hats had something to
do with their first shutout of the year, they smashed every straw

hat that appeared in their party on the way home to New York, and some dozen players walked through Penn Station Saturday night bareheaded. The Babe, of course, went unmolested as he wears an all-year-round cap.

The New York Times

AMERICAN LEAGUE STANDINGS

	W	L	PCT	GB		W	L	PCT	GB
New York	90	38	.703	—	Chicago	60	67	.472	29½
Philadelphia	73	55	.570	17	Cleveland	58	71	.450	32½
Washington	68	58	.540	21	St. Louis	52	76	.406	38
Detroit	69	59	.539	21	Boston	40	86	.317	49

Tuesday, September 6

[*On September 5, in Boston, the Yankees split a doubleheader, losing, in 18 innings, 11–12, and winning a 5-inning game ended by darkness, 5–2. Losing pitcher, Waite Hoyt (19–6); winning pitcher, Urban Shocker (15–6). Home run, Lou Gehrig (44).*]

To say that yesterday was a banner day at Fenway Park is putting it a little meekly. The crowd of 38,000 which jammed its way into the park was paying tribute once more to George Herman "Babe" Ruth's ability to draw the public everywhere. [*The crowd set an attendance record for Fenway Park, which has fewer than thirty-four thousand seats.*]

A crowd from all parts of New England, estimated as high as 70,000, tried to force its way into the enclosure. As early as 1:05 ticket selling for seats stopped, then for another 20 minutes standing room was sold, and that completed the sale for the day.

Once inside it was a question of find yourself a place. Some lined along the outfield, which necessitated ground rules [*balls falling into the crowd would be ruled as doubles*]; others climbed the fence to obtain a good view of the action; some watched from under the grandstand, while many of those unable to obtain entrance took to the high buildings overlooking the park. With such an auspicious crowd it was befitting that the Red Sox should put up a great battle and at the end of 18 innings emerge victorious.

It was 6:30 when the first game was over and most of the crowd had started home. With the sun fast sinking, Umpire Nallin called the second game at the end of five innings.

The battle between Babe Ruth and Lou Gehrig goes merrily onward, with the two deadlocked once more. In the third inning of the first game the former Columbia University star sent one of Charles Ruffing's pitches into the right field bleachers, scoring Koenig ahead of him.

Gehrig has found the Boston pitchers easier to solve than Ruth. He has totalled 10 four-base hits off the Red Sox compared to 6 made by Ruth.

Boston Evening Transcript

Out in the right field pavilion yesterday, future John D. Rockefellers were asking and getting a whole dime for the score cards across the front of which is emblazoned in red ink, "Official 5¢ Score Card." But nobody cared.

"Sportsman," Boston Globe

Wednesday, September 7

[*On September 6, in Boston, the Yankees split a doubleheader, 14–2 and 2–3. Winning pitcher, Herb Pennock (15–7); losing pitcher, Dutch Ruether (12–5). Yankee home runs, Babe Ruth 3 (47), Lou Gehrig (45).*]

Babe Ruth showed old Boston friends, to the number of 20,000, why he still is baseball's master slugger by making three home runs yesterday afternoon. Two of the smashes were epic. His first was the longest ever made at Fenway Park. It came in the sixth inning of the first game, with two on base, off the delivery of Tony Welzer and cleared the high board fence in left center field, only a few yards from dead center.

No other player has ever hit the ball over that part of the left center fence, and that the Bambino is a left hand batter adds considerably to the rating of the smash.

In the very next inning Ruth lofted a tremendously high fly

off Welzer, and it carried on and on until it just cleared the fence in front of the open space between the two sections of bleachers in right.

The Sox had a 5–0 lead when Ruth came to bat in the ninth inning of the second game. He lashed the second pitched ball to the very middle of the center field bleachers, a mighty wallop which would get first place for the day were it not for the tremendous blast over the left center field wall in the first game.

If he has many more days like yesterday, Ruth's 1921 record will go fading out and be forgotten. Home run hitting is streaky at best, and the Bam said last night that he thought he had his swing going well. He hopes to get a couple more today, his last appearance in Boston this year. He says he likes Fenway Park as a home run stage. He likes the background in center field when there is no overflow crowd to blur the vision.

Ruth's greatest home runs in point of distance are those he made in Tampa, in Detroit, and in Chicago. At Tampa against the Giants in the spring of 1919 he slammed a ball 500 feet from the plate. He then was a Red Sox. In Yankee regalia he cleared the center field fence in Detroit with a tremendous slam which broke all records in a city where slugging for years was the common thing. Only this summer he whacked a homer over the double-decked right field stand at Comiskey Park, Chicago, for what Windy City experts said was easily the most prodigious homer they had ever seen.

But the Babe's first homer yesterday probably was a more meritorious performance than any of his other gems. In the first place, it was to the left field side of center field. It cleared a wall that rises at least 35 feet and must have landed 500 feet from home. In the second place the wind was cutting across the path of this parabola. Thirdly, he was not hitting the cripple, as the count was one ball and one strike when he connected.

The count was three balls and no strikes when he made No. 46, and the ball went an amazing distance into the air and was helped by the wind. [*Ruth was one of the very few players at this time with the freedom to swing at a pitch when the count was three balls and no strikes.*] His No. 47 was made with the count one strike and no balls, and you can visualize the middle of the right field bleachers and see just what a smash it had to be to carry that far. Only the fresh memory of No. 45 prevented the enthusiastic fans from labelling No. 47 the "greatest ever."

In the fifth inning of the first game, the Babe's slugging team-mate, Lou Gehrig, got a homer with none on and temporarily went one ahead of Ruth. Then the Bam heard the fervent prayers of his New England devotees, and now he leads by two homers.

By way of keeping the records straight, the two teams divided honors, which, of course, was beside the issue, for the crowd showed interest in one thing, the Home Run Derby.

Burt Whitman, Boston *Herald*

Thursday, September 8

[*On September 7, in Boston, the Yankees won, 12–10. Winning pitcher, Bob Shawkey (2–3). Yankee home runs, Babe Ruth 2 (49).*]

Two vicious drives, one clearing the distant left field wall and the other flopping into the outstretched spaces of the center field bleachers, carried Babe Ruth within hailing distance of his home run record.

Crashing his fifth circuit wallop in two days—another record, by the way—Babe increased his lead to four over Lou Gehrig. [*The record—five home runs in three consecutive games—remained inviolate until May 23–24, 1936, when it was raised to six by Tony Lazzeri. Lazzeri's mark has been equaled but never surpassed.*]

Ruth hit his forty-eighth homer off Danny MacFayden in the first inning. It soared over the left field wall far beyond the clock. It was a mighty blow but not as long as that made by him on Tuesday.

"Slim" Harriss was Ruth's forty-ninth victim, in the eighth. This drive landed in the center field seats. Babe also made a double and a single, and then went out on strikes. Meanwhile Gehrig couldn't get under the ball, although he did hit two doubles.

The Sox should have won the game; three errors and costly passes wrecked their chances.

Eddie Hurley, Boston *Daily Advertiser*

For several weeks about the only race in the American League was between Ruth and Gehrig for the home run honors, and now it appears that the "Babe" has eliminated Gehrig and the only thing left for him to beat is his own record.

James C. O'Leary, Boston *Globe*

Baseball magnates who welcomed (?) broadcasting of ball games from their parks have not developed enthusiasm for the idea as the season progresses, and with good reason. The big objection is not that broadcasting keeps the fan from the ball park, but rather on the basis that the "announcements" by radio are doing harm in various ways and seriously prejudicing the game in general and many of its participants in particular.

The trouble seems to be that a majority of "announcers," however good they may be as entertainers, do not know enough about baseball to get by. Not only that, some of them are more "opinionated," than fair or square.

The Sporting News

Friday, September 9

[*On September 8, in New York, the Yankees defeated St. Louis, 2–1. Winning pitcher, Waite Hoyt (20–6).*]

It was Tony Lazzeri Day at Yankee Stadium yesterday, but when it was over Waite Hoyt was the golden-haired boy. For a long time it has been the ambition of the Brooklyn lad to win 20 games a season, and now the trick has been accomplished.

In setting back the Browns for the nineteenth time this year, Waite of Erasmus [*Erasmus Hall High, Brooklyn*] won his twentieth victory and, I understand, grabbed off a $2,500 bonus.

"That fellow should win me 20 games every year," Miller Huggins once told me, pointing to the Brooklyn mortician.

But heretofore Waite always stopped with 19, 18, 17, or something like that. [*In each of two seasons, 1921 and 1922, Hoyt had won nineteen games.*] Now he has made it a score and hopes to put it up several notches.

Hoyt caught Sad Sam Jones as an opponent, and the Woodsfield [*Ohio*] Sage was very good. There were only seven hits in the game, four by the Yanks and three by the Browns. Jones, however, walked eight Yanks, and two of them checked their passes into runs.

Tony Lazzeri's neighbors, kin, and admirers were there, and in such numbers that the Browns are likely to get quite an unexpectedly large check out of the series. They presented Tony with a floral horseshoe, a lot of silver, and many compliments.

What was more natural then than to have Sam Jones fan Tony with the bases full in the first inning. Sam repeated it a few innings later. [*Traditionally, whenever a player was honored with a "day," he came up with a poor performance.*] However, in the fifth Tony rocked in Babe Ruth with a sacrifice fly. It proved the winning run, so the day wasn't exactly lost to the Californian.

George Herman Ruth failed to add any homers to his collection, but he was walked three times. As for Gehrig, he walked twice and fanned twice.

Fred Lieb, New York Post

Saturday, September 10

[*On September 9, in New York, the Yankees defeated St. Louis, 9–3. Winning pitcher, Urban Shocker (16–6).*]

The king felt in the rather democratic mood to indulge in some menial labor yesterday. He hit no regal home runs, but when, early in the contest, the Yankees were in dire need of a few runs to put the Browns in their proper place, Babe Ruth thumped two vigorous singles off his loyal bat and drove in three runs, roused the Yanks out of a sound sleep, and tossed the deluded Brownies into a panic.

The Yanks ran their string of victories over Dan Howley's earnest young men to 20 in a row. The Hugmen now need only the next two games to give them the distinction of being the first major league team to sweep an entire season's series from a rival club.

Urban Shocker allowed three hits, duplicating Waite Hoyt's performance of the day before.

John Drebinger, The New York Times

Sunday, September 11

[*On September 10, in New York, the Yankees defeated St. Louis, 1–0. Winning pitcher, Wilcy Moore (17–7.)*]

Something akin, perhaps, to Mr. Tennyson's famous stream, the Yankees' winning streak over the Browns goes on and on. [*The allusion is apparently to Alfred Tennyson's* Song from the Brook, *where the stream soliloquizes: "For men may come and men may go/But I go on forever."*]

While 20,000 addicts chorused their glee, the New Yorks won their twenty-first consecutive game from the visitors, thereby establishing a record for the American League and tying the National League record. [*The record tied by the Yankees was that of the Cubs, who, in 1909, won twenty-one games against Boston while losing only one.*]

Yesterday that likeable, red-necked ancient gentleman from Oklahoma wove a spell about the helpless visitors. Wilcy pitched an impassioned, de luxe variety of armmanship, an admirable exhibition in which he grudgingly gave seven hits. Hardly less commendable was young Lefty Stewart. He, too, allowed only seven hits.

The winning run? Well, constituents, that was created in the eighth. The tall Meusel feller poked a double to left. Signor Lazzeri sacrificed him to third, and sturdy little Mike Gazella whipped a long sacrifice to center, Meusel tearing home.

That's all there was to it.

In the fifth, Prof. E. B. Combs singled to left to become the first American Leaguer to make 200 hits this year. [*On the preceding Wednesday, Gehrig had obtained hit number 199, but he had had none since then.*]

Marshall Hunt, New York *Daily News*

Cy Moore, with close to 50 games participated in this year, is as "iron" as any pitcher ever was—big and strong and with as much endurance as any pitcher since Ed Walsh's time, but he has some hard horse sense of how much work a pitcher can stand. [*In 1907, Ed Walsh appeared in 419 innings for the Chicago White Sox, and in the following year, he won 40 games while setting a record that will surely never be equaled, that of pitching in 465 innings. In 1927, Moore's total number of innings pitched was 215.*] He doesn't regard himself as super in any way in stamina. For instance, says he, "Every fourth day is often enough for any pitcher taking his regular turn. A pitcher needs three days of rest to be at his best."

"Suppose you were called on every day for a stretch? How long do you think you could do it and still deliver good pitching?"

"Well, that depends. If it were good warm weather, so you could sweat and loosen up, and you were called in the latter part of the games I think I could go in every day for seven days and be right. That, I believe, would be plenty."

Moore is a typical farmer. He lives on and owns his grain lands in Oklahoma. He is ruddy, sandy haired, with hair a bit thin, with blue eyes which tell their story of a life spent in gazing across the prairie miles, straight as a poplar, self-reliant, the soul of good humor. There are hundreds like him in the Missouri Valley and have been since the days of border warfare in the '60's, and in the Red River country, on the farms of Kansas and in the wide reaches of western Texas.

In the city he looks like a farmer on a visit to the city, but never get the notion that he's a gawk or a clod. He has a bit of a twang, but butchers no man's English. He is a big, smiling, affable, upstanding man of frank, engaging personality, with the friendly manners of a child.

He knows his soil and his irrigation. He knows about radios and wave lengths. He knows his refinements. Gorgeous hotels do not overawe him. Their silver and napery are not mysterious to him. A knife is a knife, and a fork a fork. Still, he's a farmer, a farmer and a pitcher, and real in both. I never have met a man, attaining success and fame as quickly as he has, who is more unspoiled. He is just himself.

And, the Yankees declare, "He is the greatest natural pitcher that has come into this league since Walter Johnson."

[*Moore's greatness as a pitcher was limited to 1927. He remained in the American League for 5 more seasons, but, troubled periodically by a sore arm, he won only 32 games while losing 37, with an earned run average well above 4.00.*]

W. B. Hanna, New York *Herald-Tribune*

Monday, September 12

[*On September 11, in New York, the Yankees lost to St. Louis, 6–2. Losing pitcher, Herb Pennock (15–8). Yankee home run, Babe Ruth (50).*]

Tolerant clients of this bureau, it just couldn't be done.

Your Yanks were confronted with the possibility of defeating the Browns in every one of the 22 games scheduled for them, but failed in the final.

While a Sabbath multitude of 35,000 occupied the chairs and benches of the Ruppert enclosure, Master Milton Gaston threw so admirably that the Yanks could persuade him to issue no more than five hits and no more than one in any round.

But one Yankee blow evoked a symphony of ebullience among the addicts, and that was—yes, you guessed it—a home run by that incomparable captain of the home run industry, G. Herman Ruth. It was fashioned in the fourth inning, with no colleagues on base, and we suspect it was just about one of the longest he ever clubbed in the Bronx bazaar. O, you've heard that before, but Babe's fiftieth four-base contribution found haven about ten rows below the right field advertisements and well to the left.

No. 50 for the Bambino!

Now, we are almost positive that the Bambino has clinched the home run championship. It will be an arduous job for Comrade Gehrig to catch up with him, eh?

[*For the third time, Ruth had hit fifty home runs in one season. In 1932, after Ruth had reached this plateau four times, Jimmy Foxx would become the second major league player to hit fifty home runs in a season. Ruth's hit, incidentally, was the one hundred forty-first Yankee home run for 1927, thereby breaking a major league club record set by the Chicago Cubs of 1884.*]

Marshall Hunt, New York *Daily News*

Life membership in the Elks, and a solid gold card case, studded with diamonds and rubies, was the gift drawn by Joe Dugan yesterday at Yankee Stadium. It was Dugan Day, and several hundred Elks from White Plains Lodge, No. 535, motored to the Stadium to honor Dugan, who is a member of that lodge.

New York *American*

AMERICAN LEAGUE STANDINGS

	W	L	PCT	GB		W	L	PCT	GB
New York	90	41	.701	—	Chicago	65	70	.481	27
Philadelphia	78	57	.578	14	Cleveland	60	75	.444	32
Detroit	71	63	.530	20½	St. Louis	55	80	.407	37
Washington	71	64	.526	21	Boston	44	90	.328	47½

Tuesday, September 13

[*On September 12, the Yankees were not scheduled to play.*]

George Herman "Babe" Ruth appeared in West Side Court yesterday in answer to a summons served on him by Bernard Neimeyer, sketch artist and interior decorator, of 61 West Seventieth Street, who charged that the home-run king struck him "a terrible blow in my right eye with his left fist" on the evening of July 4. [*Ruth was, of course, left-handed.*]

Ruth, expressing surprise at the charge, declared he was at Garfield, N.J., at the time of the assault. With him in court were two friends who said they had been in Garfield with Ruth on the evening of July 4. At the request of Neimeyer disposition of the case was put over until Friday to give him an opportunity to assemble witnesses.

At 11 o'clock on the night of July 4, Neimeyer said, he was walking north on Broadway at Seventy-fourth Street when two women passed him. A moment later a man brushed roughly against him and shouted to the women, "Did that guy try to speak to you?" Without waiting for a reply, Neimeyer said, "He struck me a terrible blow in my right eye with his left fist." [*Babe Ruth lived in the Ansonia Hotel, on Broadway between Seventy-third and Seventy-fourth Streets.*]

"I begged him to stop," Niemeyer continued, "and told him that I was forty-nine years old, partially blind in one eye, had a cataract on the other, and was only partly recovered from a ruptured spine. He said. 'Why did you speak to my wife? By this time one of the women had come back. She said, 'George, George, he didn't speak to us.' By this time a crowd had gathered, and I heard them whispering that the big fellow was Babe Ruth. I said, 'Grab him, somebody, grab him.' But nobody grabbed him."

Neimeyer then appealed to the traffic policeman on the corner, "but he said that sort of thing was not in his line of duty and that I would have to get the patrolman on the beat. I said the man must be of terrible importance if he could strike me and not get arrested. The policeman advised me to get a summons. I then ran after the man, who was showing the women into a taxi, and tried to get his name.

"When I asked him his name he just held up his hand and said, 'Why, brother, everybody knows me.' Then he asked the women again whether I had insulted them, and this time they said, 'Yes, he did, George.' Then the man got into the cab, the traffic policeman shooed the crowd away, and the cab drove off down Seventy-second Street."

In the days following, Neimeyer said, he had difficulty in getting a summons because he was unwilling to charge Ruth directly without seeing him again. He finally obtained a John Doe summons and served it on Ruth at Yankee Stadium on July 29. Yesterday Neimeyer was positive in his identification of Ruth saying he would "never forget that face, that physique, and that dog-trot walk."

In denying the charges Ruth said, "I'm not mad at this fellow. I feel sorry for him."

New York Herald-Tribune

Wednesday, September 14

[*On September 13, in New York, the Yankees won a doubleheader from Cleveland, 5–3 and 5–3. Winning pitchers, George Pipgras (8–3) and Waite Hoyt (21–6). Yankee home runs, Babe Ruth 2 (52), Pat Collins (7), Earle Combs (5).*]

The Yankees clinched the American League pennant yesterday, and Babe Ruth drew nearer to his 1921 record.

Waite Hoyt, former Flatbush "boy wonder," officiated in the

second game and had the honor of pitching the Yankees to the championship and Miller Huggins to his fifth American League pennant. The Flatbush boy allowed ten hits but kept them well scattered.

Ruth hit his first home run, a terrific drive into the right field bleachers in the seventh inning of the early performance, at the expense of Willis Hudlin. It came after Mark Anthony Koenig had singled. His second home run came in the fourth inning of the second game, another drive into the right field bleachers. None of Ruth's co-workers were on base at the time, but the blow started the Yankees on a four-run rally which gave them the victory and the championship.

There is still a possibility of Ruth's reaching the 59 home runs that he made in 1921. The Babe said that he believed that he would equal the record, if not shatter it, if the opposing pitchers would pitch to him in the remaining 14 games. They probably will now that the Yankees have won the pennant.

When Koenig, Lazzeri, and Gehrig completed a double play in the ninth inning of the second game and assured the Yankees of the pennant, Huggins finally smiled. When the Yankees went on their final Western trip, the little manager declared that he would not smile until the pennant was won.

He started smiling after the game but stopped when he remembered that there was a World Series to be played. Most likely Huggins will not smile again until the world's championship is won.

[*Miller Huggins had won five pennants in a period of seven years, a feat that had been accomplished by only two other major league managers, Cap Anson (Chicago Cubs, 1880–86) and Ned Hanlon (Baltimore Orioles and Brooklyn Superbas, 1894–1900).*]

William Hennigan, New York *World*

Thursday, September 15

[*On September 14, in New York, the Yankees defeated Cleveland, 4–1. Winning pitcher, Dutch Ruether (13–5).*]

Apparently little Miller Huggins is not going to give his regulars a rest before the World Series starts. Yesterday he used all of his "big guns" against the Indians. "Dutch" Ruether did the flipping, and he held the Indians runless until the ninth.

Neither Babe Ruth nor Lou Gehrig came through with a home run. The Babe helped himself to one little ordinary single in three times at bat and so did the clouting first baseman.

William Hennigan, New York *World*

On a golf basis the Yankees won the league championship by 18 up and 17 to play, a rather large margin. It's a great team. How could anybody keep them from winning? It was no trouble for them to dash off in a cloud of dust and keep going.

It was quite simple. Ruth and Gehrig hit an imposing total of home runs. Meusel, Lazzeri, and Combs were knocking over rival pitchers while Pennock, Hoyt, Ruether, Moore, and Shocker mesmerized rival batsmen. A fine team gave a great performance. Then three rousing cheers and a tiger for Babe Ruth, Lou Gehrig, Tony—whoa up! Who is that quizzical little gentleman in the corner?

"That ain't no gentleman. That's only Miller Huggins."

Huggins? The name sounds familiar. He's been with the club quite a while, hasn't he? Secretary—or something. Oh, the manager! Why, of course. Odd how it slips the memory, isn't it?

But Ruth, Gehrig, Lazzeri, Combs, and other such chaps are the important men on the club, aren't they? Certainly.

The general attitude toward Huggins is that of the rookie private who didn't know enough about army regulations to salute an elderly officer.

"Don't you know what I am?" thundered the officer. "I'm the Colonel of this regiment!"

"Well, I'll be jiggered!" said the admiring private. "You've got a darn fine job, Colonel, and I advise you to keep it."

The apology for dragging this ancient tale from the dusty archives is that it seems to fit. When Huggins is recalled to mind at all, it is with the sudden thought: There's a lucky chap with a fine job.

Well, it is a fine job, but who made it a fine job? Miller J. Huggins, Esq. He made it what it is. Everyone connected with the club seems well pleased, including not only the owner but all the individual players.

It is a pleasure to hear Tony Lazzeri discourse on the subject of the Yankee manager, done in an unusual manner.

"Huggins! That little shrimp!" roars Tony. "That skinny little guy is the greatest feller in the world. Say, that measly little runt! He knows more about baseball than any blinking lug in the business. That Singer midget has a brain bigger'n an elephant. That shriveled peanut! He treats me white! I'm for him. He's OK!"

It is agreed on all sides that Ruth, Gehrig, Lazzeri, Moore, Combs, Hoyt, and others won this year's pennant. They get the lion's share of the credit. Huggins gets what is left over, if anything.

Huggins didn't pitch a single winning ball game, and not once did he hit a triple with the bases filled. But he won two pennants without Pennock and three without Ruether or Shocker. He won three pennants before Gehrig, Combs, and Lazzeri blossomed out as stars. He won four pennants before he ever heard of Wilcy Moore.

In time the thought will crash through that this Huggins has had more than a little to do with the success of the Yankees in the last decade.

[*It is, nevertheless, true that Huggins won no pennants without Babe Ruth, and in 1925, the year of disaster for Ruth, when he appeared in only ninety-eight games, the Yankees finished in seventh place.*]

John Kieran, *The New York Times*

Friday, September 16

[*On September 15, in New York, the Yankees lost to Cleveland 3–2. Losing pitcher, Myles Thomas (7–4).*]

The Yankees missed their one hundredth victory of the season and Babe Ruth his fifty-third home run by a matter of five or six inches yesterday. Ruth's near home run came in the fifth inning with Earle Combs, the dashing Kentuckian on first. Ruth hit a high drive into right field. It had all the ear marks of a real home run, and the crowd let out a yell. Ruth trotted down to first base smiling.

Homer Summa, who was standing on the embankment in right field when the ball was hit, rushed up against the bleachers and put his back against the screen. As the ball descended, Summa leaped and caught it in his upstretched gloved hand. It was quite a spectacular catch, and the crowd cheered.

Ruth hit the ball hard throughout the game. In the third inning the big fellow hit another drive that Summa caught close to the bleachers. In the eighth he swung viciously at a curve and rammed the ball into deep center. Johnny Gill, the Indians' recruit outfielder, started up the embankment and jumped, but the ball caromed off his glove. Gill landed against the fence of the bleachers, and Ruth stopped at second with a double. Gehrig followed with his lone single of the day, and Ruth scored.

Myles Thomas started for the Yankees, and the Indians scored all their runs off him. For Cleveland's George Uhle [*the Yankee nemesis*] pitched a right smart game. He had good control of his curve ball and kept working the corner of the plate. He struck out Gehrig in the fourth, Lou missing the third strike by a foot or more. In the third, Ruth fanned on four pitches.

William Hennigan, New York World

Although the baseball season is almost over, Connie Mack, manager of the Athletics, sought to restrain legally a fan whose alleged "raspberries" and taunts broke up the morale of the team and resulted in a valuable player being traded.

The fan, whose voice is said to carry all over Shibe Park with the resonance of a "three mile loud speaker," is Harry Donnelly, 26. He was arrested yesterday by policemen detailed at the park at the request of Mr. Mack while the game with the White Sox was in progress.

At a hearing before Magistrate Down in the 22nd Street station today, Mr. Mack poured out his tale of woe.

"There are several people," he said, "who come out to the park just to ride the players and umpires and 'get their goats.' One day last week Umpires Hildebrand and Rollings stopped the game for ten minutes and refused to go on until the fans stopped their raspberries.

"On Wednesday Donnelly rode third baseman Sammy Hale [*playing in his seventh major league season*] until he had him so nervous he would have missed the ball had one been hit to him. In this game an error might have meant defeat.

"Bill Lamar was one of the best outfielders I ever had, but a group of fans, of which this man was the leader, kept riding him until he wasn't any good to me and I had to trade him away. It seems that this man pays his $1.10 to come and ride the players. Why doesn't he save it and meet them outside after the game? We want him to stay away."

Magistrate Dorn held Donnelly in $500 bail to keep the peace and threatened to fine him if he were arrested again for handing out "raspberries."

[*Bill Lamar, who had been released earlier in the season, had been a major leaguer, with four teams, for ten seasons. Only in 1925 and 1926, playing with the Athletics, did he appear in more than a hundred games. In 1925, he batted .356, and then in the following year, perhaps because of jeers from the stands, his average fell to .284.*]

Philadelphia *Evening Bulletin*

Saturday, September 17

[*On September 16, in New York, the Yankees defeated Chicago, 7–3. Winning pitcher, Wilcy Moore (18–7). Yankee home runs, Babe Ruth (53), Bob Meusel (8), Wilcy Moore (1).*]

George Herman "Babe" Ruth clouted his fifty-third home run and the Yankees scored their one hundredth victory of the season yesterday, but the real, big, gigantic event of the afternoon was Farmer Wilcy Moore's first major league home run.

Ever since he became a Yankee, Moore's greatest ambition has been to hit the ball into the bleachers and jog slowly around the bases a la Babe Ruth while the crowd cheered wildly. Ruth smashed the ball into the right field bleachers in the third inning and trotted around the bases while the crowd roared. Babe came back to the bench smiling.

"Huh," growled Moore, "I'm going to hit the ball into the bleachers before this here game is over. I've spent all my energy on pitching, but now that the Yankees have won the pennant, I'm going out and get a few home runs."

"I'll buy you the best box of cigars in town if you do," said Babe.

The big pitcher came up to the plate in the fourth inning after

Benny Bengough had flied out. He swung at a fast one on the outside of the plate, and the ball sailed into the right field bleachers. Moore jogged slowly around the bases with his chest held high and a regular Ruth smile on his face. The crowd cheered wildly.

"That don't go," yelled the Babe as Moore came back to the bench. "You had your eyes closed when you hit the ball." Farmer Moore declared that his eyes were wide open and that, as soon as he hit the ball, he knew he had his first major league home run. [*It also proved to be the last home run in his major league career, which would continue for six seasons.*]

Long Bob Meusel was the real big hitter of the day. He helped himself to a home run, a double, and a single, and drove in three runs. His Ruthian smash in the fifth was a terrific clout to deep left center [*an inside-the-park hit that became a home run by virtue of Meusel's unusually fast running*].

William Hennigan, New York *World*

The scene is the Yankees' dugout before yesterday's game. The White Sox are at batting practice. Only Arthur Fletcher, utility infielder Julian Wera, and a couple of bat boys are on the bench.

Enter Miller Huggins.

Huggins—Not much interest here these days.

Fletcher—Do you wonder?

Huggins—Nope. I'll be glad when we get started.

Enter Babe Ruth with a new glove.

Huggins—Let me see that. Why, you use a smaller glove than I did.

Ruth—Sure. I like them small. I'm going to break this one in for the series.

A group of players straggle in.

Ruth (looking out on the field)—Where's my cousin. [*A pitcher who is easy for a batter to hit against is known as that batter's cousin.*]

Ruth means Alphonse Thomas [*a nineteen-game winner in 1927, but easy for Ruth*].

Thomas is working out at third base.

Thomas—Right here, Babe.

Ruth—How the hell did he hear me? He must have rabbit ears.

Paschal—Babe wants to know how you heard him, Tommy.

Thomas—I got rabbit ears.

Ruth—Did that guy ever pitch a game against us that I didn't make a home run?

Paschal—Babe says he hopes you pitch all four games. He wants to tie his home run record.

Thomas—I'll throw him my masterpiece.

Ruth—If you do, I'll knock down one of your infielders.

Fletcher—Who's that catching for the Sox?

Durst—A guy named Battle.

Ruth—Can he?

Durst—I dunno. He's an infielder.

Fletcher—What's he catching for?

Ruth—He must be a good infielder. [*Jim Battle's major league career consisted of six games during 1927.*]

Frank Graham, New York *Sun*

George Herman Ruth stalked out of West Side Court yesterday with a pleased air of vindication when Magistrate Adolph Stern dismissed the charge of assault against him. His admirers seized him and lifted him shoulder high with shouts and cheers.

A wide grin crossed the Babe's rubicund face, and he predicted that he would "knock one over the fence" before the day was done—a prophecy promptly fulfilled during the afternoon.

Ruth arrived in court with several alibi witnesses prepared to prove that he was at Garfield, N.J., on the night of July 4 and therefore could not have assaulted Bernard Niemeyer at Broadway and Seventy-fourth Street.

Only one witness was heard—Niemeyer, who made excited and incoherent statements for an hour and 45 minutes.

Several hundred baseball fans crowded into the West Side Court to have a look at Ruth. He was as solemn as a bewildered owl when Niemeyer took the stand and made his charges. As he testified, he grew more and more excited. He was as often on his feet as in the witness chair, and the magistrate admonished him to "take it easy."

Each time Niemeyer pointed in the direction of Ruth and referred to him as "this man," the Babe stared at his accuser with a hurt air. It was only when Magistrate Stern exonerated him that he grinned and turned with relief to something he understood—the handshakes of crowding baseball fans.

When it was over, the magistrate denied the motion of the Assistant District Attorney that the complainant be committed to the psychopathic ward of Bellevue Hospital for observation.

New York *Herald-Tribune*

Sunday, September 18

[*On September 17, in New York, the Yankees won a doubleheader with Chicago, 3–2 and 8–1. Winning pitchers, Urban Shocker (17–6) and Herb Pennock (16–8). Yankee home run, Earle Combs (6).*]

The winnings of the Yankees climbed to a total of 102 yesterday.

The good hitting and spirited work of Earle Combs was one rich morsel of the afternoon, and another was the timely hitting of Meusel. The Babe did a lot of walking, too much to suit the fans.

In the first game the spitball rivals, Shocker and Faber, had a duel which was close and skillfully pitched. Both veterans of the damp delivery were in form reminiscent of their best days.

In the second game, Pennock, in effectiveness, outlasted Connally. Herbert did his stuff in a manner beyond reproach with men on base.

In the third inning of the first game, Alex Metzler hit a fluke home run off Shocker. With two out, Combs came in on Metzler's liner instead of making sure and playing it on the bounce. But he was trying and not standing there like a wooden man, as Ruth did. The $70,000 star was a 7-cent supernumerary on that play, and the hit became a homer because he didn't back up Combs.

W. B. Hanna, New York *Herald-Tribune*

Monday, September 19

[*On September 18, in New York, the Yankees won a doubleheader from Chicago, 2–1 and 5–1. Winning pitchers, George Pipgras (9–3) and Waite Hoyt (22–6). Yankee home run, Babe Ruth (54).*]

Waite Hoyt, George Pipgras, and the one and only George Herman Ruth co-operated to give the Hugmen a clean sweep of the
five-game series with the White Sox. Pipgras limited the City of
Wind aggregation to four singles in the first game, and then
Waite Hoyt, Flatbush's boy mortician, handed them twice as
many hits in the closing chapter but kept the run column the
same as his predecessor left it. [*The losing pitcher in this second
game was Ted Lyons, with whom Waite Hoyt would be tied at the ~ of
the season for the most victories, twenty-two.*]

As for the third gentleman in question, all he did was to cause
the fans who cherished the thought of keeping their straw bun-
nies for a gala occasion to throw them away when he smacked his
fifty-fourth in the fifth frame of the second game. The clout was
a ponderous one, landing far from the sight of any customer
who sat in the stands. When last seen it was travelling in the
general direction of the scoreboard.

Joseph L. Roberts, New York Morning Telegraph

AMERICAN LEAGUE STANDINGS

	W	L	PCT	GB		W	L	PCT	GB
New York	104	42	.712	—	Chicago	65	78	.455	37½
Philadelphia	84	58	.592	18	Cleveland	62	79	.440	39½
Washington	75	66	.532	26½	St. Louis	57	85	.401	45
Detroit	75	67	.528	27	Boston	47	94	.333	54½

Wednesay, September 21

[*On September 19 and 20 the Yankees were not scheduled to play.*]

Real punchers favor the punch, and always will.

Simply because they believe he packs the wallop, most of your
Yankees pick Jack Dempsey to win from Gene Tunney in Chicago tomorrow night.

Among Dempsey's strongest boosters are the twin sons of swat,
Lou Gehrig and Babe Ruth.

"I've stuck with Dempsey in all his fights, and I'm sticking with
him now," the Babe declared. "Dempsey packs the wallop—and
the wallop counts in fighting as in baseball."

"I'm for Dempsey," Gehrig said. "I believe Dempsey will wear Tunney down and put him away."

Miller Huggins, master strategist, is a Tunney man. "Tunney is too fast, too clever," Miller opines, "He'll hold Dempsey off just like clever, smart pitching can stop the sluggers."

The sluggers like the slugger, and the strategist prefers the clever boy.

Dutch Ruether also is for Tunney. But most of the other Yankees prefer Dempsey. They include Collins, Lazzeri, Koenig, Combs, Paschal, Meusel, Grabowski, Durst, and Thomas.

Ford C. Frick, New York Evening Journal

Thursday, September 22

[*On September 21, in New York, the Yankees lost to Detroit, 6–1. Losing pitcher, Dutch Ruether (13–6). Yankee home run, Babe Ruth (55).*]

There weren't many redeeming features in the playing by the Yankees yesterday. One might even say there weren't any redeeming features but for Babe Ruth's stupendous home run in the ninth inning which saved the champions from a shutout.

Babe mauled Gibson, who had pitched the Yankees into complete submission, for a drive into the far angle of the right field bleachers. He also made two singles and a fine catch, so here was one Yankee who played baseball. None of the others did, but Ruth's homer sent the crowd, which had been in a sour and sarcastic mood, home in a much better frame of mind.

The Yankees played fumbling, indolent baseball. They totaled six errors and were as keen mentally as they were adroit physically. Their infield work was mottled and doltish. Dutch Ruether pitched much better than his support. The fecund facility of the Yankees for distributing errors had more to do with the Detroit runs than Detroit hits. Koenig and Lazzeri were sleeping around second base, and Combs let a ball slip through him. The Yankees played as if they had been practicing around a pinochle table the last two days.

Ruth, by way of contrast with the others, went to the screen in the ninth inning and nabbed a big drive from little Jackie Tav-

ener. There was more action and style in that play than in all the
rest of the home defense put together.

W. B. Hanna, New York *Herald-Tribune*

Friday, September 23

[*On September 22, in New York, the Yankees defeated Detroit, 8–7.
Winning pitcher, Herb Pennock (17–8). Yankee home run, Babe Ruth
(56).*]

GENE TUNNEY KEEPS TITLE BY DECISION AFTER 10 ROUNDS;
DEMPSEY INSISTS FOE WAS OUT IN THE 7TH AND WILL APPEAL;
150,000 SEE CHICAGO FIGHT, MILLIONS LISTEN ON RADIO

Eight-column headlines, page 1, *The New York Times*

George Herman Ruth scored a clean knockout over the Detroit
Tigers in the ninth round of their battle at the Stadium yesterday. The decisive punch was a left-hand swing to the right field
bleachers, and it landed so high and far that there was no chance
for a claim of foul. The Yankees were hanging on the ropes
when Babe took his swing, and it took just that sort of punch to
carry them to victory.

Whatever wise money was in the stands must have been quot-
ing the Tigers about 6 to 1 to win when the Babe delivered his
smack. The ball landed so far up in the bleachers that it cleared
most of the spectators after it had passed the screen.

Babe had to fight his way through admiring fans as he made
his jaunt down the last quarter from third base to the plate, all
the time carrying his home run bat. [*"With rare presence of mind
the Babe clung to his bat as he loped for the first base, for the fans were
tumbling down out of the stands and had the Babe been so rash as to
have dropped his bat he never would have seen it again, since so fine a
souvenir is not be overlooked. Bat in hand, then, he made the circuit of
bases, almost hedged in by delighted fans"—Frank Graham, New York*
Sun.]

There was another fight to escape through the dugout, and
Babe had to be careful not to spike any of his public as he made
his way toward the showers. Babe's hit registered the hundred

fifth victory of the year for the Yankees, tying the American League record [*set by the Red Sox in 1912*].

Mark Koenig atoned for an earlier miscue by opening the home ninth with a clean single to right, and then came the Bambino, hitless through four previous turns at the plate. Ken Holloway was pitching, and Babe let the first two pitches glide by. He swung at the third, hit one of his hardest and highest homers, and the Tigers started moving toward the clubhouse before the ball ever landed. Right fielder Harry Heilmann took one glance, saw there was no chance, and let it ride.

Up to then, Earle Combs had been the starring player. Combs collected three triples [*raising his total for the year to a league-leading twenty-three*], and made a catch off Heilmann that took at least a triple from the Detroit slugger [*and, as it turned out, prevented Heilmann from batting .400 for the season. Earle Combs became the twelfth player to share the American League record for most triples in a game.*]

Bill Slocum, New York American

Lou Gehrig's big bat battered down another of the Babe's former major league records. The Columbian hit a triple and a single yesterday, and each knocked in a run, giving Gehrig 172 runs batted in and beating Ruth's former mark by 2. The Babe batted in 170 runs in 1921, far more than anyone had ever done. [*The RBI record that Ruth broke in 1921 was his own, 137, set in 1920.*]

Fred Lieb, New York Post

Babe Ruth has taken unto himself another movie role—not a starring part, however. When his good friend Harold Lloyd asked the Babe to assume a role in the bespectacled comedian's new picture, how could the Bambino refuse? Harold is portraying a taxicab driver in the film, who, like every other New Yorker, is an ardent Babe Ruth rooter.

The Bambino works with Lloyd mornings and is driven to Yankee Stadium in time for the big game every afternoon by Harold himself. [*Harold Lloyd was then at the height of his fame and popularity and, along with Charlie Chaplin, was one of the two most famous film comedians of the day.*]

Irene Thirer, New York Daily News

Saturday, September 24

[*On September 23, the Yankees were not scheduled to play.*]

Chicago—Commissioner K. M. Landis today completed the schedule for the world's baseball series, which will begin in the National League city on Wednesday, October 5.

Prices will be the same as last year, $6, $5, $3, and $1. All games will begin at 1:30 except on Sunday when the game will start at 2:00.

New York *American*

Sunday, September 25

[*On September 24, in New York, the Yankees defeated Detroit, 6–0. Winning pitcher, George Pipgras (10–3).*]

Outside of cracking the league record for games won in a season, the Yanks comported themselves in a comparatively quiet and dignified manner yesterday. They turned in their one hundred sixth victory while George Pipgras pitched his best game since joining the team.

Pipgras allowed but one hit for eight innings and applied as neat a coat of whitewash as has been dealt out by any Yankee pitcher this season. The Tigers were completely handcuffed.

Generally speaking, it was as fine a pitched game as has graced the Stadium this summer. [*It was a three-hit shutout; Hall of Famers Charlie Gehringer and Harry Heilmann singled in the ninth inning. Babe Ruth hit two singles, walked once, and struck out twice.*]

Murray Tynan, New York *Herald-Tribune*

Monday, September 26

[*On September 25, in New York, the Yankees lost to Detroit, 6–1. Losing pitcher, Waite Hoyt (22–7).*]

Babe Ruth and the other Yanks spent a fruitless afternoon yesterday to the complete discomfiture of 25,000 fans [*35,000, according to Bill Slocum in the* American] who had turned out to see the Babe hit a homer or two and the Yanks add another to their record of victories. The good folks got plenty of sunshine but nothing else, for the Babe hit no homers while the Yanks' attempt to impress the Tigers ended in dismal failure.

Ruth now has only four games in which to equal or surpass his 1921 mark of 59. He therefore is confronted with the task of banging an average of a homer a game. For one of Ruth's capabilities this is not altogether impossible.

The fact remains, however, that Ruth did nothing to aid his record attempt yesterday, due chiefly to the fact that the Babe, as well as the other Yanks, found the left-handed pitching of Earl Whitehill refusing to lend itself to home run hitting or, indeed, any kind of hitting. Six singles was the Yanks' total for the day.

The Babe came up five times. He struck out, bounced to the box, singled to center, and walked twice. Lou Gehrig was even less impressive. He singled, grounded out, and then fanned three times in a row.

John Drebinger, The New York Times

The Babe roamed into the right field corner yesterday and chucked out Johnny Bassler trying to stretch a single. The Babe throws out a lot of 'em trying to stretch singles.

W. B. Hanna, New York Herald-Tribune

AMERICAN LEAGUE STANDINGS

	W	L	PCT	GB		W	L	PCT	GB
New York	106	44	.707	—	Chicago	66	82	.446	39
Philadelphia	89	60	.597	16½	Cleveland	65	83	.439	40
Washington	80	66	.548	24	St. Louis	57	91	.385	48
Detroit	79	69	.534	26	Boston	50	97	.340	54½

Tuesday, September 27

[On September 26, the Yankees were not scheduled to play.]

Babe Ruth's 1927 showing is the most remarkable feat of a remarkable career. If he is swinging against soft pitching, how about the others? For that matter, the National League has had more home runs than the American, but no one in the National League is more than half way up to Ruth. [*With thirty home runs each, Cy Williams, of Philadelphia, and Hack Wilson, of Chicago, would tie for the National League lead in 1927.*]

The only way one can account for his latest showing after 14 years of service is his love for the game. The Babe could never buy as much fun with a million dollars as he gets out of baseball. He will be a lost soul when his career is over, for nothing else will ever take baseball's place in his walloping existence.

Grantland Rice, New York *Herald-Tribune*

Wednesday, September 28

[On September 27, in New York, the Yankees defeated Philadelphia, 7–4. Winning pitcher, Herb Pennock (18–8). Yankee home run, Babe Ruth (57), Lou Gehrig (46).]

Sticking grimly to his task, which calls for a homer a game if the record is to fall, Babe Ruth collided violently with a well-pitched ball yesterday and arched it high up in the right field bleachers. It was an imposing wallop, coming in the sixth inning with the bases full and Lefty Grove pitching.

When the Babe connected, there came a tremendous roar from 15,000 throats. Clearing the bases made it an ever greater spectacle, for, strange to relate, the greatest manufacturer of home runs has not often done this sort of thing. [*Prior to this game, Ruth had had seven bases-loaded home runs, four of which came when he was with the Red Sox. As a Yankee he had hit grand-slam homers against Cleveland on July 6, 1922, in the Polo Grounds; against Chicago on September 24, 1925, in Yankee Stadium; and against St. Louis on September 25, 1926, in Sportsman's Park. Ruth's career total of bases-loaded home runs was sixteen, placing him in a fifth-place tie with Henry Aaron among all major leaguers, seven behind the leader, Lou Gehrig.]*

There was another homer yesterday, in the fourth inning, by Lou Gehrig, who suddenly recalled that he too is supposed to be a swatter of considerable proportions. This was his first since September 6, in Fenway Park.

Incidentally, the Yanks broke another record yesterday. By scoring 7 runs they ran their quota for the year to 952, breaking the record of 948 runs, made by the Yanks in 1921.

John Drebinger, *The New York Times*

The radio announcer has become an interesting adjunct of baseball. The games are broadcast daily from Chicago, St. Louis, Detroit, and Boston. New York strangely has not come to it. [*As noted earlier, New York would "come to it" quite late, in 1939.*]

The announcers are stealing the trailing glory which was once attached to a baseball writer. The good folks who were wont to gather at a press box after a game and watch the animals write now pass the typewriters up cold and fawn upon the master of the mike.

The radio announcer gets shoes for his baby, cakes for his tummy, and letters for his scrapbook. The poor reporter gets the air [*in other words, is snubbed*]. Boo! Hoo! Hoo!

Frank Wallace, *New York Post*

Friday, September 30

[*On September 28, the Yankees were not scheduled to play. On September 29, in New York, the Yankees defeated Washington, 15–4. Winning pitcher, Urban Schocker (18–6). Yankee home runs, Babe Ruth 2 (59).*]

Arriving at the conclusion that he ought not to keep a palpitating world in suspense any longer, George Herman Ruth crashed out 2 home runs yesterday and with these powerful thrusts drew abreast of his own major league seasonal record of 59. The Babe has two more games in which to shatter the mark.

These two blows helped to annihilate the Senators, but no one gave much thought to the Senators. They were there merely for scenic effect.

Geared to what seemed his highest pitch, Babe lost no time closing in on the record, which he so relentlessly has pursued through the past month. The fifty-eighth came in the first inning off Horace Lisenbee, with two out and no one on base. Horace had struck two strikes on the Babe and quite craftily was trying to curve over a third one when Ruth stuck that one in the right field bleachers. It was a low, winging drive that went up only a few rows.

Then the fifty-ninth! That, countrymen, was a wallop. It came in the fifth with Paul Hopkins pitching and was an almost exact duplicate of the fifty-seventh, delivered with the bases full!

The ball landed half way up the right field bleacher, and though there were only 7,500 eyewitnesses, the roar they sent up could hardly have been drowned out had the spacious stands been packed to capacity. The crowd fairly rent the air with shrieks and whistles as the bulky monarch jogged majestically around the bases, doffed his cap, and shook hands with Lou Gehrig, who was waiting to take his turn at bat. [*Until September 27, Ruth had played for nearly five full seasons at Yankee Stadium and had hit exactly one bases-loaded home run there. Now he had performed the feat twice in two consecutive games.*]

Nor were the homers all the thrills the Babe provided his onlookers. Actually, he came perilously close to hitting four circuit smashes.

In the second inning, with Lisenbee still on the mound, Ruth hit a terrific liner to right center. It was even more of a smash than the homer in the third and easily would have cleared into the bleachers had it been pulled a trifle more to the right. It struck the barrier at the extreme left wing of the bleacher and went for a triple.

On his final turn at bat in the seventh he sent right fielder Red Barnes with his back to the wire screening in front of the same bleacher to pull down a soaring fly. A foot or two more of distance, and a new record would already be established.

[*Because of his two home runs and the two other drives that just missed* by inches, Frank Graham wrote in the New York Sun, "Not in all his spectacular years has the Babe had a greater day than this."]

John Drebinger, *The New York Times*

Saturday, October 1

[*On September 30, in New York, the Yankees won, 4–2. Winning pitcher, Herb Pennock (19–8). Yankee home run, Babe Ruth (60).*]

Well, the Babe went and did it!

Ten thousand fans shouted themselves hoarse when a terrific clout from George Ruth's bat sailed into the right field bleachers for the big fellow's sixtieth home run.

It is doubtful if anyone in that crowd ever will live to see another player hit his sixtieth home run in a 154-game season. [*As most fans know, when Roger Maris hit 61 home runs in 1961, he played in a season of 162 games. One can only speculate on what Ruth would have done with eight more games. In 1961, Maris had 590 official times at bat; in 1927, Ruth had batted 540 times. It should also be remembered that 1961 was the first year of major league expansion, and thus Maris faced numerous pitchers who were no more than minor league hurlers. In 1927, the total number of home runs hit in the American League was 533; in 1961, the total number of home runs hit in the American League was 1,534. Finally, in 3 additional seasons, Ruth hit more than 50 home runs, and altogether he had 11 seasons with better than 40 home runs. Except for 1961, Maris's best home run season was 1962, when he hit 33; in no other year did he hit as many as 30 home runs.*]

The home run was made off Tom Zachary, the veteran left-hander, and let no one get the idea that Tom was giving Ruth any of the better of it. [*Zachary would end his career with 185 victories. The man against whom Maris hit his sixty-first home run, Tracy Stallard, pitched for the Red Sox for the entire season, with a grand total of two victories. When Stallard retired from the major leagues, he had a record of 30 wins and 57 losses.*]

Ruth had been pecking away at Zachary throughout the game. Tom walked him on four straight balls in the first, and the crowd hooted and hissed. The big fellow singled in the fourth and sixth and scored both of New York's early runs. With the score tied 2–2, Koenig tripled with one out in the eighth. Zachary threw one ball and one strike to Ruth, and then the Babe swung, and another baseball sped to that favorite home run zone, the right field bleachers.

The demonstration which followed was the greatest seen in New York in years. Everybody was on his feet, cheering and yelling. It sounded like one of those Al Smith demonstrations at the last Democratic convention, but this was all spontaneous. [*This refers to the Democratic party's notoriously clamorous national convention of 1924 in New York City, when New York's Governor Smith was a leading candidate for the nomination, which went to the noted constitutional lawyer John W. Davis after 103 frenzied ballots.*]

When Ruth went out to his position in the eighth it started all over again. This time the right field bleacherites welcomed their own and started a new demonstration which was a demonstration.

Huggins continued to prime his pitching staff for the Series. He worked Pipgras six innings and Pennock three. Between them they yielded five hits. As Pennock got in with the score tied he got the benefit of Ruth's homer and won his second "soft" victory of the week.

Fred Lieb, *New York Post*

As the mighty Babe galloped around the base paths, the stands became one tumultuous ovation. Nothing like it has been seen since the Stadium was built. It exceeded the outburst that greeted Bob Meusel's hit that made the Yanks the world's champions in 1923. It rivalled anything that Broadway has ever given a visiting celebrity. No star of the great White Way was ever acclaimed so fervently. Even the veteran newspapermen, whose calloused souls have been accustomed to such demonstrations, stopped their typewriters, rose to their feet, and applauded.

The players chorused their approval. They jumped to their feet as the ball descended among the bleacherites, and they stamped their feet and slapped each other on the back.

The final big thrill came as the Babe started for the dugout after catching Walter Johnson's fly in the ninth. Fans scaled the bleacher screen and ran after the Babe; they came from the boxes and the grandstand. And as the Babe was wending his way to the dugout, those persons, among them millionaires and newsboys, slapped him on the back. And Babe liked it.

Charles Segar, New York *Daily Mirror*

The ball which became Homer 60 was caught by Joe Forner of 1937 First Avenue, Manhattan. He is 40 years old and has been following baseball for 35. As soon as the game was over, he rushed to the dressing room to let the Babe know who had the ball.

The New York Times

In the clubhouse Ruth was running around like the big kid that he is.

"No, I didn't think I could do it from the start of the season," he answered over the din. "The first time I believed I had a chance to make it was at Boston early this month, when I socked three in those two games and went ahead of Lou. We had the pennant pretty well cinched and I could afford to do a little hitting for myself. It was then that I got busy.

"The record didn't mean anything to me until I really had a good chance to make it. You remember how I tried to bat right handed against Joe Pate in Philadelphia on May 31 when we knocked the A's cockeyed? Well, I've kicked myself for that ever since, because I had two that day and then started kidding, but we had the game won, and that's all I was concerned about. Then in Chicago the last time I spent a lot of time trying to bat to left field to cross them up. I did, and we won.

"Will I ever break this again? I don't know and don't care, but if I don't I know who will. Wait till that bozo over there (pointing to Gehrig) gets waded into them again and they may forget that a guy named Ruth ever lived."

If the world forgets that a guy named Ruth lived, it will be due to universal amnesia.

Arthur Mann, New York *Evening World*

They could no more have stopped Babe Ruth from hitting the home run that gave him a new record than you could halt a locomotive by sticking your foot out. Once he had 59, Number

60 was as sure as the rising sun. A more determined athlete than George Herman Ruth never lived. With a new record in sight he was bound to make it. Ruth is like that. He is one of the few utterly dependable news stories in sports. When the crisis arises he never fails to supply the yarn. A child of destiny is George Herman. He moves in his orbit like a planet.

Succumb to the power and the romance of this man. Drop your cynicism and feel the athletic marvel that this big, uncouth fellow has accomplished.

Never mind the high fly business and the grooved ball stuff. The last two home runs that Ruth hit, the one that tied and the one that broke the record, won ball games. Do you think any pitcher would be sap enough to lay one down the gutter with a game depending on it, even one that didn't count? They all count in the pitchers' records.

That high fly stuff doesn't go either. When Ruth conks one it stays conked. Of all the home runs I have seen him hit, only one could be called a high fly, and it was so doggone high that no outfielder in the world could have snagged it. It went so blinkin' high that it looked like one of those things they drop off the Flatiron Building for a publicity stunt. The rest of them went sailing up into the bleachers on a line. [*Located at the intersection of Broadway and Fifth Avenue at Twenty-third Street, the twenty-one-story Fuller Building, built in 1902, is universally known because of its shape as the Flatiron Building and is a New York landmark.*]

I get a tremendous kick out of that egg. I like to have illusions about him. I like to believe that everything about him is on the level. I don't trust many things in sports, but Ruth I do, and I still get that silly feeling in my throat when he conks one. I'm tickled silly over his breaking the record.

Paul Gallico, New York *Daily News*

Sunday, October 2

[*On October 1, in New York, the Yankees defeated Washington, 4–3. Winning pitcher, Wilcy Moore (19–7). Yankee home run, Lou Gehrig (47).*]

In the presence of 20,000 fans, hopeful of seeing Babe Ruth

add another clout to his home run record, the Yankees closed their American League season by winning, but the Babe hit no home run.

Urged on by the crowd, the Babe tried hard to oblige, but it was just not in the cards. A left-hander, Robert Burke, passed him the first time, held him to a soaring pop fly to right field in the third and an infield out in the fifth, and in the eighth, with another left-hander, E. Garland Braxton, on the mound, Ruth's last official act of the season was a strike-out.

The crowd did see Lou Gehrig end the campaign with a parting shot into the right field bleachers, and they saw the league champions wind up the season with a total of 110 victories, a new record. [*This record stood until 1954, when the Cleveland Indians won 111 games. Cleveland then lost the World Series to the Giants without winning even one game.*]

Wilcy Moore and Waite Hoyt were called on by Huggins to pitch this final tune-up for the World's Series. Hoyt, winging through the last four innings, showed in tip-top form, but Moore was not quite so impressive.

[*The Yankees ended the season with a total paid attendance, at home and on the road, of 2,246,096, a new record for organized baseball. At Yankee Stadium the attendance was 1,264,015; on the road it was 982,081. None of the games, it should be remembered, was played at night.*]

John Drebinger, The New York Times

PIRATES CLINCH 1927 FLAG BY TRIMMING REDS

[*Now the Yankees knew who their World Series opponents would be, the Pittsburgh Pirates, who edged out the Giants and the Cardinals in a three-team fight for the pennant.*]

Eight-column front-page headline, Pittsburgh Press

Due to the impressive manner in which the Yankees outclassed the rest of the American League, there is a popular belief that the World Series will be over after the fourth game.

Rud Rennie, New York Herald-Tribune

You may sing your song of the good old days till the phantom
    cows come home;
You may dig up glorious deeds of yore from many a dusty tome;
You may rise to tell of Rube Waddell and the way he bussed
    them through,
And top it all with the great fast ball that Rusie's rooters knew.
You may rant of Brouthers, Keefe, and Ward and half a dozen
    more;
You may quote by rote from the record book in a way that I
    deplore;
You may rave, I say, till the break of day, but the truth remains
    the truth:
From "One Ole Cat" to the last "At Bat," was there ever a guy
    like Ruth?

He can start and go, he can catch and throw, he can field with
    the very best.
He's the Prince of Ash and the King of Crash, and that's not an
    idle jest.
He can hit that ball o'er the garden wall, high up and far away,
Beyond the uttermost picket lines where the fleet-foot fielders
    stray.
He's the Bogey Man of the pitching clan and he clubs 'em soon
    and late;
He has manned his guns and hit home runs from here to the
    Golden Gate;
With vim and verve he has walloped the curve from Texas to
    Duluth,
Which is no small task, and I beg to ask: Was there ever a guy
    like Ruth?

You may rise and sing till the rafters ring that sad and sorrowful
    strain:
"They strive and fail—it's the old, old tale; they never come back
    again."
Yes, it's in the dope, when they hit the slope they're off for the
    shadowed vale,
But the great, big Bam with the circuit slam came back on the
    uphill trail;
Came back with cheers from the drifted years where the best of
    them go down;

Came back once more with a record score to wear a brighter
    crown.
My voice may be loud above the crowd and my words just a bit
    uncouth,
But I'll stand and shout till the last man's out: There was never a
    guy like Ruth!

Supposedly "over the hill," slipping down the steps of Time,
stumbling toward the discard, six years past his peak, Babe Ruth
stepped out and hung up a new record at which all the sport
world may stand and wonder. What Big Bill Tilden couldn't do
on the tennis court, Babe Ruth has done on the diamond. What
Dempsey couldn't do with his fists, Ruth has done with his bat.
He came back.

Put it in the book in letters of gold. It will be a long time
before any one betters that home-run mark, and a still longer
time before any aging athlete makes such a gallant and glorious
charge over the comeback trail.

John Kieran, The New York Times

Monday, October 3

*[On October 2, the last day of the regular season, the Yankees were not
scheduled to play.]*

A visit to the Yankee dressing room before the final game of the
season revealed many interesting things. Among the first things
picked up by a roving eye was that Babe Ruth does not wear
long woolen winter undies but that Miller Huggins does, that
Herman Ruth has the queerest collection of junk in the world, in
and atop his locker, marked "Ruth" in plain white chalk just like
any other fellow's locker, and that the first thing Waite Hoyt puts
on after he has reduced himself to his rind is the gol-dingdest
red flannel shirt you ever did see.

Fascinated, your investigator watched George Herman Ruth
divest himself of his street attire and robe himself for the contest. With interest he noted the intricate ceremony of putting on
a pair of baseball pants. Picture George Herman Ruth garbed as
follows: His baseball shirt is on, so are his sliding pads. He has

donned the white socks and the long blue woolen hose. Only his pants are absent. These the Bambino carefully turns inside out and lays upon the floor with the legs facing toward his ample person. I was utterly at sea. "How," I asked myself, "is he ever going to get into those pants from that side?" Here was, indeed, a peculiar proceeding.

Observe now the beauty and simplicity of method. The Babe thrusts each of his robust dogs through the south end of his pants, pulling them up to the knee. Here he proceeded to roll pant end and stocking together as deftly as any lady of the ensemble ever twirled her sheers, until he was satisfied that all was as it should be, when, behold and lo, he now seized the other end of the knickers and pulled them up along his stately legs, turning them right side out as he did so until, in the wink of an eye, there was Ruth, pants and stockings all for one and one for all.

Fool that I was, I did not make a list of the things that crowd the Ruthian locker. Certain articles I did note—toilet lotions, arnicas and salves, baseball gloves, three Louisville sluggers there for seasoning, phonograph records of "Babe and You," telegrams and letters by the hundreds, shirts, spikes, auxiliary clothing. Atop the locker reposed an immense green gourd, at least five feet long, and what it was doing there no one seemed to know.

I remarked to Ruth that he had rather sneaked up on his record. It had all been so sudden.

"Yeah," said Ruth, "I did. I'll say I sneaked up on it. Say, kid, I never thought I could do it. You'll say you're gonna do a thing because everybody expects you to, but I just didn't think it could be done."

O, is Herman proud of that beautiful string of sixty!

"And," I said, "they weren't grooving them for you, either."

Here the Babe said something Ruthian that I cannot print, and he went on to say that if anything the pitchers worked harder on him. "What about that one I hit off Grove with the bases full?" he asked. "That feller would rather lose $100 than have me do that to him."

A small boy at this juncture claimed Ruth's attention with worshiping eyes, so he lost interest in me.

Paul Gallico, New York *Daily News*

The Yanks received a riotous sendoff when, singly and in groups, they reported at the Pennsylvania Station last night to take the Yankee Special for Pittsburgh. More than 1,000 persons jammed about the gate from which the stairway led down to the train, and among them, conspicuous for their noise-making, were some 700 boys.

Babe Ruth was singled out for the major part of the shrill cheers and whistling, but Lou Gehrig, Tony Lazzeri, Waite Hoyt, and other headliners were not forgotten.

Special policemen were pressed into service to make a pathway through the throng for the players. Red caps scurried about handling the Yankees' baggage, but ever watchful for the appearance of the burly Babe. When Ruth finally hove into view, he was almost rushed off his feet by the charge of eager youngsters, and all tried to grasp him by the hand.

The Babe shook scores of outstretched hands and told his young admirers that he felt in his bones that he would crash a few in the Series. The youngsters cheered loudly until Babe was out of sight in one of the Pullmans.

Judging by the crowded appearance of the Iron City Flier, companion train of the Yankee Special, scores of fans also were making the trip to Pittsburgh.

Hoyt, Bob Meusel, and Lazzeri were not accounted for shortly before the train was scheduled to pull out. Hoyt arrived two minutes before the Special departed, and just before the train doors were closed Meusel and Lazzeri strolled along.

As the Special moved away at 10:30 the score of fans who had managed to pass the guards and reach the platform and the squad of red caps set up a loud cheer. This demonstration was answered by a friendly wave from Ruth and his teammates.

The New York Times

ABOARD THE YANKEE'S SLEEPING CAR, EN ROUTE TO PITTS-BURGH—The Yankees are all asleep, all but Herb Pennock, who never sleeps on a train.

The Yankees occupy two cars, because this is a classy ball club and no one sleeps in an upper berth. A lower has a certain significance to a ballplayer. Putting a regular, especially a star regular, in an upper berth would be like taking a swell dame to the second balcony and riding home with her in a trolley car.

There is usually an air of dim mystery about a sleeping car. One wonders who's behind the dark green curtains that move occasionally to the motion of the train. In this instance, however, one knows that the guttural noises betray the sleeping Ruth in lower 11. The hissing sounds from lower 5 are made by Bengough while lying on his back. From the depths of lower 3 comes nothing but a vast silence, for there lies Lou Gehrig. When Gehrig sleeps, he sleeps with the quiet dignity of an Egyptian king long dead.

Huggins has the drawing-room, a sound-proof place in which it is reasonable to suppose that the mite manager has knocked the ashes out of his bedtime pipe and is dreaming of the championship of the world.

The public at large does not fully appreciate Huggins. Outside of being one of the kindest and most companionable persons in the world, he is not only a great baseball manager but a diplomat worthy of the Court of St. James's. It requires more than mere baseball management to handle the stars of the Yankee club every day of six active months.

Rud Rennie, New York *Herald-Tribune*

FINAL AMERICAN LEAGUE STANDINGS

	W	L	PCT	GB		W	L	PCT	GB
New York	110	44	.714	—	Chicago	79	83	.458	39½
Philadelphia	91	63	.591	19	Cleveland	66	87	.431	43½
Washington	85	69	.552	25	St. Louis	59	94	.386	50½
Detroit	82	71	.536	27½	Boston	51	103	.331	59

[As might be expected, the Yankees dominated the statistics for individual leaders. Lou Gehrig's batting average of .372 was third highest, behind Harry Heilmann and Al Simmons. The top three home-run sluggers were Ruth (60), Gehrig (47), and Lazzeri (18). (Curiously, Lazzeri did not hit a single home run in September.) In runs batted in, Gehrig led with a record-setting 175, and Ruth was second with 164. (In 1931, Gehrig would break his own record with 184 RBIs, a mark that still stands.) The leader in base hits was Earle Combs with 231, followed by Gehrig with 218. Ruth was tops in runs scored (158), trailed by Gehrig (149) and Combs (137). Gehrig led in doubles with 52, and his 18 triples was second to the 23 hit by Combs. In total bases, Gehrig (447), Ruth (417), and Combs (331) were the first three. In bases on balls,

Ruth and Gehrig were at the top (138 and 109). In stolen bases, Meusel was second to George Sisler, and Lazzeri tied for third.

In pitching, the top four men in winning percentages were Hoyt (.759), Shocker (.750), Moore (.731), and Pennock (.704). Hoyt and Shocker were also the two lowest in earned run averages (2.63 and 2.84), and Hoyt tied with Ted Lyons in the number of games won, 22. Moore tied with Washington's Braxton for the most saves, 13.]

Tuesday, October 4

Pittsburgh—The Smoky City is seething with excitement and suspense. The arrival of the Yanks early yesterday raised the city's pulse beat a full five points. A large crowd was at the station to greet the enemy, and the lobby of the Roosevelt Hotel was jammed from wall to wall. [*Located at the corner of Pennsylvania Avenue and Sixth Street, the Roosevelt Hotel had just opened, and the Yankees were among its first guests.*]

As the Yanks taxied to the Roosevelt they were objects of curious attention all along the route. There was much finger-pointing and staring. "There goes the Babe," shouted one native. "No, there he is in that cab," said another. "Where?" "Right over there," and so forth.

Disguised in a new brown cap, Ruth was finally run down and cornered in the hotel lobby. Later the photographers trapped him in his room and took pictures of him in a giddy dressing gown and gay slippers. The Babe posed eating a breakfast that would have sufficed for the entire Pirate infield, with the bat boy thrown in.

James R. Harrison, *The New York Times*

Pittsburgh—Two hours after the Yankees had arrived at their hotel, they were on their way to the ball park to start practicing.

One enthusiastic Pittsburgh rooter yelled at Babe as he was getting into a taxi, "You'll not hit any home runs off our pitchers." Little Eddie Bennett, the Yankees' mascot, came back with this reply: "Come out to the ball park, and Babe will show you a sample of what he's going to do in the Series."

The Pittsburgh fans did not have to wait long to see Babe hit one. The big fellow was the first Yankee on the field. He came out without his baseball shirt and stockings and without a cap. After warming up a bit, Waite Hoyt, who will probably start the first game, walked out to the pitcher's box to limber up his famous right arm.

Combs batted first, then Koenig, and Ruth followed. The crowd cheered the Babe, and he responded with a long drive into center field. Then he followed with a smash into right field. The ball found a resting place in the grandstand. The Babe hit another long drive into center field and then came back to the bench.

Then Gehrig went to the bat, and twice he succeeded in slamming the ball into the stand. The first time the ball just missed landing in the upper tier. The other smash did not have the power and drive of the first clout, but landed in the stand just the same.

When George Herman and Gehrig propelled the ball into the stand, Lee Meadows, Ray Kremer, Vic Aldridge, Carmen Hill, and Johnny Miljus of the Pirates' pitching staff were in the stands. They grunted as Babe and Lou showed them how home runs should be hit.

William Hennigan, New York *World*

The scene is the Yankee dugout at Forbes Field yesterday with the Yankees having batting practice. Babe Ruth has just come back to the bench after hitting a ball into the right field stand.

Ruth—Well, I smacked that baby.

Combs—Think the park is any longer in right field than at the Stadium?

Ruth—Yeh. About ten feet.

Paschal—Well, the way you hit 'em, ten feet won't make any difference.

Enter a young lady reporter from a Pittsburgh paper.

Young lady—Hello, Mr. Ruth.

Ruth—Hello.

Young lady—Do you remember me? I interviewed you in Elmira once some years ago.

Ruth—Sure, I remember you.

Young lady—Our managing editor bought a picture of you

eating breakfast, and now he wants me to have breakfast with you and write a story about it.

Ruth—Yeh?

Young lady—Yes. How about tomorrow morning?

Ruth—Great. I eat breakfast at ten o'clock.

Young lady—All right. I'll be there. Don't forget.

Ruth—Forget to eat breakfast? I should say not.

Young lady—I met Mr. Huggins that time in Elmira.

Ruth—Here's Hug now. Hey, Hug, here's a young lady that knows you.

Huggins—Glad to meet you, young lady.

Babe moves over, and Huggins sits down next to the young lady reporter.

Bengough—They ought to get a picture of that.

A photographer takes a picture, and the young lady exits smiling.

Huggins—This is the place I always hit the ball. I bet I hit .400 in this park.

Shocker—If you did, you must have got horse collars everywhere else to get your batting average down to .231. [*Huggins's career batting average was in fact .265.*]

It is raining briskly now, and the ground keeper's gang is spreading the tarpaulin on the field. [*In 1908, Pittsburgh was the first major league club to equip its field with a tarpaulin.*]

Ruth—Hey, never mind that. Let's play ball.

Gehrig—A little rain wouldn't hurt this ground.

Dugan—Not a bit. It's pretty fast right now.

Combs—Where's Eddie? [*Eddie Bennett*] Hey, Eddie, better get those bats in.

Ruth—Yeh, and where's my glove?

Gehrig—I got it, Babe.

Durst—How do you like the hotel, boys?

Koenig—Great. I found a lot of things in my room. A step ladder, a set of electrician's tools, and a dirty shirt. [*As noted, the hotel had just opened.*]

Ruth—No game today. Two tomorrow.

Collins—When do we get our tickets, Babe?

Ruth—They'll be ready in Hug's room at three o'clock. What's your room number, Hug?

Huggins—Seventy-one.

Ruth—I didn't ask you your age.

Huggins—You're a smart guy. I hope you don't get a hit in the Series.

Gehrig—Yes, you do. Like hell.

The downpour continues.

Huggins—I guess that will be all. Let's go.

Frank Graham, New York *Sun*

Wednesday, October 5

Pittsburgh—The Yankees' final practice yesterday was a rather hilarious affair. Babe Ruth left the field in good spirits and five balls somewhere in Schenley Park. [*Schenley Park lay beyond the outfield fences in all directions.*] The Babe's batting spree left interested onlookers, including the Pirates, open-mouthed in wonder. Most of them had never seen his majesty the ball mauler in action before.

The Yanks went through their drill in a casual frame of mind, and except for the noise of hammers, where carpenters were erecting the last of the temporary seats, and the stream of trucks bringing extra supplies of hot dogs, peanuts, popcorn, cigars, cigarettes, and chewing gum, there were no indications that they were on the eve of a struggle for baseball's highest honors and a bag of gold. [*The preceding day, in* The Times, *James R. Harrison had written, "This is the most blasé team I have ever seen go into a World's Series."*]

The Pirates were more tense. Donie Bush, the midget manager, hummed and buzzed about like a mosquito looking for a meal. He was all over the diamond, giving instructions, shouting encouragement, delivering orders. The rest of the crew were in a serious mood as they took their turns at the plate and went through a fast, impressive fielding drill. [*The five-foot six-inch Donie Bush, who had played in nearly two thousand major league games, mostly as a Detroit shortstop, was in his freshman year as Pittsburgh's manager. Previously, he had managed Washington for one year, in 1923.*]

Richards Vidmer, *The New York Times*

Pittsburgh—To most fans this is not a Yankee-Pirate World Series but Babe Ruth's. The home run king is the lone topic of conversation one hears in hotel lobbies and wherever crowds congregate. The fans are interested only in the Babe.

Charles Segar, New York Daily Mirror

Thursday, October 6

[*On October 5, in Pittsburgh, the Yankees won the first game of the World Series, 5–4. Winning pitcher, Waite Hoyt; losing pitcher, Ray Kremer.*]

Pittsburgh—The Yankees stepped through a wide-open gap in Pittsburgh's shaky defense in the third inning to bag the first game of the World Series as 43,000 spectators suppressed a number of yawns.

It was a game that Pittsburgh kicked away, a game that Pittsburgh should have won 4 to 2 with just ordinary defense, for Ray Kremer and John Miljus suppressed the thundering Yankees with six hits as the Pirates fell upon Waite Hoyt and Wilcy Moore for nine solid blows. This is supposed to be the age of wallop. But Gene Tunney proved at Chicago that the wallop doesn't always reign, and the Yankees prove the same thing this afternoon when they won through a stronger defense.

The fans expected to hear the roar of Yankee guns and the cannonading thunder of the Yankee attack. But outside of Babe Ruth they didn't hit a lick. The Babe blew himself to 3 singles, 50 per cent of the Yankee assault. The crowd looked for the Babe to lash the ball over the last outlying barriers, but he crossed the talent with three low line drives, two of which figured in the scoring.

But it wasn't Ruth's hitting or the pitching of Hoyt and Moore that pulled the Yankees through. It was the wide-open gap in Pittsburgh defensive play in the fatal third.

The Pirates had everything their way but the game itself. They had 43,000 excited fans cheering and whooping. They found the Yankees in a hitting slump. But they lacked the old pep and dash, and at the critical moment they handed the battle to their conquerors on a silver platter surrounded by green vegetable trimmings.

When the third inning started the score was tied. [*The Yankees scored in the first when, with two outs, Ruth singled and Gehrig was credited with a triple as Paul Waner in right field missed a shoe-string catch on his short fly. The Pirates came back in their half of the inning to tie the score on Lloyd Waner's triple and Clyde Barnhart's sacrifice fly.*] Earle Combs died, and then Koenig tapped a slow one to second baseman George Grantham.

Grantham booted the chance. Babe Ruth singled, and then Kremer wobbled, and both Gehrig and Meusel walked, forcing Koenig over. Lazzeri then forced Meusel on what should have been the third out, but Ruth scored on the force. A moment later Gehrig and Lazzeri started a double steal. Earl Smith, the catcher, faked a throw to second and then whipped a low peg to Pie Traynor at third. Pie made a dazzling pickup, and as Gehrig rushed for the plate Traynor made a perfect throw to Smith. The ball struck squarely in his glove and then squirted out as Gehrig crashed over with the third run of the inning sprouting from a lone single. This heavy handicap was more than Pittsburgh could get back. Pirate bats continued thumping away at Hoyt until they sent him to the cooling showers, but Moore had just enough to keep the Pirates in check. [*The Yankees' final run came in the fifth inning on Koenig's double, Ruth's infield grounder, and Gehrig's sacrifice fly.*]

It was a day and an occasion built for drama, but there was no drama. Indian summer smiled down upon the field. A surging crowd stormed the park. The rush became so great that before the game any number of steeplejacks scaled their way up the sides of the grandstands and scrambled into select $5 seats. Others discovered a rope hanging from the outside of the stands and scaled the walls after the manner of storming parties in the old Punic wars. More than $400,000 worth of admission money was sent back to indignant fans, and the attendance would have passed 70,000 if there had been room enough. It was scramble and rush and hullabaloo and stampede to look upon a gaudy spectacle which turned out to be one of the dullest games of the year.

If Pittsburgh couldn't beat the Yankees today, it may be a tough job later on.

Grantland Rice, New York *Herald-Tribune*

Play by play descriptions of the first game of the World Series were broadcast over 2 networks of 53 stations.

The National Broadcasting Company sent the game out from 43 stations, and the Columbia Broadcasting System had 10 stations in their hookup. Graham McNamee did the announcing for the National, and Major J. Andrew White was at the microphone for the Columbia system.

Officials of the National Broadcasting Company estimated that the radio audience reached as many as 20,000,000 persons.

The New York Times

Graham McNamee, announcing the game from New York to California, struggled unhappily through base hits and double plays and interrupted himself to demand plaintively, "You know what I mean?" From most of those tuned in there went up a despairing negative.

He mixed players and innings and teams. He told of the spectacle about him while players hit safely or retired to dugouts. He made right handed batters left handed and announced triumphantly on occasion that the Giants were leading—which must have been a surprise to John McGraw. He put players on bases where they weren't and left them off bases where they were.

Firmly, early in the game, he announced that Dugan and Traynor were left-handed, which neither is. He interrupted his ball by ball account of Waite Hoyt's trip to the plate to announce that One Eyed Connolly [*a famous gate-crasher*] had at last appeared. At the moment Hoyt had two strikes and three balls—when the thrill of Connolly's arrival had passed, the Yankee pitcher had gone out on an infield play.

Joe Harris hit into a double play in the second, and McNamee hit into a blind alley. He announced both men safe, he grew excited, he discovered that everything was confused. He divigated for several minutes while everybody hung breathless. Suddenly, he discovered that there had been a double play.

His announcing was filled with minor errors, sometimes amusing. In the first inning he informed his hearers that a ball pitched to Gehrig was "high for a left-handed batter." In the third he put Lazzeri on second, took him off in favor of third, and moved him back again, all in a minute or two. "You know what I mean?"

The first half of the third went along easily until there was a man on second and another on first. The announcer explained that this was the World Series being broadcast by the National Broadcasting Company. Suddenly, he interrupted himself to exclaim excitedly, "They missed it!" Some time later it developed that Smith had let a throw from Traynor go by and Lazzeri had advanced a base. Mr. McNamee then announced the score as 4 to 1 in favor of Pittsburgh. The Yanks were leading at the time.

Gehrig and Koenig became interchangeable in the fourth inning. The announcer had a tendency to exclaim excitedly over a casual pitch and to let base hits go in a monotone. "A fast ball got over just in time," he exclaimed in the fifth, referring to a pitch. But what it was in time for he did not say. Then he announced that the Giants were leading 5 to 3.

He got a number of telegrams at the start of the seventh inning and began to read them. He read a letter and interrupted himself to announce that Combs had struck out. He explained that his watch was not in the pocket he thought but in another pocket, forgetting altogether the position of the diamond.

"You know what I mean?"

New York *Sun*

Friday, October 7

[*On October 6, in Pittsburgh, the Yankees won the second game of the World Series, 6–2. Winning pitcher, George Pipgras; losing pitcher, Vic Aldridge.*]

Pittsburgh—That human traffic of organized baseball, in which men are bartered and sold in the marts of the game like cows or pigs or horses, kept George Pipgras moving around the baseball land across several seasons.

A chattel of the modern-day slave traders of sport, a pitching pawn of the New York Yankees, the big mid-Westerner was shunted about the backwoods of the pastime at the whim of others for five years.

[*These two paragraphs describe the situation in which professional baseball players existed prior to the successful challenge of the reserve clause in 1974. From 1921 through 1926, Pipgras pitched for Madison, in the South Dakota State League; Charleston, in the South Atlantic League; Atlanta and Nashville, in the Southern Association; and St. Paul, in the American Association. In a letter to the author, dated April 6, 1984, Pipgras wrote, "I was with St. Paul in 1926. The scouts told Miller Huggins that he had the best pitcher in the minor leagues and wanted to know why he didn't bring him up. I should have gone up to the Yankees in 1926, but the St. Paul owner would not release me."]*

This afternoon George Pipgras came into his big league own when he held the Pittsburgh sluggers in the hollow of his greasy old glove, a beloved relic of Atlanta, St. Paul, and the other towns of his baseball service.

Speed he fed 'em, and then more speed—blinding speed that stopped the National League champions with seven hits, no two of which were made in one inning, while the Yankees took the second game of the World's Series.

Speed he fed 'em, and more speed, until the batsmen of Pittsburgh were merely chipping with their sticks at the ball as it went hurtling past, fouling it to all corners of the field.

The Pirates got a run in the first inning, but after that they were helpless before the sizzling speed that fairly raised the fuzz on the bosoms of their white shirts as the ball zipped by.

Pipgras takes a tremendous "wind up" before letting the ball fly. He turns with his back to the batsman, then he comes 'round to deliver the ball, and all of his corn-nurtured one hundred and ninety-some-odd pounds are packed back of the delivery. And he carries on his open countenance an expression of great seriousness.

[In his previously mentioned letter of April 6, 1984, George Pipgras said, "I was primarily a fastball pitcher, but I can remember throwing slow balls that were so slow everybody had to laugh. In the second game of the 1927 World Series, I threw all fastballs except for four curveballs."]

Vic Aldridge, a chunky built, hammered down sort of a man, was on the mound for the Pirates, but finally his delivery got to drifting around aimlessly, and Donie Bush took him out. Mike Cvengros, a name you pronounce with a sneeze, and Joe Dawson finished up.

A single by Earle Combs in the third, another single by Mark Koenig, along with an error by Lloyd Waner, the youngest of the phenomenal Waner children of Oklahoma, and the score was tied. A sacrifice fly by the redoubtable George Herman Ruth, a double by Lou Gehrig, and another sacrifice fly by "Poosh 'em up" Tony Lazzeri gave the New Yorkers all the runs they needed.

True, they made three more in the eighth, but they might just as well have saved them for New York. They may need 'em there. [*The eighth-inning runs came as the result of singles by Meusel and Lazzeri, a wild pitch, bases on balls to Bengough and Pipgras, a pitch that hit Combs, and a single by Koenig.*]

You can see from my synopsis that there wasn't anything very exciting in the scoring. In fact, unless something nerve tingling transpires pretty soon, the several hundred inmates of the press section will be biting their telegraph operators in exasperation. These first two games were devoid of any features calculated to make a fellow get up on his hind legs and shriek, especially a Pittsburgh fellow.

To be candid, the home town folks are quite depressed. They can't understand why the boys cannot do something.

George Herman Ruth didn't astonish the multitude. The Pittsburgh public is commencing to wonder if George Herman Ruth obtained those 60 home runs under false pretenses, or by larceny.

The Messrs. Jumping Joe Dugan and Waite Hoyt [*who were roommates on the road*] arrived at the yard somewhat depressed because a thief crept into their palatial apartment at a downtown hotel and rifled their trouser loons of several yards in money, a yard being one hundred dollars. The Messrs. Jumping Joe Dugan and Waite Hoyt felt that this was most inhospitable in view of the fact that they are visiting firemen. [*The thief, who was never apprehended, seems to have been the only person in Pittsburgh to prevail over any of the Yankees, but then, unlike the Pirate players, he was not faced with much of a challenge. Because of the extreme newness of the hotel, the guests were not issued room keys and their closets were without coat hangers. Hoyt and Dugan thus tossed their wallet-laden trousers over a chair, and during the night someone slipped into their room and helped himself to the billfolds. (Dugan lost more than $200, Hoyt more than $300.)*]

Damon Runyon, New York *American*

Pittsburgh—In the second day of the world's dullest World Series the attitude of the Pittsburgh customers became quite as apathetic as that of the Pittsburgh team.

The hotel owners of Pittsburgh already are conceding the Series to the Yankees. The clerk at the Schenley shook hands with your correspondent as he came in from Forbes Field and said, "Guess I will not see you again until next year." When hotel clerks are conceding a Series, you can gather that it is all over but the snoring of the wearied experts.

The apathetic attitude of the fans was illustrated vividly in the fourth inning. With one out Mr. Pie Traynor drove a two-bagger to center. Then George Grantham fouled one in the direction of the boxes behind third base.

Mr. Jumping Joseph Dugan loped after it. It was one of those languid fouls that dropped slowly. Mr. Dugan pressed up against the rail of the box and reached over for it. The occupants of the box watched it come down in a moody silence. No hostile gestures were made against Mr. Dugan, even though it was quite as crucial a moment as any in this particular baseball game. The Yankee third baseman was expecting something of the sort, for he had one arm up to shield his head as he reached into the box.

But the occupants sat frozen to their seats as Mr. Dugan reached in and speared the ball with one hand. He plucked it out just as it was descending upon the head of a frozen customer and held it aloft as evidence to show the umpire.

It was at this moment that your correspondent became convinced that the Pirate customers were reconciled to the loss of the World Series. Either that or the Pittsburgh customers are the gentlest and most impartial in the world.

Persons with vision keen enough to see exactly what happened declared that the occupants of the box not only refrained from making hostile gestures but they even applauded Dugan when he prevented the ball from bouncing upon one of their skulls.

"When nobody threw anything at me I was sure that nobody cared," said Mr. Jumping Joseph Dugan after the game. And Mr. Dugan, who has been jumping round in various clubs in the American League for no little time, seems to be quite as good a guesser as your correspondent, who guessed that this would be a brief Series, with the Yankees winners.

W. O. McGeehan, New York *Herald-Tribune*

Clutching a rabbit's foot tightly in one hand and two pork-chop sandwiches in the other, John Green, negro employee of the Mint at Washington, D.C., sat last night with his back against the Yankee Stadium bleacher gate.

Green will be the first one in the grounds today or know the reason why! He arrived at the gate at 5 o'clock last night and took up his position with a determined look on his face. When Samuel Ruszer, of 876 East 118th Street, arrived at 5:30 P.M., Green said, "Since 1898 I've been trying to be the first in line at Series games and, man, if you get in ahead of me, it'll be over my dead body—Gawd forbid!"

Green said he had not missed a Series game since 1898 and that it was understood at the office of the U.S. Mint that when the games started John Green was not expected to do any work. [*The World Series, in fact, began in 1903. Although there had been other, earlier, postseason championship games, none were played from 1898 through 1902.*]

At midnight there was about a score of fans lined up behind Green. All had lunches. The gates open at 10 o'clock this morning, but there was no complaint about the long wait. Most of the early birds took it sitting down.

At an early hour today, no women had joined the line, and this was a source of considerable satisfaction to the men.

New York *American*

Saturday, October 8

[*On October 7, in New York, the Yankees won the third game of the World Series, 8–1. Winning pitcher, Herb Pennock; losing pitcher, Lee Meadows. Home run, Babe Ruth.*]

Herb Pennock's supple left arm evolved one of the pitching classics of all time in beating the Pittsburgh Pirates. The slim, graceful left-hander came as close as any pitcher ever has to pitching the perfect game in the October classic.

Up to the time the second batter came up in the eighth inning, not a Pittsburgh batter reached first. Then a single by Pie Traynor, followed by Pooch Barnhardt's double, robbed the slim southpaw of a no-hit game and a shutout. [*The first and only World Series no-hitter came on October 8, 1956, when the Yankees' Don Larsen pitched a perfect game against Brooklyn.*]

A Texas league single in the ninth was the only other hit made off Pennock. Other pitchers have allowed fewer hits in a World Series game, but no one has pitched seven such innings as Pennock.

The Yankees reached the peak of their strength in this game. Babe Ruth hit his first Series homer, a screaming line drive that landed midway in the right field bleachers and scored two runners ahead of him. Lou Gehrig hit a triple that scored two runs and missed being a homer by inches.

The Yankees' infield performed miracles to keep Pennock's hopes for a no-hit game alive. Joe Dugan, Mark Koenig, and Tony Lazzeri made plays that would be impossible but for the fact that they miraculously achieved them.

Lee Meadows, the sober looking, bespectacled right-hander of the Pirates, met the same fate as his two teammates who had presumed to stop the murderous collection of Yankee sluggers before him. He was shelled to cover in the seventh inning when the Yankees cut loose with their big offensive guns. Six runs crossed the plate in this smashing attack which Babe capped with his homer.

Pittsburgh is a crushed, spiritless club. This afternoon the Pirates make what may prove their last stand. One doesn't expect that the Yanks will bear down too hard, however, in view of the fact that tomorrow is Sunday and the Stadium is sold out. [*In 1927, as in every other year, the players shared only in the receipts of the first four World Series games.*] There is no question about the fact that they can if they want to, for there is no comparison between the two ball clubs.

Earle Combs started the Yankees off to victory in the first inning. He sent a single through the box. Koenig bounced one at Meadows, and it took a mean hop over his head. Second baseman Hal Rhyne ran in and juggled the ball, and Koenig was credited with a hit. Babe hit at a slow one and popped up to shortstop Glenn Wright. But Gehrig wasn't fooled by anything Meadows offered. Lou had just left his mother's bedside at St. Vincent's Hospital, and he knew she was listening to the radio account of the game.

"Here's where I hit one for Ma," said Lou to Eddie Bennett as he walked up to the plate. Lou took a toe hold. Next he took a wicked swing, and what the ball took was a ride to deep left field. Barnhart chased it and relayed it to Lloyd Waner. Two Yankees were already in, and Lou decided to challenge Waner's arm. The ball came to Wright, who made a good relay to catcher Johnny Gooch. Lou was a fraction late, but he had done nobly by his Yanks and his Ma.

From then until the seventh, the 60,000 odd fans saw a pitching duel that is seldom anyone's privilege to witness. Pennock was invincible. His curve ball never broke better. His change of pace had the Pirate sluggers helpless. Meadows, in the meantime, wasn't running far behind Pennock.

That kind of pitching couldn't go on forever, and it was Meadows who cracked. Lazzeri opened the seventh with a clean single. Joe Dugan dumped a bunt which Meadows unwisely elected to try for a force out, and Lazzeri was at second before the ball. Cedric Durst, batting for Grabowski, rolled a slow grounder to Hal Rhyne that served as a sacrifice, for both runners moved up a base. Pennock sent a slow roller to Rhyne, who was playing in on the grass. Lazzeri was off with the crack of the bat and slid under the throw. Koenig lashed out a double, and Pennock trotted in. Bush yanked Meadows and sent in Mike Cvengros, the southpaw Slav.

Up to that time, nothing had been contributed to the festivities by George Herman Ruth, the big record wrecker from W. 72nd Street. He welcomed Mr. Cvengros like an Eskimo welcomes the first rays of the springtime sun. Meadows had had Ruth's number and had slow-balled him to death. But there was a southpaw, and a Slavish one in the bargain. As they say at W. 72nd Street, Hot Zig.

With the count two balls and two strikes, Michael shot one down Babe's alley. A blind fan would have known it was a homer the moment ash met horsehide. That sharp crack means only one thing—a baseball finding itself suddenly in the middle of Babe's gang of idolizers in the right field bleachers. With one impulse, the mighty crowd stood and cheered the Babe. His gang in the bleachers went delirious. They gave the Babe a handkerchief waving demonstration that looked like a million generals waving flags of truce.

Dan Parker, New York *Daily Mirror*

The scene is the Yankee dugout. The time during the ninth inning yesterday. The reporter is at the foot of the steps leading from the dugout to the catacombs under the grandstand. He cannot see the action and can trace it only in the players' shouts.

Huggins—Come on, Herb. Let's have 'em, boy!

Durst—Who's that hitting?

Fletcher—Groh. Hey, Heinie! Stand up there right!

Collins—Easy now, Herb!

Chorus—Take it yourself, Herb! Herb! Herb! [*Pinch hitter Groh popped out to Pennock.*]

Paschal—Now get the little guy [*Lloyd Waner*]!

Huggins—Let's have 'em, Herb!

Chorus—Foul! Foul! [*Waner had hit a ground ball over third base, which, in fact, was called fair and went for a single.*]

Collins—One umpire says foul and another says fair. Why don't those guys get together?

Fletcher—Ice! Ice! Thought you could run. [Ice *means* ice wagon, *the term then used for slow runners. Here it is ironically directed to the speedy Waner because he did not reach second base on his scratch hit.*]

Huggins—Never mind, Herb! Let's have 'em, boy!

Gazella—Make him hit.

Wera—Lay it in there, Herb!

Fletcher—Talk it up there.

In response there is a jumble of cries, admonitions, and taunts.

Huggins—Take your wind-up if you want to, Herb! [*A pitcher never winds up with a man on base except, as in this instance, in the ninth inning with his team well ahead.*]

Grabowski—Get two, gang! [*That is, make a double play.*]

Shocker—Get one, sure!

A buzz runs the length of the dugout. [*The batter, Hal Rhyne, hit a long fly to center field.*]

Fletcher—Attaboy, Earl! [*Combs caught the fly.*] Two out! Two out!

Huggins—Let's have 'em, Herb! Let's have 'em.

Chorus—Tony! Tony! Whe-e-e-e! [*Paul Waner popped out to Lazzeri to end the game.*]

Down the steps the players tumble in the rush for the clubhouse.

Frank Graham, New York *Sun*

Well, friends, I hope you won't expect much of a story out of me in regards to yesterday's game as I was too sleepy to watch what was going on. The baseball special left Pittsburgh Thursday in pretty near a dozen sections, and yet it was my luck to be on the same section as my Oklahoma girl friend, Helma Thoke.

Miss Thoke, never having traveled on a sleeper before, had forgot to have her measurements taken for an upper, and, as she has been growing steadily taller ever since the Series started, there wasn't a berth on the whole entire train that came any-where close to fitting her. So she insisted on she and I setting out on the back platform in the moonlight watching the beautiful Pennsylvania scenery and disgusted the meaning of baseball and life. The moon was at its brightest as we rounded Horse-shoe Curve, and Miss Thoke was much impressed. She said she wished she could buy it and give it to one of the Pittsburgh pitchers.

Another thing that added to my drowsiness was two successive afternoons of gazing at the Messrs. Hoyt and Pipgras. If they was the only two pitchers Huggins had, the Yankees never would of win 110 games this season. They wouldn't of even had time to play that number. If Hoyt's first name is Waite, Pipgras must be christened "I'll call you when I get them." Between every two pitches these guys do everything but undress and be examined for life insurance. I ain't followed the Yanks very close, but experts tell me that they had a double header schedule at Cleveland in August and Huggins announced Pipgras and Hoyt as his pitchers. So the Cleveland club got permission to start the first game the day before, and even then it was called only in September on account of darkness, with the score of 24 to 1 in favor of New York at the end of the first inning. [*George Pipgras was indeed a notoriously slow-working pitcher, but Waite Hoyt, on the other hand, was usually the direct opposite of Pipgras. Hoyt and Al Schacht were mound opponents in a nine-inning International League game that lasted only fifty-five minutes, and Miller Huggins once asked Hoyt, "Why don't you slow down like Pipgras?" Hoyt replied, "Why don't you ask Pipgras to speed up like me?"*]

Speaking about following the Yanks close, Eddie Batchler of Detroit, who is a glutton for statistics, made the remark in Pittsburgh the other day that the American League set a new record this year by being the only big league that ever had seven clubs finish in the second division.

It may be recalled that in practice at Pittsburgh the other day, Cedric Durst burst a blood vessel in Pennock's leg with a line drive. [*For a while, it was thought that Pennock might not be able to pitch in the Series.*] After yesterday's game, Col. Ruppert called Cedric up in his office and signed him for next year.

"Your duties," said the Colonel, "will be to burst one of Pennock's blood vessels twice a week."

The Colonel wanted to say more, but was overcome with emotion, and it looked like he was going to burst out crying, but to save him embarrassment, Durst burst first.

Col. Ruppert himself is going to pitch today. And why not?

Ring Lardner, New York *World*

Sunday, October 9

[*On October 8, in New York, the Yankees won the fourth and final game of the World Series, 4–3. Winning pitcher, Wilcy Moore; losing pitcher, Johnny Miljus. Home run, Babe Ruth.*]

The slapstick is mightier than the bludgeon, and for that reason your New York Yankees are the baseball champions of the world, and if ever a dramatic ball game came to a sillier ending, I would like to be informed.

In the last of the ninth inning with the score tied what a dramatic setting for something stupendous, something of which you could sing through the long winter months. Miljus is pitching. Fifty-seven thousand fans begin to set up a steady, beating roar.

Combs walks. Koenig bunts safely as Traynor gums it up. The Babe is up.

They pass him purposely as the steel stadium rings with boos. [*He was walked intentionally after Johnny Miljus had thrown a wild pitch, advancing the base runners to second and third. An intentional pass would have been highly unlikely with third base unoccupied.*] Bases full, and the championship in sight. Here comes Gehrig. Ruth gives him advice. Will it be a Columbia boy, a born and bred New Yorker, who will win the championship? It will not!

Lou takes three lusty swings and strikes out. Still the bases are full. Still we have dangerous batters. Come now, Meusel. You have not had a hit all day. Remember how you broke up that Giant series? [*This refers to Meusel's single in the eighth inning of the sixth game of the 1923 World Series. The hit drove in two runs and enabled the Yankees to win the Series from the Giants, four games to two.*] Does Meusel remember? He does not. He takes three swings not quite so lusty and strikes out.

How that Miljus is pitching! The bases full and none out and he fans Gehrig and Meusel in full view of 57,000. Who is this? Ah, Tonee Poosh-em-opp—Tony Lazzeri. Sure enough, fate has stored up this moment for The Wonderful Wop. He shall be decorated by Mussolini.

He shall have free haircuts and shaves wherever he goes. He shall have as much spaghet as he can eat. O, Tonee! Tonee, poosh 'em, poosh 'em up! Wow! Wow! Wow! The ringing sound of bat and ball. No, no. Foul. Foul! Into the left field stands, but foul. [*Before Grover Alexander had fanned him in the seventh inning of the seventh game of the 1926 Series, Lazzeri had hit a hard drive into the left-field stands, which was just barely foul.*] It shows that our Tonee has his eye on the ball. Miljus is winding up again. Come on, Tonee! Poosh—!!

Does Tony connect solidly with the ball to send thousands into ecstasy? No, my friends, he does nothing of the kind, because Mr. Miljus lets go a wild pitch that hits the top of Gooch's glove and caroms to the stand, and Earle Combs gallops over with the winning run, the championship, the shekels, and the integrity of baseball. He does a little war dance, and everybody goes home.

Now, I ask you!

The championship won on a high wide pitch. Phooie! Pantaloon steps up to the bubble labeled "Drama," pulls out a long hatpin from his jeans, and Pft!

Well, anyhow, it was won, and Babe Ruth cocked a home run into the north end of the right field stand in the fifth inning with Combs on base. That was a grand and glorious home run, decidedly out of the high fly class, and it won the ball game as much as anything else the Yankees did. There was nothing fluky about it because Carmen Hill was pitching to him for all he was worth, and the one Ruth hit seemed to be an inside curve which is not usually his meat.

The game was one of those shifting things which furnishes you with a dozen stories before they are through, all of which have to be thrown away from some final absurdity such as Miljus' wild pitch.

Wilcy Moore and Carmel Hill pitched, and each team scored in the first inning. The Yankees came by theirs honestly on three consecutive singles by Combs, Koenig, and Ruth, which incidentally were followed by three consecutive strikeouts by Gehrig, Meusel, and Lazzeri.

The Pirates were presented with theirs by Ernie Quigley, who suffered a momentary case of astigmatism at first base, when he called Lloyd Waner safe after Koenig threw him out by two feet. Moore set the next two down but was not equal to four outs in an inning, and Wright doubled in the run.

From then on all was quiet until the fifth, when came the epic contributed by G. H. Ruth, which establishes definitely that the fellow is not a bust in a World Series. Two home runs in a four-game Series is not to be sniffed at. And there, you would say, was your ball game.

In fact I had some such story framed, beginning with Waite Hoyt's crack that while you can scatter singles, you cannot scatter a home run, and going on to tell how Ruth won the World Series, when what should these eyes behold in the seventh but the Yankees seized with an acute case of thumbitis, a disease which seizes the fingers and causes them to swell up until they resemble ten thumbs instead of ordinary digits. [*Moore and Lazzeri made flagrant errors, permitting Pittsburgh to tie the score.*]

From then on, Wilcy Moore was a very effective young fellow, and the baseball season of 1927 wound up with one wild heave that might have been caused by nervous, tired fingers or a damp, slippery ball. [*Light rain had fallen early in the game.*]

Paul Gallico, New York *Daily News*

Another World Series record that goes by the boards, and one that particularly gladdens the players, is that of the players' pool. Each Yankee will get a check for $5,592.17, while each Pirate will draw $3,728.11.

New York *World*

Monday, October 10

The World Series was put away with lavender and rosemary. In wildly rooting for the Yanks to win in four straight games, then meanwhile tossing more than $350,000 back into the fans' laps, the club owners and players convinced a once sceptical public that baseball is much more than a mere dollar coining industry. Its insides are not made of turnstiles and cash registers.

"It would be a nice break if the Pirates win a game, and New York has a big Sunday event," someone said to Col. Jake Ruppert before Saturday's game.

"Oh, don't say that," exclaimed the Colonel. "I won't be able to sleep until the Yanks win the fourth one."

The Colonel meant that in all sincerity. He knew that the winning of a couple of games by the Pirates would mean a half million dollars to the owners. He fought just as hard in his heart to toss that immense sum aside as the players did to win on the diamond.

As a result of the sudden termination of the event, the New York Club will not make enough money to pay the expenses of conducting the Series. Their entertainment bill alone will likely exceed the club receipts. Added to this is the enormous expense of selling and printing tickets, a job that will have to be done over again in returning $200,000 for the unplayed Sunday game.

It wasn't so much the actual loss to the magnates as the spirit they showed in rooting for the Series to end quickly. No amount of laws, rules, or regulations could do so much for baseball as that.

Bozeman Bulger, New York *Evening World*

This World Series did not lend itself to the output of heroes. The Yankees were so much better than the Pirates that there was little opportunity for individual achievement. The only chance for it was in the ninth inning of the last game, and that produced nothing but a goat. What people will remember about this Series in years to come will be the great Yankee team which won the championship in four straight games, and the wild pitch of John Miljus. You see, my dear Watson, to be a hero, one must have a heroic setting.

Rud Rennie, New York *Herald-Tribune*

Mark Koenig was the hero of the World Series.

Koenig is a particularly fitting and dramatic choice, for a year ago he was the "goat." [*In the 1926 Series, Koenig made four errors, including an especially damaging one in the last game.*]

This time Mark deserves the hero's niche. And he deserves it richly. Koenig played a flawless, swift, and intelligent game at short all the way, was the only Yankee to hit in every game, led both clubs in batting with an average of .500, with 9 hits in 18 times at bat, and batted in 3 runs. [*His fine World Series performance ended a great season for Koenig; he would have another good one in 1928. If Koenig's entire career had matched 1927 and 1928, he would surely have a plaque in Cooperstown.*]

Dan Daniel, New York *Telegram*

It is no reflection on the courage of the Pirates to say that one factor of their World Series defeat was a decided inferiority complex. They weren't afraid of the Yanks; they simply were abashed by them. In the utterances of two Pirates just before the Series opened could be read their attitude.

"Gee!" said Lloyd Waner to Paul, as he gazed upon Babe Ruth and Lou Gehrig for the first time. "They're big guys!" [*By way of contrast, Ruth's response to the Waner brothers upon first seeing them, as reported in* The New York Times *on October 4, was: "'Why, they're just kids,' he said as he blinked in amazement. 'If I was that little I'd be afraid of getting hurt.'" Each of the Waner brothers was 5 feet 8 inches in height and weighed about 150 pounds.*]

"Holy smoke!" said Emile Yde [*a left-handed pitcher who did not see action in the Series*] as he saw Ruth hammer a ball over the center field fence at Forbes Field during batting practice. "Does he do that very often?"

The Pirates had been led to believe long before they saw the Yanks that they were about to face a team that outclassed the American League and, in all probability, would outclass them. Once they took the field against this superteam they realized that the belief was sound. They couldn't pull themselves together for

the one big thrust that might have disturbed the Yanks' equa-
nimity.

Going further into the Series, there was the moment when
players of both teams streamed through the narrow passage
leading to the dressing rooms at the Stadium after the third
game. Ruth was almost the last Yank to appear, and he stalked
through a mass of Pittsburgh players.

"Well!" he shouted to a group of newspaper men. "One more
game will wind it up."

Unbelievable as it sounds, there wasn't a murmur from the
Pirates. One cannot imagine the Babe pulling a crack like that in
front of the Giants, for instance, and getting away with it. He
would have been informed by every Giant player simultaneously
that on the following day the Yanks would get their brains
knocked out, that they had been a lot of lucky stiffs, and that, to
boot, he was a ham, a bum, a clown, and a few other things
unmentionable in these chaste pages. The Pirates heard him in
silence, and by their silence gave assent.

Frank Graham, New York Sun

The plain truth is that the Yankees are one of the greatest teams
in the history of baseball. So hats off to Combs, Koenig, Ruth,
Gehrig, Meusel, Push 'em up Wop, and all the rest of the celebrated batting order. If the old Baltimore Orioles are still talked
of after 30 years, this team will be talked of for the next century,
and hats off to Huggins, the greatest lawyer who ever sat on a
bench.

New York World

Index

Items of particular significance are followed by an asterisk*.

home run, 126–27; sixth home run, 126–27; conducts band concert at St. Mary's School, 131; popularity in Chicago, 135–38; seventh home run, 140–41; eighth home run, 141–42; his views on batting in Yankee Stadium, 146; critique of *Babe Comes Home,* his film, 146–47, 282; ninth home run, 148–49; intentionally hits to left field, 154, 157–58, 164, 166, 269; tenth home run, 154–55; popularity in Cleveland, 155; dons Indian headdress, 155; 11th home run, 157; comments on his fielding, 158, 164, 184–85, 267, 274, 307, 324; 12th home run, 163; 13th home run, 165; 14th home run, 167; popularity in Philadelphia, 168; 15th home run, 169; 16th home run, 169; breaks baseball with force of his swing, 168–69; jokingly bats right-handed, 170; plays better on road than at home, 170–71; stimulated and helped by home-run competition with Gehrig, 172–73, 222–23, 255–56, 262, 289–90, 319, 327; 17th home run, 177; 18th home run, 183; dugout conver-sation, 186–87, 218, 243–44, 345–46, 368–69; 19th home run, 191, 208; 20th home run, 208; 21st home run, 209; his respect for pitchers, 213; cab-bage leaf under his cap, 214; 22nd home run, 216; games and innings missed because of injuries, 220–21, 225, 232, 234, 235, 238, 314; 23rd home run, 225–26; 24th home run, 225–26; his keen eyesight, 227–28; claims tax deduction for entertaining press, 233,

237; 25th home run, 245; his innate baseball intelligence, 248–49; 26th home run, 251; his saxophone, 257–58, 267; 27th home run, inside the park, 260; 28th home run, 261; 29th home run, 261; pop-ularity in Detroit, 261; 30th home run, 266; popularity in St. Louis, 270; his opinion on so-called "lively ball," 279; 31st home run, 280–81; 32nd home run, 283; 33rd home run, 283; 34th home run, 285; 35th home run, 295–96; 36th home run, 301; 37th home run, 308; 38th home run, 309–10; his witty retort, 313; 40th home run, 315; his destruction of straw hats, 316; loses bet to Wilcy Moore, 320–21; 41st home run, 321–22; 42nd home run, 322; 43rd home run, 324–25; 44th home run, 326; 45th home run, 330, 331; 46th home run, 331; 47th home run, 331; 48th home run, 332; 49th home run, 332; 50th home run, 337; charged with assault, 338–39, 346–47; 51st home run, 339–40; 52nd home run, 339–40; 53rd home run, 344; 54th home run, 348; picks Dempsey to beat Tunney, 348; 55th home run, 349; 56th home run, 350; acts in Harold Lloyd film, 351; praised by Grantland Rice, 354; 57th home run, 354–55; 58th home run, 355–56; 59th home run, 355–56; 60th home run, 357–60; his home-run record and that of Roger Maris com-pared, 357; praised by Paul Gallico, 360; praised in John Kieran's poem, 362–63; his locker described, 363–64; how he puts on his uniform,